ESSAYS OF FIVE DECADES

BOOKS BY J. B. PRIESTLEY

FICTION

Adam in Moonshine
Benighted
The Good Companions
Angel Pavement
Faraway
Wonder Hero
Laburnum Grove
They Walk in the City
The Doomsday Men
Let the People Sing
Blackout in Gretley
Daylight on Saturday
Three Men in New Suits
Bright Day

Jenny Villiers
Festival at Farbridge
The Other Place: short stories
The Magicians
Low Notes on a High Level
Saturn Over the Water
The Thirty-First of June
The Shapes of Sleep
Sir Michael and Sir George
Lost Empires
It's an Old Country
Out of Town (The Image Men—I)
London End (The Image Men—II)

PLAYS

The Roundabout
Duet in Floodlight
Spring Tide
Mystery at Greenfingers
The Long Mirror
The Rose and Crown
The High Toby
Bright Shadow

Dragon's Mouth (with Jacquetta Hawkes)
Private Rooms
Treasure on Pelican
Try it Again
Mother's Day
A Glass of Bitter
Mr Kettle and Mrs Moon

COLLECTED PLAYS

Volume I	Volume II	Volume III
Dangerous Corner	Laburnum Grove	Cornelius
Eden End	Bees on the Boat Deck	People at Sea
Time and the Conways	When we are Married	They Came to a City
I Have Been Here Before	Good Night Children	Desert Highway
Johnson over Jordan	The Golden Fleece	An Inspector Calls
Music at Night	How are they at Home?	Home is Tomorrow
The Linden Tree	Ever Since Paradise	Summer Day's Dream

ESSAYS AND AUTOBIOGRAPHY

Talking
Open House
Apes and Angels
Midnight on the Desert
Rain upon Godshill
The Secret Dream
Delight

All About Ourselves and other Essays
  (chosen by Eric Gillett)
Thoughts in the Wilderness
Margin Released
The Moments and other pieces
Essays of Five Decades

CRITICISM AND MISCELLANEOUS

Brief Diversions
The English Comic Characters
Meredith (E.M.L.)
Peacock (E.M.L.)
The English Novel
English Humour (Heritage Series)
The Balconinny
English Journey
Postscripts
Out of the People
British Women Go To War
Russian Journey

Theatre Outlook
The Olympians (opera libretto)
Journey Down a Rainbow
  (with Jacquetta Hawkes)
Topside
The Art of the Dramatist
Literature and Western Man
Man and Time
The World of J. B. Priestley
  (edited by Donald G. MacRae)
Trumpets over the Sea

ESSAYS OF FIVE DECADES

J. B. PRIESTLEY

SELECTED AND WITH A PREFACE
BY SUSAN COOPER

HEINEMANN : LONDON

William Heinemann Ltd
LONDON   MELBOURNE   TORONTO
CAPE TOWN   AUCKLAND

First published in Great Britain 1969

434 60356 2

The author and publishers wish to thank the following
for permission to reproduce essays which appeared originally
in their publications:

Bowes & Bowes for 'Papers from Lilliput';
John Lane for 'I for One', 'Figures in Modern Literature' and
'The English Comic Characters';
the *Saturday Evening Post* for 'Women Don't Run the Country';
and the *New Statesman* for the essays in Part XIII.

Printed and bound in Great Britain by
Bookprint Limited, Crawley, Sussex

PREFACE

Some thirty years ago, in London, the English Association published an anthology called *English Essays of Today*. Though its title was accurate enough, its contents had a curiously distant, evocative tone, for the contemporary image of the essay, then, was that of a piece of graceful, discursive writing belonging in both spirit and form to a gentler age than our own. There they all were, the descendants of Addison, Hazlitt and Lamb, in fine modern array: Hilaire Belloc, G. K. Chesterton, Max Beerbohm, Robert Lynd, E. V. Lucas, Sir Arthur Quiller-Couch. And among them was the name of a man twenty years younger than nearly all the rest: J. B. Priestley, with an essay entitled "First Snow."

. . . The first fall of snow is not only an event but it is a magical event. You go to bed in one kind of world and wake up to find yourself in another quite different, and if this is not enchantment, then where is it to be found? The very stealth, the eerie quietness, of the thing makes it more magical. If all the snow fell at once in one shattering crash, awakening us in the middle of the night, the event would be robbed of its wonder. But it flutters down, soundlessly, hour after hour while we are asleep. Outside the closed curtains of the bedroom, a vast transformation scene is taking place.

When he wrote that, the young J. B. Priestley — he must have been in his early thirties — had already arrived at the flowering of his best work as an essayist; it was no great surprise to find him anthologised in the company of all the grand old men of English letters. But there was a great deal more to come. Most members of that company were at the end of their literary careers and the end of a literary era, firmly attached in mood and outlook to the leisurely Edwardian age. Priestley, on the other hand, was only just getting into full stride. Having been born in 1894, he had his roots in the same golden world as they; but unlike them he was to go much further, to become fully twentieth-century man, travelling on into a swifter and harsher world of totally different standards and tastes. And the essay, though often said to be dying, remained alive and went with him. His work in this small, neat and peculiarly satisfying literary form covers a crucial half century in its development, and throughout those years his pieces have both reflected and influenced the changes it has undergone. For changes there have been: the essay is by no means a fossil form. The American novelist Norman Mailer recently dismissed it in tones fairly common among modern writers: "My mind wanders. It dissipates. I have no patience left for quiet exposition. In an essay you must obey formal concerns which I have not the enthusiasm to obey any longer." But he was voicing a common misconception. The essay is not the prose equivalent of the sonnet, bound fast forever to a traditional pattern; it is a piece of reflective writing whose pattern changes with the gradual and constant changing of English prose. It always has been. In the essays which J. B. Priestley has produced during the last fifty years, you can see the development more clearly than in any other man's work.

There is no prose form more personal than the essay. It may be a deliberate, often didactic, exposition of the writer's own views, like much of Montaigne, or it may be a piece of whimsical narrative like Charles Lamb's "A Dissertation on Roast Pig," but it never fails to express a distinct personality. The essayist appears often to be producing a sort of small skilled doodle, working to illustrate some essentially personal idea. This remains true in spite of the fact that the essay, being brief, has like the short story generally been written as a specifically aimed piece of merchandise, for immediate publication in a particular market. Addison and Steele wrote thus for their *Spectator,* Johnson for the *Rambler;* and the custom grew from there. These broadsheets are known now as the ancestors of the popular newspaper, and in the sense of being the only existing purveyors of current news, so they were; but they were also the ancestors of the monthly and quarterly periodicals which sprang up and multiplied long before the popular daily press. Such periodicals, like the early *Spectator,* were written for a limited public of educated readers. It was to these men that the philosophical, critical or fanciful discursions of the earliest essays had appealed; and so it was in these periodicals that the early nineteenth-century essayists — Hazlitt, Lamb, Leigh Hunt — were able to spread themselves and properly to develop the form. The essayists' public remained comparatively small, for soon the heyday of the great nineteenth-century novels — also published often in periodicals, in instal-

ment form — had arrived to satisfy the hunger of an increasingly literate
people. But still the form quietly thrived, in places like the *Saturday
Review,* for which Max Beerbohm was writing by the end of the century.
Beerbohm brought a greater informality to the essay, though for a deliberate formal purpose. "In essay writing," he observed, "style is everything.
The essayist's aim is to bring himself home to his reader, to express himself
in exact terms. Therefore, he must find exact words for his thoughts, and
cadences which express the very tone of his emotions. Himself is the thing
to be obtruded, and style the only means to this end."

By the time J. B. Priestley arrived in London to earn a literary living in
the early nineteen-twenties, this was the predominating view of the essay
— and one which had attracted the remarkable range of talents of Chesterton, Lynd, "Q" and the rest. The periodicals, not yet reeling under modern
economic pressures, still offered an encouraging level of space and readership, and some of the most fertile essayists were in fact involved in
producing them; Robert Lynd was literary editor of the *Daily News,* J. C.
Squire, editor of the *London Mercury.* Priestley wrote for both of these,
and also — in good essayist tradition   for the *Spectator* and the *Saturday
Review.* Although he was thus to some extent a journalist, in the sense (in
those spacious days not yet a pejorative one) of earning much of his living
from the journals, and although it would not have been difficult to let
natural facility take over from disciplined talent in these pieces, he nevertheless shared Beerbohm's attitude towards the essay. As he points out in
his reminiscent *Margin Released,* he took pains.

The early essays I wrote, coming out in various periodicals and
then in volume form in *Papers from Lilliput, I for One, Open House,*
were mostly literary exercises. There was nothing much I really wanted
to say, but for some years I took great pains with these pieces, like a
man learning to play an instrument. Though I kept right on into the
thirties writing weekly essays, for the *Saturday Review,* while Gerald
Barry edited it, and then moving with Barry to the *Week End Review,*
shortlived but glorious, I knew that this kind of essay, personal in tone
but elaborately composed, was already almost an anachronism. It had
had an Indian summer in the period 1900–1914, when newspapers
still published essays. Strong demand brought rich supply, as I believe
it does in all the arts. If the English switched from football to chamber
music, for example, they would soon have some masterpieces.

At this point in his career Priestley was providing a rich supply not only
of essays but of practically every other prose form. From his Yorkshire
boyhood, after a brief spell in a Bradford wool office, he had enlisted in the
army and served throughout the muddy, bloody years of World War I;
from there he had gone to Cambridge for three years, and then to London

to live by writing. By the late twenties, he had published several books "somewhere on the edge of criticism proper" — two in the "English Men of Letters" series, on Peacock and Meredith; a book on *English Humour;* and *The English Comic Characters,* a collection of critical essay-portraits in a nonacademic manner which brings its subjects brilliantly off the shelves and into their intended relationship with real life. He had written two novels, *Adam in Moonshine* and *Benighted* (a splendidly menacing tale known in the United States as *The Old Dark House*); collaborated with the English novelist Hugh Walpole on a third called *Farthing Hall,* and towards the end of the decade he wrote the long picaresque novel *The Good Companions,* which launched him into huge international fame and has to some extent moulded his reputation ever since.

Seldom has a particular success had a more misleading effect on a writer's name. For one thing, *The Good Companions* is not Priestley's best novel; it is surpassed by several others, notably *Angel Pavement* and *Festival at Farbridge.* More important, the novel itself was not a form to which he was by nature drawn. "This was not," he wrote in *Margin Released,* "a literary form in which I could work instinctively and at ease, as I had done in the essay, as I came to do in descriptive-cum-autobiographical books like *English Journey* and *Midnight on the Desert,* and as I discovered later, to my astonishment, I could do in the supposedly more difficult dramatic form. . . . What I find hard and wearisome to do is precisely what the born novelist has not to think about at all. This is the trick of maintaining an even flow of narration, steadily moving on no matter how thick and rich it may be."

This feeling did not, of course, deter him from writing more novels; quite the reverse. In the next forty years he was to write more than thirty of them. Priestley is a writer incorrigibly attracted by the challenge of a form which he finds in some way difficult, or which he has not tried before; he is the actor who refuses to be type-cast as Bottom, Falstaff and Sir Toby Belch, but must intersperse these with the roles of Brutus, Henry V, Macbeth. This is the main reason why the range of his work is so wide, making it impossible to classify him as novelist, playwright or critic; the only label you can give him is that of "man of letters," in the old sense of the all-round professional, and perhaps he is the last of that breed. It may also be one reason why his essays are not more numerous — for although they add up to a considerable collection over the space of five decades, there are long periods during that time in which they have been very thin on the ground. Perhaps this is merely chance; but perhaps too it has been caused by his finding the essay form too congenial, too undemanding. However much detailed care he gave to the writing of his essays, he still found in the form more sense of enjoyment than of challenge; and so he never stayed with it for very long at a time. The good writer always mistrusts, rightly or wrongly, any sense of his own facility; he tends to turn from the meal he can gobble — however much he may enjoy it — to the one in which he has trouble picking his way through the bones.

It is true, of course, that by the thirties the graceful, formal Edwardian essay was, as Priestley says, "almost an anachronism." But if this is true of his own early essays, then it can apply only to their form, not to their content and mood. His main essay collections had been published during the previous decade: *Papers from Lilliput* in 1922, *I for One* in 1923, *Open House* in 1927, *Apes and Angels* in 1928, *The Balconinny* in 1929. Within that period, they underwent a considerable change, developing from stiff and tentative exercises to the fluent and original pieces of the confident essayist: the writer who has learned that readers enjoy his private reflections and is thus not troubled by hesitation nor cramped by conventional choice of subject. In *Apes and Angels,* his best collection of that period, Priestley was still writing graceful, evocative pieces in the old style, like "First Snow," but also branching into reflective descriptions of the contemporary scene — in, for example, "T'Match," which foreshadows the kind of observations he was to publish in *English Journey* — and pieces of eerie narrative like "The Strange Outfitter." This kind of development was to continue during his next intensive period of work in the essay form, which came in a way he did not expect.

This was brought into being by World War II. Although Priestley was still writing for Gerald Barry's *Week End Review* during the thirties, that decade was for him given mainly to work for the theatre — his first play, *Dangerous Corner,* was produced in 1932 and rapidly followed by others — and to a lesser extent, films. Then the war began (in 1939, for the British), and at forty-six Priestley found yet another persona covering his shoulders: that of broadcaster. Alongside his other work, he began giving talks for the BBC several times a week, for both home and overseas audiences.

With the spreading of radio, and the shrinking of the printed periodicals, the time was ripe even before the war for the broadcast talk to usurp the place, form and style of the essay. The last survivor of the essayists' old guard, Max Beerbohm, had given several BBC talks in 1935, but although he gave others during and after the war he was too old to undertake much — he had, after all, begun writing for the *Saturday Review* when J. B. Priestley was only a child of three. So it was for the writer Priestley to translate the old world into the new and become the broadcaster Priestley; and he did so with a success that characteristically filled him with fury.

Those home broadcasts, those Sunday night "Postscripts". . . were . . . ridiculously overpraised. They took about ten minutes to deliver, usually between half an hour and an hour to write. They were nothing more than spoken essays, designed to have a very broad and classless appeal. . . . I didn't see then — and I don't see now — what all the fuss was about. To this day middle-aged or elderly men shake my hand and tell me what a ten-minute talk about ducks on a pond or a pie in a shop-window meant to them, as if I had given them *King Lear* or the Eroica. I found myself tied, like a man to a gigantic balloon, to one of those bogus reputations that only the mass media know how to inflate.

Here again is the writer's mistrust of his own facility: the feeling that however good of its kind a thing may be, it can't be worth much if it doesn't require much effort. It is understandable, of course, that a writer should be maddened by receiving as much praise for a talk that takes him half an hour as for a novel that takes him twelve months. But although Priestley's wartime talks no doubt gained much from their context and the manner of their delivery, there still remained their intrinsic appeal — the appeal of the essay. These were, indeed, "spoken essays," and in them Priestley, first among a number of writers working for radio during its heyday, did much to affect the change which has taken place in the written essay since the beginning of this century. The older form had been personal, with informality expressed through formal grace; but it had depended largely upon artifice. As Lord David Cecil says of Max Beerbohm:

> Like Lamb's Max's are the "pure" type of essay; that is to say, they are not written to instruct or edify but only to produce aesthetic satisfaction. As much as a poem or a piece of music, they are the expression of a creative impulse. What Max creates is a personality. Because it is a creation, it is not a self-portrait; Max the essayist is not the same as Max Beerbohm the man any more than Elia the essayist is the same as Charles Lamb the man. In each case the writer projects on to his page a personality not identical with his own, though founded on it, a figure made up of elements selected from himself and then rearranged and displayed for his aesthetic purpose. The result is an intensely vivid impression of a living individual. But paradoxically the life comes from the fact that he is not drawn directly from nature, that he is a creation, rather than a reproduction.

This passage could be applied word for word to the J. B. Priestley of the essays written before 1940; they were created by the same means. Already then they had been moving gradually in another direction, so that the pieces in *Apes and Angels* are far more vivid and direct than those in *I for One*. But they still belonged to what Priestley himself had described as a dying form. Now, the approach which he adopted for his broadcasts — albeit in an exaggerated form, since the spoken word must sound "natural"

in a way that words written for the eye never can — steered him further
from the formal pattern-making of the earlier essays and into a more
genuinely personal framework and mood. The ducks on the pond looked
less like an exquisite water-colour and more like real ducks. And though
one cannot claim much for radio as a literary influence, it is undeniable
that the broader audience which Priestley was now reaching on the air was
also rapidly producing a broader readership for him, and other essayists, in
print. At all events, by the end of the war he and the essay were firmly
headed in a new direction; and although this newer essay sacrificed none of
the virtues of the old, it had acquired some additional ones which had
much in common with those of the spoken word.

For Priestley, the combination resulted in 1949 in a book called *Delight*.
It was an enchanting piece of work, taking as motto a stanza from Walter
de la Mare's "Fare Well" which might serve as an admonition to all general
essayists, or for that matter all artists.

> Look thy last on all things lovely
> Every hour. Let no night
> Seal thy sense in deathly slumber
> Till to delight
> Thou have paid thy utmost blessing:
> Since that all things thou wouldst praise
> Beauty took from those who loved them
> In other days.

Delight is not a conventional collection of essays; it might almost be said
to consist of one long essay in kaleidoscope form. Beginning with a
"Grumbler's Apology" in penitence for a lifetime of apparent scowling
discontent, Priestley marvels his way through a considerable number of
pieces — to be precise, one hundred and fourteen — on people, moments,
places, things which have ever brought him the swift dazzle of delight.
None of the pieces is long; some are very short indeed; but each is an essay
in miniature — or one facet of the composite essay on delight, which is
after all an emotion definable only through its many causes. The range is
huge, from the nostalgic glow of remembering performers, writers, conductors from the faraway past, to highly contemporary pleasures like
"quietly malicious chairmanship" or "frightening senior civil servants."
But above all every piece is of course intensely personal; there is no
deliberate seeking for effect here, nor formalised creation of a paper
personality; only one writer burbling happily away to himself with a
genuine pleasure that brings its own grace to the style.

The coming of the *Idea*. There is nothing piecemeal about its arrival.
It comes as the ancient gods and goddesses must have manifested

themselves to their more fortunate worshippers. (And indeed it comes from the same place.) At one moment the mind knows it not. The next moment it is there, taking full possession of the mind, which quivers in ecstatic surrender. I have been accused — and not unjustly — of having too many ideas. "More hard work, more patience," they tell me, "and not so many ideas, my boy." But although hard work and patience may bring rewards I shall never know, where is the ravishing delight in them? Lord, let me live to welcome again with all the old abandon, not knowing whether I am dressing or undressing, whether it is Tuesday morning or Friday evening, the sunburst of the Idea!

Within the five decades of Priestley's essays, *Delight* forms a sunny domestic interlude; not surprisingly, most of the pleasures it records have to do with the family, with recollections of boyhood, with the encounters and observations of the private man. The essays which he produced during the next twenty years have been of a different kind; written mainly for the London political review *The New Statesman and Nation,* they are generally polemical in tone, written, as their author remarks, "to challenge and provoke." Some were published as *Thoughts in the Wilderness* in 1957; some as *The Moments* in 1966; others, included in the present volume, have not been reproduced before. In their total effect, they add up to an expression of what has perhaps always been J. B. Priestley's fundamental preoccupation as a writer: a concern that the life of the people — and particularly the people nearest at hand, in England — should contain a proper human dignity; that we should all, as it were, be given enough to eat not only with our mouths but with our minds.

It is an appeal for a life with some fire in it; a repeated warning against the perils of Mass Communication, Block Thinking, and the stifling of creative thought by grim inflexible political structures, whether of the Right or the Left. Whether he is making bitter fun of politicians or denouncing the culture-consuming octopus he calls Admass, Priestley is continually and dexterously here turning the essay, that most personal form, to social ends. He is not merely entertaining or reflecting; he is also trying, sometimes most wrathfully, to make his readers think. And the style of these later essays, pared down to a deceptive simplicity, reinforces their solemn matter with the gaiety of a Chesterton or a Thurber. You can find all the old and new virtues of the essay mingling in, for instance, Priestley's piece on "The Unicorn," with its warning that the British, who seem still unaccountably to believe in the roaring grandeur of their Lion, had better accept the fact that the poor old beast has in fact lost not only his voice but all his teeth. Like all of us of all nationalities, they had better turn before it is too late to a less grandiose side of their national character:

So — up with the Unicorn! Make way for the unsound types, all those who made such a bad impression on the committee! Forward the imaginative men, the creators and originators, even the rebels and cranks and eccentrics, all those with corners not rubbed off, bees in their bonnets, fire in their bellies, poetry in their souls! It's nearly now or never. For if we don't back the Unicorn against the Lion, if we are not a boldly imaginative, creative, inventive people, a world that expected more of us will soon not even let us keep what we have now. The only future we can have worth living in is the one we greet, bravely and triumphantly, riding on a Unicorn.

It is the new touch brought to an old form; a modern master giving a bright relevance to a style that might have gone out of date. This time, you can certainly call it the English Essay of Today.

Susan Cooper

April 1968

CONTENTS

Preface by Susan Cooper

B

X. From THOUGHTS IN THE WILDERNESS 1957

XI. From the SATURDAY EVENING POST December 12, 1964

I. From PAPERS FROM LILLIPUT 1922

THREE MEN

The first is (or was) a schoolmaster. When he was in his later teens, long before I met him, he had worked for an Oxford scholarship, and he had worked so hard that a few days before the examination he was found at a late hour babbling incoherently over his books, a nervous wreck. He never took the examination and never went to Oxford, but, when he recovered, passed into a little day-school. Nevertheless, Oxford had entered into his soul. To me, he was more like an Oxford man, or what an Oxford man ought to be, than any other person I have ever met. He had all the larger and more genial traits clearly marked, with just the least delicious hint of pleasant caricature, like a good actor presenting a character study of a younger don. There were little peculiar traits too, as of some mythical college, of a ghostly Balliol or an unsubstantial "House." It may have been the result of deliberate cultivation, or it may have been the gift of one of the younger gods, a compensation for that disastrous breakdown; I do not know, but it was harmless enough, and delicate fooling for a spectator.

I have not seen him for years, but I can call him well to mind even now; a little man with hair loosely parted in the centre and falling over his temples, and eyeglasses insecurely perched halfway down a long nose. In the small town in which he (and I too) lived at that time, there were in all five working-men's clubs. He was a member of all five. Why, I do not know, except that beer was very much cheaper in these places than it was elsewhere. But even that does not explain why he was a member of them all. But so it was. Nightly into one or other of these working-men's clubs, he carried his insecure eyeglasses and his Oxford manner, and was well received, with the respect due to "a character," rather than with the hardly suppressed laughter that followed him elsewhere. There he would take a friend, and over the beer (which was both cheap and excellent) he would talk at length, letting the ball of conversation roll easily down the long cadences of his speech. His favourite theme, I remember, was the utter worthlessness of the middle classes, to which he belonged, and he was the first person of my acquaintance to speak of them as "the bourgeois." It is years since I last saw him, but I trust that some school still knows him, chalky and pedantic, day by day, and that at least five working-men's clubs still see him, magnificent over his beer, night by night.

The second man was a spectacled smoky fellow, getting on in years, whom I knew but slightly. His trade was the writing of boys' stories, not for expensive illustrated books but for penny dreadfuls. What else he had done to earn his bread, when he was only an aspirant, I do not know, but that was his trade when I knew him. Year after year, he chronicled the adventures of Dick This or Jack the Other at School or among Pirates or Red Indians; and his pay was one guinea for every thousand words, which was not bad, for he could turn out a good many thousand words in a week and could also fill up with Boom! Crash! Bang! a kind of writing that boys like. Although the scenes of his tales were laid in all parts of the world, there was no nonsense about him; he did not travel in search of local colour, but used a gazetteer and trusted to his powers of invention, which were well tried and excellent. But his heart was not in the work and he took no pride in it. At regular intervals he would simply send off so many thousand words to the Boys' Monster Tales Publishing Company Limited, and his stories came out under many different names, not one of which was his own. He had a wife but no family, few friends, and belonged to no club or society. The thing he lived for was a great work in metaphysics, at which he had been engaged for many years, and which was to be called "The Mind of the Universe." All his spare time and energy were given to thinking out the problems that he had set himself, and he would weary his few visitors with interminable talk in a philosophical jargon of his own making. Years before, he had read a little handbook on Spinoza, which had brought a new set of problems into his world, and which had so intrigued him that he had determined to devote the remainder of his life to metaphysics. But he had also made up his mind not to study the philosophers because their theories might keep him from original thought: he meant to think everything out for himself. When he had erected his system, the world would recognise it for what it was, and forgive his preposterous stories of "Jack Marraway and the Terror of the Prairie" and the rest. He was wrong. I am no metaphysician but I know that his stories were better than his grand original system of metaphysics. For, after years of labour, he had only succeeded in enunciating paradoxes that were stale jokes in Ionia, in dragging out cumbersome creaking theories that even the long extinct State University of Hochensteilschwarzburg would have rejected at a glance; and all written in that terrible jargon of his. Yet it was a manly thing to do, and though all his labour was worth little, it was not in vain, for it gave him secret incommunicable pleasure and he felt himself to be a man marked off from the common run of men; which he was. For the rest, he smoked prodigious quantities of Meadowsweet Flake — a vile tobacco, grossly doctored and scented.

The other man I never knew personally, but I received many accounts of him, and his reputation, the legend of him, has been very dear to me. He was a shopkeeper and sold, at a considerable profit, optical instruments, spectacles and whatnot. But what set him apart from other men was that he had had more bad verse through his hands than any other person in these islands. It was his one great hobby to collect bad verse and publish it in anthologies. He must have known more poetasters than any other man living or dead. On the death of a well-known politician, or immediately after any great public event, he would set to work and gather up all the offscourings of the "Poets' Corners" of obscure country papers. Thus, he it was, and no other, who edited *The Best Poetical Tributes to the Late Joseph Chamberlain* and many other anthologies. His system was, I fancy, to compel every contributor to become a subscriber and take several copies of the volume in hand, so that it was ensured a sale. The verse was always bad, the very worst conceivable, for no one who wrote good verse would have suffered him to live. Why he did it — and he produced innumerable volumes — is a mystery, for there could not have been much money in it, and the same energy and impudence would have given him a fortune in the quack medicine business. I have thought sometimes that he was a satirist of a particularly deep kind, but I have been assured by those who knew him that he was entirely serious and innocently proud of the good work he was doing. Nor did he allow his literary service to interfere with his trade. In the centre of his shop-window there was a coloured life-size bust of Shakespeare with a pair of eyeglasses on its nose. The bust hinted delicately to all passers-by that though our man was but a shopkeeper, he too had served the Muse and was the editor of the Hundred Best, etc.; the eyeglasses, through which one caught the mild glance of the poet, indicated the nature of the shop. It was admirable! And though the man himself is dead, the shop remains and with it the bust. I saw it only a short time ago, and was gladdened; indeed, there seems something lacking now when I see Shakespeare without his eyeglasses; but one cannot, of course, be dogmatic about such matters of taste.

All three men lived in one town, where I too lived for a season. And there were others, more wonderful still, whom I cannot describe in this place, nor perhaps in any other, for I write to be believed.

ON A MOUTH-ORGAN

For the past half hour, someone, probably a small boy, has been playing a mouth-organ underneath my window. I know of no person under this roof peculiarly susceptible to the sound of a mouth-organ, so that I cannot think that the unknown musician is serenading. He is probably a small boy who is simply hanging about, after the fashion of his mysterious tribe, and whiling away the time with a little music. Why he should choose a raw day like this on which to do nothing but slide his lips over the cold metal of a mouth-organ must remain a mystery to me; but I have long realised that unfathomable motives may be hidden away behind the puckered face and uncouth gestures of small boyhood.

I have not been able to recognise any of the tunes, or the snatches of tunes, which have come floating up to my window. Possibly they are all unknown to me. But I think it is more likely that they are old acquaintances, coming in such a questionable shape that my ear cannot find any familiar cadence; they have been transmuted by the mouth-organ into something rich and strange; for your mouth-organ is one of the great alchemists among musical instruments and leaves no tune as it finds it.

It has been pointed out that whatever material Dickens used, however rich and varied it might be, it was always mysteriously transformed into the Dickens substance, lengths of which he cut off and called Novels. It seems to me that the mouth-organ, though a mechanical agent, has something of this strange power of transformation; whatever is played upon it seems to come out all of a piece; whatever might be the original character of the tunes, gay, fantastical, meditative, stirring, as their sounds are filtered through the little square holes of the instrument, their character changes, and they all become more or less alike. "Rule, Britannia!" "Annie Laurie," and the latest ditty of the music-halls somehow or other lose their individuality and flow into one endless lament, one lugubrious strain, that might very well go on for ever.

For this reason, the sound of a mouth-organ has always succeeded in depressing me. It must have been invented by an incorrigible pessimist, who sought to create a musical instrument that would give to every tune, no matter how lively, some touch of his own hopeless view of life; and probably the only time that he laughed was when he realised that he could leave this thing as a legacy to the world. I have never played a mouth-organ because I know that my own native optimism would not be strong enough to resist the baneful influence of the music it makes. To hear it now and again is more than enough for me.

To one who is filled with the joy of life — a small boy, for example — such hopeless strains may prove only invigorating, may serve as a wholesome check upon his ebullient spirits, like the skeleton at the Egyptian feasts. But to most of us weaker brethren, frail in spirit, music that is unillumined by even a glimmer of hope is intolerable.

For the past half hour, I have been trying to concentrate all my attention upon some fairly cheerful matter, and I have failed. It has been impossible to keep out the sound of this mouth-organ. Its formless, unknown, unending tune, only fit for bewailing a ruined world, has gradually invaded my room, penetrated through the ear into my brain, and coloured or discoloured all the thoughts there. There is in it no trace of that noble sadness which great music, like great poetry, so often brings with it; the mouth-organ knows nothing of "divine despair." It seems to whimper before "the heavy and the weary weight of all this unintelligible world."

"Oh de-ar!" I seem to hear it crying, "No hope for yo-ou and yo-ours; me-eserable world! Oh de-ear!" It has brought with it a fog of depression; my spirits have been sinking lower and lower; and under the influence of this evil mangler of good, heartening tunes I have begun to think that life is not worth living.

Most music worthy of the name has such beauty that it will either raise us to a kind of ecstasy or give us a feeling of vague sadness, which some delicate persons prefer to wild joy. Sir Thomas Browne, you remember, has something to say on this point, in a passage that can never become hackneyed no matter how many times it is quoted: "Whosoever is harmonically composed delights in harmony; which makes me much distrust the symmetry of those heads which declaim against all church music. For myself, not only from my obedience, but my particular genius, I do embrace it; for even that vulgar and tavern-music, which makes one man merry, another mad, strikes in me a deep fit of devotion, and a profound contemplation of the first composer."

But these mouth-organ strains will make a man neither mad nor merry, nor yet strike in him a deep fit of devotion; but if his ear is like mine, they will make him sink into depression and dye his world a ghastly blue.

It is curious that certain other popular musical instruments seem to have the same characteristics as the mouth-organ. The concertina and the accordion, good friends of the sailor, the lonely colonist, and rough, kindly fellows the world over, seem to me to possess the same power of transforming all the tunes played upon them into one long wail. I have read about their "lively strains," but I have never heard them. The sound of a concertina a quarter of a mile away is enough to shake my optimism. An average accordion could turn the Sword Theme from *Siegfried* into a plea for suicide. A flageolet or a tin-whistle has not such a shattering effect; nevertheless, both of them can only give a tune a certain subdued air, which is certainly preferable to the depressing alchemy of the other instruments, but which certainly does not make for liveliness.

The bagpipe, which has been so long the companion of the lonely folk of northern moors and glens, can produce at times a certain rousing martial strain, but, even then, a wailing air creeps into the music like a Scotch mist. Its very reels and strathspeys, which ought to be jolly enough, only sound to me like elaborate complaints against life; their transitory snatches of gaiety are obviously forced. At all other times, the bagpipe is frankly pessimistic, and laments its very existence.

There is probably some technical reason why these instruments produce such doleful tones. Perhaps our sophisticated ears rebel against their peculiar harmonies and discords. But it is certainly curious that mouth-organs, concertinas, tin-whistles, and the rest, so beloved of simple people, should be intolerable to so many of us. Is it that we have no miseries to express in sound? Or is it that our optimism is so brittle that we dare not submit it to the onslaught of this strange music? I do not know.

All that I do know is that at the present moment I am sitting in my armchair before a bright fire, depressed beyond belief by the sound that floats through my window; while outside, in the cold, there stands a small boy, holding a mouth-organ in his numbed hands and bravely sliding his lips over the cold metallic edges of the thing; and by this time he is probably as gay as I am miserable.

AN APOLOGY FOR BAD PIANISTS

Ignoring those musical labourers who are paid so much per hour, at cinemas and dance-halls, to make some sort of rhythmical sound, all pianists, I think, may be divided into four classes. There are, first, the great soloists, the masters, Paderewski, Pachmann, and the rest, who would seem to have conquered all difficulties. With them the piano, a dead thing of wires and hammers, becomes a delicately responsive organism; its hammers are extra muscles, and its strings added nerves, running and leaping to obey every fleeting impulse; their playing is as saturated with personality as their gait or speech. Not so with the members of the second class, which is, to my mind, a dubious fraternity. They may be called the serious amateurs. Very often they take expensive lessons from some professor, who undertakes to "finish them off." But they never are finished off. The sign and mark of the serious amateur is that he practises assiduously some piece of music, maybe a Chopin study or a Brahms sonata, until he has it by heart; after which he assembles a number of friends (or, more often, new acquaintances), squashes their attempts at conversation, and, amid a tense silence, begins to play — or, as he would say, "interpret" — his laboured solo. The fourth class consists of odd strummers, vampers and thumpers; young ladies who play waltzes and old ladies who play hymns; cigarette-in-mouth youths with a bang-and-rattle style of performance; all inexorable, tormenting noise-makers, from those who persist in riveting — rather than playing — Rachmaninoff's C sharp minor Prelude to those who buy Sunday newspapers in order that they may pick out with one finger the tune of a comic song. All such are the enemies of peace and harmony, and as they cannot be ignored in any other place, here they can be quickly dismissed with all the more pleasure.

It remains now to say something of the third class of pianists, which, if it were reduced to such straits, could count me among its members. To write at some length of one's own class after perfunctorily dismissing others may seem to savour of egotism, but the truth is, we — I speak fraternally — have been so much maligned and misunderstood up to now, we have endured so many taunts in silence, that we have a right to be heard before we are finally and irrevocably condemned.

It is only on the score of technique, the mere rule-of-thumb business, that we stand below the serious amateurs; we belong to a higher order of beings and have grander souls; in spirit we come nearer to the great masters. The motives of the serious amateur are not above suspicion. In his assiduous practice, his limited repertoire, his studied semi-public style of performance, is there not a suggestion of vanity? Is his conscious parade of skill, taken along with his fear of unknown works, the mark of a selfless devotion to music, and music alone? I doubt it.

But our motives are certainly above suspicion. Music has no servants more disinterested, for not only do we gather no garlands in her service, but daily, for her sake, we risk making fools of ourselves, than which there can be no greater test of pure devotion. We, too, are the desperate venturers among pianists; every time that we seat ourselves at the keyboard we are leading a forlorn hope; and, whether we fall by the way or chance to come through unscathed, the only reward we can hope for is a kindly glance from the goddess of harmony.

It is hardly necessary to dwell on the fact that our execution is faulty, that we are humanly liable to make mistakes, seeing that our weaknesses have been for years the butt of musical pedants and small souls. In the dim past we received some sort of instruction, perhaps a few years' lessons, but being bright children with wills of our own we saw no use in labouring at scales and arpeggios, at the tepid compositions of Czerny, when there were balls to throw, stones to kick, and penny dreadfuls to be devoured. An unlocked door or an open window — and we escaped from the wretched drudgery, thus showing early that eager zest of life which still marks our clan.

Now, it is enthusiasm alone that carries us through. Our performance of any "piece of average difficulty" (as the publishers say) is nothing short of a series of miracles. As we peer at the music and urge our fingers to scurry over the keys, horrid gulfs yawn before us, great rocks come crashing down, the thick undergrowth is full of pitfalls and mantraps, but we are not to be deterred. Though we do not know what notes are coming next, or what fingers we shall use, if the music says *presto,* then *presto* it must be; the spirit of the tune must be set free, however its flesh may be lacerated. So we swing up the dizzy arpeggios as a hunted mountaineer might leap from crag to crag; we come down a run of demi-semi-quavers with the blind confidence of men trying to shoot the rapids of Niagara. Only the stouthearted and great of soul can undertake these perilous but magnificent ventures.

Unlike the serious amateurs, we do not pick and choose among pieces until we have found one to which we can give the cold glitter of an impeccable rendering. We attend concerts (for, above all, we are the concert-goers and dreamers of dreams, as O'Shaughnessy might have said) and come reeling out, intoxicated with sound; for days we are haunted by a lovely theme or an amazing climax until we can bear it no longer; we rush off to the music-shops to see if it is possible to capture this new lovely thing and keep it for ever; more often than not we return home in triumph, hardly giving ourselves time to flatten out the music before plunging into the opening bars. Nothing that has been arranged for the piano or that can be played in some sort of fashion on the instrument comes amiss if it has once aroused our enthusiasm; symphonies, operas, tone poems, string quartets are all welcome. Nay, we often prefer the arrangements of orchestral things, for we do not think of the piano merely as a solo instrument; to us it is the shining ivory and ebony gateway to the land of music. As our fingers wander over the keys our great dream-orchestras waken to life.

I believe that at the very end, when the depths of our folly and ignorance are fully revealed, when all our false notes have been cast up into one awful total by the recording angel of music, it will be found that we, the bad pianists, have been misjudged among men, that we, too, have loved and laboured for the divine art. When we file into Elysium, forlorn, scared, a shabby little band, and come within sight of Beethoven, whom we have murdered so many times, I believe that a smile will break through the thunder-cloud of his face. *"Ach!* Come you in, children," he will roar, "bad players, eh? . . . I have heard. . . . Very bad players. . . . But there have been worse among you. . . . The spirit was in you, and you have listened well. . . . Come in. . . . I have composed one hundred and fifty more symphonies and sonatas, and you shall hear them all."

ON TRAVEL BY TRAIN

Remove an Englishman from his hearth and home, his centre of corporal life, and he becomes a very different creature, one capable of sudden furies and roaring passions, a deep sea of strong emotions churning beneath his frozen exterior. I can pass, at all times, for a quiet, neighbourly fellow, yet I have sat, more than once, in a railway carriage with black murder in my heart. At the mere sight of some probably inoffensive fellow-passenger my whole being will be invaded by a million devils of wrath, and I "could do such bitter business as the day would quake to look on."

There is one type of traveller that never fails to rouse my quick hatred. She is a large, middle-aged woman, with a rasping voice and a face of brass. Above all things, she loves to invade smoking compartments that are already comfortably filled with a quiet company of smokers; she will come bustling in, shouting over her shoulder at her last victim, a prostrate porter, and, laden with packages of all maddening shapes and sizes, she will glare defiantly about her until some unfortunate has given up his seat. She is often accompanied by some sort of contemptible, whining cur that is only one degree less offensive than its mistress. From the moment that she has wedged herself in, there will be no more peace in the carriage, but simmering hatred, and everywhere dark looks and muttered threats. But everyone knows her. Courtesy and modesty perished in the world of travel on the day when she took her first journey; but it will not be long before she is in hourly danger of extinction, for there are strong men in our midst.

There are other types of railway travellers, not so offensive as the above, which combines all the bad qualities, but still annoying in a varying degree to most of us; and of these others I will enumerate one or two of the commonest. First, there are those who, when they would go on a journey, take all their odd chattels and household utensils and parcel them up in brown paper, disdaining such things as boxes and trunks; furthermore, when such eccentrics have loaded themselves up with queer-shaped packages, they will cast about for baskets of fruit and bunches of flowers to add to their own and other people's misery. Then there are the simple folk who are for ever eating and drinking in railway carriages. No sooner are they settled in their seats but they are passing each other tattered sandwiches and mournful scraps of pastry, and talking with their mouths full, and scattering crumbs over the trousers of fastidious old gentlemen. Sometimes they will peel and eat bananas with such rapidity that nervous onlookers are compelled to seek another compartment.

Some children do not make good travelling companions, for they will do nothing but whimper or howl throughout a journey, or they will spend all their time daubing their faces with chocolate or trying to climb out of the window. And the cranks are always with us; on the bleakest day, they it is who insist on all the windows being open, but in the sultriest season they go about in mortal fear of draughts, and will not allow a window to be touched.

More to my taste are the innocents who always find themselves in the wrong train. They have not the understanding necessary to fathom the time-tables, nor will they ask the railway officials for advice, so they climb into the first train that comes, and trust to luck. When they are being hurtled towards Edinburgh, they will suddenly look round the carriage and ask, with a mild touch of pathos, if they are in the right train for Bristol. And then, puzzled and disillusioned, they have to be bundled out at the next station, and we see them no more. I have often wondered if these simple voyagers ever reach their destinations, for it is not outside probability that they may be shot from station to station, line to line, until there is nothing mortal left of them.

Above all other railway travellers, I envy the mighty sleepers, descendants of the Seven of Ephesus. How often, on a long, uninteresting journey, have I envied them their sweet oblivion. With Lethe at their command, no dull, empty train journey, by day or night, has any terrors for them. Knowing the length of time they have to spend in the train, they compose themselves and are off to sleep in a moment, probably enjoying the gorgeous adventures of dream while the rest of us are looking blankly out of the window or counting our fingers. Two minutes from their destination they stir, rub their eyes, stretch themselves, collect their baggage, and, peering out of the window, murmur: "My station, I think." A moment later they go out, alert and refreshed, Lords of Travel, leaving us to our boredom.

Seafaring men make good companions on a railway journey. They are always ready for a pipe and a crack with any man, and there is usually some entertaining matter in their talk. But they are not often met with away from the coast towns. Nor do we often come across the confidential stranger in an English railway carriage, though his company is inevitable on the Continent and, I believe, in America. When the confidential stranger does make an appearance here, he is usually a very dull dog, who compels us to yawn through the interminable story of his life, and rides some wretched old hobbyhorse to death.

There is one more type of traveller that must be mentioned here, if only for the guidance of the young and simple. He is usually an elderly man, neatly dressed, but a little tobacco-stained, always seated in a corner, and he opens the conversation by pulling out a gold hunter and remarking that the train is at least three minutes behind time. Then, with the slightest encouragement, he will begin to talk, and his talk will be all of trains. As some men discuss their acquaintances, or others speak of violins or roses, so he talks of trains, their history, their quality, their destiny. All his days and nights seem to have been passed in railway carriages, all his reading seems to have been in time-tables. He will tell you of the 12:35 from this place and the 3:49 from the other place, and how the 10:18 ran from So-and-so to So-and-so in such a time, and how the 8:26 was taken off and the 5:10 was put on; and the greatness of his subject moves him to eloquence, and there is passion and mastery in his voice, now wailing over a missed connection or a departed hero of trains, now exultantly proclaiming the glories of a non-stop express or a wonderful run to time. However dead you were to the passion, the splendour, the pathos, in this matter of trains, before he has done with you you will be ready to weep over the 7:37 and cry out in ecstasy at the sight of the 2:52.

Beware of the elderly man who sits in the corner of the carriage and says that the train is two minutes behind time, for he is the Ancient Mariner of railway travellers, and will hold you with his glittering eye.

II. From I FOR ONE 1923

ON BEGINNING

How difficult it is to make a beginning. I speak of essay-writing, an essentially virtuous practice, and not of breaking the ten commandments. It is much easier to begin, say, a review or an article than it is to begin an essay, for with the former you attach yourself to something outside yourself, you have an excuse for writing and therefore have more courage. If it is a review that has to be written, well, there, waiting for you, inviting your comment, is the book. Similarly with an article, you have your subject, something that everybody is excited about, let us say the Education of Correlates or the Bearing of Teleology on the Idea of God, and thus you know what is expected of you and (though it may sound difficult to common sense and physiology) you can take up your pen with a light heart. But to have nothing to cling hold of, to have no excuse for writing at all, to be compelled to spin everything out of oneself, to stand naked and shivering in the very first sentence one puts down, is clearly a very different matter, and this is the melancholy situation in which the essayist always finds himself. It is true that he need not always be melancholy; if he is full of himself, brimming over with bright talk, in a mood to take the whole world into his confidence, ready to rhapsodise about music-halls to Mr. Bertrand Russell, Dean Inge, and the Lord Chief Justice, or to soliloquise on death and the mutability of things before the Mayor and Corporation of Stockport, if he is in such good fettle the essayist will find his task a very pleasant one indeed, never to be exchanged for such drudge's work as reviews and articles; and he will step briskly on to the stage and posture in the limelight without a tremor. But such moments are rare, and the essayist at ordinary times, though he would eagerly undertake to defend his craft, cannot quite rid himself of the feeling that there is something both absurd and decidedly impudent in this business of talking about oneself for money; this feeling haunts the back of his mind like some gibbering spectre, and it generally produces one of three effects. According to his temperament, it will prevent him from doing anything at all that particular day or perhaps any other day, or it will allow him to write a few brilliant opening sen-

tences and then shut him up, or it will keep him from making a start until
the last possible moment.

For my own part, I am one of those who find it difficult to begin; I stand
on the brink for hours, hesitating to make the plunge; I will do anything
but the work in hand. This habit is certainly a nuisance, but perhaps it is
not quite so intolerable as that of some other persons, men of my acquaintance, who fall into the second category mentioned above and always find
themselves making dashing openings and then coming to a stop. Without a
moment's hesitation, they will take up their pens and write on the top of a
clean sheet of paper — "On Massacre," and will then begin at once: "It is
only as a means to an end that Massacre can be adversely criticised. As an
end in itself, something that is its own reward, there is nothing to be said
against it and everything to be said for it. It is only since the gradual
overclouding of the purely aesthetic view of life that Massacre has come to
need any defence. It is true that we still talk of art, but actually we care
nothing for its values, and in particular for those of Sublime Art, which
asks for the whole of life upon which to experiment. Thus it is that we have
come to misunderstand Massacre, a manifestation of the Sublime, and have
lost sight of the true Herod." At this point, they will stare at what they
have written, well pleased with it as an opening, and then discover that the
flow has ceased. They will write "Albigenses" — "Sicilian Vespers" —
"St. Bartholomew" on the nearest sheet of blotting-paper, but all to no
purpose; they will have come to a stop, and horrible hours will pass, and
perhaps many more dashing openings will have been made, before any real
progress will have come about and their essay taken some sort of shape.
Such writers seem to me even more unfortunate than I am, for I do at least
go forward once I have made a beginning; as soon as I have summoned up
courage to ring the bell I am at least admitted into the house of my choice,
and am not, like these others, left kicking my heels in the vestibules of half
a dozen houses perhaps without ever seeing the interior of any of them.

Nevertheless, though there may be worse things, my own habit of procrastination is undoubtedly a great nuisance. Fear, indolence, and a plain
incapacity to concentrate for more than a few seconds, all play their parts.
In the end, it is true, they delay my beginning so long that they succeed in
destroying themselves, for I become so desperate at last that my fear and
indolence are willy-nilly driven out of court and I even achieve some sort
of concentration. But in the meantime I have wasted hours and hours. I
begin, usually in the morning, with the fullest intention of settling down
immediately to work; an essay has to be written; it has been left too long
already, and I have no time to waste. But no sooner have I arrived in my
room than I begin to do a great many things that I never do at any other
time. I clean a pipe or two, all the while pretending to myself that I am
eager to get to work, though it is curious (to say the least of it) that I never

scrape and clean my pipes at any other time. After having lovingly filled and lighted one of these beautifully clean pipes, I sit down, but get up again almost immediately to straighten one of the pictures, to restore a few books to their proper shelves, or to clear away any odd papers that may be lying about. Then instead of sitting at my table on a hard little chair, whose unyielding surface and ungracious angles would serve to remind me that life is real and earnest, I bury myself in an enormous basket-chair of the kind that is exceedingly popular (and not without good reason) at the universities. This chair is so long and low that I always find it necessary to have my feet off the ground when I am sitting in it, so in this thoroughly comfortable posture, with slippered feet up somewhere near the fire-place, knees slightly bent, head well back, I prepare myself to grapple with the work in hand. I reach for my fountain-pen and a stiff writing-pad; my pipe is going beautifully; now, if ever, is the time to concentrate. But alas! — I cannot concentrate. I can follow another man's thought, in a book or out of it, as long as it should be necessary, but left to its own devices my mind does nothing but wander aimlessly, for I am of a discursive habit of mind, with strong but eccentric powers of association. Mr. Pelman and his friends would weep over my puling attempts to keep my thought to its proper theme; and I sometimes think that I would seek their assistance had I not somewhere at the back of my mind a fear that they would contrive to turn me away from scribbling altogether and convert me to Salesmanship, whatever that may be.

Gloriously at ease, then, lying in my big fat chair, I consider the prose masterpiece in miniature that must be born into the world during these next few hours. In bed last night, when I ought to have been asleep, I had the whole thing worked out; it was there down to the last comma, and it was wonderful; the bed-posts were festooned with noble thoughts and the counterpane glittered with bright miraculous phrases; there can be no doubt that I surpassed myself last night. No wonder that now, when the work has actually to be done, I feel so sleepy. And unfortunately, though the subject itself remains, I can hardly remember a word of what I invented last night, and the few snatches I do remember seem crude and thin. It does not even appear a very promising subject now. What is there to be said about it that has not already been said? Little or nothing. But something must be done, so I write down the title and draw a line underneath it, and contrary to my usual practice I do this very slowly and carefully, merely to waste time and retard the evil moment when I shall have to take thought. But long before I have finished drawing the line, my mind has wandered whole continents away from the subject. Drawing the line so slowly has made me think of an old master I once had at school who was always pointing out that the best way to draw straight lines without the aid of a ruler was to draw them very quickly; and from him my mind has rambled round to

other masters I had, and from them to holidays, and to friends and California and paint-brushes and Whistler and Chelsea and my friend X and
Devonshire cream and finally to Coleridge. And now that I have arrived at
Coleridge, I suddenly remember that I want to look up some passage in the
Table-Talk, so with a not ignoble effort I scramble out of my chair and
search for the book and the particular passage. And now it is nearly half an
hour since I read that passage, but the *Table-Talk* is still in my hands and I
am still reading. But I put it down because I recollect an old project of
mine, a book on the criticism of Coleridge, and now I begin to plan that
book all over again and detached phrases for the introductory chapter
come into my mind; and now I decide that I must sketch my plan for this
book on paper, and I take up my pen and paper again, but only to remember that I have an essay to write. . . . Lunch has come and gone. . . .
And now I will settle down and get my work done. But first I must put
away the copy of Coleridge's *Table-Talk* still lying in my chair. So I put it
away, but when I withdraw my hand it has taken out the second volume of
Leslie Stephen's *Hours in a Library,* and for no accountable reason I find
myself still standing by the bookshelf reading his essay on Horace Walpole.
This will never do, and rather angrily I put Stephen away and fling myself
down in my chair once more. My manhood is at stake; I must take the
plunge; so without more ado I seize hold of my pen and paper and write:
"How difficult it is to make a beginning. I speak of essay-writing, an essentially virtuous practice, and not of breaking the ten commandments. . . ."
And then, with only a few halts, I go forward to the end. But what the end
is, I cannot tell you, for it has all become very complicated.

HAUNTED

It has come back again, and I suppose that I shall have it with me now for
the remainder of the day. Ta tumti tumti tumtiti — there it goes — tumtiti
tumtitee. This is to be tune-haunted, one might almost say hagridden, only
that a melody, however much of a nuisance it may become, cannot possibly
be described as a hag; and to be tune-haunted is my constant fate. Poets
and novelists are for ever talking of people who are haunted by a face, but

for my part I have never been haunted by a face, and, indeed, agree with Sir Thomas Browne and some others among my betters in declaring that I can never summon up a satisfactory image in my mind of any face that is really dear to me. Tunes, little snatches of melody some two bars long, are my oppressors. As I am setting down these words, there is a monotonous concert taking place somewhere at the back of my mind, and it is ta tumti tumti tumtiti all the way. I will describe, as far as I can, what happens. I go to a concert, we will say, and come away with a swarm of melodies humming and buzzing under my hat. After a little while they leave me in peace, but then, during the next few days, I discover that my mind is continually groping for something, continually adding one note to another in its search for one particular delightful sequence. Unless I happen to be fully occupied, I feel a faint dissatisfaction: something is missing. Then suddenly, as if a room had been flooded with light, a melody, one of the tunes I have just heard, sings clearly in my mind, and I am enraptured with it. No other art could give me such a moment; it is a sudden undreamed-of caress from the Muse herself, Euterpe or Terpsichore; and the world and I, golden lads, move on to the sound of ta tumti tumti tumtiti. But alas! the melody only comes back for a few moments, and unless I should happen to examine it carefully while I still have it in my grasp (and it is as if one should happen to count the feathers of the Phoenix) and obtain some idea of its notation, it vanishes as suddenly as it first appeared, and I am left to wander in a tuneless void. Where it goes to I do not know, but I should not be surprised if it did not sink into my unconscious mind and there, in that dim region, serenade the sick and groaning complexes. What is certain is that for a space I have it not.

Then begins an intolerable game of hide-and-seek, sometimes lasting for days and days. Though outwardly I am as other men, and eat, sleep, work when compelled, talk with my friends, sneer at my enemies, perform great acts of self-sacrifice in my imagination and innumerable mean, petty, rather selfish little acts in actual practice, in short, though I behave as other men do and would appear even to someone who knew me very well in no way different from what I usually am, nevertheless I am a man living in a queer dream, a man for ever occupied with the most foolish quest imaginable. If the tune is in my unconscious mind all the time, then nothing could better illustrate the doctrine that the will has little or no power to bring anything up from the unconscious to the conscious mind than this game of hide-and-seek. Sometimes, after great concentration, I manage to lay hold of ta tumti or it may be tumti tumtiti, but the full glory of ta tumti tumti tumtiti baffles all my efforts. "Ta tum" it calls mockingly from one corner of my mind, and off I go in hot pursuit, beating among the woods and thickets of memory, but all in vain. It has fled, but not far, only far enough to call

"Tumti tumtiti" somewhere close behind my back, and then to escape me again. Even an iron will (and mine is not metallic at all) would not be able to command such an elusive mocking thing; though I suppose it is also true to say that a person with an iron will would not engage in such foolery with tunes, would neither hunt them nor be haunted by them, and thus would never make the test. Then when I have given up all hope, and perhaps deliberately shut all thought of the matter out of my mind, the tune comes floating back and I am in possession of it once again. And this time, it remains.

There is now no end to the tune, which goes on singing itself over and over at the back of my mind. It forms a kind of background, for the time being, for my whole life, and all things flow to its measure. I pass ta tumti tumtiti days and nights, and move and have my being in a recurring tumti tumtitee. Curiously enough, no matter what the original character of the various tunes might be, they always take on one particular kind of significance before I have done with them and always have precisely the same effect upon me. The odd bars of melody that have haunted me from time to time have been of many different kinds, only alike in that none of them has been a really massive theme, like many of those in Beethoven's Nine or Wagner's *Ring*. Unfortunately, I have never kept a record of them, but I am quite certain that they would make a very odd list, in which all kinds of music, good, bad, and indifferent, would be represented. With one or two exceptions, the music I like best and can always listen to with delight has never haunted me, perhaps because it is its superb development and general structure that appeal to me; and though I have often enjoyed such music in my mind after I have come to know it very well, it does not haunt me in the fashion of these separate snatches. I am rather glad, too, because once a melody has given me a thorough haunting I have never any further use for it afterwards; it seems to me absolutely devoid of beauty and significance, a bone with all the marrow sucked out, and I fling it away, and this is clearly not the way to treat great music. I wish I could remember all the tunes, or parts of tunes, that I have lived with for a short hectic season in this fashion; but I am sure that at best I can only recall a few. There was, I remember, the queer little waltz-tune that figured as a serenade and an intermezzo in Wolf-Ferrari's *Jewels of the Madonna;* and one of Elgar's "Enigma" variations, the one in three flats; and the jerky little theme that the orchestra plays when the sacristan (or whatever he is) hobbles across the stage in the first act of *Tosca;* and the refrain of an old French song that I once heard Mr. Plunket Greene sing and that had some such words as *"D'ou venez vous promener vous promener vous belle";* and a lilting open-air sort of theme from the first movement of one of Grieg's violin sonatas; and a snatch from a silly music-hall song that went "Oh I do love you, my Orange-Girl"; and, an exception to the general rule for I have never tired of it, Schubert's "Litany"; and the first few bars, a trifle lighter than air and exquisitely coloured, of a certain capriccio by Brahms; and many another that I could whistle but probably could not name. My ta tumti tumtiti of the moment is, I fancy, from somebody's imitation Old English dance; it is not Edward German's, of that I am sure, but for the rest, I do not know who wrote it, what it is called, how it begins or follows on (for it is just a few bars in the middle that are haunting me), or even where I have heard it played.

I notice that it is going the same way as the others. As it repeats itself endlessly, it is losing all its brightness and eager lilt and is becoming, by some hocus-pocus, curiously wistful, the expression of vain regret, still a little mocking perhaps but now gathering tenderness and settling into a not unpleasing melancholy. However blithe they may be at first, these tunes all have precisely the same effect in the end; they ta tumti me into a sort of inner mood of melancholy so that even when I am laughing and talking I am still doing it to their rather mournful lilt. It is curious that music, once it has filtered into the memory, should always lose any gaiety it might have once had and turn regretful, softly hymning a world of lost endeavour. Nothing can express gaiety, happiness, and even ecstasy as music can, but we must be listening to it and not remembering it (at least snatches of it), or otherwise it will soon flow back into the main stream of melancholy, to which most music (taking the art in its entirety) seems to belong. Perhaps this is because the happy kind of music does not depend on its melodic structure but on the manner in which it is developed, the way in which it rushes to a climax, and also on the irresistible appeal of polyphony, one theme answering another, escaping and returning, and so forth; whereas all of this is lost and nothing but the melodic outline, endlessly retraced, remains to the little tunes that haunt the mind. This repetition of one little tune gives us music in its primitive form, and music in its primitive form, the naïve folk-music of every race, always seems subdued and mournful. A tune may have a quick dancing lilt with it and so appear jolly enough at a first hearing, but let it once sink into the mind and its very superficial bustle and cheerfulness only heighten the real strain of regret or disillusion that soon makes its appearance: music has its irony too. My imitation Old English dance, which is still buzzing at the back of my mind, and of which, by the way, I am now heartily sick, for it has long outstayed its welcome, is certainly an ironical little caper, and might have been composed by one of Shakespeare's musical clowns had it been a better tune, for it has something of their spirit. If I cannot discover any other way of ridding myself of this bitter-sweet carolling, which is ta-tumti-ing the world away, I must fall back upon my old remedy, a remedy that has never failed even in the most desperate instances. I must find out the name of the piece, and then, if it is arranged for the piano, buy it and play through these particular bars about half a dozen times. When I have done this, I shall be able to walk abroad once more without a care or a ta or tumti in the world, a free man until the next tune leads me into philandering again, and I desire, pursue, capture and sicken once more. O fickle weak humanity! Ta tumti tumti tumtiti.

ALL ABOUT OURSELVES

"Now tell me," said the lady, "all about yourself." The effect was instantaneous, shattering. Up to that moment, I had been feeling expansive; I was self-confident, alert, ready to give a good account of myself in the skirmish of talk. If I had been asked my opinion of anything between here and Sirius, I would have given it at length, and I was quite prepared to talk of places I had never seen and books I had never read; I was ready to lie, and to lie boldly and well. Had she not made that fatal demand, I would have roared like the sweet little lion she imagined me to be, roared as gently as any sucking-dove or nightingale: for, unlike that haphazard impresario Peter Quince, I had, you may say, "the lion's part written." But to tell her all about myself. My expansive mood suddenly shrivelled to nothing; every richly dyed shred of personality was stripped from me and there remained only my naked, shivering mortality. Nothing but a jumble of memorable old phrases haunted my mind: I was, like Socrates in the first syllogism, a man and therefore a mortal, such stuff as dreams are made on, born of a woman and full of trouble, one whose days are as grass. . . . What was there to be said? I stared at my sprightly companion, who was still smiling, half-playfully, half-expectantly, and I must have looked like a child peering from the ruins at the squadrons of an invading army. Then I mumbled something so unsatisfactory that, despairing of any intimate avowals, she passed on to some other topic, while I, donning my cloak and wig, my cap and bells, left the naked six feet of ground to which her demand had confined me, and made haste to follow her. Yorick was himself again.

The request, so framed, was undoubtedly preposterous. Indeed, it was so obviously calculated to silence any normal human being that one may reasonably suspect the motive that lay behind it. To confess one's terror at meeting such a demand is not necessarily to hint at an engaging modesty. It was so all-embracing, so ultimate, that only a megalomaniac or a great genius could have coped with it. A request to know what I had been doing for the past year or intended to do in the next twelve months, to know whether I approved of William Shakespeare or liked early rising, would have set my tongue wagging for an insufferable length of time. I am ready to talk about myself, that is, about my opinions, my likes and dislikes, my whims, my experiences, my hopes and fears, at any and every season. I have my own share of that windy, foolish, but, I hope, not too unpleasant vanity which is common to most people who do little tricks with words and pigments and fiddle-strings; I can fly my little coloured balloons of conceit with the next scribbler or chorus girl or cabinet minister. But even if we only need the merest shadow of an excuse to talk about ourselves, there must be something interposed between the universe and our bare selves; there must be bounds assigned to our flow of egotism; we must be given some idea of ourselves to work upon, to build up or knock down. To tell *all* about ourselves in one vast breath is really to press the whole round world in the lemon-squeezer of our minds, to explain the sum total of things in terms of ourselves, to raise the ego to a monstrous height. The very thought of it flips the mind with "a three-man beetle" and stuns a man into humility.

Perhaps with most men there comes a time when they are able to give a reasonable sort of account of themselves; but I, for one, am free to confess that I have not yet travelled so far. I am still busy trying, unsuccessfully as yet, to piece together the various impressions and opinions of myself I gather from other people to make up the fragments of my portrait. I am still noting, with amazement, the broken reflections and queer glimpses of myself that I catch sight of in other people's minds. This I conceive to be the third stage of one's progress in self-knowledge: how long it lasts and whether there is a fourth stage at all are questions that I cannot answer. But I can vouch for the two previous stages. When we are very young, not only has the earth and every common sight (to plunder Wordsworth) the glory and the freshness of a dream, but we ourselves have something of the same glory and freshness; we gulp experience and do not question ourselves, and this golden age lasts until we realise, with something of a shock, that there are other selves who see us from the outside just as we see them. It is when we become conscious of other selves that we become self-conscious. Then we pass on to the second, most disquieting stage, which, for most people who are impressionable and imaginative, covers the whole period of their later teens and early twenties, and may even last considerably longer.

At this time we do nothing but question ourselves; rosy little Hamlets, we are for ever busy with self-communion. Never are we so anxious to discover what we are and never do we make so little of the matter as we do then. We examine ourselves in the light of everything we read, and become weathercocks swinging before the changing wind of ideas. An hour of Swinburne turns us into magnificent pagans and sensuous lovers, but before the day is out, a few pages of Carlyle have promptly transformed us into sturdy philosophers or roaring men of action. We can be Stoics before breakfast, Epicureans after lunch, and uncertain but hopeful Platonists before nightfall. Then gradually we lose heart, for though every philosophy attracts us and seems to have been almost designed to catch our eye, though we can always read so much of ourselves into every character we admire, yet there is always something essential wanting in us. We might be anything: we are nothing; nothing but a bundle of impulses, a rag-bag of discarded ideals and wavering loyalties. We are convinced that other people will never understand us, will never be subtle enough to appreciate that curious quality which, for all our wretched lack of anything like character, our instability of purpose, our wandering will, somehow makes us splendid and unique. Meanwhile, we can make nothing of ourselves, for we seem radically different from hour to hour, according to the company we are in. If we are with some great lout of a fellow, then we see ourselves dapper, fragile, precious, and, in a flash, decide the path we will take for the rest of our lives. But no sooner do we fall in with some little dandy than we hear our own voices, cutting through his mincing accents, and recognize in them the notes of strong determined men who will make their way in the world. So we go on, until we feel that we can show nothing to the world but this dance of shifting selves.

But we grow up, and then either we cast off introspection in engaging to do the world's work or we still try to puzzle it all out. Perhaps we begin to remark the figures we cut in the minds of our friends and acquaintances, and try to live up to the best of them; though how we discover which are the best of them is a question I am not prepared to answer. This may lead us into vanity, a swelling eager sort of vanity, restless in pursuit of praise, a characteristic that is not so bad as it sounds. As some wiser men have already pointed out, vanity is at least warm, human, social, frankly dependent upon sympathy. There is an infinitely worse alternative, easy to fall into if we strongly approve of ourselves and yet shrink from soliciting other people's suffrages, and this is the solitary and desolating vice of pride. Many a man is praised for his reserve and so-called shyness when he is simply too proud to risk making a fool of himself. The vain man will cut capers in order to obtain notice and applause, the proud man asks for notice and applause without being willing to cut the capers, while the very proud man has such a miraculous self that he does not even want the applause. Some philosophies make this last state of complete self-satisfaction their goal, but one and all omit to mention the obvious advantages enjoyed by the oyster on such a plan of life. But unless we are victims of such icy folly, we discover, perhaps to our astonishment, that our greatest moments come when we find that we are not unique, when we come upon another self that is very like our own. The discovery of a continent is mere idle folly compared with this discovery of a sympathetic other-self, a friend or a lover. Where now is the sickly pleasure in not being understood, in being unique, miraculous, entirely self-satisfying, in shutting the painted doors and windows of the mind? Before this solid smashing happiness of thus being understood, all our walls go down and the sunlight comes streaming in. And then, and not until then, begins that endless tale which seems to be merely about this and that, but is really all about ourselves.

A COINCIDENCE

Although we talk so much about coincidence, we do not really believe in it. In our heart of hearts, we think better of the universe; we are secretly convinced that it is not such a slipshod haphazard affair, that everything in it has a meaning. If, let us say, a man rises on New Year's morning, takes up his newspaper, and, opening it casually, finds himself staring at a name identical with his own in the column of Deaths, it is a thousand to one that he will be shocked and strangely apprehensive. Afterwards, he will relate the incident to his friends, call it a curious coincidence, and laugh, loudly though not heartily, over it, and his friends will call it a curious coincidence too, and they will all laugh loudly together and slap one another on the back and feel convinced that they are fine strong fellows with no nonsense about them. This, at least, is what the men will do; the women, who are realists and less given to deluding themselves, will be more openly dubious. None of them will feel entirely comfortable at heart; they will all find it difficult to dismiss the notion that somehow or other such an incident is significant, that behind it lies the finger not of chance but of fate.

C

As we go through the year we light upon quite a number of these "co-incidences" that we choose to interpret one way or the other; and whether they promise good or ill fortune, it is certain that they always promise something. Even the smallest, things so trifling that we do not consider them worth mentioning to our friends, are not without their effect. The old wondering, peering, superstitious creature that crouches at the back of all our minds sees them as light straws borne along the wind of fortune. Even the most trifling of all will yet induce a mood, a mood that may lead to a quarrel or a reconciliation, to the revocation of a will or the beginning of a masterpiece. It is very foolish and even dangerous to imagine that we are reasonable beings; such notions, in view of what we think we know of the history of our species, are themselves highly unreasonable. So it will do us little harm openly to confess for once the quite irrational influence that certain curious incidents, sometimes spoken of as coincidences, have upon our minds. If it is a weakness, it is probably a universal one, and so need not trouble anyone.

Having thus, rather cunningly I think, put everybody into the same boat, I am ready to admit what I should not admit without some such preamble. I am ready to admit that I have been oddly troubled for the past week by the memory of a very absurd little coincidence. Unhappily it was not a pleasant one; it has left a nasty flavour in the mouth; and though nothing may come of it (for I cannot really see that it has any recognisable significance) I do not feel so sure of myself as I did. Something, I feel, is rotten, somewhere, and I can only hope that it is still in the state of Denmark. What I call a coincidence insists upon assuming, somewhere in the darker regions of my mind, the form of an accusation, until I feel vaguely responsible for all manner of evils, like a man who imagines that he has done murder in his sleep.

Last week, I was staying in the north of England, and set out one day to visit an old friend of mine who lives in one of those little industrial places, half towns, half villages, that are to be found in the neighbourhood of the great manufacturing cities. This particular village is perched on the summit of a hill and lies on the edge of a wide moor. It is a grim, forbidding country, bleak and desolate before the coming of the tall factories, and still more inhuman and terrifying to the eyes of a stranger now that its surface is pock-marked with the unlovely signs of industry, looking as if the great hills had broken into small-pox. The factories thrust up their long slender chimneys and show their thousand and one windows, like blind eyes, to the cold light; the few green fields are harshly framed in black walls; great cinder heaps abound there; monotonous rows of little houses run sharply this way and that, up or down from the dirty roads; in front are the brown wastes of moorland, with their scattered clumps of hard jagged black rock silhouetted against the sky. The moors frown on the mills, and the mills frown on the men. Such country cannot be ignored; it grips hold of the mind; it is unique. Human nature being by no means a tender plant, it flowers there as elsewhere; indeed, this part of England is a great breeding ground for massive virtues and odd humours.

Only at night does it become tolerable to a stranger. On a fine clear night, all its harshness disappears, and it achieves an unfamiliar beauty of its own. When the sun has finally gone down, a few strange lights, pale amethyst, green, deep orange, linger above the moorland. The hills fade into the sky; the distant tram-cars, climbing the hills, look like shining golden beetles; the street-lamps across the valley seem to bring new and pretty constellations into the sky. Unhappily, it was not night when I boarded a tram-car that would take me to my friend's ugly village on the hill, and though a tram ride there is rather exciting, for the track is almost that of a mountain railway, and the trams are like top-heavy creaky galleons, I felt depressed as I stared out of the window. The tram made one last groaning effort and succeeded in scaling the rise that leads to the village. We passed mournful and ill-shaped football grounds, groups of little allotment gardens, sufficiently unlovely to smirch the innocence even of a vegetable, and what was worst, any number of those hideous little hen-runs in which the submerged tenth of the race of fowls peck out a miserable existence. We passed a public-house or two, and then were soon into the village. I remarked the dreary little shops, the short streets that ran sharply down from one side of the road, and the houses, built of stone and now nearly black. The tram stopped and I descended into the street, in no humour for an encounter with the representative of any lower civilisation, such as a bland Chinaman or a tall smiling South Sea Islander.

Facing me, as I descended from the tram, was a little street that immediately attracted my attention. It had only four or five houses on each side, almost windowless dwellings with the colour and lines of coal trucks. They had no gardens, nor even yards, railings or a few steps; the hapless folk who lived in them walked straight from the street into the house or from the house into the street. Only a small part of the roadway was paved, the rest being a dreadful mixture of grass, cinders and mire. It ended in a patch of waste ground, from which the grass had long been worn. There was the road at the top, with the trams groaning by, and the patch of waste ground at the bottom, and two little rows of dark cottage houses looking at each other. There seemed to be no children there, or cats and dogs, or even open doors: nothing but an unbroken silence. It seemed to me, as I stood there, to be the most unpleasant street I had ever seen, the very last street in the world I would ever choose to live in. It was not one of your picturesque, lurid slum streets, ever ripe for either a spree or a murder; it was perfectly respectable, and always would be; no Sunday newspaper would ever make good copy out of its doings; it kept itself to itself. But what a place, inconceivably dreary, suffocating! Everything that had gone to make that street was clearly wrong; there could be no argument about it, no question of this system or that system; something stood plainly indicted. There behind those walls, living and loving, dwelt Man, the dream of the swarming protozoa, how noble in reason, how infinite in faculties!

But what of the coincidence that has disturbed me in secret for this past week? Why, at that moment, when I had just begun to mutter "There, but for the grace of God . . . ," it suddenly occurred to me to look for the name of this street, fully expecting to discover in it some last ironical stroke, some mention of Lavender, Acacia or even Paradise. I looked up, and there, above my head and plain for all the world to see, was the name in bold white letters — Priestley Street.

III. From FIGURES IN MODERN LITERATURE 1924

WALTER DE LA MARE

On their last evening together on Beechwood Hill, it will be remembered, Miss M. tells Mr. Anon. of a ghost that came to a house near Cirencester: "And when it was asked, 'Are you a good spirit or a bad?' it made no answer, but vanished, the book said — I remember the very words — 'with a curious perfume and most melodious twang.' " Mr. de la Mare himself is not unlike that ghost, for when we approach him as critics and ask him if he is this or that he, too, seems to vanish — "with a curious perfume and a most melodious twang." He is one of those writers who have a few obvious characteristics known to everybody, characteristics that are complacently indicated by the reviewer whenever such writers publish a book; but if we wish to press forward and examine him more closely, he becomes curiously elusive, almost playing Ariel to our Caliban. There is no difficulty if we are simply prepared to enjoy and not to analyse, for we can always recognise his hand; the work is all of a piece, and no one who has once known it can fail to appreciate that curious perfume and that most melodious twang. Superficially, his work may appear somewhat fragmentary and casual, the spasmodic creation of a gifted dilettante — a few bundles of short lyrics, some short tales, and a fantasy or two, so many lovely and quaint odds and ends; but nothing could be further from the truth, for actually his work is one of the most individual productions this century has given us, every scrap of it being stamped with its author's personality and taking its place in the de la Mare canon. If Mr. de la Mare were to wander into half a dozen literary forms that so far have not known him, if he were to bid farewell to poetry and fiction and do nothing but essays, criticism, and even history, the new work would promptly link up with the old and take on a quality different from that of any other essays, criticism, or history, so marked is his individuality. Nevertheless, he remains to criticism an elusive figure, whose outline and gestures are not easily fixed in the memory — a shadowy Pied Piper.

One fairly common misconception must be brushed aside before we can begin to examine Mr. de la Mare, and that is the notion that he is primarily a creator of pretty fancies for the children. Because he has occasionally produced a volume for children, many persons regard him merely as the latest and most delicate of nursery poets, an artist for the Christmas Tree. Nor is this notion, except in its crudest form, confined to the uncritical, for even at this late hour there is a tendency on the part of many critics to treat Mr. de la Mare as if he were not an artist with a unique vision, a man of strange delights and sorrows, but a rather gentlemanly conjurer they had engaged for their children's party. There is, of course, an element of truth in this view, but at the moment it is hardly worth while disengaging it, though, as we shall presently see, this element of truth happens to be of supreme importance. Regarded as a general view this popular misconception is so preposterous that if we go to the other extreme, if we argue that Mr. de la Mare is a writer that no child should be suffered to approach, we shall not be further from the truth. We could point out that his work is really unbalanced, decadent, unhealthy, poisonous fruit for any child's eating. Consider his subjects. *The Return* is the story of a man who is partly possessed by an evil restless ghost, who comes back from a meditation among the tombstones in the local churchyard, wearing the face of a long-dead adventurer — a nightmare. The poetry is filled with madness and despair, wonders, and witchcraft, lit with a sinister moonlight; some crazed Elizabethan fool sitting in a charnel-house might have lilted some of these songs. The *Memoirs of a Midget* is the history of a freak who moves elvishly in the shadow of some monstrous spirit of evil; it is a long dream that never turns to the waking world, but only changes, when it does change, to nightmare. The tales in *The Riddle* are worse; they are the chronicles of crazed or evil spirits, Miss Duveen, Seaton's Aunt, and the rest; their world is one of abnormalities, strange cruelties and terrors, monstrous trees and birds and dead men on the prowl; their very sunlight is corrupt, maggot-breeding. And is this, we might ask, the writer of pretty fancies for the children? — as well might we introduce Webster, Poe and Baudelaire into the nursery and schoolroom. Such an account of Mr. de la Mare as an unwholesome decadent is manifestly absurd, but on the whole it is probably less absurd than the more popular opinion of him as a pretty-pretty children's poet. Yet we can use his work for children as a kind of jumping-off place in our pursuit of him.

We can begin with the large and very successful anthology of poetry that Mr. de la Mare has brought out recently, *Come Hither,* "a collection of rhymes and poems for the young of all ages." This very personal and delightful anthology has a curious introduction, in which very characteristically the author, by the use of quaint anagrams, makes a kind of story out of his account of Nature and Poetry; and it also contains an enormous number of rambling notes and quotations from all manner of curious old books. And this happy volume makes it clear that when he set out to please the "young of all ages," he also set to please himself and brought together all the poetry he loved, whether it was something by Shakespeare or Milton, or an old jingle of nursery rhyme. There is about this anthology, though it contains some of the most solemn and moving passages in our literature, something of the golden spacious air of childhood, something a thousand leagues removed from the atmosphere of most anthologies of this kind, and one realizes that this is not merely the result of good taste, a sense of what is fitting, and so on, but of something much rarer, an imagination of an unusual kind, one that is infinitely wider and more sensitive than a child's, and yet, in one sense, still is a child's imagination. It has been said that a keen remembrance of childhood, the ability of a man to see again at will the world as he saw it when a child, is a test and sign of genius. But imagination, it is clear, includes the ability to recapture former states of mind, whether they belong to childhood, youth or later life, and the childhood theory of genius is obviously much too wide. It is probably true to say that geniuses of the first rank, the Homers and Shakespeares and Dantes, feed imaginatively on all their experience and are no more dependent on childhood than they are on any other period of their life; they are for ever gorging on existence, and as they age, their vision widens, or at least changes. But there is a lesser order of geniuses who create worlds for themselves that have a distinct life of their own, but are obviously different, running obliquely, from the actual world we know, and it appears to me that such writers (Dickens is the type) build up their little universes from their childish impressions and carry forward with them into manhood their early imaginings and memories. What they do not understand and cannot enter into imaginatively during their youth they never do understand, not, at least, for the purposes of their art. The world of the imaginative child is made up of impressions that are largely at the mercy of his reading. Thus the boy who has pored over the *Arabian Nights* soon discovers when he walks abroad that his London is beginning to look like Bagdad, and if this impression is sufficiently strong the years may drive it away from the surface of his mind, but they will never completely destroy it; and if our boy becomes a man of letters, then the caliph, the barber, and his brothers, and all the rest will probably find a way, beneath some disguise, into all his chapters. Dickens spent his childhood among the odd figures that loafed about Portsmouth, Chatham, and Camden Town, and his earliest reading, particularly his rapt study of Smollett, gave him a pair of spectacles through which these odd figures looked even more grotesque than they actually were, so that for the remainder of his life he moved in a world of queer shapes and violent ever-recurring gestures. Afterwards he met many new types of men and women, counting some of them among his intimates, that he tried very earnestly to portray, but he never succeeded in dowering them with that superhuman vitality which animates his other characters, for the simple reason that such persons, belonging as they did to a world he only knew later in life, never entered into his childish memories and imagination, which represented the animating principle, the pulsating heart, of all his work. A Shakespeare could have swept them all in, a Dickens could not. One mark of all the writers who belong to this class is their weakness in portraying normal, somewhat commonplace and sensible persons, who hardly exist in a child's world. Figures of terror and figures of fun, fearful or adorable monsters like Fagin and Micawber or Quilp and Mrs. Gamp, the vast shadows thrown by a few odd personages in the flickering taper-light of a child's terror or glee, these alone are the characters to which they can give an intense life of their own.

It is only when they are compared with the very greatest, the demi-gods of creative literature, that such writers are found to be faulty, for the very intensity of their imagining lifts them high above the great mass of authors. Their work has a personal vision and a curiously fascinating "glamourie" that delights the more imaginative reader. Nor must they themselves be supposed to be "childish" (in the looser sense of the term) merely because the world of their imagination was put together during childhood, for they may have, and often do have, the deepest feelings to express, the most subtle emotions to convey, and their work may be quickened with the touch of a sublime philosophy. The world they show us may not enlarge its limitations, may present the same colours, surfaces and shapes, but as time goes on and their vision widens, this world becomes more and more symbolical, just as in the childhood of a race men people the earth and the heavens with images of beauty and dread, the gods, demi-gods, demons, and fairies, and these figures persist and retain their ancient lineaments while the race that imagined them ages and changes, making ever-increasing demands upon the spirit, until such figures symbolise a whole universe of complicated values: the tale, in its outline, remains the same, but interpretation succeeds interpretation and its significance ever deepens. Now Mr. de la Mare, in his finest and most characteristic work, shows himself to be a writer who belongs to this order. The world he prefers to move in is one that has been pieced together by the imagination of childhood, made up of his childish memories of life and books, nursery rhymes, fairy tales, ballads, and quaint memorable passages from strange old volumes. Behind this, using it as so many symbols, is a subtle personality, a spirit capable of unusual exaltation and despair. There is nothing conscious and deliberate, I fancy, in all this; his mind instinctively seeks these forms in which to express itself; his imagination, when it is fully creative, instinctively avoids the world of common experience and runs back to this other world it created long ago. As a poet, he has often been compared and contrasted with Mr. W. B. Yeats, and the comparison is of special interest in this connection. Now Mr. Yeats's poetic history may be discovered in one little verse of his:

> I made my song a coat
> Covered with embroideries
> Out of old mythologies
> From heel to throat;
> But the fools caught it,
> Wore it in the world's eyes
> As though they'd wrought it.
> Song let them take it,
> For there's more enterprise
> In walking naked.

There is a pretty little chapter of literary history in these few arrogant lines. Mr. Yeats's earlier poetry used the picturesque figures and symbolic imagery of the Celtic myths and certain mystical or pseudo-mystical cults because it found them convenient; it wore them as a man wears a coat, and could, and did, step out of them and walk "naked" when a whole school of poets began to be attracted towards such easy and picturesque matter. Having deliberately adopted the Celtic gods and fairies, the secret roses, and what not, Mr. Yeats, who is actually nothing if not deliberate, could with equal deliberation discard such things and, further, give his reasons for doing so in verse. There is nothing instinctive here; Mr. Yeats decided that it was high time his poetry expressed his moods under the guise of a shadowy drama of gods and fairies, and when he had had enough of it he stopped; he has always been a very sophisticated, self-conscious artist, and appears to have always held the opinion that it was part of a poet's business to take up attitudes and play for an hour or so with the nearest mythology or the most picturesque cult. He has always been a poet who has merely dabbled in mysticism, just as his compatriot "AE" has always been a mystic who has dabbled in poetry. Whatever there is in Mr. Yeats, there is certainly as little of the child as there could be in a man who is a genuine artist, and the world of his imagination owes little to the impressions and dreams of his childhood. Now the world we discover in Mr. de la Mare's poetry has some superficial resemblance to that in Mr. Yeats's, but Mr. de la Mare could not casually wave away his fairies and witches and ghosts and Arabias and Melmillos and Princess Seraphitas, not because they are really anything more than exquisite images and symbols, but because they are part of a world to which his imagination instinctively turns, in which it probably actually lives, not so much a beautifully embroidered coat that his Muse wears for a season, but her actual form and presence. (Perhaps I need hardly point out that this comparison does not involve any judgment as to which is the better poet, a question that demands an altogether different approach.) One of the most beautiful and significant of Mr. de la Mare's earlier poems, "Keep Innocency," puts before us the paradox of innocent childhood's love of what seems to its elders terrible and cruel, such as warfare:

> *He, with a mild and serious eye*
> *Along the azure of the years,*
> *Sees the sweet pomp sweep hurtling by;*
> *But he sees not death's blood and tears,*
> *Sees not the plunging of the spears.*
>
> *And all the strident horror of*
> *Horse and rider, in red defeat,*
> *Is only music fine enough*
> *To lull him into slumber sweet*
> *In fields where ewe and lambkin bleat.*
>
> *O, if with such simplicity*
> *Himself take arms and suffer war;*
> *With beams his targe shall gilded be,*
> *Though in the thickening gloom be far*
> *The steadfast light of any star!*
>
> *Though hoarse War's eagle on him perch,*
> *Quickened with guilty lightnings — there*
> *It shall in vain for terror search,*
> *Where a child's eyes beneath bloody hair*
> *Gaze purely through the dingy air.*

And we may say that there is a central core in Mr. de la Mare's imagination that has "kept innocency," though his spirit should walk the awful borderlands and proclaim its despair; a man has *felt* the world he shows us, but a child's eyes have *seen* it, lit with strange stars or bright with unknown birds.

I know nothing of Mr. de la Mare's personal history, and even if I did know something it would be sheer impertinence to make use of such knowledge here (this business is impudent enough as it is), and actually such writers whose imagination still feeds on the experience and impressions of their childhood (and by childhood I mean throughout the period up to and including adolescence) might easily have little or no common ground in their personal histories. But in order to see roughly "how it works" we can allow ourselves to indulge in a little of that not unpleasant guesswork which our newest psychologists, who are, we understand, men

of science, indulge in so frequently. Here is a man, not Mr. de la Mare or
another, but simply a man, who developed very early and lived more
intensely than most men during his childhood, lived, let us say, in the
country, and what with the sights and sounds of the country-side, old
books, old houses, and quaint old people, had his fill of beauty and
romance. Every object in this world would be linked with half a hundred
feelings and would remain bright and clear in his memory. Everything
would be significant and would not only be associated with beauty and joy,
but in some instances, this being the penalty of the sensitive spirit, with
terror and despair. And this boy is not only observing very closely the real
world about him, discovering so many things linked up with his emotions
that his very remembrance of them is infinitely suggestive, standing him in
good stead in after years, but is also brooding over romance and wonders
wherever he finds them, in scraps of song or tales at the fireside, and the
objects and figures of romance and wonder, though they are not "real"
objects and figures, take their place in his world, too, and go through the
very same process that the others did, except that, as time passes, their
beauty and elusiveness gives them a greater potency as symbols. His life,
then, is filled, brimming over, miraculous. Then comes some disastrous
change, a move from the country into some great ugly city, the death of
beloved persons, the necessity of earning a living by some dull grinding
occupation, and so on and so forth, and now though his life may flow
evenly enough, he is already an exile. Adam has been cast forth. He begins
to write, and then, like Dickens, he may release the whole flood of childish
memories and impressions, or like, let us say, Hawthorne, he may make
little progress at first, may begin by trying to write like the persons he
happens to admire at the moment and not find himself. The young man of
our psychological anecdote follows the latter course, and for a time, though
he produces work of exceptional interest, does not find himself; but then,
as time goes on, by some chance or other, the company of children of his
own, some work undertaken for children, he gradually gropes back to this
central flame in his imagination and restores, or rather rediscovers for the
purposes of his art, the world he has carried over from his childhood. His
poetry not only makes use of the figures and situations so familiar in that
world, burdening them more and more with spirit, deepening their significance, but makes more and more use of the idea of exile itself, seeing all
beauty as the flaming sign that the Paradise from which we are all exiled
still stands, remote but not entirely unglimpsed, and pitying all men
because they are not where in their hearts they would be. His prose fables
turn back more and more to that bright, clear, significant past, still burning
undimmed in the memory; almost unthinkingly the very houses and furniture it describes are houses and furniture out of that boyhood; the old

quaint figures come bobbing up again, the creatures of childish terror and wonder come creeping out of their holes; and every tree and bird and figure will not only be as significant as they once were, but will actually become more significant. And the work of such a man will have an unusual strength and a curious magic of its own. It will also have its own peculiar weaknesses. It will not describe with success, despite its author's knowledge of his craft, those things that only enter into adult life and the imagination of a mature man; it will fail, as I have already suggested, with the so-called normal, in which there is no easily recognisable element of the strange, the beautiful, the terrible, the grotesque; and in the poetry, this work will have strange weaknesses, at first unaccountable, because, though it is so concrete, like all good poetry, and dramatises so exquisitely the fluctuations of the spirit, it will break down and lose itself in woolly abstractions when trying to express certain partly philosophical ideas, simply because such ideas are outside the range of that imaginative world; have not, so to speak, been accepted by it, and cannot be adequately symbolised and made concrete through its agency.

So much for the theory and its pretty guesswork. A short examination of Mr. de la Mare's work, without regard for all manner of literary qualities and questions that lie outside the scope of the enquiry, will enable us to discover how closely we can apply the theory and what it is worth. But first it is worth remarking that the later work is better and more personal, more characteristic than the earlier, both in poetry and prose. Thus, both the *Memoirs of a Midget* and the collection of short tales called *The Riddle* are better, on any count, than — to go no further back — *The Return*. This last is, of course, a fantasy, but it differs from the later work not so much in its theme but in its treatment, which brings it nearer to the ordinary realistic fiction of the time than the later stories are. The style is not so mannered, not so subtly cadenced and bright with imagery, as the style of the other two volumes, and it does not lure us on to forget this world of offices and the witness-box as the later one does, but really has the contrary aim of making the one fantastic stroke credible. Mr. de la Mare has not boldly entered his own world, and the result, for all the art he has plainly lavished on the story, is unfortunate; the story itself is one, or at least is of the kind, that we are more accustomed to seeing treated comically, in the manner, say, of Mr. Anstey, than treated tragically as it is here, and though this would not have mattered in the least had the author lured us away into his own world, it matters a great deal when he is making terms with this one. For example, seeing that the translated Lawford and his wife are compelled to deceive everyone about them in the most elaborate fashion, we wonder why it did not occur to them that Lawford, who was his own master and not without means, could easily settle the matter by quietly

slipping away from the district for a time. This procedure would not have
pleased Mr. de la Mare, it is clear, but it was the obvious thing to do. And
the author, by his method of treatment, aiming at some kind of verisimili-
tude, invites such questions, which would be mere prosaic quibbling,
nothing more than evidence of the questioner's lack of imagination, if they
were raised in connection with one of the later stories. Then again, Mrs.
Lawford, a commonplace, conventionally minded wife, is the kind of
character the ordinary realistic novelist sketches in between a few puffs of
his (or her) cigarette; but just where such inferior chroniclers are happily
in their depth, Mr. de la Mare is well out of his, and Mrs. Lawford is
appalling, a crude monster from a first novel by a third-rate writer. Her
friend and their conversations are on the same level of crudity. In short, the
conventional element, which would not be present at all in the later stories
since the whole pack of characters, with their houses and furniture, would
be subtly translated, is so badly done that it almost wrecks the fantasy,
which is presented with some characteristic strokes of genius. Here, then,
the normal, with its commonplace tangle of adult relations and interests,
has baffled our author's imagination.

Then in his next story he boldly obliterated all the common relations and
affairs of life by choosing a theme that was bristling with difficulties, that
probably every other story-teller we have would have rejected at a glance,
but that required just such an imagination as his and no other for its successful treatment. The *Memoirs of a Midget* overshadows *The Return* not
so much because it is later and the author has improved his craft, but
because he has now boldly entered his own world and has left off trying to come to terms with that of most novelists. Many people have
wondered why Mr. de la Mare should choose such a queer subject, the
history, in autobiographical form, of a year or so in the life of a freak, for
what is easily his most ambitious single performance, a novel on the old
heroic scale. But if our account of him has any truth in it at all, he could
hardly have done better; the choice of subject itself, let alone his treatment
of it, was a stroke of genius. What more effective dramatisation of the
mind of an adult who still retains the imagination of his childhood could
there be than the person of Miss M. the Midget, who is so diminutive that
even the child, to whom daisies and buttercups are platters and chalices, is
a hulking clodhopper when compared with her, who sees an ordinary
garden as a kind of enchanted jungle:

> My eyes dazzled in colours. The smallest of the marvels of flowers
> and flies and beetles and pebbles, and the radiance that washed over
> them, would fill me with a mute, pent-up rapture almost unendurable.
> Butterflies would settle quietly on the hot stones beside as if to match
> their raiment against mine. If I proffered my hand, with quivering

wings and horns, they would uncoil their delicate tongues and quaff from it drops of dew or water. A solemn grasshopper would occasionally straddle across my palm, and with patience I made quite an old friend of a harvest mouse. They weigh only two to the half-penny. This sharp-nosed furry morsel would creep swiftly along to share my crumbs and snuggle itself to sleep in my lap. . . .

And yet, despite her wonder and innocence, moving as she does in a world that is like the child's, only much stronger and brighter, she is not a child, but a poetical sensitive adult, with all the thoughts and emotions of an adult who is shut off from most common activities. And now, because it is she who tells the story, things that would have been blemishes in another and different story, nearer to common life, are here in their right place; the grotesque towering figures, whether of Dickensian humour or of late Byronic sentiment and tragedy, are at home in this world, which has a reality of its own even if it is not the one we know best, and so is entitled to its own humour, sentiment and tragedy. The style is now heightened, being very artfully cadenced and bright with pictures, particularly in the earlier, more descriptive and less dramatic chapters, which constitute, in my opinion, the best part of the book and contain the most exquisite and memorable passages, notably the description of Miss M. in the deserted house on her last evening there. All the chapters that relate to her experience at home and her early days at Mrs. Bowater's, in which she is shut off from the great world, but lives in a bright little world of her own, are magnificently done, the work of a genius; but as her circle of acquaintance widens and she moves about more, until she queens it in London, the poetical gradually gives place to the grotesque; the child is there and is ruthlessly inventing; so that at times across those scenes of fashionable life, as seen by the Midget, there flutters the shadow of Mr. Salteena.

At first sight it may appear that our theory of Mr. de la Mare's imagination will break down when we pass from the *Midget,* which triumphantly proclaims its truth, to the collection of short stories in *The Riddle.* In these tales the author creeps along the borderlands of the human spirit, and in a style that is even more artful, mannered and highly coloured than that of the *Midget,* he describes the corroding evils and moonstruck fantasies that visit those on whom the world's common burden of affairs presses most lightly, the very young and the very old, and those whose reason has been fretted away and whose ordinary faculties have fallen into desuetude; it is a book of "atmospheres," of adventures on the edge of things, crumbling away the homely and comforting reality, and confronting us with the heaving and crawling darkness. But not all the stories are set in this queer spiritual twilight; some of them seem little more than exquisite memories, clustered about some slight theme, and have something of the bright loveli-

ness, the happy magic, of those clear dreams that only too rarely visit our
sleep; their brightness and their suggestion of old ways and scenes point to
their author's having made a poetical kind of camera obscura out of his
memory. Many of them are related as the experiences of childhood,
notably two of the most exquisite, "The Almond Tree" and "The Bowl,"
both of which have the air of being fragments from some greater context
(though perhaps existing only in the writer's mind); and none of these
things could have been created by a man who had not kept alive his
childhood and never lost sight of its world. Some of the tales have the
appearance of bright nursery pictures that have suffered some curious
change and become symbolical representations of a spiritual life that no
nursery ever knew. And even the stories that seem furthest away from
anything we can connect with childhood reveal, after some scrutiny, their
indebtedness to the kind of imagination that has already been described.
No reader of that excellent tale, "The Tree," is ever likely to confuse Mr.
de la Mare's Fruit Merchant with the actual elderly wholesale greengrocers
who do business in the neighbourhood of Covent Garden, for this Fruit
Merchant, with his triangular nose and small bleak black eyes, first appears
to the imagination like one of the quaint figures in a toy-book and finally
remains in it as some kind of bad fairy, who could only traffic in apples of
glass and oranges from the Dead Sea. Only the trade directories in the
kingdom of Oberon can have known the fantastic firm of Lispet, Lispett
and Vaine. And there could hardly be a better example of the way in which
it is possible to utilise a figure from the world of the imaginative child,
making it return with all its suggestion of terror, but deepening its significance, than the figure of Seaton's monstrous aunt in the story of that name.
The spiritual background of the story can only be understood by an adult,
but the principal figure, this eccentric old woman with her long face, big
head, and enormous appetite, who is somehow a witch and a devil, comes
straight out of childish memory and imagination, and no man who has
completely lost his childhood will feel any terror in her presence: in our
maturity we meet eccentric old ladies, but no such aunts as this; but our
early days and nights, if we had any imagination at all, were peopled with
such creatures. There is a curious suggestion throughout these stories (as I
pointed out in another place when *The Riddle* first appeared) that this
world of Mr. de la Mare's is, as it were, the other half of the Dickens's
world, the poetical, mysterious, aristocratic half that Dickens, with his eyes
fixed on the democratic, humorous, melodramatic elements, never gave us.
This suggestion was something more than an odd fancy, for both these
lovable geniuses (Mr. de la Mare is certainly a genius), different as they
are in almost every essential, have at least one thing in common, their
method of building up their worlds, the process of the creative imagination.

Fortunately Mr. de la Mare's poetry has been more frequently noticed and more widely quoted than his prose, so that we need only touch upon its essentials. Its world, as we have seen, is one that has largely been made up of the impressions of childhood. Nursery rhyme, ballad, fairy tale, quaint memories have run together and formed a world that is filled with curious symbolism, romantic images, and a haunting elusive music that is like nothing so much as the exquisite stammer of some elfin-hearted girl. And nothing less than music and strange imagery that hangs upon one miraculous adjective could express what the poet has in his heart. We have seen already that such a poet would make more and more use of the idea of exile itself, and an examination of the poetry only confirms the opinion. In his very acute short study, Mr. Shanks remarked:

> He is, in the first place, the poet of lost paradises. Almost all his poetry expresses dissatisfaction with this world, with this life, and a straining towards something more to be desired, which is indescribable, almost unimaginable, of which an image is evoked as it were between the words of his poems. If he has one constant and recurring thought about the world it is this — that there is a better place to be in than the one in which we now find ourselves. . . .

This is very true. It is, after all, but a step from the exile from childhood to the exile from Paradise. Mr. de la Mare's delight in the world (and some of his loveliest poems are expressions of that delight, and what is perhaps his very finest poem, "Fare Well," is noble praise of it) only leads him away from life, that is, not the whole cosmic process, but the battle between belly and worm that stirs the surface of this planet; and every lovely thing only increases his desire to glimpse:

> *Pure daybreak lighten again on Eden's tree.*

And when he wishes to praise music, as so many poets have done, it is characteristic of his most constant mood that he should praise it because it remakes the world or lifts the shades of the prison-house for an hour:

> *When music sounds, gone is the earth I know,*
> *And all her lovely things even lovelier grow.*

He will put his songs into the mouths of those who are "simple happy mad," because such Fools, carolling on the blasted heaths of life, are still as children, have kept innocency. In the volume called *Motley*, the influence of the war is apparent everywhere, and yet it takes a form different from that in the work of other poets. Characteristically Mr. de la Mare prefers to treat it as a child might treat some inexplicable calamity, like the sudden death of a parent; his momentary despair takes on the character of a child's outraged innocence, and a catastrophe that was brought about by the human will can only force its way into his world in the guise of some insane and hardly credible intrusion, as if a mad bull had rushed into Miss M.'s garden. Not that he is wanting in ordinary human sympathy, coldly detached; on the contrary, as some critics have already pointed out, pity, a boundless noble charity, is probably the dominant note of his work. Whatever it is that he has lost and now regrets, whether it is childhood, platonic pre-existence, eternity, Paradise, that the flash of a bird's wing or the glimpse of a burning face recalls for a moment, it is not merely for the saved or the sensitive; if he is an exile, then so are all men, and so his pity is universal. And his greatest weakness, as I suggested in an earlier passage, is his failure to express certain ideas in the concrete imagery that poetry demands, his tendency to find refuge in vague and woolly abstractions; and this weakness is easily understood when we realize that a poetic imagination like his is clearly limited and is unable to grapple with ideas that belong entirely to maturity. If there ever was a body of lyrical verse that embodied, with exquisite precision, a definite philosophical attitude towards life, it is the poetry of Mr. A. E. Housman, yet no contemporary verse is more concrete, less given to abstractions. But Mr. Housman's imaginative world is not the product of childhood (and so lacks the romantic glamour, the fascinating strangeness of Mr. de la Mare's) but of early manhood, and is thus able to provide the appropriate dramatic and concrete setting (or body) for his ideas. But this weakness is less marked in Mr. de la Mare's last volume, *The Veil,* which is stronger and harsher, not without traces of growing pains on the part of its author, so that it may well be that he will make this theory of his genius, sketched in so crudely, out of date before it has been more carefully stated and developed. In the meantime he remains one of that most lovable order of artists who never lose sight of their childhood, but re-live it continually in their work and contrive to find expression for their maturity in its memories and impressions, its romantic vision of the world: the artists whose limitations and weaknesses are plain for any passing fool to see, but whose genius, and they are never without it, never mere men of talent, delights both philosophers and children; the artists who remember Eden.

IV. From THE ENGLISH COMIC CHARACTERS 1925

THE ILLYRIANS

If you take ship from the coast of Bohemia — having made your last bow to Perdita and Florizel — and sail for a day in a westerly direction, you will presently arrive at Illyria. There you will find the love-sick melancholy Duke, seated among his musicians, polishing his images and doting upon the "high-fantastical"; and go but a little way out of the city and you will come upon the stately Countess Olivia among her clipped box-trees, pacing the lawns like some great white peacock, while her steward Malvolio, lean, frowning, and cross-gartered, bends at her elbow. There too, if you are lucky, you may catch a glimpse of the rubious-lipped lovely Viola, stretching her slim legs and swinging her pert page's cloak between the Duke's palace and Olivia's house, delicately breathing blank verse. And if there should come to your ears the sound of drunken catches, and to your nose the smell of burnt sack and pickled herrings, then look for Olivia's uncle, Sir Toby Belch, and his friend, Sir Andrew Aguecheek, and with them, it may be, that dainty rogue, Maria, darting about like some little black and white bird, and Feste the Clown, with his sharp tongue, bright eyes and strange bitter-sweet songs. In and out of doors, there is good company in Illyria, good company whether it is high or low, sober or drunk.

Our present inquiry takes us into the society of the low, the drunken and disreputable company, the comic Illyrians. (It is difficult even to sound the name and remain sober.) Whether Malvolio, who was himself neither drunken nor disreputable but essentially a "grave liver," should have place in the company, is a very debatable question. Most of the comic scenes in the play revolve around him, and it is his antics, his sudden rise and his awful collapse, that form the basis of most of the broader comedy of the piece; his self-love and swelling vanity, which make him an easy butt for Maria and her grinning troupe, his gravity and pompous airs, are all served up, without mercy, for our entertainment. Yet Malvolio, strictly speaking, is not a comic character. He stands outside the real comic tradition. Although Shakespeare gives some of his speeches a most delicious flavour of absurdity, he does not treat Malvolio as he treats his purely comic figures, whom he regards not merely with a humorous tolerance but with positive delight and relish, encouraging them, as it were, to indulge their every whim. The difference between, let us say, Malvolio and Sir Andrew Aguecheek is that Shakespeare handles the one and dandles the other. Sir Andrew is really a much more contemptible figure than the serious and capable steward, but then he is so manifestly ridiculous that he evades criticism altogether, escapes into a world of his own, where every fresh piece of absurdity he commits only brings him another round of laughter and applause. Times change, and we are more likely to regard Malvolio with some measure of sympathy than was Shakespeare; indeed, in spite of his vanity, to us he is a figure not untouched by pathos, for the possibility of Olivia falling in love with him (and she admits his value as an employee) appears to us not entirely preposterous, nor do his portentous gravity and puritanical airs seem to us so offensive, now that our Sir Tobies have been steadily rebuked in the manner of Malvolio for at least two generations. Sir Toby's famous reply — "Dost thou think, because thou art virtuous, there shall be no more cakes and ale" — cuts the ground from under the feet of a very large number of our energetic fellow-citizens, whose apparent business it is, Malvolio-like, to attend to our private affairs and superintend our morals; and Sir Toby was fortunate in being able to make such a rejoinder without being suppressed. Malvolio, we may say, has been steadily coming into his own for a long time, so that it is difficult for us to regard him as an unpleasant oddity as Shakespeare did. And perhaps it says something for our charity that, sitting as we are among ever-diminishing supplies of cakes and ale, we can still see something pathetic in this figure.

Shakespeare's sympathies were so wide and his dramatic genius so universal that it is always dangerous to give him a point of view and dower him with various likes and dislikes. Nevertheless it is true to say that certain types of character very clearly aroused his dislike; and it is also true to say that these are the very types of character that appear to have some fascination for our world. In short, his villains are rapidly becoming our heroes. Thus, Shakespeare clearly detested all hard, unsympathetic, intolerant persons, the over-ambitious and overweening, the climbers and careerists, the "get-on-or-get-outs" of this world. When the will and the intellect in all their pride were divorced from tolerance, charity, a love of the good things of this world, they formed the stuff out of which the Shakespearean villains were made. But the Bastard and Iago and Richard the Third are the very characters that some of our modern dramatists would select to adorn three acts of hero-worship. So too, to come down the scale, our friend Malvolio, the pushing puritan, is, under various disguises, the hero of almost one-half of all the American novels that were ever written. Shakespeare, looking steadily at Malvolio with his self-love

("O, you are sick of self-love," cries Olivia to him) and his intolerance, contrives that he shall be covered with ridicule, but never regards him as a comic figure. In spite of his absurdities there are fermenting in him too many of those qualities that Shakespeare detested for him to be a figure of fun. While this conceited and over-ambitious steward struts cross-gartered on the lawn for our entertainment, there flutters across his path, for one fleeting moment, the terrible shadow of that other ambitious underling, Iago. So Malvolio is deceived, abused, locked up and treated as a madman for a short space, and this is his purgation, for Shakespeare saw that his soul was in danger and so appointed for him two angels of deliverance, namely, Maria and Sir Toby Belch.

In the very first speech that Sir Toby makes, when we discover him talking with Maria, he remarks that "care's an enemy to life," and this we may take to be his philosophy. His time is spent in putting a multitude of things, oceans of burnt sack, mountains of pickled herrings, between himself and the enemy, Care; and he may be shortly described as a Falstaff without genius, who would have made the fat knight a very able lieutenant. Undoubtedly, he is a very idle and drunken old rip, who forgets his position, which, as the uncle of the Countess, is considerable, his years and his manners, and passes all his time in low company, in the society of his inferiors, either because, like Maria, his niece's chambermaid, they devise entertainment for him, or because, like Sir Andrew, they serve as butts and cat's-paws. But notwithstanding his devotion to sherris-sack — and it is doubtful if we ever see him sober — unlike Falstaff Sir Toby does not live altogether in an ideal comic world of ease and merriment; by much drinking of healths and singing of catches and fool-baiting, and with the assistance of a kind of rough philosophy, a tap-room epicureanism, he certainly tries to live in such a world; but common-sense and a knowledge of this world's uses keep breaking in from time to time. In spite of his idleness and love of mischief, he is shrewd enough on occasion. Thus, he does not propose to deliver Sir Andrew's ridiculous challenge to the supposed Cesario, because, he declares, "the behaviour of the young gentleman gives him out to be of good capacity and breeding; his employment between his lord and my niece confirms no less: therefore this letter, being so excellently ignorant, will breed no terror in the youth — he will find it comes from a clodpole." He is in no doubt as to the capacity of his admiring dupe, Sir Andrew, who is only encouraged to remain as the suitor of Olivia in order that Toby may amuse himself and mulct the foolish knight of his ducats. His apparently innocent defence of Sir Andrew in the opening dialogue with Maria ("He's as tall a man as any's in Illyria" — and the rest) is, of course, mere impudence, one wag winking at another. Then later, when the confusion between Viola and her brother complicates the action, Sir Toby changes his mind about Cesario, as he has a right to do on the evidence before him, and remarks: "A very dishonest, paltry boy, and more a coward than a hare: his dishonesty appears in leaving his friend here in necessity, and denying him." And he it is who has the wit to see that the joke against Malvolio has gone far enough — "I would we were well rid of this knavery." Although he vastly enjoys stirring up unnecessary strife and egging on two apparent cowards to fight one another, he shows no reluctance to taking part in any quarrel himself and is certainly no coward. When he himself is hurt, it will be remembered, he makes no complaint ("That's all one: 'has hurt me, and there's the end on't. — Sot, didst see Dick surgeon, sot?"), and though this stoicism simply covers a fear of being ridiculed, it does argue a stout nature.

Sir Toby, then, is by no means a simpleton. Nor is he, on the other hand, a comic genius like Falstaff, whose world has been transformed into an ideally comic world, whose whole life, whose every speech and action, are devised to further ease, enjoyment and laughter. Sir Toby, in his own coarse, swashbuckling manner, is witty, but he is not the cause of wit in other men. He does not transform himself into an object of mirth, content so long as men are laughing and the comic spirit is abroad, but like any bullying wag of the tap-room, looks for a butt in the company. He is really nothing more than an elderly schoolboy with a prodigious thirst and far too much spare time on his hands: the type is not uncommon. Having a more than usual amount of energy, both of brain and body, and no serious powers of application and no sensible objects upon which to expend such energy, his one problem is how to pass the time pleasantly. As he happens to have his existence in a romantic and idyllic world of love and dalliance and fine phrases that offers no employment to a robust and prosaic middle-aged gentleman, and as he, unlike our country squires and retired majors, cannot turn to golf and bridge, there is nothing for it but cakes and ale, the roaring of catches, verbal bouts with the chambermaid and the clown, and mischievous antics played at the expense of such creatures as Malvolio and Sir Andrew. Men so situated always seek out low company and are never at ease among their equals. But once among his cronies, Toby enjoys himself with such rollicking abandon that he communicates his enjoyment to us, so that we would not for the world have him different. There is about this drunken, staggering, swaggering, roaring knight such a ripeness and gusto that his humours are infectious, and once we are in his riotous company decency and order seem intrusive and positively ill-natured. He has leave to keep us out of bed all night and we would not stint him of a drop of sack or a single pickled herring. Falstaff apart, there never was a better bear-leader of a fool. With what a luxury of enjoyment he draws out and displays to us the idiocies of the guileless Sir Andrew:

SIR ANDREW. I'll stay a month longer. I am a fellow o' the strangest mind i' the world; I delight in masques and revels sometimes altogether.

SIR TOBY. Art thou good at these kickshawses, knight?

SIR ANDREW. As any man in Illyria, whatsoever he be, under the degree of my betters; and yet I will not compare with an old man.

SIR TOBY. What is thy excellence in a galliard, knight?

SIR ANDREW. Faith, I can cut a caper.

SIR TOBY. And I can cut the mutton to 't.

SIR ANDREW. And I think I have the back-trick simply as strong as any man in Illyria.

SIR TOBY. Wherefore are these things hid? wherefore have these gifts a curtain before 'em? are they like to take dust, like Mistress Mall's picture? why dost thou not go to church in a galliard, and come home in a coranto? My very walk should be a jig; I would not so much as make water but in a sink-a-pace. What dost thou mean? is it a world to hide virtues in? I did think, by the excellent constitution of thy leg, it was form'd under the star of a galliard.

SIR ANDREW. Ay, 'tis strong, and it does indifferent well in a flame-coloured stock. Shall we set about some revels?

SIR TOBY. What shall we do else? were we not born under Taurus?

SIR ANDREW. Taurus! that's sides and heart.

SIR TOBY. No, sir; it is legs and thighs. Let me see thee caper. . . .

Once in his cups, how magnificently he overrides mere precision in speech and common-sense and rises into a poetical kind of nonsense of his own: "To hear by the nose, it is dulcet in contagion. But shall we make the welkin dance indeed? shall we rouse the night-owl in a catch that will draw three souls out of one weaver? shall we do that?" With what gusto does he enter into the matter of the duel between Sir Andrew and the disguised Viola, alternately breathing fire into them and then damping it with a report to each one of the other's fury and prowess. He bustles from one to the other in a very ecstasy of pleasure. Sir Andrew, he tells Fabian, "if he were open'd, an you find so much blood in his liver as will clog the foot of a flea, I'll eat the rest of the anatomy" — a remark worthy of Falstaff himself — Sir Andrew is not anxious to fight, but Toby fans his few smouldering embers of courage into a blaze and compels him to send a challenge:

Go, write it in a martial hand; be curst and brief; it is no matter how witty, so it be eloquent and full of invention: taunt him with the license of ink: if thou *thou'st* him some thrice, it shall not be amiss; and as many lies as will lie in thy sheet of paper, although the sheet were big enough for the bed of Ware in England, set 'em down: go, about it. Let there be gall enough in thy ink; though thou write with a goose-pen, no matter: about it.

Then gives him some further encouragement when the challenge is written:

> Go, Sir Andrew; scout me for him at the corner of the orchard, like a bumbaily: so soon as ever thou see'st him, draw; and, as thou drawest, swear horrible; for it comes to pass oft, that a terrible oath, with a swaggering accent sharply twang'd off, gives manhood more approbation than ever proof itself would have earned him. Away!

We can almost hear Toby smacking his lips over the vision of Sir Andrew letting fly a terrible oath, with a swaggering accent sharply twang'd off. Then, with an ever-increasing relish for the situation and with his images swelling at every fresh turn of the farce, Sir Toby confronts Viola with a tale of her incensed opponent awaiting her, "bloody as a hunter," "a devil in private brawl: souls and bodies hath he divorced three; and his incensement at this moment is so implacable, that satisfaction can be none but by pangs of death and sepulchre: hobnob is his word; give't or take't . . ." — a terrifying picture. Back again he goes to Sir Andrew, now to damp the knight's faint ardour with an equally terrifying account of his adversary: "Why, man," roars the mischievous old toper, "he's a very devil; I have not seen such a firago. I had a pass with him, rapier, scabbard, and all, and he gives me the stuck-in with such a mortal motion, that it is inevitable; and, on the answer, he pays you as surely as your feet hit the ground they step on. They say he has been fencer to the Sophy." "Pox on't," cries the startled Sir Andrew, out of his simplicity, "I'll not meddle with him." But there is no escape for him, even though he should part with his horse as the price of that escape. It is only the unexpected entry of Antonio that robs us of the climax and, possibly, Sir Toby of the horse, but the artful and mischievous knight, who has known something of the satisfaction of those lesser gods who prompt our tyrants and prophets and further our wars and revolutions to pass pleasantly their idle aeons, has had his fun. He has contrived a tale that, with humorous embellishment, will keep any company uproarious between one round of sack and the next, between chorus and chorus.

But if we have enjoyed Sir Toby's antics so much that we have no desire for his immediate amendment, we must leave him with some misgiving, for at the conclusion of the piece we plainly see that those very gods of mischief whom he has emulated in this affair of the duel have now selected him as the victim of their sport. They who have allowed him to season his sack with so many herrings in pickle, have now devised for him a rod in pickle. This is nothing less than his marriage with Maria, of which we learn from Fabian's explanation of the joke against Malvolio at the end of the play. We are

told: "Maria writ the letter at Sir Toby's great importance (i.e., impor-
tunity — though this is not strictly true); in recompense whereof he hath
married her." Alas! — poor Toby. We had seen the possibility of such an
alliance throughout the play; indeed, scene after scene had shown us Toby
edging nearer and nearer to his doom. We had heard him declare, "She's a
beagle, true-bred, and one that adores me," in all his fateful masculine
complacency. When the Malvolio jest was at its intoxicating height, we had
heard him shower compliments on the artful little soubrette, "Excellent
wench" and the rest, had caught him declaring to Sir Andrew and Fabian,
in the ecstasy of his enjoyment, "I could marry this wench for this device,
and ask no other dowry with her but such another jest." We have heard
him cry to her, "Wilt thou set thy foot o' my neck?" and "Shall I play my
freedom at tray-trip, and become thy bond-slave?" Yet, with the sound of
such dangerous speeches, verbal gun-cotton, still ringing in our ears, we
had thought that the old fox might yet sniff the air, scent danger and then
bolt for freedom. But no, he has walked into the trap. He has been snared,
like many another man, not only by a woman but by his own philosophy.
"Care's an enemy to life," he has told himself, and with so much idleness
on his hands, with so rich an appreciation of japes and jests, with so great a
capacity for mischief and the staging of whims, what could be better than
an alliance with Maria, who has proved herself the very queen of humorous
strategy, a "most excellent devil of wit," and a most generous purveyor of
cakes and ale? Alas! — had this been any other man's reasoning, he would
have seen the folly of it. As it is, he marries, so that the perfect life of
comic ease and merriment that he is always attempting to build up may
have another prop, and does not realise that he is simply bringing it all
down in one awful crash. Who doubts for a moment that what Olivia, with
her stately displeasure, could not do, Maria, the erstwhile accomplice and
fellow mischief-maker, but now the wife, will accomplish within a very
short space; that Maria the chambermaid, with a comically sympathetic
view of sack, catches, and late hours, is one thing, and Maria the wife, with
a husband to reform, is another; that the very wit that could devise such
unseemly jests will henceforward be occupied, not in devising others, but in
schemes, equally efficacious, for preventing husband Toby from reaching
that large freedom he hitherto enjoyed? As a last bulwark against care, he
has taken Maria to wife, and now, without a doubt, the old freedom has
vanished and care is about to return in an undreamed-of measure. Toby's
philosophy has undone him, and he falls; but he falls like a great man. We
have caught his days at their highest point; nevermore shall we see him,
free, spacious, as rich and ripe as a late plum, all Illyria his tavern, a prince
of gusto, good living, and most admirable fooling; from now on he will
dwindle, take on a cramped and secretive air, and lose his confidence and

zest, for now he will always be discovered, his Maria's reproaches still shrilling in his ear, a cup too low.

Of one of Sir Toby's boon companions, Feste the Clown, there is little to be said. Viola, after a bout of wit with him, sums up the matter admirably:

> *This fellow's wise enough to play the Fool;*
> *And to do that well craves a kind of wit:*
> *He must observe their mood on whom he jests,*
> *The quality of persons, and the time;*
> *Not, like the haggard, check at every feather*
> *That comes before his eyes. This is a practice*
> *As full of labour as a wise man's art:*
> *For folly, that he wisely shows, is fit;*
> *But wise men's folly, shown, quite taints their wit.*

This is an accurate description of Feste's own practice, for as he lounges in and out of the scene, it will be noticed that always he plays up to his company. He is a professional entertainer and gives his audiences what he knows will please them. The love-sick Duke feeds upon melancholy, and so to him Feste sings "old and antique" songs and takes delight in his art, but as soon as he has finished the last note of "Come Away, Death," like the brisk professional he is, he himself shows no trace of melancholy or of any emotion, but is his usual self in a moment, detached, observant, critical, taking his leave with a sly dig at the Duke's melancholy and inconstancy. With the other serious characters, he acts the professional fool but always with a certain reserve and dignity and always with one eye upon the main chance, conjuring another coin into his hand with an ingratiating witticism. Malvolio he really dislikes because the proud and puritanical steward has a contempt for both him and his office (a contempt that Shakespeare himself had probably met with in some Malvolios of his acquaintance), and so he does not scruple to play Malvolio the cruellest trick of all by pretending to be Sir Tobas the parson. With Sir Toby and Maria, Feste appears at his ease and, as it were, with his wit unbuttoned, bandying broad jests with them; while for the delectation of Sir Andrew, a great admirer of his, he utters the first nonsense that comes into his head. Indeed, in this company of boon companions and midnight caterwaulers, his humour is all for wild nonsense of a Rabelaisian cast. Such ridiculous speeches as "I did impeticos thy gratillity; for Malvolio's nose is no whipstock; my lady has a white hand, and the Myrmidons are no bottle-ale houses" cast a spell over the rural wits of Sir Andrew, who pronounces it to be "the best fooling, when all is done." (There is apparently a lower level of intelligence and humour than Sir Andrew's; it is to be found in those commentators who have pored for hours over these nonsensical speeches of the Clown's and have then complained that they could make little of them.) And though we may not agree that this "is the best fooling, when all is done," most of us have regretted that we were not present at the previous meeting of Sir Toby, Sir Andrew, and the Clown, when, according to Sir Andrew, the Clown was in very gracious fooling and spoke of Pigrogromitus and of the Vapians passing the equinoctial of Queubus. Perhaps this is one of the delights that Heaven has in store for us, or for those of us who are only fit for a Heaven slightly damaged and humanised. Wind and rain outside; indoors a clear fire and a few tall candles, with sack in plenty; Sir Toby, straddling and with nose aglow, on one side; Sir Andrew gaping on the other; and the Clown before us, nodding and winking through his account of Pigrogromitus and the Vapians passing the equinoctial of Queubus; the whole to be concluded by the catch of "Hold thy peace, thou knave," with the possibility of being interrupted at any moment by a Malvolio in his nightshirt — here is a hint for the commander of the starry revels.

Sir Andrew Aguecheek is one of Shakespeare's family of simpletons: he is first cousin to Slender and Silence. Life pulses so faintly in this lank haired, timid, rustic squire that he is within a stride of utter imbecility. He is really the very opposite of Sir Toby, who is for ever in mischief simply because he has more energy and brains than he knows what to do with, being without any serious purpose, whereas Sir Andrew follows Toby into mischief simply because he is deficient in both energy and brains, and for ever takes the line of least resistance. Without a shred of either self-respect or self-confidence, without volition, courage or sense, he is any man's prey, a toy-balloon blown hither and thither by the slightest breeze. His social standing and wealth are just sufficient to leave him independent of any occupation or control, a free agent, but being what he is, it means that they are just sufficient to leave him at the mercy of the first rascal he meets. At first sight, it seems astonishing that a comic character of any dimensions could possibly be created out of such material, and, indeed, only a great genius could have taken these few straws and made of them a creature whose every odd remark and quaint caper is a delight. But it is Sir Andrew's amazing simplicity, his almost pathetic naïvety, his absolute lack of guile, that make him so richly absurd. And with these there goes a certain very characteristic quality, the unanalysable factor, that is present in every remark he makes; every speech has a certain Aguecheek flavour or smack that is unmistakable; even as we read we can hear the bleating of his plaintive little voice. His best trait is one that he shares with every simpleton, and that is a childlike capacity for enjoyment, which is really born of a sense of wonder, the ability to marvel at and relish the commonest things, to see the world innocently and freshly, a sense that withers among brighter wits and natures richer in experience but blooms for ever with the extremes of humankind, the utter simpletons and the great geniuses. Sir Andrew has this capacity, and it entitles him to a place at the revels. In spite of his starts and frights, his loss of two thousand ducats and his broken head, it is clear that he has enjoyed himself hugely in the company of his admired Sir Toby, and that he will return to his distant estate bubbling with a confused tale of strange happenings and great personages that will be meat and drink to him for years. It is true that he has been everybody's butt, but then he does not know it; he is happily protected from all such discoveries and will be all his life; so that he might almost be said to have the best of the laugh, for whereas the others are living in this world, he is still dwelling in Eden.

There are a thousand things that could be said of this simple creature, for there is probably no better text than a fool, but one particular aspect of him invites our attention. What really tickles us about Sir Andrew, over and above the unanalysable drollery of his speeches, is not what he thinks and feels but the fact that he should not be able to conceal what he thinks and feels. There is somewhere at the back of all our minds a little Sir Andrew Aguecheek, giggling and gaping, now strutting and now cowering, pluming himself monstrously at one word and being hurled into a fit of depression by the next; but most of us contrive to keep this little fellow and his antics carefully hidden from sight for the sake of decency and our own self-respect. Some of Sir Andrew's ingenuous remarks have the same effect, or should have the same effect, upon us as the sight of a monkey, which presents us with a parody of human life that is highly diverting but that leaves us somewhat shamefaced: after seeing so many things done openly that we ourselves do in secret, we blush, partly for the monkey that it should make a public show of itself, and partly for ourselves who have so much that is better concealed. The mind of Sir Andrew, such as it is, is as plain to sight as the dial of the parish clock. Almost every remark he makes, innocently revealing, as it does, the ebb and flow of his poor self-esteem, is not only a piece of self-revelation but also a revelation of all our species: this zany, naked to our sight, is uncovering the nakedness of statesmen and philosophers, popes and emperors. How delicious in its candour is his reply to Sir Toby's bantering charge of being "put down": "Methinks sometimes I have no more wit than a Christian or an ordinary man has: but I am a great eater of beef, and I believe that does harm to my wit." How swiftly following the thought that he may be no better than the ordinary in some particular comes the possible explanation, the eating of beef, to raise the phoenix of his vanity again from its ashes. He remains, at some charge to his purse, with Sir Toby as a suitor to Olivia; and yet it is clear that the whole idea is Sir Toby's, for Olivia plainly does not favour Sir Andrew, and he knows it, nor does he himself feel any passion for the

lady: he has simply allowed himself to be persuaded, caught in the web of
Sir Toby's imagination and rhetoric. How swiftly too his vanity plumes
itself again at Sir Toby's artful prompting in the matter of his accomplish-
ments; he can cut a caper, he tells us with a delicious affectation of
detachment, and thinks he has the back-trick simply as strong as any man
in Illyria.

In the matter of scholarship, which most gentlemen of his time affected,
his simplicity and candour are nothing less than wholesome and refreshing.
When Sir Toby declares that "not to be a-bed after midnight is to be up
betimes" — and then, plunging into the depths of his learning, brings
forth an adage from Lily's grammar — "And *diliculo surgere,* thou
know'st —" Sir Andrew provides us with the rare spectacle of a man acting
honestly in the face of a classical quotation, by replying: "Nay, by my
troth, I know not: but I know, to be up late is to be up late." So too when
Sir Toby asks if our life does not consist of the four elements, he replies,
indifferently, "Faith, so they say; but I think it rather consists of eating and
drinking" — a notable answer. Again, when the Clown asks whether they
will have a love-song or a song of good life, and Sir Toby decides for the
former, Sir Andrew speaks for all the novel-readers of our circulating
libraries but with more sincerity than they can ever muster when he adds:
"Ay, ay: I care not for good life." Most excellent too is his critical
observation in reply to the Clown's remark that the knight, Sir Toby, is "in
admirable fooling": "Ay, he does well enough if he be disposed, and so do
I too: he does it with a better grace, but I do it more natural." And what
could be more revealing than his cry at the indignation meeting after the
visit of Malvolio. Maria has said that the steward is sometimes a kind of
Puritan. "O!" cries Sir Andrew, "if I thought that, I'd beat him like a
dog." When pressed for his exquisite reason, he confesses to having none:
indeed, he has no reason at all, but the excitement of the occasion has
heated his poor wits and he wishes to make some full-blooded declaration
and stand well with the company, like our Sir Andrews who sit in their
clubs and tell one another they would "shoot 'em down." How pathetically
he echoes Sir Toby. Even when the latter remarks that Maria adores him,
Sir Andrew, not to be left out, instantly lights a pitiful rushlight of amatory
remembrance: "I was adored once." Yes, he, Sir Andrew, was adored
once: it is not true, but for the moment he thinks it is and so contrives to
take his place among the swaggering fellows, alongside Sir Toby. And
perhaps best of all, the very sweet distillation of ingenuousness, is his
whisper in the shrubbery when Malvolio, having read the letter, is rehears-
ing his part as the Countess's husband. As soon as mention is made of "a
foolish knight," Sir Andrew is in no doubt as to the person — "That's me,
I warrant you." And when his guess is confirmed by the actual sound of his

D

name, he is almost triumphant — "I knew 'twas I, for many do call me fool," a remark that smacks more of complacency than resignation, as if to be known as a fool did at least single him out for some notice. And how revealing, too, is his conduct during the duel episode. He has been told that Olivia has only shown favour to Cesario in order that her more backward suitor, the knight, should be encouraged to accost: he must redeem his credit either by valour or by policy; and so he declares for valour, for policy he hates. And so he sends a challenge that, notwithstanding his complacent view of its "vinegar and pepper," deserves a prominent place in any collection of diplomatic documents:

> Youth, whatsoever thou art, thou art but a scurvy fellow. Wonder not, nor admire not in thy mind, why I do call thee so, for I will show thee no reason for 't. Thou comest to the Lady Olivia, and in my sight she uses thee kindly: but thou liest in thy throat; that is not the matter I challenge thee for. I will waylay thee going home; where if it be thy chance to kill me, thou kill'st me like a rogue and a villain. Fare thee well; and God have mercy upon one of our souls! He may have mercy upon mine; but my hope is better, and so look to thyself. Thy friend, as thou usest him, and thy sworn enemy,
>
> ANDREW AGUECHEEK.

Never, in the whole history of the duello, was such good citizenship exhibited in a challenge. And when Sir Andrew learns that his adversary has been fencer to the Sophy and is a fire-eater, he is swift to declare that he will not meddle with him, and that had he known that the fellow had been so valiant and so cunning in fence, he would have seen him damned before he would have challenged him. And, of course, Sir Andrew is only talking sense: it would have served the fellow right not to have been challenged. Later, when he has struck Sebastian and has received a pummelling in exchange, he tells Sir Toby to let Sebastian alone: "I'll go another way to work with him; I'll have an action of battery against him, if there be any law in Illyria: though I struck him first, yet it's no matter for that." No matter at all: he feels, as we all do, that the law is on his side. Our last glimpse of him is somewhat moving, for he has a broken head, received in the company of Sir Toby, who has himself been given "a bloody coxcomb," but nevertheless his admiration and faith are undiminished; had Sir Toby not been in drink, he tells the company, things would have fallen out very differently; and at the last, he cries: "I'll help you, Sir Toby, because we'll be dressed together." But his idol turns and rends him, calling him an ass-head and a coxcomb and a knave, a thin-faced knave, a gull. These are hard sayings but not too hard for Sir Andrew to swallow, and perhaps they made their peace together afterwards. If not, we can only

hope that our simpleton went on his travels and somehow in the end
contrived to find his way into Gloucester and into the orchard of Justice
Shallow, for there he would find company after his own heart, the great
Shallow himself and Silence and Slender, and take his place among such
boon companions, seat himself at the pippins and cheese and try to
disengage from his tangled mind such confused memories as remained
there of Illyria and the roystering Illyrians, his foolish face aglow beneath
the unfading appleblossom.

MR. MICAWBER

It is odd to think of the sinister Mr. Murdstone as the tool of Providence,
acting unwittingly as its compensating finger, restoring the balance in the
affairs of poor little Copperfield. But that is what he was. The ten-year-old
David is immured in Murdstone and Grinby's warehouse, with its dirt and
decaying floors and scuffling old grey rats. But he must have lodgings,
cheap lodgings, and so Mr. Murdstone bethinks himself of a certain not
very successful agent of the firm who has a room to let in Windsor Terrace,
City Road, and decides that David shall go there. David is taken into the
counting-house and introduced to his new landlord:

> A stoutish, middle-aged person, in a brown surtout and black tights
> and shoes, with no more hair upon his head (which was a large one,
> and very shining) than there is upon an egg, and with a very extensive
> face, which he turned full upon me. His clothes were shabby, but he
> had an imposing shirt-collar on. He carried a jaunty sort of stick, with
> a large pair of rusty tassels to it; and a quizzing-glass hung outside his
> coat, — for ornament, I afterwards found, as he very seldom looked
> through it, and couldn't see anything when he did. . . .

It is Mr. Micawber, the inimitable, the unique Mr. Micawber. Henceforward, we know that once our bottle-washing and label-pasting is done,
in that dark warehouse at Blackfriars, there will be this god-like creature
waiting for us at home; and that when Murdstone and Grinby's is nothing
more than an evil memory and we have almost forgotten Windsor Terrace,

City Road, we have not yet done with the great Micawber, who will continue to pop up in odd places and send us letters when we are least expecting them, letters that are worth more than all the money he will contrive to borrow from us from time to time; and in short — as the great man himself would say — an account has been opened for us in the Bank of Humour where we have been given unlimited credit. Our whole existence has been enriched by the flavour of Micawber so that it can never taste quite the same again, can never be entirely flat and saltless whatever may happen to us. Little did Mr. Murdstone imagine that by an idle choice of a landlord he was to wipe off all our scores against him and actually leave us in his debt. Micawber has arrived, and the balance has been more than restored. Perhaps this is the only occasion in the life of that hard-pressed gentleman on which he and a credit balance have arrived together.

Mr. Micawber is unquestionably the greatest of all Dickens's comic figures. Unlike so many of the others, he is droll both in character and in speech; he would be vastly entertaining if he were only described to us, if we were only allowed to see him from a distance and never met him face to face or heard him speak; the idea of him is comic; but in addition to that, of course, he is infinitely droll in speech, always saying the kind of thing we expect him to say but always saying it better, being more himself, so to speak, every time we meet him, as such persons are in real life. He is not only the greatest of Dickens's comic figures, but, with the one exception of Falstaff, he is the greatest comic figure in the whole range of English literature, a literature supremely rich in such characters. Falstaff is greater because he is himself a comic genius; in him the two familiar types of characters, the comic rogue and the comic butt, are combined, for he is a comic rogue who is his own butt, and as such he is unique. To this must be added his extraordinary versatility, the teeming abundance of his wit and humour, ranging from crude horse-play to a kind of comic philosophy, which is only displayed within a comparatively small compass (and perhaps necessarily so, for no man, not even a Shakespeare, could have kept the Falstaff of *Henry IV, Part One,* going long — only a god could have fed the furnace of that wit) but makes him tower above any other comic character. Micawber must be included in quite another category, namely, that of the great solemn fools, who do not offer us their wit and humour but only themselves, who do not make jokes but are themselves one endless joke. If Micawber — and all the persons of his kind (and most of us have known a few) — should realise even for a moment that he is funny, he would be ruined for us; but happily he does not, and while we are actually in his presence — and what a presence — we too must be as solemn as he is, the greatest of all the great solemn fools. It is only when his majesty has departed that we can break into inextinguishable laughter.

The story that Micawber adorns is different from the other Dickens novels in having a certain autobiographical basis: Dickens is making direct use of a number of his own childish experiences. There strolled magnificently through all the memories of his childhood and youth one extraordinary figure, his father, John Dickens, and it was he who became Mr. Micawber. So close at times are the two, the "Prodigal Father" (as Dickens called him) and the great comic character, that the description of Micawber sitting in state with his petition to the King in the Marshalsea, at the end of the eleventh chapter, is taken almost word for word from his own autobiographical notes describing an identical scene in the Marshalsea in which his father figured prominently. Thus we can say that in the creation of this monument of humour, Nature herself laid the foundations and was responsible for the general lines of the structure, while Dickens simply added the decoration, those touches of art necessary when cold print has to take the place of warm breathing reality. It is more than likely that all the most successful characters of fiction and drama are created in this way, they are neither elaborate pieces of portrait painting, on the one hand, nor examples of pure creation, creatures dropped from the blue, on the other; but, if they are comic characters, have their origin in persons long known and humorously and lovingly observed, pondered over, rolled — as it were — on the author's palate until he has the very flavour of them, and then subtly transformed by art, the non-essential parts pared away and the essential coloured and heightened, until at last we have characters who, in a short acquaintance begun and ended in a few chapters, have the same effect upon us that their originals would have in real life if we had known them for years. It is a pity that we have not chapter and verse for this creative process, the real person and the fictitious one side by side, so that we could actually observe the transformation.

Comic figures created in this fashion seize hold of our imagination so strongly because not only have they the wild absurdity that a humorous and fanciful author, like Dickens, can give to the speech of his figures, they have also a certain solidity, a psychological richness, that sets them far above those brittle creatures who, like so many of Dickens's later characters, are simply an eccentric trick of speech and gesture and nothing more, characters that have no insides but are merely masks, clothes and wires. Thus Micawber, in his talk, has all the wild absurdity of a comic individual, and particularly, of course, a comic Dickens individual, and he has too the psychological richness and solidity of a universal type and is therefore, unlike so many entertaining characters, a fruitful theme for any man's discourse. Volumes passing a score of philosophies under review could be written on the Micawbers.

Really great absurdities of speech are like really great passages of poetry, they cannot be analysed, no more than a scent can be analysed; they are simply miraculous assemblages of words. Why they should be so ridiculous is, and must remain, a mystery. Faced with them, we can only enjoy and give thanks, taking our analysis elsewhere. In the last resort, speech and character cannot, of course, be separated, one being the expression of the other, and concerning Mr. Micawber's character there is a great deal to be said, so that his delicious conversation, which in its highest flights of absurdity, as we have seen, is beyond analysis, can be very briefly examined in passing. Its most obvious characteristic is its trick of anti-climax. Mr. Micawber indulges in a very florid and theatrical rhetoric that always breaks down; just when his fantastic bark appears to be safely launched on the flood of oratory, we hear the grating of the keel and discover that he has run aground; his habit of giving everything a false dignity in his talk (which perhaps reaches its climax in his reference to the man from the waterworks as a "Minion of Power"), as if he were not an impecunious commercial traveller chatting with his friends but a statesman addressing the senate of some vast empire, is ridiculous enough, but it is made still more ridiculous by the fact that he cannot keep it up, his invention or his vocabulary not being equal to the demand, so that he inevitably flounders and breaks down. But a further touch of absurdity is added by the fact that though — so to speak — the matter breaks down, the manner does not: we can realise that at the moment when his oratory is crashing down into the commonplace, his pompousness is becoming even more marked, that "certain condescending roll in his voice" and that "certain indescribable air of doing something genteel" being more noticeable than ever. Nothing, we imagine, that he ever says can be delivered with such a dignified and genteel air as that "In short" which always arrives when his first gushing stream of oratory is drying up and he is casting about — usually in vain — for other springs of noble and resounding speech. We have only to take a single scene, let us say that in which he says good-bye to David before leaving for Plymouth in the earlier part of the book, to discover several excellent examples of this oratorical anti-climax and bathos. Mr. Micawber, with his capital histrionic sense, is aware of the solemnity of the occasion and is in a rather mournfully didactic mood. "Procrastination," he remarks to David, "is the thief of time. Collar him." Touching on Mrs. Micawber's father, who has been hurled into the conversation by Mrs. Micawber, he observes: "Take him for all in all, we ne'er shall — in short, make the acquaintance, probably, of anybody else possessing, at his time of life, the same legs for gaiters, and able to read the same description of print, without spectacles." And then later when he gives us his great contribution to economics and ethics: "Annual income twenty pounds, annual expenditure nineteen six, result happiness. Annual income twenty pounds, annual expenditure twenty pounds ought and six, result misery. The blossom is blighted, the leaf is withered, the God of Day goes down upon the dreary scene, and — in short, you are for ever floored. As I am." And when he had said this, we are told, Mr. Micawber drank a glass of punch with an air of great enjoyment and satisfaction, and whistled the College Hornpipe. And well he might, for, having expressed the misery of his position in what he considers such excellent rhetoric (for he himself soars high above bathos), he is perfectly happy, for he is an orator, an artist; he has the so-called "artistic temperament," and is indeed perhaps our very best example of it.

It is significant, however, that Mr. Micawber is not an artist by profession but a commercial gentleman. But just as many artists, perhaps the majority of them, have not even a glimmer of the artistic temperament, so many gentlemen engaged in business, particularly in its vaguer and looser forms, on its fringes, in dubious agencies and so forth, are, like Micawber, almost perfect specimens of the temperament. One of the greatest and most astonishing Bohemians I have ever met was a certain dissipated watchmaker of the town of Maidstone in Kent. It is on the lounging and strange borderlands of trade, where blossom for a season the odd little companies in odd little towns, that our Micawbers are to be encountered. "The truly gorgeous and great personality," Mr. Chesterton remarks very rightly, "he who talks as no one else could talk and feels with an elementary fire, you will never find this man on any cabinet bench, in any literary circle, at any society dinner. Least of all will you find him in artistic society; he is utterly unknown in Bohemia." No, he is tucked away in the general office of the Bristol Leatherworks, or may be found in East Lancashire, acting as the local representative of the Imperial Patent Mat Company. In such places, behind a door in some dingy provincial street, unhonoured and unsung, are our Micawbers, personalities like sunsets, and we are unfortunate, to say the least of it, if we have not known at least one of them.

Too much has been made of Mr. Micawber's mere hopefulness: the phrase about "waiting for something to turn up" seems almost to have hypnotised everybody. Not that he was not supremely hopeful, one of the ripest of optimists, but he cannot be explained merely in terms of optimism: the analysis must be carried much further. His temperament is, of course, extremely elastic; his moods are like quicksilver, and much of his drollery arises from his astonishingly rapid changes from the very depths of despair to the height of gaiety and good-fellowship. When creditors, dirty-faced men for the most part, called at his house and shouted "Swindlers" and "Robbers" up the stairs, Mr. Micawber, it will be remembered, "would be transported with grief and mortification, even to the length (as I was once made aware by a scream from his wife) of making motions at himself with a razor; but within half an hour afterwards, he would polish up his shoes with extraordinary pains, and go out, humming a tune with a greater air of gentility than ever." And when little David visited him in the Marshalsea, Mr. Micawber wept and solemnly conjured his youthful visitor to take warning by his fate, but then immediately afterwards borrowed a shilling, sent out for some porter, sat down to his room-mate's loin of mutton, and was his glorious self again. He positively juggles with his moods, and can touch the extremes within the space of a single sentence. One of the most amusing, though by no means one of the quickest, of his changes is that at Canterbury when he and David meet for the first time since the early days in London. The three of them (for Mrs. Micawber is there — seeing the Medway) sit down to fish, roast veal, fried sausage-meat, partridge, and pudding, wine, strong ale and, after dinner, a bowl of hot punch; the evening is decidedly festive, healths are drunk all round, Mr. Micawber delivers an eulogium on the character of Mrs. Micawber (as well he might), and they end by singing "Auld Lang Syne" and "Here's a hand, my trusty frere" — Mr. Micawber throughout being the very picture of conviviality and high spirits. Yet David receives the following letter, early the next morning, a letter clearly written within quarter of an hour after his departure the previous night:

MY DEAR YOUNG FRIEND,

The die is cast — all is over. Hiding the ravages of care with a sickly mask of mirth, I have not informed you, this evening, that there is no hope of the remittance! Under these circumstances, alike humiliating to contemplate, and humiliating to relate, I have discharged the pecuniary liability contracted at this establishment, by giving a note of hand, made payable fourteen days after date, at my residence, Penton-ville, London. When it becomes due, it will not be taken up. The result is destruction. The bolt is impending, and the tree must fall.

Let the wretched man who now addresses you, my dear Copperfield, be a beacon to you through life. He writes with that intention, and in that hope. If he could think himself of so much use, one gleam of day might, by possibility, penetrate into the cheerless dungeon of his re-maining existence — though his longevity is, at present (to say the least of it), extremely problematical.

This is the last communication, my dear Copperfield, you will ever receive

From
The
Beggared Outcast,
WILKINS MICAWBER.

On receipt of this startling communication, David immediately runs to the hotel in the hope of being able to comfort his friend, but on the way there

he meets the London coach — "with Mr. and Mrs. Micawber up behind;
Mr. Micawber, the very picture of tranquil enjoyment, smiling at Mrs.
Micawber's conversation, eating walnuts out of a paper bag, with a bottle
sticking out of his breast-pocket." The Beggared Outcast had promptly
vanished once he had written that heart-rending letter, and his place had
been probably taken at once by Mr. Micawber the genteel man of the world
and, for the nonce, the complacent author.

The secret of Mr. Micawber is that he does not really live in this world at
all: he lives in a world of his own. It is a world in which he himself is
clearly a man of talent, for whom great prizes are waiting round the next
corner, where an IOU clearly set out and given to the proper person or an
entry in a little notebook is as good as cash down, where everything is
larger and simpler and richer and more romantic than the things of this
world. In short — to echo him once more — he lives entirely in his
imagination: he has the real artistic temperament. Let circumstances cast
him down ever so little, then he cries farewell and plunges headlong into
the dark gulf of despair; but within a short space of time he has not only
climbed out of that gulf into the common daylight of ordinary cheerfulness,
he has soared away into the very empyrean of human happiness: he will
have no half-measures in his moods, because a robust, romantic, and (to
speak truth) somewhat theatrical imagination takes no delight in half-
measures; it demands either the green limelight and the muted strings or
every light in the house ablaze and the full orchestra crashing in triumph.
But the real world, observing that Wilkins Micawber will not consent to
live in it, plans a hearty revenge. It contrives that the said Micawber shall
be for ever in difficulties; that his talent shall pass unrecognised (except by
Mrs. Micawber) and his offers — as she herself tells us — received with
contumely; that neither corn nor coals shall sustain him, and that he shall
be for ever head over ears in debt, existing in a wilderness of notes of hand,
discounted bills, and IOU's; and so, eternally jostled by creditors and
bailiffs, in and out of the debtors' prison, exchanging one set of miserable
lodgings for another, pawning the few remaining possessions in order to
pay for the next meal, he and his wife and their ever-increasing family are
for ever driven from pillar to post, can never breathe freely, clear themselves, settle down as decent citizens willing and able to look any man in
the face; and thus would seem to be in a truly wretched condition. Short of
actual crime — and borrowing on such a scale appears to be dangerously
near a criminal proceeding — it is hardly possible to imagine an existence
more squalid, uncomfortable, and hopeless. This world, it would seem, has
revenged itself very thoroughly.

But actually it has done nothing of the kind, for Mr. Micawber remains
unscathed, living as he does in some other world of his own. The above
account of his way of life is true enough as it is glimpsed from the real

world; but Mr. Micawber himself does not really see it like this, as we may gather from his talk, nor does his wife, nor, indeed, does any one who is under the spell of his glamourous imagination and walks with him for a space in his own private Eden. If a man who has just been quarrelling with the turncock from the waterworks can dismiss the matter with a reference to "the momentary laceration of a wounded spirit, made sensitive by a recent collision with the Minion of Power," he is beyond the corroding touch of bitter circumstance; the slings and arrows of outrageous fortune whistle by, leaving him unhurt; his imagination has provided him with one of those fairy cloaks that enable their wearers to brave all dangers. Mr. Micawber sees himself as the central figure in some colossal wild romance, to which even the most disastrous events do but add an intensely absorbing and moving chapter or so and call for nobler attitudes and more magnificent rhetoric on the part of the principal actor. Once things are seen in that romantic haze, so that they loom splendid or sinister and run riot in scarlet and black and gold, the dreariness, the hopelessness, of the petty tale that is the world's report of Mr. Micawber's life completely disappear: he goes his way to the sound of epic drums, the trumpets of tragedy, and the flutes and violins of romance. To him, the present is always a crisis, whether of good or ill fortune matters not, a crisis to be enjoyed as the latest and strangest scene in the drama; the past, far from being a hopeless record from which remembrance turns her face, is an Othello's tale of battles, sieges, fortunes, of moving accidents by flood and field, of hairbreadth 'scapes i' the imminent deadly breach; the future, shining round the next corner, is a happy ending.

What chance has poverty, with its poor shifts and wretched limitations, its dinginess and drabness, with a mind so wedded to high romance, so intoxicated with opulent images and phrases, so richly nourished by the milk and honey of words? What does it matter what facts have to be faced if they are first sent to the carnival of the romantic imagination and so always return the strangest and most fascinating company, still moving to music in their tragic and comic masks? David was a poor little fellow of ten, a timid little washer of bottles, when he lodged, dingily and precariously like a mouse, with the Micawbers; but Mr. Micawber, meeting him again after a lapse of years, can drink "to the days when my friend Copperfield and myself were younger, and fought our way in the world side by side." On their first meeting again, at Canterbury, when David tells him that he is now at school, he can remark: "Although a mind like my friend Copperfield's does not require that cultivation which, without his knowledge of men and things, it would require, still it is a rich soil teeming with latent vegetation." Later, when they meet in the company of Traddles, Mr. Micawber refers to his affairs as a somewhat romantic historian, engaged in

the chronicle of the whole world, might refer to the position of some great
empire at a crisis in its history:

"You find us, Copperfield," said Mr. Micawber, with one eye on
Traddles, "at present established, on what may be designated as a
small and unassuming scale; but, you are aware that I have, in the
course of my career, surmounted difficulties, and conquered obstacles.
You are no stranger to the fact, that there have been periods of my
life, when it has been requisite that I should pause, until certain unexpected events should turn up; when it has been necessary that I
should fall back, before making what I trust I shall not be accused of
presumption in terming — a spring. The present is one of those mo-
mentous stages in the life of man. You find me, fallen back, *for* a
spring; and I have every reason to believe that a vigorous leap will
shortly be the result."

And his subsequent review of the situation, his parting speech, in the
manner in which it succeeds in casting a curious glamour over everything,
transforming the most trumpery and prosaic matter into something rich
and strange, gives us the complete Micawber, soaring high above this world
of "offices and the witness-box":

"My dear Copperfield, I need hardly tell you that to have beneath
our roof, under existing circumstances, a mind like that which gleams
— if I may be allowed the expression — which gleams — in your
friend Traddles, is an unspeakable comfort. With a washerwoman,
who exposes hard-bake for sale in her parlor-window, dwelling next
door, and a Bow-street officer residing over the way, you may imagine
that his society is a source of consolation to myself and to Mrs.
Micawber. I am at present, my dear Copperfield, engaged in the sale
of corn upon commission. It is not an avocation of a remunerative description — in other words, it does *not* pay — and some temporary
embarrassments of a pecuniary nature have been the consequence. I
am, however, delighted to add that I have now an immediate prospect
of something turning up (I am not at liberty to say in what direction),
which I trust will enable me to provide, permanently, both for myself
and for your friend Traddles, in whom I have an unaffected interest.
You may, perhaps, be prepared to hear that Mrs. Micawber is in a
state of health which renders it not wholly improbable that an addition may be ultimately made to those pledges of affection which — in
short, to the infantine group. Mrs. Micawber's family have been so
good as to express their dissatisfaction at this state of things. I have
merely to observe that I am not aware it is any business of theirs, and
that I repel that exhibition of feeling with scorn, and with defiance!"

An excellent example of our friend's Front Bench manner, in which every
polysyllabic phrase suggests at least five thousand a year and a substantial

pension. What is an empty pocket compared to such verbal riches? Selling corn upon commission may be a poor business, but once it is referred to as "not an avocation of a remunerative description" it somehow suggests that immense wealth is lying only just beyond the speaker's grasp; it takes us immediately into an atmosphere of prosperity. What is a balance at the bank to a man who has only to open his mouth to shower riches about him like someone in a fairy tale, whose very tongue is an alchemist?

Living in the world as he does, not as some poor devil trying to patch together a bare existence and evade his creditors, but as the central and heroic figure in that amazing chronicle, The Life and Times of Wilkins Micawber, Lover, Husband, Father, Financier, and Philosopher, Mr. Micawber instinctively seizes hold of every situation, good or evil, that presents itself and makes the most of it. Faced with such romantic gusto, so fine an appreciation of a crisis, revelling even in profound despair and last farewells, ill fortune, try as it may, can hardly make itself felt. And the commonplace, that drab stuff which is the fabric of most of our days, vanishes entirely: it is hardly conceivable that Mr. Micawber can ever have had a dull moment. It would be difficult to imagine anything more dreary than the prospect of being a clerk to a petty solicitor in a small cathedral town, or anything less exciting and romantic than a family removal from London to Canterbury; but Mr. Micawber, on the eve of his removal to Uriah Heep's, stands before us as a man who has just seen Troy burn and is now about to embark on an Odyssey. And so, of course, he is: it is we who are blind and deaf and spiritless in our boredom. "It may be expected," the great creature declares to his friends, "that on the eve of a migration which will consign us to a perfectly new existence, I should offer a few valedictory remarks to two such friends as I see before me. But all that I have to say in this way, I have said. Whatever station in society I may attain, through the medium of the learned profession of which I am about to become an unworthy member, I shall endeavour not to disgrace, and Mrs. Micawber will be safe to adorn." Being able now to cast off his disguise (the name "Mortimer" and a pair of spectacles — and who can doubt that he enjoyed both immensely?), he speaks as one who has long been an exile or spent half a lifetime in remote hiding-places, and his language leaps up to grapple with the romantic moment: "The cloud has passed from the dreary scene, and the God of Day is once more high upon the mountain tops. On Monday next, on the arrival of the four o'clock afternoon coach at Canterbury, my foot will be on my native heath — my name, Micawber."

No sooner is Australia mentioned ("the land, the only land, for myself and my family" — though he has obviously never given it a thought before) than he sees a new part for himself and plunges into it. Within an hour or so, we are told, he is walking the streets of Canterbury — "expressing, in the hardy roving manner he assumed, the unsettled habits of a temporary sojourner in the land; and looking at the bullocks, as they came by, with the eye of an Australian farmer." And as the plans for emigration mature, he becomes still more wildly colonial. What could be better than the steps he has taken to familiarise himself and his family with the conditions of Australian life?

"My eldest daughter attends at five every morning at a neighbouring establishment, to acquire the process — if process it may be called — of milking cows. My younger children are instructed to observe, as closely as circumstances will permit, the habits of the pigs and poultry maintained in the poorer parts of this city: a pursuit from which they have, on two occasions, been brought home, within an inch of being run over. I have myself directed some attention, during the past week, to the art of baking; and my son Wilkins has issued forth with a walk- ingstick and driven cattle, when permitted, by the rugged hirelings who had them in charge, to render any voluntary service in that direc- tion — which I regret to say, for the credit of our nature, was not often; he being generally warned, with imprecations, to desist."

Once on board the ship, he combines, with great skill, both the colonial and nautical characters. With a low-crowned straw hat, a complete suit of oilskins, a telescope, and a trick of "casting up his eye at the sky as looking out for dirty weather," he is nothing less than an old salt, and we can be sure that he carried out his intention of spinning an occasional yarn before the galley-fire. And he has also provided himself and his family with enormous clasp-knives and wooden spoons, and insists upon their drinking out of "villainous little tin pots" although there are plenty of glasses in the room, so determined is he that they shall stand before Albion as "denizens of the forest." "The luxuries of the old country we abandon," he an- nounces with an intense pleasure that is the very height of luxury. Happy Mr. Micawber, with every hour adding pages to his romantic history, moving sublimely in a world of his own creation, clad in the armour of his soaring fancy, the conqueror of circumstance, merely adding its variations to his swelling moods as he adds the lemons to the punch. He is a greater figure in the history of romantic idealism than most of its professors, for he lays bare more of its secrets, as he rolls out his "few remarks" and points his single eyeglass over the steaming bowl, than whole volumes of our Schellings and Schlegels. Happy Mr. Micawber, joyously combining the rôles of financier, sailor, and pioneer, but, in truth, only travelling in a dream, from an England that was never there to an Australia that he will invent, sailing from moonshine to moonshine.

It was a fortunate day for Mr. Micawber when he visited a certain house (presumably in Plymouth) and heard the daughter of the family sing her two ballads, "The Dashing White Serjeant" and "Little Tafflin," for by the time he had heard "Little Tafflin," we are told, he had resolved to win the fair singer or perish in the attempt, and, as we know, was successful, so that Emma became in due course the companion of his travels, his partner in joy and sorrow, Mrs. Micawber. He could not have made a better choice. Mrs. Micawber is entitled to a place, by the side of Lady Macbeth, among the great wives of literature. Micawber himself is a great man, but we must not allow our appreciation of that fact to blind us to another fact, namely, that great as he is, he would be like a ship robbed of its compass without "that pervading influence which sanctifies while it enhances the — in short, the influence of Woman in the lofty character of Wife." There never was a man more suitably and happily mated. If an unswerving loyalty, an unconquerable fidelity, are necessary to the character of a good wife, as they are, then Mrs. Micawber takes her place among the best, for her loyalty and fidelity are almost matchless. Though buffeted by the world, pursued by duns, hampered by her ever-increasing family, at odds with her relatives, she will never desert Mr. Micawber. If there should be any cynic who should doubt the strength of her attachment, let him read once more the chronicles of the Micawbers, and he will be compelled to agree: Mrs. Micawber will never desert Mr. Micawber. If a certain similarity in tastes and temperament is one of the conditions of a happy marriage, as it is, this similarity is not difficult to find in the Micawbers. Fortunately, Mrs. Micawber has all her husband's elasticity, his power of rising from the depths of despair to the heights of conviviality in an incredibly short space of time. Had she been a woman of another temperament, a creature of fixed moods, gazing with stony eyes at the rapidly oscillating needle of her husband's humour, all her loyalty would have been to little purpose: the God of Day would inevitably have gone down upon the dreary scene. But she is as elastic as he is. "I have known her," David tells us, "to be thrown into fainting fits by the king's taxes at three o'clock, and to eat lamb-chops breaded, and drink warm ale (paid for with two teaspoons that had gone to the pawnbroker's), at four. On one occasion, when an execution had just been put in, coming home through some chance as early as six o'clock, I saw her lying (of course with a twin) under the grate in a swoon, with her hair all torn about her face; but I never knew her more cheerful than she was, that very same night, over a veal-cutlet before the kitchen fire, telling me stories about her papa and mamma, and the company they used to keep." But a happy marriage demands not only unity but variety. The two partners must not be identical in character, a mere reflection of one another, but must be sufficiently diverse so that each one can put something into the joint concern that the other partner lacks, so that they can act as both a check and a stimulus upon one another. Does this final condition clang the gates before Mrs. Micawber's face, barring her out of the ultimate Eden? It does not.

If Wilkins is the imaginative partner, the rhetorician, of the Micawbers, Emma is the logician. Her task it is to stand behind her fiery and impetuous spouse, restraining him until she has pointed the way. Never was a devoted woman better equipped for the task. "Emma's form is fragile, but her grasp of a subject is inferior to none," her father was in the habit of saying, and undoubtedly her father was a man of some discernment. Mrs. Micawber's grasp of a subject compels our admiration. Mr. Micawber, with his swelling and opulent imagination, is capable of conceiving the most colossal projects and of hurling himself into the fray, but to Mrs. Micawber is left the arduous task of clearing away, with a ruthlessness that appals lesser intellects, the nonessentials of a problem and then of stating it, in its barest terms, with an exquisite and almost superhuman lucidity. Not even in the early days of Political Economy, the days of the Economic Man, when the textbooks were as repulsive as they are today but differed from our modern works in being intelligible, were economic problems stated so clearly as they are by Mrs. Micawber. Her approach to the matter of the Medway Coal Trade is a model of reasoning:

"We all came back again," replied Mrs. Micawber. "Since then, I have consulted other branches of my family on the course which it is most expedient for Mr. Micawber to take — for I maintain that he must take some course, Master Copperfield," said Mrs. Micawber, argumentatively. "It is clear that a family of six, not including a domestic, cannot live upon air."

"Certainly, ma'am," said I.

"The opinion of those other branches of my family," pursued Mrs. Micawber, "is, that Mr. Micawber should immediately turn his attention to coals."

"To what, ma'am?"

"To coals," said Mrs. Micawber. "To the coal trade. Mr. Micawber was induced to think, on inquiry, that there might be an opening for a man of his talent in the Medway Coal Trade. Then, as Mr. Micawber very properly said, the first step to be taken clearly was, to come and see the Medway. Which we came and saw. I say 'we,' Master Copperfield; for I never will," said Mrs. Micawber with emotion, "I never will desert Mr. Micawber."

I murmured my admiration and approbation.

"We came," repeated Mrs. Micawber, "and saw the Medway. My opinion of the coal trade on that river, is, that it may require talent, but that it certainly requires capital. Talent, Mr. Micawber has; capital, Mr. Micawber has not. We saw, I think, the greater part of the

Medway; and that is my individual conclusion. Being so near here, Mr. Micawber was of opinion that it would be rash not to come on, and see the Cathedral. Firstly, on account of its being so well worth seeing, and our never having seen it; and secondly, on account of the great probability of something turning up in a cathedral town. . . ."

Apart from that one emotional outburst on this subject of never deserting Mr. Micawber, not only excusable but even admirable in itself, showing as it does that the crystal-clear brain is only the servant of a woman's warm heart, a treatise by a master of the subject could not achieve greater lucidity. Equally good is her later survey, at the dinner-party given by David, when she goes into the whole question of her husband's prospects with characteristic thoroughness and grasp. Coals are not to be relied upon; and corn, we are told, though gentlemanly is not remunerative — "Commission to the extent of two and ninepence in a fortnight cannot, however limited our ideas, be considered remunerative." Brewing and banking are both discussed by this devoted and clear-sighted helpmate, but both have shown themselves adamant in the face of Mr. Micawber's offers. It is clear, as Mrs. Micawber remarks, that we must live. What is to be done? Let us hear the lady herself on the subject, and so discover her at the height of her powers:

"Very well," said Mrs. Micawber. "Then what do I recommend? Here is Mr. Micawber with a variety of qualifications — with great talent —"

"Really, my love," said Mr. Micawber.

"Pray, my dear, allow me to conclude. Here is Mr. Micawber, with a variety of qualifications, with great talent — I should say, with genius, but that may be the partiality of a wife —"

Traddles and I both murmured "No."

"And here is Mr. Micawber without any suitable position or employment. Where does that responsibility rest? Clearly on society. Then I would make a fact so disgraceful known, and boldly challenge society to set it right. It appears to me, my dear Mr. Copperfield," said Mrs. Micawber, forcibly, "that what Mr. Micawber has to do, is to throw down the gauntlet to society, and say, in effect, 'Show me who will take that up. Let the party immediately step forward.' "

I ventured to ask Mrs. Micawber how this was to be done.

"By advertising," said Mrs. Micawber — "in all the papers. It appears to me, that what Mr. Micawber has to do, in justice to himself, in justice to his family, and I will even go so far as to say in justice to society, by which he has been hitherto overlooked, is to advertise in all the papers; to describe himself plainly as so-and-so, with such and such qualifications, and to put it thus: 'Now employ me, on remunerative terms, and address, postpaid, to W. M., Post Office, Camden Town.' "

Does Mr. Micawber think of taking up the Law — then Mrs. Micawber is quick to ask whether, in applying himself to a subordinate branch of the profession, he will place it out of his power to rise ultimately to the "top of the tree," seeing him, in her mind's eye, as a Judge or a Chancellor. When Australia is suggested, she is on hand to inquire as to the climate and the circumstances of the country — are they such that a man of Mr. Micawber's abilities would have a fair chance of rising in the social scale? When they are actually on the boat, how nobly she devotes herself to the task of making her husband (who has declared that "Britannia must take her chance") see that his duty, in this distant clime, will be to strengthen and not to weaken the connection between himself and Albion. No wife could do more in furthering the best interests of her husband and of society at one and the same time. How inspiring is her very last piece of advice:

"I wish Mr. Micawber to take his stand upon that vessel's prow, and firmly say, 'This country I am come to conquer! Have you honours? Have you riches? Have you posts of profitable pecuniary emolument? Let them be brought forward. They are mine.' "

Mr. Micawber, glancing at us all, seemed to think there was a good deal in this idea.

"I wish Mr. Micawber, if I make myself understood," said Mrs. Micawber, in her argumentative tone, "to be the Caesar of his own fortunes. That, my dear Mr. Copperfield, appears to be his true position. From the first moment of this voyage, I wish Mr. Micawber to stand upon that vessel's prow and say, 'Enough of delay: enough of disappointment: enough of limited means. That was in the old country. This is the new. Produce your reparation. Bring it forward!' "

After this, there is no excuse for Mr. Micawber if he does not "wield the rod of talent and of power in Australia." A fine fighting spirit, womanly wit, and a devoted heart can do no more for him.

Mrs. Micawber is one of the severest logicians with whom we have ever been acquainted; but she is not really reasoning about this world at all; she lives in Mr. Micawber's world, and, indeed, represents the logical and scientific point of view in that world. Existing as she does in the fire and light of Mr. Micawber's rich imagination, walking for ever in his gigantic shadow, it naturally follows that she has long since lost sight of common reality, which has been swallowed up by the strange and romantic world created for himself by Mr. Micawber. And since there is no reason why such a world, however strange and romantic and shadowy it may be, should not have its own logicians, we find Mrs. Micawber in the part, thereby supplementing her husband's more emotional, rhetorical, and imaginative outlook, manner, and speech, completing — as it were — his world for him just as she rounds off his life by her partnership in their happy marriage. Nor is it strange that a lady who, notwithstanding her fragility of form, has a grasp of a subject inferior to none, should be so consistently and happily moonstruck. The rich and fiery imagination, incessantly creating, must always acquire the ascendancy: the most austere and determined logic can never, in the last resort, be anything more than its willing servant. Ourselves both creations and creative, living half in and half out of some gigantic tragi-comedy of black night and unnumbered stars, in which we willy-nilly play a part laid down for us and yet contrive before we have done to have some tiny say in its authorship, putting in a cry here, a gesture there, that are our own, we must instinctively recognise and do homage to the creative imagination, bearing as it does the marks of divinity, so that sooner or later we come under its spell and are wetted by its spectral rain and warmed by its fabulous suns. In the fable, perhaps the loveliest and most significant of them all, of the crazy knight, Sancho Panza is most grossly and realistically minded, a man of common-sense, with his eyes fixed on solid objects; and yet after he has jogged behind his master down so many winding roads, he becomes in the end as high fantastical as the Don himself and capers among enchantments. So too Mrs. Micawber, for all her fierce feminine lucidity, has taken to her bosom not only the person of Mr. Micawber but all his host of dreams and legends, so that she too moves happily among enchantments, the picture of a good wife and a fitting subject for innumerable parables.

Nothing has been said so far about the part that Mr. Micawber is made to play in the story, a part that has been severely criticised, not least by his greatest admirers. Of the emigration and Mr. Micawber's purely material success at the end of the story, Mr. Chesterton has remarked: "But how did it happen that the man who created this Micawber could pension him off at the end of the story and make him a successful colonial mayor? Micawber never did succeed, never ought to succeed; his kingdom is not of this world." This is well said; but even if we agree with this view of Micawber, it is possible to defend Dickens. If the material success is offered us as a kind of poetic justice (and the choice of the Colonies suggests this, as the Victorians seemed to regard the Colonies as a rough-and-ready kind of Christian Heaven, with a scheme of poetic justice that would reward, let us say, the Squire's son, who has been wrongly accused of forgery and promptly exiled, with ten thousand head of sheep), then it is entirely unnecessary, for Mr. Micawber himself is a kind of poet, who lives in poetry, and does not need poetic justice. But if it is simply regarded as a new setting for Mr. Micawber, giving him, as it were, more scope for his Micawberishness, then it can be justified. Our last news of him is as "a diligent and esteemed correspondent" of the *Port Middlebay Times,* and obviously he was entirely at ease, as happy as a king, dashing off leaders for that influential organ. Is there anything nearer Micawber in this world than the early Colonial and American Press, existing sumptuously on magnificent phrases, rhetoric, and capital letters? Once the actual work had begun and the pioneers were busy, Micawber was worth his weight in diamonds and rubies to any colony (not merely as a character — as that, he was worth his weight anywhere) as a rhetorician, a fount of glorious phrases, an ever-gushing spring of eloquence, as the very embodiment of the romantic outlook upon life, of unconquerable faith and hope. Hard labour and easy rhetoric have tamed many a wilderness. Pioneering demands, first, the great workers, and then, afterwards, the great talkers; and it is not merely a coincidence that of all modern states America should have produced the largest crop of orators and offered them the greatest rewards. Mr. Micawber, I have no doubt, talked Port Middlebay into existence, and so deserved its highest honours.

But of his part as a detective in the history of David Copperfield it is impossible to put forward any defence. It is impossible to read those chapters without feeling that Micawber is being constrained by his creator: even the humour is forced and unreal. Indeed, the whole episode is preposterous. Uriah Heep would never have dreamed of employing such a person; Mr. Micawber would never have remained in the office a week; and, even supposing that both actions were possible, he would never have been able to conceal his knowledge of Uriah's shady transactions or, what is yet more unlikely, have been able to ferret them all out, tabulate them in a formal document, and then bide his time until the proper moment for disclosure had arrived. Mr. Micawber as a financial detective is no more convincing than Shelley as a Bow Street runner. This trick of hurling his great drolls into the plot of the story and compelling them to play some quite unlikely part is, of course, one of the most notable defects in Dickens. Nor can we understand how a man could have the wit to create such creatures and yet the folly to treat them so badly, until we reflect that we do not regard a Dickens tale as he regarded it. We think the stories exist for the sake of the characters; we do not care what happens so long as the delicious creatures make their appearance from time to time; many of us, who know the Dickens characters as we know our friends, could not set down on paper a single plot of his, having long since forgotten the machinery of the tale. But Dickens, an extremely conscientious author, thought that the characters existed for the sake of the stories — it is only in *Pickwick* that the characters exist for their own sweet sakes; and so when he had created some colossal droll, a Micawber, a Pecksniff, a Skimpole, and the like, he felt that he had to justify the space taken up by the great creature and so forced him to further the interests of the plot, usually in some outrageous manner. This was only the view of the conventional author, the superficial Dickens; the real man knew better and, in his heart of hearts, realised that these great comic figures of his were their own excuse and needed no complicated intrigue to justify their existence. Had he not realised this, he would never have allowed them to occupy so much room in his story, but would have curtailed their antics and bound them fast to the plot.

There is only one thing better than a story, and that is — a character. A character is half a hundred stories at once, the source of endless fables; and it is something more, particularly if it is a comic character. The tragic figures can hardly be separated from their particular chronicles, for we envisage them in the awful light of their destiny and doom; but the great comic figures wander out of their books, which are only so many introductions to them, for they are nothing if not children of freedom, and so we find them and their starry folly at large in our minds. The books themselves we may have forgotten, their very names may have faded out of our memories, but these figures, long since our friends that we are ready to laugh and cry over, we do not forget. Their happy absurdities have added something to the whole flavour of our existence: these great fools, dissolving us into laughter, have touched our minds with the mellow philosophy of their creators: leaving their company, the parlour door closed behind us, the tavern lights that illumined them now blurred in the wind and rain, we question the night, which has swallowed our last peal of laughter, more curiously, and await, in a heightened mood of expectancy, the pageant and comedy of the approaching day. Only this humour of character can stir the depths. The humour of incident and situation that does not proceed from character, however artfully it may be contrived, is at its best only an elaborate play, making a glitter and commotion on the surface of things. But the humour of character goes down and touches, surely but tenderly, the very roots of our common human nature.

V. From OPEN HOUSE 1927

THE BERKSHIRE BEASTS

I found myself walking through a large park with an old family friend, let us call her Miss Tweedletop, a somewhat characterless, colourless lady whom I had not even seen for years. Such persons have a habit of popping up in dreams years after we have apparently ceased to give them even a passing thought. They travel, by what devious ways we cannot imagine, into our subconscious minds, look around them bravely and then, shaking the mud off their shoes and taking a deep breath, they somehow contrive to jump up into our dreams. Miss Tweedletop and I, then, were walking through this park, and I knew somehow that we were really one unit of a fairly large party of friends who had all come out for a day's pleasure and sight-seeing. How I knew this I do not know, because the dream seemed to begin at the point when we had either lagged behind or outdistanced the main body, which I never saw at all. All my dreams appear to be tiny instalments of an enormous *feuilleton:* I never know the beginning or the end, although I am one of the chief actors, and also, they tell me, the dramatist, producer, and scene-shifter. But I always know a little of what has gone before; I give myself, as it were, a hint of the situation before I set myself on the stage; and on this occasion I knew that we were both members of a sight-seeing party.

We were strolling down a sort of carriage drive that swept forward, as such things usually do if there is space for it, in a vast curve. The place was not unlike Richmond Park but rather more trim and well ordered, perhaps the private park of some duke or other. We had walked slowly forward for some time, slowly because Miss Tweedletop is (or was) an elderly woman; and had been idly talking of this and that, when suddenly I saw, only a little way in front, a most curious group, a herd of the most unlikely creatures. They were of various sizes, but the largest would be easily twice the size of a full-grown elephant. They were not unlike elephants in appearance, except that they tapered more noticeably from head (their heads were enormous) to tail, and though they had the same huge flopping ears, they had no trunks. I am no lion tamer and I confess to being nervous in the presence of all strange animals, but I think that even a lion tamer or an elephant hunter might have felt rather diffident about approaching such creatures, who looked as if they had strayed out of the early chapters of the *Outline of History*. Miss Tweedletop, however, walked on even after she had noticed the astonishing brutes we were gradually approaching.

"Ah," she exclaimed, but rather slowly, like one who makes small-talk, "there are the Berkshire Beasts." She said it quite casually, just as people say "There is the County Court" or "There is the Albert Memorial" when they are not excited about the matter themselves nor expect you to be excited about it, but are simply making talk. I could see that Miss Tweedletop thought I knew as much about the Berkshire Beasts as she and everyone else did. By this time they were much closer, and I could see that they were a dark green colour and rather wrinkly and shiny, not unlike something between a cheap kind of lady's handbag and one of those foul and unnatural editions of the poets that are bought only as presents; but many thousands of times bigger than the most capacious handbag or the largest edition of Tennyson ever known. They looked bigger than ever. And then I noticed that every one of them, male or female, old or young, was wearing spectacles. Yes, spectacles, rimless spectacles of the kind affected by very intelligent, well-informed persons. They were, of course, much larger than our spectacles; indeed, I noticed that each lens of the spectacles worn by the adult monsters was about the size of an ordinary dinner plate. As the creatures turned their heads, their glasses gleamed and flashed in the sun. I did not see anything very droll in all this; I remember that I thought it a little odd at the time, but nothing more; indeed, unless I am mistaken, it appeared to me that the creatures, peering through or over their glasses at us, looked more sinister than ever.

All this I noticed, of course, during the brief interval of time when Miss Tweedletop made her remark. And then, instead of owning that I knew nothing about the Berkshire Beasts and thus giving myself the opportunity of learning something worth knowing in the natural history of dreamland, like a fool, and a cowardly fool, I allowed a bad social habit to overmaster me, and replied, equally casually, "Ah, yes. The Berkshire Beasts." I might have been their keeper for years; I might have spent half my lifetime tracking them down and capturing them in their native haunts (and what haunts they must have had!); I might have been the crazy oculist who had fitted them with their spectacles; so casually did I reply. But meanwhile, I had come to the conclusion that it was high time we turned back. One or two of them were moving in a leisurely but awe-inspiring fashion in our direction, and we were still walking towards them, as if they had been mere cattle or sheep and not monstrosities twenty feet high. True, their spectacles suggested that they were not ordinary monsters, that they knew something of the decencies and courtesies of life, and even hinted, as glasses always do, at a bookish pacifism, a ferocity strictly confined to polemics and debate. Why we should generally associate short sight with good nature is rather a mystery, but we do, and there is always something peculiarly revolting and unnatural about a spectacled murderer, just as there would be about a baby who was caught trying to poison its nurse.

One monster detached itself from the others, perhaps it was the leader as it was certainly one of the largest, and moved gigantically to meet us and then stood, with lowered head, looking at us over the top of its glasses, not ten yards away. I can see it yet, with its incredible head, dark green wrinkled skin, its spectacles stretched across a broad flat nose that was at least eighteen inches from side to side. Now or never was the time to turn round and run for it, even though there was no cover, no hiding place, for quite a distance. But the protest died in my throat, for Miss Tweedletop never turned a hair but strolled on with no more concern than she would have had in passing a tobacconist's shop. She did not even seem particularly interested in the creatures; and of course if she knew them and was not afraid, there was no reason for me to fear. But I do not think it was any such piece of reasoning that led me to walk forward by her side without any protest; it was merely the fear of being laughed at by a little old maiden lady. I saw myself being squashed as a boy squashes a black beetle; in a moment or so, those astonishing spectacles would be splashed and reddened by my blood.

But nothing happened. We passed almost under the leading monster's nose and he did nothing but survey us a little sadly and sceptically. It was incredible; the rimless spectacles had won. Perhaps that is why the creatures were made to wear them; before, when they were merely ordinary monsters without glasses, they were probably the most ferocious and dangerous creatures in the world, but now, simply with the addition of these contrivances of glass and wire, they were more gentle than most of our fellow humans. Probably the females were learning to knit monstrously, and the males were cultivating philosophical interests and debated among themselves as to the Knower and the Known. But as to that, I shall never be sure. Something, however, I did learn, for Miss Tweedletop made two more remarks before she tripped back into the lumber room of my uncared-for memories. "You know," she said, as casually as ever, "they're only kept now for their singing."

If she was as casual, I was as foolish as before, for instead of boldly pressing for an explanation after admitting my ignorance, I still concealed it and remarked: "Really? Only for their singing?" No doubt I thought that, later, perhaps when we had joined the others, by putting a question here and there I could learn all I wanted without confessing my ignorance. If so, I was sadly disappointed, and was rightly served for my foolishness.

Miss Tweedletop seemed faintly indignant, as if the tone of my reply cast a shade of doubt upon the ability of the beasts. "Yes," she said, rather reproachfully, "but they sing so beautifully." And then not a word more, for suddenly she and the monsters and the park and the bright summer day were all huddled away into the playbox of the night and I found my nose sniffing at the cold morning, and myself further from that park than I am from Sirius. Somewhere in the limbo of dreams, there is a park in which, perhaps, the Berkshire Beasts, like the morning stars, are singing together, singing so beautifully.

HAVING COVERED THE CARD TABLE

Everybody agreed that the card table needed a new covering. In place of that smooth green sward which makes the tournament of hearts and spades a delight to the eye, our card table had long been showing us a field that looked like some dreary recreation ground in a little industrial town, all faded, patchy, grey, fit for nothing better than sixes of clubs. There was talk of calling in the local carpenter, but I would not hear of it. I told them I would do it myself. They were surprised, humorous, indulgent, but I persisted. I had already examined the table and had come to the conclusion that it would furnish me with a pleasant little job, well within my very limited range of craftsmanship. The sides, which apparently held in position the baize or felt (actually it is felt, though everybody thinks it is baize), were screwed on, so that they could easily be removed, and the old cloth torn off and the new tacked on without much difficulty. I was not to be defrauded of so much happy screwing and tacking, so much stretching of smooth bright green cloth, by any bored artisan. I bought some felt and came hurrying back with it almost as if it were some new music or a parcel of books, and then, having surrounded myself with screwdrivers, scissors, hammers, tacks, pipes, tobacco, and matches, I spent a solidly happy morning.

It is very odd that I should thus find myself more and more interested in working with my hands. I would seem to have reversed the usual progress in the hobbies of men, who commonly begin with the boy's carpentering outfit (complete on card) and gradually find their way to books and ideas.

When I was a boy, however, I hated handiwork, and cared for nothing but books and games. The *Boy's Own Paper* showered instructions on me in vain, and I could pass by the most glorious set of tools, rows of gleaming chisels and gouges, without a thrill. No lop-sided boat of my laborious creation ever waddled out from the shore to heel over in the middle of the park lake or village pond. I never made anything, and did not possess even a pocket-knife. Christmas and birthdays brought me books, footballs, cricket-bats, single-sticks, and the like, and the only time I ever received anything to build up (it was a gigantic loop-the-loop contrivance, made up of hundreds and hundreds of little pieces of stiff cardboard: my father finally erected it), I was disgusted. At one high school that I attended for a season there was a period set aside for what was called "manual work," when pencil-boxes and iron paper-weights came clumsily and mournfully into being, and this period was a misery to me, whose shapeless bits of wood and pieces of battered metal were for ever held up to derision. In all other matters but this of craftsmanship, I was the conventional boy, a ferocious fullback, a slogging batsman, a rapturous student of pantomime, good for three helpings of suet pudding, but for the rest I preferred the inside of a book to the inside of a steam engine and never even touched a hammer if I could avoid it.

When I say that I bought my first box of tools only a few years ago, a light will be thrown on my curious history. It seems as if I am becoming more and more interested in those things that I neglected in my boyhood. Nowadays I like to know why the wheels go round. I have something of a passion, if not an openly declared one, for what my friend the etcher happily calls "gadgetry." I have not only mended a gramophone and a typewriter, but am frequently to be found boasting about it. As yet I have not achieved a workshop, but I am rapidly becoming one of those men who do the little jobs about the house. By the time I am an old man, I shall probably be completely indifferent to books, having taken to fretwork and Meccano sets. As a craftsman, I am still a blundering novice, but the enthusiasm is there and time will ripen all. My planing is still contemptible; my sawing is weak; but my screwing and nailing are now almost up to professional standard, being sure, cool, masterful. This covering of the card table was my opportunity, for there were fourteen trim screws to be taken out and put in again, and tacks innumerable to hold the smooth green felt in position. It would be hard to say which gives me the more pleasure, the tack, that little epigram of the nailbox, demanding only a tiny push with the finger and then a jolly crack with the hammer, or the screw, so subtle and so enduring, with its initial outburst of wilfulness followed by its gradual submission, until at last it seems to conquer the material almost of its own accord.

Perhaps, though, the screw gives us the finer pleasure. I enjoyed every moment with those fourteen, enjoyed their brief effort at resistance, their crescendo of easy exit, their snug re-entry. Compelled as I am to deal so largely in human stuff, is it to be wondered at that I should find such delight in screws? I spend my days poring over the records of men's thoughts and dreams, wondering at their courage and timidity and impudence and vanity, praising here and blaming there, losing myself in the shadowy Walpurgis Night that we call literature. I see my fellow-creatures pretending to be better and wiser than they are or more base and foolish, counterfeiting emotions they have never really known or hiding feelings that have shaken them for years. I spend hours and hours spinning theories or absorbing some other man's ideas, only to find, on looking back, that all is moonshine. I take mind and heart to this subject and that, pour myself out and then wrestle with the stubborn sheets, yet at the end I do not know whether anything has been created, whether it is not all idle vanity. There are perhaps a few moments of intense satisfaction for me while the work is in hand; there is a brief delight in the turning of a dangerous corner; and then nothing but fret and labour that is at once hard and yet fantastic until the work is done and I am free to juggle lazily with the next dream. If I get no praise for what I have done, then I am heartsick; but if praise does come my way, then it seems to me foolish and fulsome and I am irritated or embarrassed. So it goes on. This way of life is my own choice and I would have no other, not even though I should have my "yachts and string quartets"; but sometimes there is a joy in taking leave of it, in stretching green felt across the top of a card table, in turning home a good solid screw.

With a screw, biting its way into the woodwork and staying there if need be for half a century or, if you will, returning to your hand, the very same screw, within the next five minutes, you know where you are. It was devised for one kind of work, and that work it will do. It cheats neither itself nor you, is as definite, as rigid, as this other stuff with which I commonly deal is shifty and shadowy, maliciously protean. When you have tightened the last of your handful of screws, you can survey your work with solid contentment: something new has been created, if only the cover of a card table, and its existence cannot be argued away. My screwing and scissoring and hammering are done, and now our shining kings and queens and knaves have a new smooth lawn for their strange encounters. A man with such jobs to do daylong, measuring the work with a wise eye, now taking up his screwdriver, now his scissors, now his hammer, is in no bad case, if, that is, he has enough in his pocket at the day's end for his steak and beer and baccy and occasional visit to the play. A man so situated is a churl if he grumbles. On the other hand, if he is bundled into a roaring great factory and there has to pass the whole day holding or cutting the felt, or hammering in tacks, or putting screws in holes while another man turns the screwdriver, then we can hardly blame him if he comes to the conclusion that he is being cheated, if he turns into a man with a grievance. He thinks that he is being cheated out of money, but whether he is or not, the fact remains that he is certainly being cheated out of something even more important, namely, a decent and amusing job, that honest and engrossing work which is also great fun. There was a time when all work was of the kind that most of us at some time or other have performed purely to amuse ourselves, just as I covered the card table: we have — I speak for both sexes — dug up gardens, mown grass, picked fruit, woven and dyed cloth, sailed boats, made shelves and cupboards, knitted stockings, soled boots, cut down trees, printed books, and so forth. But I have yet to meet anybody who went to work in a factory for fun, who spent his leisure in taking part in mass production. The world will not be happy when all the economists have agreed together and have regimented us into equal hours and equal wages, but when everybody has more work, real work, to do, when we are all happily covering card tables through the long day and have just leisure enough for an odd rubber or two before we go to bed.

THE INN OF THE SIX ANGLERS

This morning, for the first time in my life, I wished that I was an angler, a real angler, not one of those fellows (as the fat man said last night) "who'll fish for an hour and then want to go and pick blackberries." As we rode away from the inn and left the lake idly lapping behind, with all six anglers happy on its bosom, I told myself that I had missed my chance of happiness in old age by not fishing steadily through all my youth. Perhaps, however, it was really the inn that did it, the inn and the lake together. There is no resisting an inn that is small and quaint and good, a place that is shelter and fire and food and drink and a fantastic journey's end all in one. Nor is there anything in nature more enchanting than a lake. Rivers I have loved, and with them the restless sea, so magical and yet so melancholy, perhaps because it seems the symbol of our desires; but it is those lovely lapping sheets of water, neither seas nor rivers yet having the charm of both with something added, some touch of quiet, peace, soul's ease, that really possess my heart. You travel over leagues of hulking and stubborn land, then suddenly turn a corner and find a space where there is no earth but only a delicate mirroring of the sky and that faintest rise and fall of waters, the lap-lap-lap along the little curving shore. Where else can you find such exquisite beauty and tranquillity? May I end my days by a lake, one of earth's little windows, where blue daylight and cloud and setting suns and stars go drifting by to the tiny tune of the water. There is no mention of a lake in Wordsworth's strangely magical lines:

> The silence that is in the starry sky
> The sleep that is among the lonely hills,

but I will wager that they were written by some lake-side, for there is in them the lake spirit, the quiet enchantment, the heart's ease.

It may, then, have been the inn and the lake that made me wistful of angling. All yesterday we were travelling north through Central Wales, a lovely country, filled with an antique simplicity and kindness, that few people seem to know. I had heard of this lake and was determined to go there and, if possible, spend the night by its side. It is the one virtue of a motor-car that it can gratify such whims. We rushed north, then, and saw the hills grow in majesty and the sky darken over our heads. Where we stopped for tea there was some talk of a landslide, a road washed away by a recent storm, along the way we wished to travel, but by this time we were determined to see our lake or perish. (It is this spirit alone that saves the soul of the motorist, who would otherwise be a mere beast.) We discovered some kind of road on the map and were very soon bumping along it. The next two or three hours were Homeric. I was at the wheel and, you may be sure, innumerable smoking-rooms will find me at that wheel again, will have to travel with me down that road. I have now a story that is a fit companion for that other story of mine, that account of how I once changed down to low gear with a screwdriver, when everything began to break in the middle of a Buckinghamshire hill.

The road dwindled to a mere tattered length of tape threading itself through the hills. There were great holes everywhere, and at times the steering-wheel was nothing better than a rattling useless ring of metal. The hills piled themselves all round us, great screens of slaty rock threatened to overwhelm our trumpery shivering craft, and the narrow bitten track went twisting this way and that, offering steeper gradients every five minutes. And now the mere drizzle, which had accompanied us for the last hour or two, darkened into a torrential downpour, blotting out everything but the next few yards of road. I had to open the windscreen because it was impossible to see through it. Big drops would hit me in the eye, so that at times I saw nothing at all. The track got worse, the rain fell more heavily, the car rattled and roared and leaped and bumped, and we laughed and shouted to one another, being now in that state of curious and half-sickening exaltation which visits us when sudden death is apparently just round the corner. But as the nightmare track lengthened out and the rain still fell in sheets, completely drenching us, smashing through hood and cap and coat, we settled down to the grim business of getting anywhere at all. At last there came a long descent and a slackening of the rain. We swerved down through a misty fissure into a grey and ghostly place, where we heard, once the car had achieved its easy hum again, the faint noise of water. We were in a hollow in the mountains, a hollow almost entirely filled with the dim grey sheen of water. Here then was the lake. Another ten minutes of twisting and turning and we were shaking ourselves, like dogs from a pool, in front of a low building that seemed nothing more than three brown cottages joined together. This was the inn.

There never was a better journey's end. A Pimlico boarding-house would have seemed paradisal after that shattering ride, but here was a place in a million. We seemed to have rattled and bumped our way clean through this modern world into another and more lovable age, where "they fleet the time carelessly." It was not long before we were snug and dry, sipping sherry in front of the fire. We caught vague glimpses of elderly men, anglers apparently, for the place was full of rods and baskets of trout. Then came dinner in a low lamplit room. There was no nonsense about little tables and simpering maids handing round snippets of food. We found ourselves at a long table with all the other guests, and all the other guests were six jovial old anglers, the oldest and most jovial at the head of the table. The dishes, vast tureens of soup and joints of mutton, were placed in front of these two, who cut and carved and cracked their jokes. The dinner was good, made up of clean, honest, abundant food, and the company was even better. I have not had such a strange and satisfying meal for years. It was just as if one had somehow contrived to merge *The Compleat Angler* and *Pickwick Papers*. Outside, mist gathered on the lake, so remote that it might have been in the heart of another continent, and darkness fell on the hills. Inside, in the kindly and mellow lamplight, we sat snug, and ate and drank and listened, still half-dazed, still with the rain and wind in our ears, like people in a dream.

I saw it all in the clear light of morning, a morning of thinning mist and faint sunlight on the lake, when the mouth watered for the fried trout and bacon that the two oldest anglers handed round. It was only this morning. Yet, as I look back upon last night, it still seems like a dream. The journey, the place itself, the inn, the six old anglers — the whole experience is more like the memory of some happy chapter in a leisurely old-fashioned tale than a piece of reality. I can hardly believe that that valley and lake are on the map, that in some directory of hotels that inn may be found. It seems as if that remote place had slipped through some little crack in time, so that the years had rushed by without avail, leaving it brimmed with its old-fashioned spirit of leisure and courtesy and kindness. Its guests, the six old anglers, were not quite of this world. They were, or had been, I believe, schoolmasters, doctors, musicians, but one could only see them as anglers, living for ever at this inn, for ever strolling down to the boats in the morning and returning with their trout in the evening to carve the mutton and exchange their long and leisurely stories (like those that hold up our older novels for whole chapters) round that lamplit board. One of them, the one who mastered the joint, had been going there for at least forty years, and the others seemed to remember the place twenty or thirty years ago. Not that they did not know other places too, for they exchanged reminiscences about them, remote little lochs in Scotland, unknown Irish rivers, wherever there were trout and salmon to be had. They always gave one another all the facts, precise directions for finding places, the names of all the inns and innkeepers and gillies, and talked on as if life lasted a thousand years, kindly years of sunlight and mist and lapping water and leaping fish and golden hours about the dinner-table. They showed me, in the jazz pattern of our years, this silver thread of peaceful and quiet days that old Izaak Walton knew so long ago; so that I too would be an angler at last, and find my way again to that inn, this time to be one of their confraternity, and then perhaps I too could quietly angle my way out of time altogether. Yet even now it is all so unreal that I have a feeling that I could not find that lake and that inn again, and I am sure that by the time I am old and grey they will have vanished for ever.

OPEN HOUSE

There was a man having dinner near me who looked like someone I used to know, and I puzzled and puzzled until suddenly I remembered. Uncle George! I knew that it could not actually be Uncle George, who must be quite old now or may, indeed, be dead; but this man looked like the Uncle George I remembered from long ago, and the sight of him started all manner of queer things from the thickets of memory. He was not my own uncle, you must understand, but the uncle of my old schoolfellow, Harold Thorlaw, and the greatest man in the Thorlaw circle. He did not live in our own little provincial town — and now I come to think of it, I never knew where he did live — but at irregular intervals he used to descend upon us, perhaps during his travels, for I remember that his business took him about a good deal. In our provincial circle he was a grand cosmopolitan figure. To his nephew and me, then in our teens, and indeed to all the Thorlaws, Uncle George was the great world. London, Paris, and New York spoke to us through him. He it was who told us about music-halls and head waiters and card-sharpers and those lordly expresses, those ten-somethings that do it without a stop, that are the very soul of rich cosmopolitan life. You always knew when he had arrived at the Thorlaws', for you felt his presence even in the hall, and were not surprised when Harold, or his sister, or his mother, came out to you and whispered, "Uncle George's here!" There he was, oracular in the large armchair near the piano, perhaps having his little joke, asking the girls a riddle, suggesting a song (he liked a light cosmopolitan sort of music, and would occasionally produce a copy of something that was going well at the Gaiety), or telling us a queer thing that had happened at his London hotel, amiably keeping up a pretence of being one of us but clearly as far removed from us — and he knew that we knew — as Harun al-Rashid himself.

It was with the Thorlaws themselves, however, rather than with Uncle George, that my memory began to play. They were the kind of people we seem to run across only in early life, perhaps because they only blossom in provincial towns and wither and change in the air of London. The shortest way of describing them is to say that they were hospitality, real warm hospitality, incarnate: they kept open house. They were worlds away from the kind of lavish entertainers you encounter in London, the lion-hunting ladies and the vulgar rich whose houses have really been turned into railway hotels. They loved nothing so much as being surrounded by relatives and friends, and the friends of their relatives, and the relatives of their friends. It was not that they had plenty of money; they were anything but rich, and Mrs. Thorlaw's worn little housekeeping purse must have been drained of its last sixpence many a time to provide such hospitality as they proffered. They never sat you down solemnly to dinner, and could not have done even if they had wanted to, for there always seemed to be three times as many people there as the tiny dining-room could possibly have held. No, their great meals were tea, in which the oddest of odd cups and saucers came floating out on a tide of hot water; and a sketchy and peripatetic kind of late supper, when there was always an enormous bustle and you were so occupied getting out of people's way and handing things round that you never noticed if you were actually having anything to eat.

Yet there shone through that house so bright a spirit of generous

E

hospitality that it seemed to snow meat and drink there and you took part in a perpetual feast. What may have been in cold fact a cup of lukewarm tea and half a sandwich seemed a solid hour's happy guzzling. A small glass of cheap port in that house was worth whole bottles of vintage wine anywhere else. So strong was the atmosphere of festivity that material facts, actual cakes and ale, were of little or no account. You called there — "popped in" was the phrase for it — on an ordinary Saturday or Sunday evening and, if you had not known what to expect, you would have supposed that it was Christmas Eve or Old Year's Night, or that a birthday or a wedding was being celebrated. There would be two or three people in the hall, a few others having a snack in the dining-room, probably a group of ladies chattering in the best bedroom, and the drawing room would be full. I have never known any other room like that drawing room, for it was certainly not very large and yet there seemed to be no limit to the number of visitors it would hold. To say that it would be "full" does not mean that it would not hold any more people (it always did), but merely that it looked full — indeed, fuller than any room you had ever seen before. You would see a swarm of faces on three different levels, for some people would be standing up, others seated on chairs, and the rest would be on the floor. My friend Harold, whose idea of pleasure in music was limited to the notion of taking something very fast and loud and trying to play it faster and louder than anyone else had ever played it, would be pounding away at the piano; and everyone there would be very noisy, very hot and flushed, very happy.

The Thorlaws could create this atmosphere wherever they went. I remember now that they took a tiny cottage on the edge of the moors during the summer months of one year, and that I called there after a long walk on either a fine Saturday or Sunday afternoon. I could hear them shouting and laughing long before I got to the door. The tiny cottage was simply bursting with people, who were eating and drinking and passing plates and filling teapots and putting kettles on the fire and being sent for water or returning with more milk. Everyone would be explaining to everyone else how it happened that he or she had "popped in," and at the sight of each newcomer a tremendous shout would go up. (I have a vague idea, though my memory may be the dupe of my innate poetical desire to have everything perfect, that Uncle George was there.) The Thorlaws, I believe, could have filled a plague-stricken hovel on a blasted heath with such a laughing crowd of visitors. It was not merely that they had a passion for gathering people round them — for many have that whose houses are visited once and then for ever shunned — but they radiated such a spirit of friendliness and good cheer that instantly they put all their visitors at their ease, made it impossible to be stiff, supercilious, or shy, and transformed every chance gathering into a kind of hilarious family reunion. With them, if you were asked to sing a song, you immediately stood up and sang it without any more ado. I myself have sung comic songs there by the hour, without shame, and may be remembered to this day by all manner of people in remote places as a budding Henry Lytton, as "Harold's friend, you know, who used to sing the comic songs." I was always being button-holed in odd places by people who had seen me there, people whose very faces I had forgotten, let alone their names, who asked me if I had any more comic songs and were obviously prepared to roar with laughter at every remark I made.

I would give something to be able to call there again tonight, now that they have all returned so vividly to my remembrance. To see Mr. Thorlaw, a humorous and pugnacious little man with blazing blue eyes, moving round with the doubtful port, chaffing the girls and bullying their young men. To see his wife, one of those little thin, dark women who seem to be made of wire and catgut, smiling, tireless, who would go flicking in and out of the throng like a radiant shuttle; and all those flushed, noisy, and happy people I would meet there, most of whose names I never knew, whose names and faces, one and all, I have now forgotten. Foolish, funny little people, nothing like the beautiful, the clever, the distinguished persons whose acquaintance I can boast today, but dimly consecrated in my memory by a happiness that something seems to have withered away, shining there in a queer kind of Golden Age, strangely compounded of provincial nobodies and cheap port and chaff and comic songs. I wonder if that house, like the hospitality that gave it so much light and warmth, has gone the way of so many things and is now given over to loneliness, to darkness and dust. Here, at least, for an hour in my memory, the lights have been turned up, the fires poked into a blaze, and the doors opened wide again, the place itself a guest in the open house of remembrance.

VI. From APES AND ANGELS 1928

THE FLOWER SHOW

It is our annual flower, fruit, and vegetable show, and a great event. It may not look to you like a great event — for you can only see two marquees in a field — but you ask Quince, our gardener. He has been thinking and talking about nothing else these past four weeks. You will find him in one of the marquees, looking strangely clean (and somehow smaller) in a new suit. We — that is, Quince and our garden — have won nine prizes, including the first prize for onions. Quince is radiant. He has been after that onion prize from the first, partly because it had been won for seventeen years by the same man, Mr. Snug, who lives near the station, and partly, I suspect, because he must have talked expansively about his onions one night at the Duck and Drake and have been chaffed about them. So he set to work to grow some Ailsa Craigs (for that's our heroine's name) that would smash this seventeen years' record. "Oi don't care what happens, sur," he has said to me more than once, "so long as Oi gets the proize for them thar onions." He has spent whole days tending them and, latterly, gloating over them. After great deliberation, he chose nine of the largest, made a little stand for them, cutting a hole in the wood for each onion to rest in, so that they made a very fine show indeed, though I must confess that they looked to me like some new garden game, distantly connected with bowls. But there they are now, with the red label on them that dethrones Mr. Snug, who must be content with a blue label and the second prize. Quince cannot keep away from his onions; sometimes he takes a look at the apples (Second Prize) or the tomatoes (Second Prize); but he soon returns to the onions. It is really nothing to him that we had no award for our mixed vegetables (though they were as good as Snug's, which were given a First), that our carrots have not had a look in, that our roses only managed a Third. He has won nine prizes in all, and a First for onions: his ship is in harbour.

Now you can hear the Plumborough Brass Band. They are here in all the bravery of blue and silver uniforms and peaked caps, though it cannot be said they look quite at home in them. There are certain kinds of faces and figures — soldiers and policemen have them — that seem to belong to uniforms, and these honest fellows from Plumborough have not acquired such faces and figures, so look sheepish in their blue and silver. Moreover, a brass band should be loud and careless, made up of men who believe that this is the best of all possible worlds and that life can be generously saluted by brazen sounds in waltz time and the clashing of flagons; but the Plumborough Band seems too earnest, thoughtful, scrupulous, and picks out the notes as if it were not certain they ought to be touched, like visitors fingering bric-à-brac. They are telling us now that two for tea and tea for two is their ideal, but they are so uncertain and doubtful that we feel that this view of life is too shallow for Plumborough. We will leave them and visit the man who is dressed in a jockey's cap and silk vest. He is a stout, middle-aged man, and looks ridiculous in this shimmering red and black; and what is more, he is the only man in the field in fancy dress; but he does not care, and has evidently long outgrown self-consciousness. He offers us three darts for twopence — there are prizes for the highest scores of the day — and we all throw darts, and some of them hit the board and some of them do not; but one of us, knowing no more of darts than the rest, makes 107, the highest score of the day so far. Such are darts, and such is life.

We are asked to guess the weight of a pig, and when we go to look at it, we find that it is a mere pigling, no bigger than a fox-terrier. Like most of the pigs in this part of the world, it is mottled, brown and black, and therefore — to my mind — quite unreal. That is probably why I find it impossible to imagine what its weight will be, and anyhow, it is eating all the time, and may be any size before the show is over. We try bowling at skittles, and I do very badly and laugh with the rest, but find myself pointing out that the ground is very uneven and that the bowls themselves are absurdly misshapen. The man we see dodging in and out of the little coal office at the station, a man who looks like a troll, asks us to pay sixpence each and put a stake, with one's name written on it, into a circle of ground where treasure is buried. (This must be a coalman's idea of life.) When we have done this, we are all weighed by the jovial gentleman-farmer in whose field the show is always held. This is something of an ordeal. There is nothing in being weighed if you step onto one of those automatic machines that send a pointer briskly round to a figure on a dial. But when you are weighed by a leisurely human being, who slowly puts one chunk of metal after another into the scale and then carefully announces the final result, it is quite a different matter. I am rather ashamed of my thirteen stone and five pounds, not because I really feel there is anything disgraceful in being a little heavier than most people, but because there is such a thing as the pressure of public opinion, and the world, which gets sillier, is now given over to banting and to people made out of cheese-parings after supper. We have a word with the retired schoolmaster who is one of the officials of the show. He is going about putting down names and figures in a notebook, and is quite happy, feeling that he is back again in harness. Schoolmasters never really retire; there is always, at the back of their minds, an unconquered, never-to-be-surrendered fortress of pedagogy.

We must try the other marquee. The cook, who entered the meat pie and the cake (to cost less than two shillings) competitions, has not won a prize. She did not trouble about the third competition, which is for the best dish of boiled potatoes. They are all here, these dishes, and very unappetizing they look too in the middle of the afternoon — unlike the meat pies and the cakes. You have to be hungry to appreciate a potato, and this is a fact that historians ought to remember. Whenever or wherever the potato is much talked of, hunger is stalking abroad. Opposite the meat pies and the cakes are the exhibits from the school, for the most part pages from copybooks and mats and tiny dolls made of crinkled paper and raffia, the kind of dolls that children prefer to the expensive and eyelashed beauties from the toyshops. On the table that runs down the centre are more fruit and vegetables, and an old man is measuring beans with a piece of string. I am surprised, and rather aggrieved, to discover that George, our giant pumpkin, is here. There is no mistaking him. What he is doing here, I cannot imagine, for there is no prize for which he could compete. Indeed, he serves no common uses, and was grown neither for the kitchen nor the drawing-room. He is to the garden what Falstaff is to the drama of *Henry IV*. He is its comic poetry, and he has given me more pleasure than any other vegetable or fruit, not excepting those rounded maidens, Rubens creatures, that are the darlings of Quince's heart, the Ailsa Craigs. If ever I visited the kitchen-garden, it was to see George the pumpkin, to mark his ever-increasing girth, to admire his golden and rotund magnificence, to give him an affectionate slap. Can you wonder that such a one figures in a fairy tale? Quince must have brought him down here because he felt obscurely that the garden should be also represented by its great comic character. Let us give pumpkin George a farewell slap.

Quince is still in the first marquee, trying — for he is a good modest fellow — not to look too like a man who has broken a long record for the onion prize. But he cannot disguise the fact that he is the happiest man at the show. His father is with him now, a very ancient retired gardener, who looks as if he had grown out of the earth, like a grand old tree. He puffs at his short pipe and pretends to philosophic calm, but you can see that he too is rejoicing over the great onion victory. Quince's brother is here too, the signalman, very brisk and natty in a blue serge suit, and seeming to belong to a later (and perhaps less enduring) civilisation than the other Quinces. He tries to make fun of the whole thing, this man of machines, but I know that he was helping Quince all morning and really has the cause at heart.

The small son and the smaller daughter of Quince are also here (one got a prize for a mat and the other for a copybook page — it has been a great day), and keep pushing their apple cheeks, which ought to have had prizes too, as close as they can to their father's sleeve. I am positive that Quince will not leave this marquee until the end of the day, that he will be the last man in it. Here is the scene of his triumphs, and here he remains. I congratulate him again on the onion victory. "They shouldn't ha' talked at me," he says; and I foresee his having a triumphant pint or two tonight at the Duck and Drake, where they thought he could not grow Ailsa Craigs. There is nothing more for us to do now. The fifteen men from Plumborough are proclaiming, through their instruments, that they are "Less than the du-ust beneath (pom-pom) his chariot whee-eel," but they do not proclaim it with much conviction, except the drummer, who is coming into his own in this riot of Oriental passion. As we wander down the road we can still hear him tom-tomming, and we leave the day to him and Quince.

T'MATCH

If you are in Bruddersford on Saturday afternoon, you go to t'match. I was in Bruddersford last Saturday afternoon, and quite automatically set out for t'match. As a matter of fact, there were several football matches, of varying codes, to choose from, and when I marched out of the hotel I had no idea at which particular match I should arrive. I simply followed a grey-green tide of cloth caps, which swept me down streets that grew meaner at every turn, past canals and gas works, until finally we came to the edge of the town. In that part of the West Riding, the Bruddersford district, there is not a very marked difference between town and country. When the last street brings you to a field, you are not aware of any dramatic contrast, simply because the field is not one of your pretty lush meadows, peeping and smiling, but is a dour slab of earth that keeps its grass as short as a wool merchant keeps his hair. This countryside, an angry spur or two of the Pennines, valleys full of black rock, does not regard the local handiwork of man with disfavour. If there must be men about, it says, then let them build factories and railway sidings and gas works: and so all these things seem to flower naturally out of that grim country. There are some parts of the West Riding that do suggest to you that industry is the supreme vandal, that the fair face of Nature has been blackened; but none of these fine thoughts come to you in the neighbourhood of Bruddersford, where it is obvious that town and country are all of a piece and the tall black chimneys seem inevitable if fantastic outcroppings of rock on those steep hillsides. Moors and mills, smoke and stone: I need say no more, because either you know or you don't. (And let us have no talk of the Brontës, who did not live in this particular district, who were not Yorkshire people, and who should be given a close season.) It is a country, whether it expresses itself in fields or streets, moors or mills, that puts man on his mettle. It defies him to live there, and so it has bred a special race that can live there, stocky men with short upper lips and jutting long chins, men who roll a little in their walk and carry their heads stiffly, twelve stone of combative instinct. If you have never seen any of these men, take a look at the Yorkshire cricket team next summer. Or come to t'match.

I paid my shilling and then discovered that it was a rugger match, presumably the Northern Union, the professional, thirteen-a-side, all scrimmage game. I was annoyed to find that the match had started. There were about ten thousand people there, including a thousand little boys all screaming in a special pen, but I was disappointed at the lack of enthusiasm. Nobody apart from the boys seemed to be paying much attention to the game. I noticed too that the players, though sufficiently well-built fellows, were not the giants I expected to find in Northern Union rugger. It was all very disappointing. "Who are they?" I asked the man on my right. "Nay, ah doan't knaw," he replied. "It's t'lads' match. Under twenty-one." I began to see light. "This isn't the proper match, then?" I remarked to him. He stared at me: "This is nowt," he said, dispassionately. "T'match begins in a minute or two. Bruddersford versus Millsbury." This explained everything; the afternoon had not yet begun.

I cast a complacent eye on t'lads, who very soon cleared off to the sound of an odd cheer or two. Then there was silence. We all waited for Bruddersford and Millsbury to appear. I could feel a difference in the atmosphere. Then they came running on and we all shouted. Bruddersford were in red, and Millsbury were in blue. The forwards on both sides were colossal fellows, fit to engage in a scrum with a few elephants. A minute later t'match had begun. The Bruddersford back immediately performed several miracles, and we all applauded him and called him Joe. "That's right, Joe!" we told him, though I cannot say he took much notice of us. Then Number Eight of Millsbury, who looked like a bull in a blue jersey, grabbed hold of Joe a minute or two after he had rid himself of the ball and threw him several yards. Joe did not seem to care very much, but we were very angry. "Mark him, Joe!" we cried: "Watch Number Eight, Joe!" These tactics, however, could not prevent Bruddersford from scoring. Ginger began it. There is always a red-haired man in every team — or if there is not, then the manager does not know his business — and this one was a little wiry fellow, who played three-quarter. (At least, he was always waiting outside the scrums to pick up the ball, and frequently one saw him emerging from a heap of humanity, looking none the worse for having had about half a ton of bone and muscle piled on him.) Suddenly, then, Ginger went through like a little red shuttle, and we all shouted away as the ball sailed between the tall posts a minute afterwards. Then the game was lost for half an hour in a desert of scrimmages. There are too many scrimmages in this Northern Union game. I got tired of seeing those twelve men pushing and heaving.

The man on my left, whose cap was too small and moustache too large, was disgusted. "Nay, Bruddersford," he kept shouting in my ear, "lake foitball." He was angry, passionate, a man with shattered ideals. He had come to see foitball laked and it was not being laked properly. Bruddersford were winning, but being something more than a mere partisan, being a critic of the art, he was not comforted. "They're not passing, not passing," he told my left ear-drum. "Look at that! Nay, Bruddersford!" he would cry. He appeared to suspect that my left ear-drum entertained views of the game quite different from his own. Just before half-time, a man in front of me but some distance away, a man with a cap at the back of his head, a red muffler, and an angry unshaven face, above which he tilted a beer bottle from time to time, suddenly created a diversion. He was, I think, a Millsbury supporter, one of those men who have no money but yet contrive to follow their football teams wherever they go, and he must have entered into an argument with some Bruddersford enthusiast. I do not know what they were arguing about; all that I do know is that suddenly this man turned round to face us and cried at the top of his voice: "Neck and ankles, that's what I say. Neck and ankles." He seemed to be in a towering rage. Then he turned round again to look at the game, but a moment later, still more furious, he cried to us his mysterious slogan: "Neck and ankles!" Then he added, as an afterthought: "You can't get away from it. Neck and ankles!" He took another long pull at his bottle. "Ger aht wi' yer!" we said to him. This roused him to a frenzy, and putting down his bottle and raising his voice, he yelled: "B——y neck and ankles! B——y neck and b——y ankles!" And he glared defiance at some three thousand of us. "Put a sock in it!" we yelled back to him, and turned our attention to the game.

The two great events of the second half were Nosey's try and the sending off of Millsbury's Number Six. Nosey had done very little up to the time he received that pass, and I had come to the conclusion that he was not a man worth watching. He got the ball, however, well in his own half, and began to race at a prodigious speed down the touchline. Millsbury made a rush at him, but, after he had pushed away one or two and swerved from two or three more, he gathered speed and simply outran all the others, curving in exquisitely at the last to plant the ball neatly between the posts. You should have heard our shouts for Nosey. Even the critic on my left was impressed, and was very satirical at the expense of some unknown detractors of the great Nosey. "And then they say 'e can't run. Can't run!" he sneered. "Beat 'em all. Beat 'em all." He liked this phrase so much that he kept repeating it at odd moments during the next quarter of an hour.

But he was not so repetitious as the little man in the macintosh behind me. It was the sending off of Millsbury's Number Six that set him going. This Number Six had completely lost his temper and made a rush at a Bruddersford man when the ball was far away. The Bruddersford man contrived to throw him down, but the referee determined to make an example of this Number Six — for the play was becoming very rough — and so ordered him off the field. We gave him a boo or two as he left. But the little man in the macintosh was still indignant, and proclaimed, in those flat tones that are sometimes discovered in fanatics, that if he, Number Six, had tried it on with Mulligan (the burliest of all the Bruddersfords) Number Six would not have walked off but would have had to have been carried off. The game began again, and blues and reds charged one another and fell in heaps. "If 'e'd tried it on with Mulligan, 'e'd 'ave been carried off," came the flat voice from behind. Another try for Bruddersford: Ginger again! But Joe couldn't convert it. Hard lines, Joe! "If 'e'd tried it on with Mulligan" — yet once more. The blues are tiring now, and they are bad-tempered, but we are giving them as good as we get. Nearly time, now. Another try? No. Time. We give them a cheer. "If 'e'd tried it on with Mulligan" — but no, we must get out. The little man with the macintosh, we feel, will be the last spectator to leave the ground. He will tell the man who closes the gates what would have happened if Number Six had tried it on with Mulligan. The rest of us are out now, swarming down the narrow road, towards the trams. We are all talkative, amiable, relaxed: our combative instincts put to bed for a little space. We can turn a more gentle regard upon the gloomy hills, the factories and gas works and railway sidings; for the time being they do not trouble us; we have been to t'match.

FIRST SNOW

Mr. Robert Lynd once remarked of Jane Austen's characters: "They are people in whose lives a slight fall of snow is an event." Even at the risk of appearing to this witty and genial critic as another Mr. Woodhouse, I must insist that last night's fall of snow here was an event. I was nearly as excited about it this morning as the children, whom I found all peering through the nursery window at the magic outside and chattering as excitedly as if Christmas had suddenly come round again. The fact is, however, that the snow was as strange and enchanting to me as it was to them. It is the first fall we have had here this winter, and last year I was out of the country, broiling in the tropics, during the snowy season, so that it really does seem an age since I saw the ground so fantastically carpeted. It was while I was away last year that I met the three young girls from British Guiana who had just returned from their first visit to England. The two things that had impressed them most were the endless crowds of people in the London streets, all strangers (they emphasised this, for they had spent all their lives in a little town where everybody knew everybody) and the snow-covered landscape they awoke to one morning when they were staying somewhere in Somerset. They were so thrilled and delighted that they flung away any pretence of being demure young ladies and rushed out of the house to run to and fro across the glittering white expanses, happily scattering footmarks on the untrodden surface, just as the children did in the garden this morning.

The first fall of snow is not only an event but it is a magical event. You go to bed in one kind of world and wake up to find yourself in another quite different, and if this is not enchantment, then where is it to be found? The very stealth, the eerie quietness, of the thing makes it more magical. If all the snow fell at once in one shattering crash, awakening us in the middle of the night, the event would be robbed of its wonder. But it flutters down, soundlessly, hour after hour while we are asleep. Outside the closed curtains of the bedroom, a vast transformation scene is taking place, just as if myriad elves and brownies were at work, and we turn and yawn and stretch and know nothing about it. And then, what an extraordinary change it is! It is as if the house you are in had been dropped down in another continent. Even the inside, which has not been touched, seems different, every room appearing smaller and cosier, just as if some power were trying to turn it into a woodcutter's hut or a snug log-cabin. Outside, where the garden was yesterday, there is now a white and glistening level, and the village beyond is no longer your own familiar cluster of roofs but a village in an old German fairy tale. You would not be surprised to learn that all the people there, the spectacled postmistress, the cobbler, the retired schoolmaster, and the rest, had suffered a change too and had become queer elvish beings, purveyors of invisible caps and magic shoes. You yourselves do not feel quite the same people you were yesterday. How could you when so much has been changed? There is a curious stir, a little shiver of excitement, troubling the house, not unlike the feeling there is abroad when a journey has to be made. The children, of course, are all excitement, but even the adults hang about and talk to one another longer than usual before settling down to the day's work. Nobody can resist the windows. It is like being on board ship.

When I got up this morning the world was a chilled hollow of dead white and faint blues. The light that came through the windows was very queer, and it contrived to make the familiar business of splashing and shaving and brushing and dressing very queer too. Then the sun came out, and by the time I had sat down to breakfast it was shining bravely and flushing the snow with delicate pinks. The dining-room window had been transformed into a lovely Japanese print. The little plum-tree outside, with the faintly flushed snow lining its boughs and artfully disposed along its trunk, stood in full sunlight. An hour or two later everything was a cold glitter of white and blue. The world had completely changed again. The little Japanese prints had all vanished. I looked out of my study window, over the garden, the meadow, to the low hills beyond, and the ground was one long glare, the sky was steely, and all the trees so many black and sinister shapes. There was indeed something curiously sinister about the whole prospect. It was as if our kindly country-side, close to the very heart of England had been turned into a cruel steppe. At any moment, it seemed, a body of horsemen might be seen breaking out from the black copse, so many instruments of tyranny, and shots might be heard and some distant patch of snow be reddened. It was that kind of landscape.

Now it has changed again. The glare has gone and no touch of the sinister remains. But the snow is falling heavily, in great soft flakes, so that you can hardly see across the shallow valley, and the roofs are thick and the trees all bending, and the weathercock of the village church, still to be seen through the grey loaded air, has become some creature out of Hans Andersen. From my study, which is apart from the house and faces it, I can see the children flattening their noses against the nursery window, and

there is running through my head a jangle of rhyme I used to repeat when I
was a child and flattened my nose against the cold window to watch the
falling snow:

> *Snow, snow faster:*
> *White alabaster!*
> *Killing geese in Scotland,*
> *Sending feathers here!*

This, I fancy, must have been a north-country charm (for that grey upland
region is full of wizardries) to bring down the snow. And though we are
told by the experts that as much snow falls now as ever it did, we know
better, and I suspect that the reason is that there are fewer children with
their faces pressed against their nursery windows, chanting: "Snow, snow
faster!"

This morning, when I first caught sight of the unfamiliar whitened world,
I could not help wishing that we had snow oftener, that English winters
were more wintry. How delightful it would be, I thought, to have months of
clean snow and a landscape sparkling with frost instead of innumerable
grey featureless days of rain and raw winds. I began to envy my friends in
such places as the eastern states of America and Canada, who can count
upon a solid winter every year and know that the snow will arrive by a
certain date and will remain, without degenerating into black slush, until
spring is close at hand. To have snow and frost and yet a clear sunny sky
and air as crisp as a biscuit — this seemed to me happiness indeed. And
then I saw that it would never do for us. We should be sick of it in a week.
After the first day, the magic would be gone and there would be nothing
left but the unchanging glare of the day and the bitter cruel nights. It is not
the snow itself, the sight of the blanketed world, that is so enchanting, but
the first coming of the snow, the sudden and silent change. Out of the
relations, for ever shifting and unanticipated, of wind and water comes a
magical event. Who would change this state of things for a steadily
recurring round, an earth governed by the calendar? It has been well said
that while other countries have a climate, we alone in England have
weather. There is nothing duller than climate, which can be converted into
a topic only by scientists and hypochondriacs. But weather is our earth's
Cleopatra, and it is not to be wondered at that we, who must share her
gigantic moods, should be for ever talking about her. Once we were settled
in America, Siberia, Australia, where there is nothing but a steady pact
between climate and the calendar, we should regret her very naughtinesses,
her wilful pranks, her gusts of rage and sudden tears. Waking in a morning
would no longer be an adventure. Our weather may be fickle but it is no
more fickle than we are, and only matches our inconstancy with her
changes. Sun, wind, snow, rain, how welcome they are at first and how

soon we grow weary of them! If this snow lasts a week, I shall be heartily sick of it and glad to speed its going. But its coming has been an event. Today has had a quality, an atmosphere, quite different from that of yesterday, and I have moved through it feeling a slightly different person, as if I were staying with new friends or had suddenly arrived in Norway. A man might easily spend five hundred pounds trying to break the crust of indifference in his mind, and yet feel less than I did this morning. Thus there is something to be said for leading the life of a Jane Austen character.

THE DARK HOURS

This last week I have had a succession of bad nights. It is not merely that I cannot easily find sleep. This I never could do, except during those times when I have spent the whole day in the open. Who, having enjoyed them, does not remember those hours of sleep, a divine unconsciousness, that fell on him, came down like a vast benevolent sandbag on the top of his head, at the Front? Sleep then was not simply a dark little ante-room through which one passed in order to arrive at the next morning's breakfast table, but a sojourn in the Blessed Isles. I remember — it must be twelve years ago — the best sleep I ever had. We had been three weeks or so in the trenches, the clayey kind, full of water and with hardly a dug-out; and though there had been no real fighting, there had been any number of those daft alarms and excursions that hearty generals, talking over the wine and cigars in some distant château, praised to one another, in the belief that Englishmen always preferred magnificence to war. We had been so long without adequate sleep that our eyes were for ever hot and staring under leaden lids. Well, one dark night we were relieved at last, and went swaying down miles of cobbled road. Some of the fellows dropped out, others slept as they staggered on, and finally a remnant of us arrived at some place that was nothing to us but a dark assemblage of barns and windowless houses, familiar enough yet as unreal as a place on the moon. A gulp or two of hot sweet tea, a moment's glow of rum, then down we fell so mud-caked that we were as stiff as mummies on the hard floors, and down too came the lovely velvet curtain, blotting out the whole lunatic show of babbling statesmen and lads with glazing eyes. I slept for eighteen hours.

In the ordinary way, however, I have to woo my sleep, and that is one reason why I have read so many books, chasing Morpheus down innumerable labyrinths of eighteenth-century moralising or twentieth-century introspection. Those no-sooner-have-I-touched-the-pillow people are past my comprehension. There is something suspiciously bovine about them. When they begin to yawn about half-past ten, as they always do when I am with them (and I make you a present of the inevitable comment), I feel that they forfeit all right to be considered as fellow-creatures, spirits here for a season that they may exchange confidences at the hour when all the beasts that perish are fast asleep. I do not complain about having to approach sleep so stealthily, tip-toeing through a chapter or so. After all, this is only to prolong the day, and I cannot help thinking that such a reluctance to part for ever from the day, though it be only an unconscious reluctance, is proof of an affectionate nature, unwilling to dismiss a servant, however poor a thing. Nor do I complain — though I like it less — about waking too early, beginning the day before it is fairly ready for me, nothing but a grey little monster with the chill on it and still opposed to all our nobler activities. I have been told that as the years wither me away, I shall have more and more of these early wakings, and I cannot say that the prospect pleases me. But for the moment I will submit to it without complaint, for there are worse things, and all this last week I have been suffering from them. I have been finding myself awake, not at the end of one day nor at the beginning of another, but sometime between them, in the mysterious dark hours.

Now this I do most bitterly resent. I have accustomed myself to prolonging the day, and I will try hard to resign myself to beginning it before it is worth beginning, but this other thing, this awful interloping piece of time, neither honest today nor splendid tomorrow, is a horror. You suddenly wake up, open your eyes, expecting welcome daylight and the morning's post and the savour of breakfast, only to discover that it is still dark, that nothing is happening. You roll over, turn back, then over again, curl your legs up, stretch them out, push your hands under the pillow, then take them out, all to no purpose: sleep will not come. You have been thrust, a dreadfully alert consciousness, into some black No Man's Land of time. Reading, for once, fails as a resource. Frequently your eyes are so tired that the lines of print become blurred and run into one another. But even if you have no difficulty in seeing, it is still hard to read because all the savour seems to have departed from literature. You feel as if you were trying to attack a dish of cold potatoes. Even a new play by Shakespeare would leave you indifferent. I remember spending one very hot night in a London hotel. The place was full and I was a late-comer, so that I was given a tiny bedroom not far from the roof and looking out on nothing but a deep narrow court. I got off to sleep very quickly, but awoke about two and then vainly tossed and turned. There was nothing for it but to read, and I switched on my light. As a rule I have a book in my bag, but this night I was completely bookless, and the only reading matter in the room was that supplied by two evening papers. I had already glanced through these papers, but now I had to settle down to read them as I have never read evening papers before or since. Every scrap of print, sports gossip, society chit-chat, City Notes, small advertisements, was steadily devoured. There I was, in my hot little aerie, reading those silly paragraphs about Lord A leaving town or Miss B the musical comedy star making puddings, while the night burned slowly away. For weeks afterwards the sight of an evening paper made me feel depressed.

Yet it is even worse when your eyes refuse to help you and even the silliest reading is impossible. You are left with your thoughts, as I have been several nights this last week. It is not possible, I find, on these occasions to think constructively or amusingly at all. You cannot plan anything. You cannot even lose yourself in an entertaining reverie. The dark hour, belonging to no day, swoops down and claims you as its own. No longer do you float easily on the kindly tide of ordinary human affairs. There is nothing tangible that you are afraid of, and, indeed, a burglar or a little outbreak of fire would seem a blessing. Nor are you, in melodramatic fashion, the prey now of your conscience. But you are alone, completely alone, really feeling for once that you are imprisoned in your consciousness. At ordinary times we seem able to reach out of ourselves, sometimes entirely forgetting ourselves; and that way lies happiness. In these dark hours there is no escape, not even by any dizzy ladder of thought, and your mind goes round and round, drearily pacing its cage. Life is nothing but a pulse beating in the darkness, or, if not that, then only the remembrance of a vague happy dream, bright faces fading and suddenly dwindling laughter, surrounded and conquered by terrible night. But this is only life, as it were, outside yourself. Inside you, there is life too, something alive, sensitive, shuddering, a bird beating its wings against the bars.

This self-consciousness of the dark hours, unable to fasten on anything outside itself, for ever denied communication, its thoughts wearily jangling round the old circus ring of the mind, is a glimpse of Hell. These are the terrors with which the preachers should threaten us. The old-fashioned place, we know, would soon become companionable. I have no doubt that it would not take us long to develop a taste for molten metal and brimstone, and that the fiends themselves would soon prove to be most entertaining companions. But these dark hours of the night and the spinning mind, if prolonged, would only gain in terror and despair. They are the true nightmare. The very thought that even now they are probably lying in wait

for me is infinitely depressing. And, for the time being, I am avoiding a
certain kind of fiction, if only because it has a curious suggestion of this
torment. The kind I mean consists of quite clever stuff by youngish contemporary novelists, who work entirely and very elaborately through the
mind of one central figure, whose self-consciousness, inability to escape
from self, are so extreme that he or she is really a solipsist. Never once do
these unhappy creatures forget themselves. They are for ever watching
themselves, and relating everybody and everything to that image. And
always they are depressed and depressing. In theory these novels would
seem to grapple very closely with life, but somehow in practice, as actual
representations, they fail badly, as everybody who still clings to the un-
fashionable practice of comparing literature and life must recognise. I
realise now, however, that they do represent something with tolerable
accuracy, and that is the night's vengeance on the unsleeping consciousness, the dark hours.

SEEING STRATFORD

"You must admit you haven't been there," they said. I told them I had
been *through* the town more than once. But that was nothing, they retorted,
because I hadn't *seen* anything there, didn't know where Shakespeare was
born or buried or where Anne Hathaway lived, had never sat on the edge
of the second-best bed. I told them I didn't care. "We know you don't care
for the sight-seeing part of it," they confessed, "but that won't last long.
It's a delightful run, and look what a lovely morning it is." And it *was* a
lovely morning; spring in blue and gold; not the smallest pocket-handker-
chief of cloud in the whole sky. Not only did I agree to visit Stratford-on-
Avon but I also helped to take down the hood and the screens of the car,
for apparently the moment had arrived for it to be converted into an open,
summery affair. The five of us packed ourselves in, together with a great
deal more lunch than we should ever require. Is there anything more terrifying to a person with sense and sensibility than a day's pleasure, what some
people call a "little jaunt"? The fuss and scurry and discomfort and egg sandwiches and dust and nipping winds — to be acquainted with these things is
to prefer a day's work to a day's pleasure. Before we reached Stratford, the

other two sitting at the back with me agreed that they never remembered a
colder journey. It was very odd and very annoying. You appeared to be
travelling through the very pomp of June itself; the sky was a midsummer
blue; the roads shone in the bright sunshine; you passed old men sucking at
their pipes, sitting on the grass and wearing no overcoats; and to the eye
you seemed to be happily roasting in the golden oven of summer. But the
cold was frightful. The wind, a dry north-easter, cut across the whole way,
numbing our cheeks and making our chins really ache with cold. Yet
whenever our watering eyes allowed us to see anything, there was the
lovely lazy day spread in front of us. It was just as if we were bewitched.

The real literary shrine is, of course, a library. For the rest you may at
times come close to an author's spirit in various odd places and atmospheres, it may be in an autumn wood, on a bare moor, in a bar-parlour,
within sight of a palm reef and a line of breakers. But the official literary
business, with its documents of birth, marriage and death, its museum and
antique shop airs, its array of beds and pens and desks and chairs, its
visitors' books and picture postcards and glib custodians, is simply so much
solemn nonsense. The persons who really enjoy this cultured and hushed-
voice sight-seeing are never people who care very much about books and
authors. Stratford is their Mecca. I hope Shakespeare himself knows all
about it, that he is keeping an immortal eye on his birth-place. How he
must enjoy the fun! I can hear him roaring with laughter. I can see him
bringing other immortals (probably Cervantes among them, for if those
two are not hand-in-glove, then there is no friendship among the shades) to
see the local branch of the Midland Bank, which tries to look Elizabethan
and romantic and even has some scenes from the plays drearily depicted
round its walls. He will show them how everything in the place is con-
scientiously thatched and beamed. He will watch us paying our shillings in
this place and that to gape at an array of articles that have really nothing to
do with him, rooms full of Garrick and Hathaway relics. His attitude
towards all solemn and pompous official persons and bores was always
touched with a light malice and his own irony, and he must delight in the
fact that he contrived to leave behind him so few facts about his life and so
few things to admire. He must enjoy watching his biographers compiling
their works, when they know only too well — poor fellows — that all the
facts could be set down on two or three sheets of notepaper and that they
will have to write page after page beginning, "We can imagine the young
Shakespeare" or "No doubt the poet at this time" or "Is it not likely that
the dramatist" — feverishly padding.

Having left little or nothing of his own behind him, he must take a
malicious pleasure in the efforts of his townspeople to provide visitors with
Shakespeare museums. I hope he watched them ransack every corner of the
place and dubiously install documents relating to the wood of his mulberry

tree and portraits of the mayor of 1826. And I am sure he delights in some of the custodians of these places. There is the good lady — and very helpful and courteous she is too — who repeats all the facts she knows in a most fascinating whispering sing-song and always ends every little speech with a comment in exactly the same tone: I know that I could have listened to her all day. Then there is the man who has a passion for saying "in the summer months," just as if the case were entirely altered in winter. "Here is a document that interests a lot of people in the summer months," he told us; and again: "That's the inspiration chair. In the summer months ladies like to try it."

We did not pay all the attention to him that he deserved because we were obliged to keep glancing out of the window. We were convinced that three men outside (and two of them were undoubtedly Bardolph and Nym) were wanting to steal our car. When we first drove up to the place, they had approached us with some trumpery excuse, had indeed talked about taking photographs. Now amateur photographers and Shakespeare pilgrims are an innocent race, and these three, Nym and Bardolph and another, were very seedy and shifty-eyed. We waited for a few minutes, during which time they hung about suspiciously, vainly trying to look as if they were about to take a photograph any moment, and then at last we locked the car (a poor protection, I am told, against thieves), went in, and asked one of the curators to keep an eye on it for us. Naturally, however, we also kept an eye on it ourselves.

But what, it may be asked, were Nym and Bardolph doing there? We soon found the answer, in a dense and dusty stream of cars and cycles and char-a-bancs that passed us on the main road. The local races were on that afternoon, and Birmingham had descended upon the town. Perhaps Shakespeare himself might have been found up there, mingling sedately yet humorously with the crowd. I certainly caught sight of Ancient Pistol (in a bowler) hanging over the side of a char-a-banc. He was probably going to meet Falstaff (now haunting the "silver ring"), who had no doubt suggested to friends Nym and Bardolph that a car might be "conveyed."

Yes, Shakespeare himself would laugh all night if he spent a day in his little town now. He would be amused at the solemn arts and crafts persons who have set up shop in the kindly shadow of his great fame; at the expensive hotels that try to delude Missouri and California into the belief that they are hostelries lately removed from Eastcheap; at the Shakespeare This and the Hathaway That meeting the eye everywhere; at the transformation of his bustling little town into a shrine where Justice Shallow guides the feet and eyes of Judge K. Shallow. He would laugh but he would understand too. He would turn wise yet wondering eyes upon the little yellow man from Cathay who was looking down upon that flat tombstone in the old parish church. He would understand the middle-aged American woman (she had that curious dried look that comes to some American women and suggests they have been specially prepared for export, like dried fruit), who walked up to the curator of Anne Hathaway's cottage and cried: "Well, I've had a lovely time in there and I wouldn't have missed a minute of it." He would understand this, although he himself probably did not have a lovely time in that cottage. He would laugh but he would go down at once to the precious human stuff that is lying underneath all these solemn antics and mummery.

And there was one moment, the other afternoon, when I did really feel I was treading upon his own ground. It was when we were in the gardens of New Place, very brave in the spring sunlight. You could have played the outdoor scene of *Twelfth Night* in them without disturbing a leaf. There was the very sward for Viola and Sir Andrew. Down that paved path Olivia would come, like a great white peacock. Against that bank of flowers the figure of Maria would be seen, flitting like a starling. The little Knott Garden alone was worth the journey and nearer to Shakespeare than all the documents and chairs and monuments. It was a patterned blaze of tulips, the Elizabethan gentlefolk among flowers. The white ones, full open and very majestic, were the great ladies in their ruffs; and the multi-coloured ones, in all their bravery of crimson and yellow, were the gentlemen in doublet and striped hose. The little crazy-paved paths added a touch of pride and fantasy and cross-gartering, as if Malvolio had once passed that way. And then, to crown all, there were tiny rows of sweet-smelling English herbs, thyme and sage and marjoram, and misty odorous borders of lavender. I remember that when we left that garden to see the place where Shakespeare was buried, it didn't seem to matter much. Why should it when we had just seen the place where he was still alive?

MR. PICKWICK RETURNS

There are, I know, any number of "Green Dragons" in the land, but I wonder if you know the one I mean. It is no great distance from where I live, though actually it stands at the junction of two main roads, a few miles from the nearest village, in appealing isolation. It is, indeed, a noble old coaching house, brave yet with good beef and beer, old wood and shining pewter. There it lies in the very bottom of those green and grey saucers of rich country-side, for ever mellowed with haze, that are England herself. Once in that valley you must inevitably walk into the kindly maw of the "Green Dragon." Well, the other night, as I climbed the hill from Little Chanbury and dropped down through Long Moulford, I told myself there would be just time for a leisurely drink there before the place closed. It was the magical hour of dusk, of purple air and vaguely glimmering fields; a time, you may say, when anything might happen. And when I had nearly reached the inn, something did happen. I saw a great shadow come stealing silently up the road, approaching the inn from the opposite direction. Clearly it was some kind of vehicle, but there was something curiously huge and ghostly about it. It came gliding on and I walked steadily forward, and it chanced that we arrived before the "Green Dragon" together. Now I saw that it was an enormous motor-coach, the largest I had ever seen. But the odd thing was that it showed no lights nor made any sound. Yet it was filled with people; I could see rows of heads, a vague blur of faces through the dusk. It swung round in a lumbering yet spectral fashion and then stopped only a yard or two from where I was standing and staring. The light from the inn showed me a large device or monogram painted on the side of the coach. I made out the letters "P.C.".

There was not a sound, not another movement now, and as I stood staring there I began to feel creepy. "Hello!" I cried, aloud. It was just as if the word had broken a spell. Instantly the coach was filled with bustling, bewildering life. The blurred rows of faces turned into very energetic people, who all stood up and began talking at once. I could not see them very clearly, but they appeared to be a most astonishing collection of persons, who looked as if they were returning from a pageant or a masquerade. Then above the babel I heard a voice that sounded strangely familiar. "Sit down, old codger," this voice cried. "Sit down and keep still or you'll break your neck, as the church bell said to the vethercock." It happened too that I caught the reply to this extraordinary command. "Vy, Sammy," said a husky voice, "we're 'ere, an't we? And you're a-gettin' down yourself." "And what if I am, old 'un?" cried the first speaker. "You keep still. I'm a-getting out to 'elp the Governor down. Your turn'll come, as the leg o' lamb said to the cab 'orse." A moment later I saw an agile figure jump over the side, disappear for a second or so, and then return carrying some steps, down which a number of persons descended. The leader seemed to me a rather short, plump, elderly man, with a round face. He came nearer and I caught the flash of spectacles. "This looks a capital inn," I heard him declare to one of his companions. "I think they might find room for us all here, what do you think?" Other voices chimed in now. "A most beautiful night," one of them murmured, "when all Nature, except the lovelorn nightingale, seems asleep." He might have continued in this strain, but he was interrupted by the fellow who had brought the steps: "And the pike-keepers, sir. Don't forget them. They're not asleep, though p'raps you wouldn't say they vos part o' Natur." "That will do, Sam," said the elderly gentleman. "Mr. Snodgrass hasn't asked for your opinion." Did this Sam then touch his hat and say, "Sorry, sir"? I am not prepared to say that he actually did, for by this time I was lost in a maze of wonder and the ground beneath my feet seemed to be the shifting territory of dreams.

Other people had come crowding out of the motor-coach, and could be dimly seen in the dusk, stretching themselves and slapping one another on the back. Everybody seemed to be talking at once, but now and then I would hear a voice that was raised above the general babble. "Where's Bob Sawyer?" I heard somebody cry, but I never discovered if he was there. A thin young man, a very fantastic figure, pushed his way through the crowd, looked up at the inn sign, and was now addressing the gentleman who seemed to be the leader of the party. "Stop here, eh? — just the place — know it well — 'Green Dragon' — plenty of bedrooms — good beer — rounds of beef — apple tart and Stilton — famous for 'em; I'll go in — tell 'em who we are — big party — distinguished travellers — special prepara- tions — beds aired — supper on the table — no waiting — best of every- thing — otherwise business ruined for ever — shut up shop — sold up — children in workhouse — do their best and made for life — influential guests — know a good inn — tell everybody — great opportunity for land- lord — special terms — next week crowded out — curious tourists — next year two guineas a night — Americans come — fortune made — retire for life — country gentleman — boys at Oxford — girls at Court — happy ever after." When he had done, I heard that husky voice raised somewhere in the back of the throng. "Wot did 'e say vos the name o' this 'ere public?" After having had the name repeated to him, the speaker called out: "D'hear that, Sammy? 'Green Dragon'." This Sammy, not without a touch of impatience, called back: "Well, wot of it, old Nobs?" "On'y this, Sammy," the husky voice went on. "I never knowed a 'Green Dragon' yet as wasn't kept by a vidder and 'adn't a stuffed parrot in the tap." This statement had reached the ears of the elderly spectacled gentleman near me, who cried: "That's a most curious circumstance, Mr. Weller," and seemed to be on the point of pulling out a large notebook when there was another interruption.

This came from a man in coloured glasses, who had fussily made his way to the front of the party. "Bless my soul, Mr. Pickwick!" he cried. "Are we staying here? And is this the 'Green Dragon'? Do you know that I've never stayed at an inn of that name before? Isn't that extraordinary, really re- markable? You knew I was here, of course, one of the party? Magnus —

Peter Magnus. Who's this, Mr. Pickwick? A friend of yours?" He was
staring at me. They were all staring at me. Uncertainly, I moved forward a
pace or two. "Dear me," said Mr. Pickwick, blinking at me. "I can't say I
remember this gentleman." At that moment the thin young man, with the
jerky manner of speech, came closer, and I thought he was about to shake
my hand. "Nonsense!" he said. "Know him well — no strangers here —
knows me too — Alfred Jingle, Esquire — come to welcome us — deputa-
tion of one — represents the county — deputy sheriff — going to read
official address — got in left-hand coat pocket — pay attention — all
ready for you, sir." Mr. Pickwick turned to one of his companions, and
whispered: "I dare say Jingle's right. The news of our return here, after a
hundred years, has reached these people." He turned to me now. "Well, sir,
here we are, stopping for the first night of what you might call a centenary
tour, for it's just a hundred years since we began our journey. Only now, of
course, all our friends are with us, as you may see for yourself if you look
around you. We are ready for you, sir." Did they suppose I was about to
give them an official welcome? Apparently they did, for there was neither a
movement nor a sound now, and every face there was turned towards me.
But how still, how ghostly they were!

"Here's that new chara of young Bardsley's," cried a loud voice behind.
"Isn't it a size? Cost him something, that. Calls it the 'Pickwick.' " The inn
was closing and men were coming out. There was the huge motor-coach,
silvery in the queer half-light, but all the Pickwickians had vanished. The
man who had just spoken and one or two companions were looking
curiously at the coach, and that was all. Where now were Mr. Pickwick,
Tupman, Snodgrass, the two Wellers, Jingle and the rest? Evidently the
motor-coach was solid and real enough, though it was strange that it had
come gliding up apparently without lights or driver. Perhaps my little dusk-
dream, in which my old friends had returned so surprisingly, had begun the
moment I set eyes on the vehicle, which had thus rolled straight through
into my dream, shedding its lights and driver in the moment of transition.
But what had Mr. Pickwick meant by his talk of a centenary? I thought
over these things as I walked home, still a little dazed, and it is hardly
necessary to say that when I arrived there I immediately took out a copy of
Pickwick. In the second chapter I read how the Pickwickians began their
never-to-be-forgotten tour on 13th May 1827, and then I began to wonder
if I had dreamt it after all.

THE STRANGE OUTFITTER

This morning I had a dream and the memory of it has been with me ever since, so that I feel already that I have had a tremendous day. I look back on the morning and see it stretching away, across two worlds, this one and another, wherever that outfitter's shop may be. I first opened my eyes, however, in this world. The room was full of sunlight, and I was sufficiently wakeful to wonder if it was late and then to look at my watch. It was three minutes past eight; I remember that distinctly. I don't remember how long I remained awake; all that I do know is that I dropped off to sleep again and that the next time I looked at my watch it was twenty minutes past eight. That wicked little extra sleep cannot have lasted longer than a quarter of an hour, but it lasted long enough for me to visit an outfitter's shop in some fantastic town of dreams. I have a vague idea that the adventures in that shop were only the concluding chapter of the dream, and that I had had a day or two's travelling, of the mysterious dream kind, very dark and crowded, before I ever decided to visit the Gent's Outfitter. But of all that went before I can remember nothing that is sufficiently distinct to be worth describing so that my dream may be said to begin in the shop. Once there, it is vivid enough. I have not, however, the least idea why I had entered the place at all. I may have gone there to buy something or I may have walked in for fun.

The shop was small and square, very cosy and rather old-fashioned, the kind of establishment you would find in a market town, a one-man shop. It appeared to be lavishly stocked, for all the walls were piled high with those flat cardboard boxes (usually white with green edges) that hold shirts and collars and ties and braces and are so often lifted down and deftly spread over the counter that they have the air of being part of a juggling apparatus, first cousins to those shining things that the attendants bring on to a variety stage. It had only one window, which was small, rather low, and looked out upon a wide street. There was nothing remarkable about the place. We have all visited dozens of shops like it, I imagine, when we have been away from home, and have discovered that we were in need of studs

or dress ties. The proprietor was not quite so commonplace in his appearance. He was very tall and thin, swarthy, with a large nose and flashing
teeth, but not a Jew, quite English. He looked about forty. He was very
much the gentlemanly shopkeeper, dignified in black coat and striped
trousers; without that unpleasant mixture of superiority and servility in his
manner which is so common, and in its place a mingling of deference with
a curious eagerness that was at once odd and attractive.

He wanted to mend the little straps at the back of my waistcoat. It didn't
seem strange that he should know they were torn (they always are, for
reasons that are now supposed to be discreditable); but I remember that I
had no particular desire to have them mended. He insisted, however, and
brought out needle and thread, saying that he could easily do it while I was
wearing the waistcoat. We argued about this in an amiable fashion, and at
last, finding that he was on the point of starting behind my back, I said that
I would take off the waistcoat so that he could repair the straps at his ease.
This I did and he helped me on with my coat again and I remained
waistcoatless for the rest of the time. He sat down and presumably began
stitching up the straps. I am not sure about this because I turned my back
on him. Moreover, I never saw the waistcoat again.

"I think I'd like a cap," I said, though why I cannot imagine.

"Caps? Certainly, sir. There you are," he cried, but without stirring from
his seat behind me. But there I was indeed, for the counter, right under my
nose, was now heaped with caps. A moment before there had not been a
single cap in sight. His voice came over my shoulder again: "Nice lot of
caps there, sir," he was saying complacently. I cannot say they were a nice
lot of caps, and I remember that I did not like the look of them at the time.
They were all very large and loud and had enormous flaps, so that they
appeared to have been designed for persons who were not sure whether to
stalk a deer or attend a cup-tie. However, I looked them over and decided
to try one on, singling out the nearest, a very woolly, ginger-coloured affair.
There was a mirror at one end of the counter, and now, with the cap
perched on my head, I turned to look at myself.

What I saw there rather astonished and — to be frank — delighted me.
I had fine dark eyes, but all the rest of my face was dazzlingly fair. Not
only was I handsome beyond the dreams of Hollywood, but I boasted a
piquant kind of good looks, a contrast in colouring, not to be matched in
this island. And, of course, the cap itself, which had worked the magic,
looked admirable. I took it off and then a quick glance at the mirror
showed me what I always see there, if not something a trifle worse; so
hastily donned the cap again and stared once more at that bright face,
which seemed to have newly come from the mint of faces.

"I like this cap," I told the man.

"They're very good caps," he replied, still from somewhere behind my back.

"I'll take it then," I said. I took it off, this time without another glance at the mirror, and put it down on the counter. The next moment there weren't any caps. I was just standing there, staring idly at the bare counter and puffing at a pipe.

"I'm sorry, sir," said the man, who was now at my elbow, "but there's no smoking in the shop."

"Then you ought to have a notice of some kind," I told him. I looked round the shop and waved my hand. "You see, there's absolutely nothing here to tell me that smoking is not allowed." I was very annoyed, but after a moment I quietened down and pipe in hand, made him a long speech. "The fact is," I began, "you don't understand my point of view. If I have once lit a pipe, I hate to leave it unfinished. I don't mind not smoking at all, if I know that I can't smoke, but it's annoying to light a pipe in the street outside and then to have to take it out in here." There was a great deal more in this vein, I vaguely remember, all about the striking of matches and the taste of tobacco that is only half-smoked, and so and so forth. I explored the subject very thoroughly. Meanwhile, I was not looking at the man himself but at the shelves and boxes in front. When I had concluded my speech, however, I turned to see how he was taking it, for he had been very quiet.

He had a pipe in his mouth, and was smoking it calmly and with every appearance of enjoyment. His eyes met mine without a trace of embarrassment.

"I thought you said there was no smoking allowed here," I said.

"Not here," he replied, puffing away. "In the shop. There's no smoking in the shop."

I looked round and then I understood what he meant. The shop had gone. We were still in the same place; there was the same low window and the same street outside; the room itself was neither larger nor smaller; but all the outfitting part of it, the counter and shelves and cardboard boxes, had vanished. It was now a little sitting-room, with panelled walls, an armchair or two, and a low settee under the window. I turned round and round examining the place, and seemed to lose sight of my companion. At last, however, while I was staring at something, with my back to the window, I heard a terrific chattering behind me.

The man was sitting on one end of the settee under the window, and on the other end was a very tall woman. Both of them were wearing huge masks. These masks were not unlike those worn by Indian witch-doctors. They seemed to be made of carved wood and were painted a bright red. The most surprising and frightening thing about them, however, was that they had movable mouths. And now both mouths were opening and shutting prodigiously in a very rapid and loud and quite incoherent conversation. Neither the man, that once innocent-looking outfitter, nor his sinister companion took the slightest notice of me, and I stood there staring at them while they gibbered away at one another. Then I chanced to raise my eyes. There were crowds of people in the street outside, parading up and down, singing and dancing, and one and all of them wore masks. I saw none like the hideous pair in front of me, but nevertheless the whole strange town went masked. What did it mean? Where was I? I stared so hard that I stared myself out of the masquerade and the town altogether, into Oxfordshire at twenty past eight in the morning. I had been there and back in less than a quarter of an hour. But I wish I knew exactly where I had been.

THE MAN WITH THE FLARE

It was the flare I noticed first. It was lying beside a bundle of painted canvas and short poles on the station platform at Banbury. Had it been the usual paraffin flare (and by "flare" I mean those crude lamps that seem to be simply a canister of oil with a long spout), so much dingy metal, it would probably have been merged into the background of the station. I might not have noticed it at all; and even if I had, I should probably have taken no interest in it. A dirty and oily flare would only have suggested the drab chaffering of little market-places, and I should have thought no more about it. But this flare was painted a bright orange, and was easily the most conspicuous and the most cheerful object on Banbury platform. It looked like a symbol of jovial and picturesque vagabondage, and stood out from the mass of luggage as a John drawing of a gipsy woman stands out in a room full of sedate landscapes. I kept my eye on it and waited for the owner to appear. The bundle at its side was obviously a little stall, the kind of stall at which you are offered a watch or half a crown if you perform some quite impossible feat with disks or a swinging ball.

Presently the owner arrived, carrying a black wooden box that apparently contained whatever else he possessed. The man was worthy of his flare. He was a shortish nippy fellow, wearing a scarf of the same bright orange as his flare: it relieved him from the necessity of carrying collars and ties and studs and also it proclaimed a challenge to life. His suit and his big cap were faded, but I caught a glimpse, as he fussed about with his box and bundle, of a red round face that was even more lively than the scarf. When the north-bound train came in, he saw his flare and stall into the van and took himself and his black box into an empty smoker. I followed him, and tried to read my papers while he brought out needle and thread from his box and did a little mending; but the very sight of him made the papers seem duller and sillier than ever, and I waited for him to speak.

It was not long before we were in talk, and we yarned away — or rather, he yarned and I listened — across some hundred and fifty miles of English country and in several refreshment rooms of Midland junctions over hurried bottles of Bass. It is impossible to capture him and pin him to a sheet of paper. You have to hear his voice, so eloquent and yet so rusty (he had been talking at the top of it for years, drowning the neighbouring steam organs and sirens: he was good at the "patter," he told me, and I could well believe it), with its twang of the fair-ground and the barrack-room and the boxing booth and its faint Scots burr. You have to see his dancing black eyes for ever punctuating his remarks with winks, and the gestures that amply illustrated his recital, whether it was a matter of taking a drink or winning a light-weight championship. You have to feel his nudges, for he was given to stressing a point with his elbow. His winks and nudges took you into his confidence, showed you that whatever was being said was between the two of you: his voice had taken the whole world into its confidence for so long that now it could not confine itself to one listener, so that the winks and nudges had to be called in as allies.

He was nothing if not dramatic, and he could people a railway carriage or a refreshment room with soldiers and boxers and showmen and crowds. If he talked (as he did) of a friend of his who ought to have been world's champion at some weight or other — "Fight anybody. Beat the Dixie Kid. Beat Birmingham Jack. Beat the Fighting Fireman. Beat 'em all. Fight anybody. But a fool, a mug. Do it for nothing. Never got in with the click [the clique]" — you really saw this man going about and fighting anybody and beating everybody, a whole epic of disinterested pugilism reeled through your mind. What is impossible to capture — unless he were dis-played at great length — is the immense liveliness of him, that quality which made the commercial travellers and workmen who travelled with us seem by comparison the drabbest figures, men made out of wood.

He was a wandering Scot, one of five brothers. (I can tell you about them: one was killed in the war; one is a bricklayer, earning seventy-five dollars a week somewhere in Massachusetts, U.S.A.; one is a donkey-man

on a trawler; and the other is the mate of a collier.) Years ago, he had
been in the militia and then he became a professional boxer, a light-weight,
and he had a good deal to say about boxing. He was running a booth just
before the war, but he joined up at once and got a bullet wound at Neuve-
Chapelle. (We talked war, of course, and found that our respective divisions had been neighbours, that we knew the same trenches and had been
billeted in the same flour-mill.) Since the war he had travelled the length
and breadth of England, Scotland, Wales and Ireland, and — as he put
it — all the islands too, "Isle o' Lewis, Isle o' Arran, Isle o' Man, Anglesey,
Isle o' Wight, Channel Islands (first time I landed in Jersey with fourpence,
four pennies. Second time, with a hundred and four pounds, hundred and
four)," and had even worked his way through France and Belgium, sometimes with a boxing booth, sometimes as a quack doctor, sometimes with a
"Try Your Skill" stall. He and O. Henry's "Gentle Grafter" — wasn't it
Jeff Peters? — would have been comrades-in-arms in two minutes. His
various adventures were merely hinted at in the course of conversation.
Thus, talking of Negroes, he would say: "Very good fellers, some of 'em.
There was So-and-so, came from Plymouth. Went round Devon and Corn-
wall and Somerset with him. Made him into a wild man. I'd say 'Walla-
Willa-Walla' and he'd say 'Willa-Walla-Willa,' and I'd tell 'em we were
talking in his own lingo. Marvellous, isn't it?" And there was another
Negro, from Manchester, he had with him once in a boxing booth: "Nice
quiet feller. Died o' consumption. Fight anybody for three rounds, just
three rounds, no more. Quid to anybody who could stand up to him for
three rounds. Couldn't do any more. Been a great fighter if he could have
stood it. Died o' consumption."

   At present he is running a ball on a string game, but does not think much
of it. "I'm in the wrong line," he said. "Not enough money about. You've
got to sell 'em something. Feller I was stopping with last night, pal o' mine,
is coining it. Sells rubber dolls. Ninepence in the shilling profit. Took a
hundred and fifty quid in three days, a hundred and fifty. Spends it all.
Tarts, booze, gives it away — good feller. Always has stock, though.
Hundreds o' quids worth, stock, see it piled up in a corner of the caravan.
Rubber dolls. That's the game. Sell 'em something."

   He travels for nine months out of the year — from fair to cattle-show,
from regatta to race-meeting, meeting old pals at every turn, and then for
three months, from January to March, I think, he goes back to his home in
Scotland — "drinking beer and whusky." Then he takes a free passage on
his brother's collier to Sunderland, and begins all over again, with his little
black box and his orange flare. He had no overcoat, which is probably the
test of the real vagabond. I asked him where he stayed. "Anywhere," he
said. "Always get in somewhere. Don't bother much about eating. Can't eat

breakfast — too much booze. Eat at the stalls — whelks — good for you, you know — chips and fish — anything. I'm all right." And he looked all right, too, ruddy and brisk and twinkling.

He had a craftsman's delight in the tricks of the trade, and told me a hundred and one stories illustrating them. Here is one of them, though I cannot possibly reproduce his manner of telling it. "Cleverest thing I ever saw or one of 'em," he began, "was at Such-a-place. D'you know it? Well, there's a race-meeting there, not much of one, farmers' meeting. I'm here with my stall, next to me is the boozing tent, and next to that there's a crowd running the three-card trick. They've one dressed as a parson, another as a farmer, and another as an old woman. They're just getting going when up comes a plain-clothes man, 'tec. He looks them over." And he gave me an imitation of a plain-clothes man looking them over. "This 'tec raises his hand, to beckon to two policemen. But the feller running the game clips him under the jaw and down he goes. The old woman falls on top of him, screaming. They all start shouting: 'Leave her alone!' 'He's drunk!' 'Old enough to be your mother!' 'Shame!' All the click's shouting away. In a minute the crowd's so thick the coppers can't get through. All the crowd's shouting now. The feller running the game pulls the old woman away, and them and the rest of the click slip to the back while the crowd's shouting at the 'tec and the coppers are pushing their way through. 'He's drunk. Lock him up.' And they get hold of him, and it takes them a minute or two to find out who he is. Clever, wasn't it? Never saw anything neater. All got clean away. Marvellous!"

His flow of talk uncovered for me a whole parasitic underworld of which you and I have only obtained odd glimpses, a world of fairs and little race-meetings and boxing booths and low pubs, of cheapjackery and pugilism, of "tarts and booze." It was as if he held that paraffin flare of his to the face of another England. Yet it was better talk than I hear in most places, and not only because it was more picturesque and dramatic, more full of the sap and savour of life, Hogarth and Morland instead of the artists of the magazine covers, but also because it had more genuine sense and sensibility, more downright humanity, whether he was talking of the war or Ireland or Communism or Capitalism, poor men and rich men, rascals and good fellows, drink and fighting and comradeship and death, than you are likely to discover in the talk of fifteen hundred railway carriages stuffed with newspaper-made opinions. The little man may not have seen life steadily and seen it whole by the light of his orange flare, but he had at least taken a good look at it for himself; and I think Henry Fielding, after wagging a finger at him in the dock for being a vagabond and something of a cony-catcher, would have given him a slap on the back and a guinea afterwards. Just before we parted, he discovered that I "wrote for the

papers." This excited him: "I've got a fine subject for an article for you,"
he cried. I was all curiosity. "The cultivation o' the tomato in the Channel
Islands," he went on. "There's a subject for you. The tomato. Marvellous."
He left me marvelling.

VII. From THE BALCONINNY 1929

THE BALCONINNY

One of my ambitions has been realized at last. For the past two months we have been living at the very edge of the sea and — this is the point — are the temporary owners of what the youngest member of this family, a neologist of something like genius, calls a "balconinny." If you saw it you would see at once that it is a balconinny rather than a balcony, being just large enough to hold three comfortably seated people. You could have tea on it — at a pinch — but not lunch or dinner. There is only room for one bed. If this is not a balconinny, then what is it?

You can slip out of either the drawing-room or the best bedroom onto this balconinny. I never fail to enjoy the thrill of it, for I have always wanted to have a balcony overlooking the sea — and here it is, even though it is only a balconinny. There is always something dramatic and heart-lifting about the contrast. One moment you are in the drawing-room, which is full of mysterious water-colours and little tables that must not be touched; or you are in the best bedroom, which is full of enormous wardrobes and photographs of people you don't know; and the very next moment you are a thousand miles away from such things, looking at the sea and sky. It is true there is a road or promenade below, but you need never notice that; look straight ahead, or for that matter to left or right — anywhere, in fact, but downwards — and you might think you were on a ship, a large, steady, clean ship. Staying here, indeed, is a sea voyage artfully shorn of its disadvantages, the rust-coloured bath-water and the stewed tea, the miseries of bunkdom, and such problems as "Does the cabin steward really deserve more than the dining-room steward?" I have done eight thousand miles at sea and found less to look at than I find here in a single afternoon.

Moreover, we overlook no common waters. This is the corner of England where everything except woad-painting and cairn-building began, for here Julius himself beached his ships and Augustine landed. These are the Downs, where the old merchantmen and men-o'-war found an anchorage. Out there are the Goodwins, which are lighted like a park every night. If you want an atmosphere of wrecks and lifeboats (did I not first make the acquaintance of this place in the heroic pages of *Chatterbox,* ages ago?) and smuggler and pigtails and tarry trousers, haunted by the ghost of a jolly lyric by Charlie Dibdin, then this is the place for you.

Not that we have to amuse ourselves here by dreaming of the past — a miserable business. Something is always happening, here and now. You never know what will be conjured onto this shining mirror. The other night, returning from a day in London, a long hot dusty futile day, which can only be compared with that of a mite revisiting the interior of a large cheese, I saw in the blue hollow of sea and sky two white yachts lying out there, close together, like two mysterious beautiful ladies whispering together and idly flashing their jewels; and when I rushed out onto the balcony, early next morning, these yachts had gone, stolen away, and I half wondered if I had dreamt them. But that very morning, in came a Dutch mine-layer or mine-sweeper, looking like the fat brother of that French Fisheries boat we had seen a few days before. And this is to say nothing of the regular traffic of this magic street: the great P. & O. and Union-Castle liners, the tankers and grain-ships and tramps and tiny coasting steamers, the brigs and luggers and little racing yachts. Sometimes we take the day's papers onto the balcony, but we find it hard to give them any serious attention; their politicians and millionaires and criminals and bright young people are only the vaguest of spectres; and soon, so soon — as Shakespeare might have said — their gaudy, babbling and remorseful day has crept into the bosom of the sea.

When I looked out from the balcony this morning, there was neither day nor sea, just vaguely shining space, as if we were hanging over the world's edge. The hooting of the invisible lightship might have come from some doomed star. We breakfasted on the very margin of all substantial things. More light stole through, and in place of that vast nothing there was so much shimmering silk, grey below and palest blue above, and on this fabric were tiny moving shapes, delicate as moths, yet most of them, it may be, crammed with fish and iron bars and bales of cotton, full of men making stew or smoking cut plug. Tomorrow morning, if the glass falls and the wind freshens, there will not be a trace of all this ghostliness. The horizon will have come back again, a long green line, broken into a white jumble here and there where the Goodwins set the water creaming. The whole flood will be running stormily at us, smashing at the shingle, throwing handfuls of salt into the whistling air, and churning round the ships, now as hard and clear to sight as black paint and red paint can make them. And the whole place will look as if the sea had washed all over it during the night, for everything will be clean and have a salty sparkle. What a show to have a private box for, a box you can use any time of day! Even Mr. Cochrane must admit his defeat. He has his dancers, but what did Prince

Florizel cry? "When you do dance, I wish you a wave o' the sea, that you might ever do nothing but that." And here they do nothing but that.

Perhaps the best time of all is after dinner, especially on these warm and windless nights, when you can take one of those glorious long cheroots out on the balcony and watch the ash reach its third half-inch. You can also watch for some of the last signs of picturesque romance left to this world. Last night I was up there, when it was nearly dusk, and saw far out, nearly on the horizon, a full-rigged ship. And that is by no means an everyday affair, seeing a full-rigged ship. But that was not all. Somewhere an artist was at work. The house, the promenade, the foreshore, were all settling into dusk, and the sea itself was fading and darkening; but out there, where the ship was, the last gleams of sunset were falling, and for a minute or two she was irradiated, and even when her hull was no longer flushed, her great sails were still golden, and even when they paled and sank, her masts still seemed tangled with the sunset. Then, in the deeper dusk, she turned ghostly, and at last she vanished, just flitted away when our heads were turned, like a ghost. Perhaps she was a ghost.

The lights of the Goodwins came twinkling on, a little uncertainly at first, as if they were not quite sure they were wanted. Away on the right, the pier put on its little coloured spangle of lights, which dropped long trembling reflections into the water. On the cliff to the left our neighbouring town turned itself into a bracelet of glimmering yellow points. The whole traffic of the sea became a pattern of lights, fixed or wandering, in a mystery of purple air and indigo waters. You saw something that looked like a distant row of houses on the move and you knew that a liner from Calcutta or the Cape had passed by and that hundreds of your fellow-countrymen were staring over the rails and hearing the great engines go humming, *Home-in-the-morning, Home-in-the-morning*. And little lights, as lonely as a few fireflies in a desert, crept by, going the other way, and you know that a tramp or two had slipped out of the Thames, bound perhaps for Montevideo or Callao.

These and many other things we saw last night, as we sat on our little balcony. And our neighbours had set some works in motion in a box, and out of this box there came some familiar and great music, and in this music we saw Siegfried and the dragon and the leaping fire and the deep enchantment of the forest; and all this too flowed easily into the night and was one with it. Long after we have left this house I shall still use its balcony. They will tell me this and that; they will argue and fuss and sweat; they will point out that Jones is overpraised and Smith underrated, that Brown should go out and Robinson come in; and it will not matter; I shan't hear them. I shall be back on this balconinny.

MY DEBUT IN OPERA

I am one of the very few authors who have ever appeared with the
Beecham Opera Company. It is true that I was not expected to sing —
though I did sing. It is also true that I played with the Company for one
night only. I was not asked to appear again, but then, on the other hand, I
never asked to be asked again. Once was quite enough; I have no serious
operatic ambitions; and now nobody can say I have never appeared in
opera just as they cannot say I have never been to Africa; I have had my
night with the Beecham Company just as I have had my half-day in
Algiers.

The time is ten years ago, the spring of 1919. The place — a provincial
city. I am newly returned from that dismal progression — heroics, endur-
ance, boredom, disgust — known up to the present as the Great War. I am
writing articles and reviews for the local paper at a guinea a column. In one
of the principal streets of my city I encounter an old acquaintance of the
ranks and we have what he calls, very inaccurately, "a gill." He tells me
that this week he is assisting the Beecham Opera Company. I remember
then that it is his practice to "walk on" at the local theatres. I myself had
seen him as an Eastern domestic, a policeman, member of a jury, a
forester, and as the Bishop in *Richard III*. Indeed, it was a poor week at
our Theatre Royal when he did not walk on as somebody or other, always
dumb. Six of them, it appears, are walking on this very night in Gounod's
Romeo and Juliet. This is one of the few operas for which I have not
booked seats. I do not want to see *Romeo and Juliet,* but I should like to
appear in it. I am even willing — so eager, so rash, are we amateurs — to
hand over the night's pay, the whole two and sixpence, to the man whose
place I take. The matter can be arranged. I am to be at the theatre at seven-
thirty, to meet my acquaintance at the stage door.

I am there and he is there, and the two of us, with a last glance at the
waiting crowds, march in through the stage door. We go up steps and down
steps and along so many corridors that I am completely bewildered. At last
we arrive at a dressing-room that is as hot as an oven — and well it might
be, for it must be somewhere near the centre of the earth. The room

contains one long mirror, several large theatrical baskets, an overpowering smell of grease paint, and one bored little man in his shirt-sleeves. There is a notice: SMOKING STRICTLY PROHIBITED. We all light up at once, all, that is, except the little man, who was smoking when we entered and seems to have been smoking without cessation for about forty years. He opens one of the baskets, and begins throwing costumes at us.

I find myself wearing a yellow and black doublet or whatever it is, and one black tight and one striped yellow and black tight; and I look like a rather plump wasp. The little man takes our faces, one by one, and rubs red and brown into them. Then we put on brown or black wigs, thick and bobbed, and crown them with little round hats, Beefeater style. To complete our discomfort — for the wigs are very hot and the hats do not feel as if they were on — we are now given pikes about eight feet long. We are, it seems, the town guard of Verona, and I have no doubt we look the part or, indeed, something better than the part. We have all been in the army, and I will wager we could have mopped up the real town guard of Verona — and Vicenza and Padua — in a jiffy. But not, I must confess, with those pikes. When an opera company as big as the Beecham concern is playing in a provincial theatre there is no room behind the scenes for a walking stick, let alone half a dozen eight-feet pikes. As we trail our pikes down steps and up steps and along corridors, we are cursed by Montagues and Capulets together. "A plague on both your houses!" we mutter, trying in vain to disentangle ourselves.

We arrive in the wings. The opera has begun, but we are not wanted for some time. To walk into that brightly lit space looks a fearsome enterprise, yet we see fellows dashing on and off and never turning a hair. Mercutio — or some other bearded gallant — waves his arms and reaches a top note, then comes out into the wings and lights a cigarette. But now we are summoned. The stage manager has remarked our existence. He is the most worried-looking man I have ever seen. Everything he does appears to be one last desperate effort. Night after night he dies a hundred deaths. Now he seizes a pike and shows us how it should be carried.

Our duties, he explains, are simple. We make two appearances. The first time we march on, we stand, we march off. Nothing could be easier, though it is clear that as he says this he does not believe we shall find it easy. He only means that if this were the world he thought it was when he first undertook stage management, it would be easy. As it is, if we were to go prancing round the stage, tearing the scenery with our pikes, he would not be really surprised. He alone is sane in a lunatic world. Now comes a big scene. More and more people crowd onto the stage and make more and more noise. At last we are the only performers left in the wings. It is our turn now? It is. Affairs in Verona are at a crisis. There is nothing for it but to summon the town guard. But will the town guard come? They will. At this moment they are fearfully carrying their six pikes in the tiny space between the drop and the back wall of the theatre, to appear through a central arch. There we were. No applause greeted us; nobody paid much attention to us, either on the stage or in the audience; but we did what we had to do manfully. We marched on; we stood; we marched off. Half the opera was saved. Back in the wings I hear a thunder of applause, and I wonder if the audience is aiming some of it at us, if they are saying to one another, "The principals and chorus are not very good, but the town guard is magnificent, especially the third one with the black tight." What would happen if I insisted upon taking a curtain with Romeo and Juliet? I see myself standing between them, pike in hand, bowing gracefully. What I do, however, is to retire to our subterranean dressing-room with the other five. The little man is still there, sinking into a more profound boredom. He must have always been there. Perhaps the theatre was built round him.

It is almost time for our second and final appearance. We are back in the wings, and the stage manager, now far beyond hope, a man resigned to his fate in an idiotic universe, gives us our instructions. There is to be an admirable little variation in our movements. This time we have to march on, *to spread ourselves,* to stand, to march off. Before, the audience saw us in a dense mass: now, they will see us in scattered groups. No doubt there will be a great deal of talk afterwards, some people preferring us in a solid body, others delighting in the scattered effect, in which individual features, the fit of a black tight, for example, are brought into greater prominence.

Here is the second big scene — the wedding. All Verona is turning out. We see to it that our hats are not on straight, we grasp our pikes and on we go, spreading ourselves superbly. The post of honour falls to me. I am on guard at the church door itself, actually between it and the footlights, which are not two feet away. I am standing gracefully at ease. I am also wondering what would happen if I dropped my pike, which now seems about twenty feet long. Would it brain the *cor anglais* player in the trench below? Very busy they are too, down there. I can see them all quite plainly. I can see rows of faces in the stalls and the circle. All the people in the chorus are singing now, so I join in, finding Gounod well within my powers. It is absurd perhaps that the pikeman on duty should sing, but then it is equally absurd that anybody else there should sing. The drama moves. I have a strong desire to drop my pike or alternatively to play a bigger part in the action. Why shouldn't a humble member of the town guard — the one with the black tight — suddenly become the hero of *Romeo and Juliet?* Again, why shouldn't we pikemen take charge of the whole drama, beginning by clearing the stage? That would be a welcome diversion. What would happen if we passed a note on to the management saying that we would clear the stage with our pikes unless we were given five pounds apiece? After all, we hold the opera in the hollow of our hands.

We also hold our pikes, and I for one am tired of mine. There, it is finished. At least, the real opera is finished — the pike part of it — for there is still a little for Romeo and Juliet and other minor characters to do. We return to the depths, pikes at the trail; we throw black and yellow tights and bobbed wigs at the little bored man; we wash and dress and receive our money; we depart for beer.

Such was my debut in opera. This is exactly what happened, just ten years ago. I have invented nothing; I have neither exaggerated nor embellished; yet I do not expect to be believed.

CARLESS AT LAST

I suppose there are thousands of people in this country who are now telling themselves that they are happy because at last they have cars. But what is their happiness compared with mine? At odd moments throughout the day I remember that I have no car, and there is more music in my heart than ever came out of Daventry Experimental. Sometimes I forget that it has really gone for ever. I think of it being away in some garage, eating its head off; I imagine that I shall soon have to go once more and hear the lying reports of the mechanics; I take up my letters expecting to find among them those bills for repairs that are as crazy and vindictive as the proclamations of Oriental tyrants. And then I remember. It has gone for ever; there are no more garages, mechanics, bills for repair; I am no longer an owner-driver but a free man. There is an astonishing feeling of lightness and ease about the shoulders. No longer have I to support a huge and dubious piece of mechanism and its sneering and shrugging attendants in overalls. The thing may have made me look richer than I am, but it certainly made me feel miserably poor. Now that it has gone, I seem to be quite comfortably off again. I take trains and buses and taxis (without having to ask myself "Why don't you use the car?") and I am amazed to find how cheap they are. It is a pleasure to travel now. It is also a pleasure to stay at home, for now there is no five-seater open tourer on the premises to remind me that I ought to be going somewhere in it in order to get my money's worth.

My mind to me a kingdom is. The R.A.C. and the A.A. are fading into

meaningless initials. Double Shell is something in an ugly dream. I pass
Dunlop and Michelin without so much as a nod. The Golden Pump is one
of the innumerable blots on the landscape, nothing more. If any more
young men don overalls and dirty their faces, they will not do it at my
expense. I am indifferent to the real character of Ethyl. Four, six, eight, or
twenty cylinders, it is all one to me now. What they do to the gallon is a
question that leaves me shrugging, and at last I have enough spare cash to
discover, if necessary, what I can do to the gallon. I can look at the country-
side again like a man and not like a mere slave of the wheel. I can afford to
dislike your long straight roads, to welcome the narrowest and most
winding of lanes. I like to see trams in a town. The sight of cattle in the
streets gives me pleasure again. I smile at old ladies who wander into the
middle of the road and then decide to turn back. The cyclist seems to me
an innocent creature, not without a certain quaint beauty. I have shed a
whole foul tangle of contempt and envy. The people who sit in long shining
pieces of mechanism no longer seem any better than the people who are
packed into a tiny box on wheels. I raise no more hats to the Rolls or the
Daimler: neither do I put out my tongue at the oldest Ford. In that daft
world of wheels and smells I am Gallio himself. I am happy and free,
careless and carless. It is as if my mind — the metaphor comes to me from
some vague dream — had been decarbonised.

I was never at ease in that world. True, the first car I had was an
unusually incompetent, if not downright malicious, vehicle. It was a very
good argument for mass production, for it was of a make so rare that I
never found anybody who had ever heard of it, and most people seemed to
imagine that I had invented the name — and probably made the car. There
was always one part of the mechanism that was not working, and towards
the end hardly anything was working; I remember taking one visitor to the
station in it when neither footbrake nor handbrake, clutch nor gears, were
doing duty, and even the steering-wheel was all loose — we simply rolled
down to the station. The only advantage the car had over ordinary cars was
that it required virtually no feeding. I never remember giving it any oil, and
it only asked for a mere drop of petrol. I suspect that it was not an internal-
combustion engine at all, but a car on a new principle — years before its
time — and really worked by will-power. Probably in a century or two
there will be nothing but cars like that, which will simply be *thought* along
the road. Unfortunately, my own will was not strong enough, though undoubtedly I worked miracles with it. Men in garages regarded me with wonder and awe after they had examined it, and I have no doubt the more intolerant of these mechanics would have had me burned as a wizard if I had
stayed in the neighbourhood.

My second — and last — car was very different. It was the product of a very well-known firm, and it looked imposing enough. It worked in the ordinary way, and so long as various expensive operations were performed upon it from time to time, it continued to work. But instead of being an ascetic, it was a downright glutton. Petrol it consumed as fast as it could, but oil was its passion. It demanded the most extravagant brands, and it could never have enough of them. It would hardly visit the station under a quart, and when we went touring in it you could have followed our route simply by observing the trail of empty oil drums. I could never afford to buy myself a book or a cigar or a bottle of wine when I had that car, for as soon as I had a spare pound or two it cried out for more oil. It was like entertaining for ever a drunkard who touched nothing but champagne. Imagine the relief at seeing him reel away at last, and you can form an idea of my present state of mind. I cannot pass a garage without jingling the shillings in my pocket and feeling comparatively rich.

That I am a bad driver I will cheerfully admit. I think the trouble about driving is that it requires just the wrong amount of attention — at least from me. It is not absolutely a full-time job, needing all your concentrated powers, but neither is it a thing you can do properly while thinking about something else. This was always my mistake: I would go on so merrily that after a time I would begin to think about other things, and when I did return to the matter in hand I was always a few seconds too late. I was too late at High Wycombe, when I bent the front axle; at Ealing when I hit the tram; at Northwood when I ran into the oldest Ford in the world (it belonged to a bill-poster and smashed my radiator); at Newport, that horrible November afternoon, when I cracked the electric standard and gathered round me all the people of Monmouth. When I was not too dreamy I was too impatient. Thick traffic exasperated me. My friend P. actually likes driving through thick traffic, and spends many a happy hour reversing in the most crowded London thoroughfares. Such a taste is incomprehensible to me. It is as if a man liked putting in a morning doing up the most awkwardly shaped objects into parcels, at the risk of being fined or maimed if they were not absolutely neat. My own experiences were so unpleasant that merely to be a passenger in a car that is being driven through a tangle of traffic makes me sweat; and in Paris I shut my eyes and offer up a prayer. It is not that I am afraid of being killed or of killing anybody else (I was never in danger of doing that even when I drove myself); it is simply the thought of that familiar and sickening crash, the crowd and the questions and the fuss, that appals me, remembering as I do my own adventures.

Now I am well out of it, a free man again. I suffer no inconvenience, for there is no longer any pleasure in motoring itself and there are trains and buses and taxis enough to take me wherever I want to go. No more taxes

and garage fees and bills for petrol and oil. No more maddening conferences with mechanics who know no more about cars than I do, and no
more staggering charges for repairs. No more worries about good roads
and bad roads and trams and policemen. I can no longer drop you anywhere. You will have to drop me, and when I go, notice how jaunty my
step, how lively the tune I whistle, all so carless and free.

LITTLE TICH

Of all the deaths that occurred last year — and how rich it was in
mortuary — the one that troubled my imagination most was that of Little
Tich. Hardy, Haig, Asquith, these are a nation's losses; we bared our heads
in the streets or went black-plumed to the Abbey; our very mourning was
large, cool, and dignified, a state pageant. The poet, the soldier, the statesman, these have had their being in a world where death kept his throne,
and to go to the grave is for them only the inevitable last journey. No
sooner have they gone than we fall to estimating and praising, making new
entries in the ledgers of fame; but unless we stood close to these great
departed, knew them and loved them as men, we do not find ourselves
staring anew at this life, bewildered by mortality. But it is inconceivable
that a famous droll should ever leave us. We cannot believe that he and
Death could ever meet. To go from the Alhambra to the grave — there is
nothing inevitable in this, but something bewildering, shocking. That is why
Hamlet, questioning this life, brooding over mortality in the graveyard of
Elsinore, finds the skull of Yorick in his hand. Therefore I make no
apology for saying that none of these deaths we have had lately has
troubled me more than that of Little Tich.

It has been said that the passing of these men has brought an age to an
end. Thus, with Hardy, goes the last flicker of the Victorian Age of
Literature. Nearly as much might be said of Little Tich, whose very name
takes us back to the distant idiocy of the Tichborne Case. He was a legend
in his later years. He was capering in his long boots when some of us,
myself included, were in the nursery. I heard about him — from uncles
who did not disdain to share the good news of life — long before I ever set

foot in a music-hall. He was one of the figures of the Nineties. He had set in a roar whole audiences of quaint extinct creatures, "boys" with their bowler hats, yellow canes, and short, pearl-buttoned, fawn coats, and "girls" with flounces and feather boas and dashing busts. Indeed, to the last, one of his songs used to bring him on in the character of a "masher," with short fawn coat and tiny cane, one Johnny Green, or, as he himself gave it out in the chorus, "Ja-horny Gréen, Ja-horny Green." He came to us, unspoilt, from the great days of the halls. He was a piece of social history. Something has departed with him, too. While we could still go and see him of an evening, we were in touch with another age. Now, the link has been broken.

These, however, are minor pedantries. I saw Little Tich many times, but never went with any thought of social history or past ages in my head. I can well remember the first time I saw him. I had heard so much that I had come, with all the cool arrogance of youth, to the conclusion that I should be disappointed. I suspected the hocus-pocus of memory working in my elders. The chap would probably be some mere freak, who made a name in drollery when such names were easy to make. The lights at the side flashed out the number of his turn; the band played very quickly and loudly; up went the curtain and there — in the middle of the enormous gold cavern of the stage — was a diminutive steeple-jack, complete with climbing apparatus. But he was no steeple-jack of this world; he had climbed into it from some other and infinitely droller world. There was something irresistibly comic in the foreshortened figure he presented. The head was of normal size, quite large as to nose; the body was trumpery; the legs were nothing, mere wisps. At once this astounding elf plunged into an account, illustrated by a wealth of passionate gestures, of the whole business of steeple-jackery; he seemed to climb, to tremble upon heights, to fall through space, before our very eyes; and there was in this manikin the fiery energy, the spirit, of ten men. In two minutes everybody was laughing. In five minutes I was laughing until the tears rolled down my cheeks. And many an hour have I laughed since, though never perhaps with that complete abandon of the first encounter. After I had seen him a few times, he did not make me laugh so much as keep me in a constant happy chuckling.

It was his habit to present a number of characters, a lady in court dress (perhaps his favourite), a grocer, a jockey, "one of the boys," and so on; and it was impossible not to be tickled by such a series of daft miniatures. You may say he drolly foreshortened all humanity. This trick helped, but it was not the secret of his attraction. Nor was it to be found in the obvious material of his turn. Thus his songs mattered not at all. You hardly ever caught the words of them, and when you did you found you had been listening to no purpose. The matter of his songs and talk was the old traditional stuff — mother-in-law, the lodger, kippers and beer, dubious sausages and dangerous cheese; an ancient round of japes. But all this was mere fodder for the unsophisticated, bait for the groundlings. On a far higher level were his actions, his sudden gestures.

The actions by means of which he illustrated his little chronicles of triumph or woe were adorable. Indeed, they did not illustrate his tales, they brought them to life. He would say, "So I went in," and then he would show you how he went in, his feet going pitter-patter-pitter-patter and his tiny legs seeming to vibrate rather than move as ordinary legs move. It was the essence of all going in that he proffered you. He was magnificent when he suggested a righteous indignation. Beginning with some such remark as "I told him what I thought about him," he would then proceed to show you his disapproval in rich dumb-show, and as he careered fiercely about the stage, kicking and lunging, the empty air was filled with retreating giants. He had a trick of becoming entangled with things — the train of that court dress, for example — that few mimes in the world can have bettered; and I will swear that his mounting fury, the old anger of the human spirit baffled by stubborn things, has never been surpassed. And his gestures, so quick and neat, so energetic and intelligent, were like little epigrams in a new language. No wonder he was so popular in Paris, where he numbered among his most enthusiastic admirers the Guitrys themselves. Now I come to think of it, there was something Gallic about this fiery little man. At times he would cock a knowing droll eye, taking a whole vast assembly into his confidence in a second, that said as much as two hours of French farce. But he was English too, cheerfully inconsequential. We talk of people "breaking into" a dance, but the verb flatters them. Little Tich, however, really did break into dances. He was into a dance, fifty fantastic little steps, and out of it again almost before you knew what was happening.

There was in him an admirable sophistication in music-hall funny business. He really stood away from his songs and jokes and silly clothes and obvious fooling, and all the time merely offered them with a wink and a grin. The drollery was not in his doing these things but in his pretending to do them. He did not really act a man telling you something about his mother-in-law, but a man pretending to be a man telling you something funny about his mother-in-law. You were all behind the scenes with him, or at least one set of scenes, for behind another was a little hard-working actor called Relph, with a stout sense of his dignity and importance in the profession and a taste for painting. Thus he would offer a joke and then shake his head over its reception, remarking that it "went better last night." He would drop his hat and then not be able to pick it up because he always contrived to kick it forward. This might or might not make you laugh. But when, having done this a few times, he would say blandly: "Comic business with chapeau," then, if you shared with him a free human intelligence, you shouted with laughter. I think that was the innermost secret of this little droll's appeal. In the antics of this gargoyle there was all the time a suggestion of a companion spirit winking and nodding and shrugging at you over the crazy jumble and tangle of things. And the things remain, but he has gone. Let us remember him with affection.

MY FORCHERN

I saw the sign up a side-street: Madame Dash — Palmist. I decided at once to have my character, my destiny, unveiled. The way led up a narrow flight of stairs, shared by a number of people such as Poppleworth & Sons, Surveyors, and J. G. Burton & Co., Enquiry Agents. At first I could not find Madame Dash. There was no door bearing her name. I went up three flights of stairs that were narrower and dustier at every turn, and I found and refound Poppleworth & Sons and J. G. Burton & Co., but no Madame Dash. I returned to the street and looked up at the windows. One of them was draped in lace curtains. There, I told myself — and J. G. Burton could not have done better — there is Madame Dash. I climbed the stairs again, discovered the door that seemed to be nearest to the lace curtains, knocked, and was asked to enter.

The room was very dim because the end nearest the window had been partitioned off. A head appeared round the curtain of the partition and said: "D'you want a reading? Just wite a mowment, please." So I sat down in the remains of a leather armchair and waited in the dim room, which was very stuffy and reeked of cheap incense. I examined its four vases of artificial flowers and its two prints, *The Star of Bethlehem* and *Westward Bound: with the Compliments of the Canadian Shipping Line*. I sat there not one minute but ten, during which time there was a continual whispering behind the partition. Then at last two subdued-looking middle-aged women, who, I will swear, kept little sweets and tobacco shops and had husbands who disappeared ten years ago, crept round the curtain, and I was invited to take their place near the window, with Madame.

There was nothing of the alluring or sinister sibyl about Madame, who was short, plump, middle-aged, with a round red face and eyeglasses drolly supported by a very snub little nose. She was wearing a black dress and a rather dirty grey woollen jersey without sleeves, and looked like the owner of a cheap seaside boarding-house who occasionally attended meetings of the local Theosophical Society in winter. She had, however, a pleasant open face, and out of hours, with another sympathetic middle-aged woman and a cup of tea or a bottle of stout by her side, no doubt she would prove to be a very genial companion. At the moment, however, she was earnestness itself. She faced me across a little table, gave me a crystal, told me to cover it with my hands and think about those affairs that I wished her to discuss. Then she looked at my left hand. "Well, yes, of course," she began. It was just as if we had been talking for hours. Her voice had plunged straight into an easy, intimate tone. A very clever opening, I thought it.

"Well, yes, of course," she said, "you've always been sensitive and reserved, and so of course you've been misunderstood. You've reelly an affectionate niture, but people don't think so. Thet's how it is with you. And you've lost fythe. You're one as can see through people. You know what's at the beck of their minds when they're talking to you, you know if they're lying, if they're guilty or not. But being sow reserved, it's got you misunderstood a good deal, it has. And then you've lost your fythe. You follow me, downcher?"

This, extended afterwards to "You follow me now, downcher?" was her favourite phrase, and sometimes she put it in sadly, sometimes it came out briskly, sometimes it arrived with a triumphant ring. What she would do without it, I cannot imagine, for it served all manner of purposes. It kept me nodding like a mandarin. So far I agreed with everything she said. Her view of my character was singularly like my own.

It was now the turn of my right hand. "Yes," she said, "you've had to work hard, but up to now you've not had all you've been entitled to have from your work. Other people been getting the benefit. You follow me, downcher? People have picked your brains before today. Professional, aren't you? It's written here in your hand that you're professional. You'll do better this year than you've ever done before. The months of My and June'll be good for you, specially good. You'll arrive at a position of great responsibility, you will, before long. Up to now, though you might have done fairly well, you reelly haven't had your chance. You follow me, downcher?"

Yes, I was following her. All these were, emphatically, my sentiments. At the moment I could not think of the names of the rascals who had been picking my brains and stealing the fruits of my endeavour, but I had no doubt at all that they existed.

"And another thing," Madame pursued. "Anybody looking at you would think you were a gentleman who had the best of health, but you haven't, you know, reelly. You've not been as well as you might have been since last November, nothing like so well as you look. You see what I mean?"

I agreed with enthusiasm. It is perfectly true that I am hardly ever as well as I look, and I have the misfortune to be surrounded by people — relatives, friends, and even doctors — who simply cannot understand this, who do not realise what I suffer in my own quietude.

She had finished with my hands now, and began gazing into the crystal I had been holding. "I see a Nightch," she announced, impressively. "A Nightch!" I cried, startled. "Yes, the letter Ightch," she said. "D'you know anybody whose nime begins with a Nightch?" But this did not take us far because I know so many people whose names begin with that letter. She mentioned several other initial letters too, but this was easily the least valuable part of the séance. I refused to take an interest in these vague alphabetical creatures.

"I see money coming to you from two directions," she said, peering in the crystal. "It's in here, two different directions. Can you understand what that means? It's money coming to you soon." I am accustomed to seeing money depart in all directions, but the thought of it coming, two shining streams converging upon me, was new and distinctly pleasant. I did not understand what it meant (or if I did, I do not see why I should tell everybody), but for a moment I enjoyed the thrill of one about to be rich.

"I see a tall gentleman, very straight he is — he stands up in here — oldish gentleman, and he means well to you. You can trust him. And there's a younger gentleman, dark with a thin fice, and he's to be trusted too. And these two'll bring you in a lot of money. And you're doing a lot of signing, a lot of signing. You follow me, downcher?" "Well," I said, hesitantly, "as a matter of fact, I always have a good deal of signing to do." "But we don't see here anything you do in the ordinary way of things," she said. "This is special signing, something that'll please you." She stared again in silence for a few moments. "You're in a city with narrow streets and very tall buildings, you've had to go there on business, and it's very lucky for you. Very narrow streets and very tall buildings. Liverpool or Manchester, p'raps."

"I hope not," I murmured. It is one thing to be told you are to be lucky in some strange city, and it is quite another thing to be told you will be in Liverpool or Manchester. I felt disappointed, but clung to the hope that topography was not her strong point.

Her next remark was rather reassuring. "The streets mayn't be so narrow," she observed, "because it may be only the buildings that are so high. Anyhow I see you there, and it'll be lucky for you." Which left me with a conviction that the city was New York, that I was to be there signing contracts for plays, films, serial stories, short stories, five-hundred-dollar articles on The American Woman as I See Her, with men straight as ramrods standing by, looking after my interests. "Now, you can ask me anything you like," she said, but really by this time I felt there was little to ask. After a minute or two, during which she told me again that I was reserved, sensitive, affectionate, misunderstood, witty and keen-brained, unlucky so far but about to be very successful, and that all I wanted was a little fythe, I did put a question, but it was only to ask her what I owed her. "It's half a crown, that is, if you're satisfied," she replied.

Satisfied! I should think I was. Without knowing my age or profession, anything of my personal history, she had yet contrived to tell me all the things that I want to be told, the things I have always secretly believed to be true of myself and that nobody but me — and this kindly oracle — ever seemed to understand. The session was worth a hundred half-crowns. It was a daydream of oneself suddenly conjured into an oracular utterance. It was a visit to a magic mirror.

As I went out, I saw two people waiting their turn. I only had a glimpse of them, but it was enough to show me that they too would prove to be reserved, affectionate, sensitive, misunderstood, unfortunate perhaps up to now but about to rush into prosperity, immense good fortune. I thought of them pleasantly as I passed the doors of Poppleworth & Sons, Surveyors, and J. G. Burton & Co., Enquiry Agents, and descended into the world again.

COMMERCIAL INTERLUDE

I am staying in an hotel in a Midland town, and it has turned me into a Commercial. When I arrived yesterday — that is, when I walked down the road from the station — I saw that the hotel called itself Family and Commercial, but as soon as I had spent five minutes in the place I realised that it was purely Commercial. It cannot have seen a family for twenty years. But Commercial is no idle boast. The coffee-room was full of Commercials and I became one myself simply by engaging a room here. "Is there a place," I asked the maid, "where I can sit and write in the morning?" "Just the Coffee Room — for Commercials," she replied. I am still wondering what would have happened if I had said that I was not Commercial but Family. (And, after all, I can easily prove that I am more of a family man than a commercial one.) Would rooms shuttered and shrouded these twenty years have been thrown open for me? Would the Boots have gone round blowing the dust from Family armchairs? The maid, however, never hesitated a moment: I was obviously a Commercial.

Her method of reasoning, I imagine, was that no man who was not a Commercial would ever dream of staying at this hotel. No doubt, too, I have the look of a bagman, one of the less prosperous kind, travelling in some antiquated line of fancy goods. (And there are times when I see myself in that melancholy part.) For the moment, then, I am a Commercial. I sleep in Number Eight, and eat, drink, smoke, read, write, in the coffee-room; and I am trying to summon up courage to cry, very loudly and snappily as the others do, "Good-morning, gentlemen! Good-evening, gentlemen!" I hope to bring it off once before I go. Already I am being regarded with suspicion because I mumble the greeting and leave out the "gentlemen." The other Commercials are probably asking one another what the place is coming to.

That is a question I can answer. If all the other bedrooms are like mine — and I see no reason why they shouldn't be — then the hotel is tottering into ruin. My room is reasonably clean, but that exhausts its virtues. It is as cheerful as the interior of an old trunk that has been put away in the boxroom these fifteen years. Its ancient wallpaper is faded and stained beyond recognition as a colour or a pattern; in one corner there is plaster wandering across, like a river on a huge map; and high up the wall opposite my bed the damp seems to have crumbled away paper, plaster and all. The two windows, which look out upon the backs of warehouses but occasionally offer a glimpse of a passing train, are draped with yellowed lace curtains and very old blue roller blinds. Last night I could not persuade the blinds to stay down and this morning I had an even greater difficulty in cajoling them up again.

The toilet set is chipped, cracked, or broken. The jug has no spout. The soap-dish is completely severed into two halves. And there is a certain missing handle that cannot even be discussed. In the corner by the washstand is a row of coathooks, but most of the hooks are either leaning forward at a ridiculous angle or are not there at all, and anyhow you cannot hang your clothes over a washstand. The bed is very high and very lumpy and very cold. Climbing into it is not going to bed but to Tibet. The single electric light is in a distant corner, removed as far as possible from the bed, the washstand, the mirror. A notice informs you that "The electric light will be turned off at 11.30 p.m. Candles are placed in each bedroom," and the first statement is true. The candles, I suspect, went out with the Family. The only towel you receive is a very small face towel, and so far as I can see, any other would be useless. The Commercial apparently is supposed to take a bath whenever he returns to his distant home. This hotel sees the Commercial as a man who almost completes his dressing on first rising, shaves and washes his face and hands in the pint of warmish water brought to him, and after that does nothing but a little rinsing and dabbing with cold water and a slimy face towel.

I have never occupied a prison cell, but I imagine it to be rather more cheerless than this bedroom of mine. But I defy any other kind of apartment to compete with it in desolating discomfort. The moment you arrive, it announces: "I am simply so many cubic feet of bedroom space. My little iron grate has never had a fire in it and never will have. Nobody here has ever really looked at me, given me a thought. The sooner my walls crumble away, the better." And when you return at night — and in Midland towns you return quite early — the room is even more expressive: "I'm a chill and cheerless hole," it cries at once. "Nobody has ever really lived in me. Get to sleep immediately — if you can. But listen to those trams, groaning and groaning away. Plenty of noise here, isn't there? Not a cheerful noise though. What d'you think of life, eh? Care for it much? You're a damned fool to be sober, if you ask me. Trying to read, eh? Haven't seen much of that, I must say, but it won't work. Lights out soon, you know. Cold, isn't it? You're not so young as you were, are you? Getting many orders, business good? I thought not."

Something like that, I will swear, it said to me last night, when I turned in at the early hour of ten-thirty. I had been to the local Hippodrome, where I had been saddened by the spectacle of a fifth-rate revue, a show without a single gleam of talent or high spirits, simply so many overworked and underdressed girls and hoarse-voiced and perspiring men. I had had a drink downstairs in the public smoking-room where the usual semi-circle of patrons were drearily chaffing the fat barmaid. Then I tried the coffee-room, joining the three Commercials who were sitting round the little fire at the far end of the room.

There was the young man in blue laboriously reading the *Daily Mirror;* the red-faced man in brown, who was yawning over a glass of stout; and the elderly bald man who sucked an empty pipe and did nothing else until the maid came in, whereupon he brightened up and addressed her as Minnie. I could see that bald man going round, year after year, to all the commercial hotels in England, calling the maid Minnie here, Gertie at Nottingham, Mabel at Leicester, Gladys at Birmingham. I filled a pipe and stared in front of me, first at the fire, then at the two monstrous engravings, *The Jubilee Celebration in Westminster Abbey, June 21, 1887,* and *Ramsgate Sands (circa* 1850), and when I had tired of these, at a glass case of stuffed humming-birds perched upon a gilt tree. I remember thinking how incredible it was that there really were places where such creatures, gorgeous in vermilion and sea-green and amethyst, were alive, actually flying about. (We Commercials have the oddest thoughts sometimes.) The young man in blue still pored over his *Daily Mirror;* the red-faced man produced wider and wider yawns; the elderly one sank into an apathetic pipe-sucking again; and outside the Midland trams departed noisily and lugubriously into the deeper night of the suburbs. So I went up to my room, and when I heard what it had to say, I told myself that I would never even hint a fault in commercial travellers again.

Fortunately, I had a book with me. It was Adlington's translation of *The Golden Ass.* About eleven o'clock, when a little warmth was creeping down towards my toes, I was reading the following passage: "And so, in this sort I went to supper, and behold I found at Byrrhena's house a great company of strangers, and of the chief and principall of the city: the beds, made of Citron and Ivory, were richly adorned and spred with cloath of gold, the Cups were garbished pretiously, and there were divers other things of sundry, fashion, but of like estimation and price: here stood a glasse gorgeously wrought, there stood another of Christall finely painted. There stood a cup of glittering silver, and here stood another of shining gold, and here was another of amber artificially carved and made with pretious stones. Finally, there was all things that might be desired: the servitors waited orderly at the table in rich apparell, the pages arayed in silke robes, did fill great gemmes and pearles made in forme of Cups, with excellent wine. Then one brought in Candles and torches, and when we were sat downe and placed in order we began to talke, to laugh, and to be merry. And Byrrhena spake unto me and sayd, I pray you, Cousine, how like you our countrey? Verily I thinke thoro is no other City which hath like Temples, Baynes, and other commodities, which we have here. Further we have abundance of household stuffe, we have pleasure, we have ease, and when the Roman merchants arrive in this City they are gently and quietly entertained. . . ." An idle tale of a distant place and a long time ago, when the wolves were howling in the deep forests of these Midlands. There are no wolves now, only trams, which still go groaning to their sheds long after a Commercial's light has been extinguished.

RESIDENTIAL

At first it seemed hard luck that our house should not be ready for us. After such a magnificent return to town, what an anti-climax to spend a week or two in an hotel! But now I cannot help thinking that this, after all, is the best approach. With a fortress of domesticity at our backs, we should have begun our life here by merely making raids on Vanity Fair, by rushing out, grabbing a bit of experience and then hurrying back home with it. As it is, we have no home. I see these days at the hotel as a kind of little gateway, a darkish place, overhung with foliage, where you may stand for a moment and catch a glimpse of the mad gala of life in town. The curtain is trembling and all its folds are brightening, but first there is a brief prelude for muted strings and muffled horns. Our stay here is the prelude. With a place of our own we should not have felt the same queer glow of anticipation. Besides, we should have been too real. Now, it is London that is real and we are shadowy; and that, I maintain, is a good way to begin all over again.

This is a residential hotel. You realise that at once when you talk to the manageress. Every profession or trade has its great phrase that comes so roundly and comfortingly to the speaker's tongue. In the world of the theatre, for example, managers and others bring out their great phrase when they say they have Played To Capacity, and vaudeville artistes produce theirs when they announce that their act was so well received that it Stopped The Show. Ten minutes' conversation with the manageress of this hotel left me in no doubt as to what the great phrase is in residential hotel circles; it arrived time after time, always in triumph and capital letters: Booked Right Through The Winter. If manageresses of residential hotels ever hold a conference, I imagine that the hall will be decorated by a banner on which will be emblazoned in letters of crimson and gold — Booked Right Through The Winter. Spring, summer, autumn — what are these? Nothing; a few dreamy weeks of leaf and cloud; seasons so vague, so attenuated, that even the most opulent retired tea-planter, in search of a permanent south bedroom and corner table in the dining-room, could not book right through them. But Winter — that grand bulk of weeks and months — ah, what a thick, heavy, solid season! — and how delightful to see good guests, quiet maiden ladies and jolly grey-haired bachelors, all with suitcases stuffed with preference shares, booking right through, spiring their way from October to April!

It follows that we ourselves are nothing here. Surrounded as we are by people who have Booked Right Through The Winter or may do so at any moment, we are mere outlines of human beings. Our beds must be made and our rooms tidied; food must be placed before us; but on our forms and faces is not that steady light of B.R.T.T.W.: we are ghosts. And we feel like ghosts. Everything in the hotel conspires to rob us of any lingering traces of substantial humanity. I have no desire to complain of the place, which is, I have no doubt, one of the best residential hotels in town. It is clean and comfortable. In place of the usual ironmonger's assistant or retired cloakroom attendant, a chef is employed in the kitchen. The lighting arrangements are such that you can read in bed and see your face in the mirror. There are three large public rooms, and they have an adequate supply of armchairs, card tables, ash trays, to say nothing of wireless sets and the grand piano, the gramophone, and the Ping-Pong table. What more could a guest, even a B.R.T.T.W., require?

Strange as it may appear, however, I must confess that I for one cannot sit in any of these rooms for more than ten minutes. They are rooms that demand proudly to be thoroughly inspected when you are first looking over the hotel, but once you are a guest they do not ask you to sit in them. Indeed, they contrive to resent your presence. You can sit on the edge of one of their huge armchairs, waiting for somebody, but that is all. If you try to settle down, you find after five minutes or so that you are so uneasy you are compelled to get up and walk about or try another room. The walls, the carpets, the empty chairs, these things stare at you, ask one another what you are doing there, and finally tell you to go. You feel as if you had sneaked into the window of a furniture shop and were sitting in one of the chairs there. I have yet to see a card on one of the card tables, and the only time I left a little ash in one of the ash trays I hurried out the moment afterwards, like a man who had just committed sacrilege.

Sometimes there are people in these three public rooms. In the smoking-room, which has as much chill leather in it as any club in London, I have seen three men talking in a corner. I have caught them there three times now, and each time they appeared to be talking about laundry shares. What a staggering creative artist there must be behind reality! If you and I had to find a topic for three men in a corner of a smoking-room, we might rack our brains for six months and then not light on one so strange. Shares, or laundries — yes; but not laundry shares. In the drawing-room, I once caught two dim middle-aged women sitting very close together and whispering, and on another occasion I found a young girl there, standing in front of the piano and idly picking out a tune with one or two fingers. She was obviously not a guest at the hotel, not of British birth and parentage, and very reckless. It is the foreigners who grapple with these rooms. I have actually seen two Germans playing Ping-Pong in the third room, and making nearly as much noise as they did in the dining-room. And last Sunday I heard an incredible din in this Ping-Pong chamber and discovered that it was being made by a party of about fifteen members of some Latin race. They had put two tables together and were apparently holding a family conference round them. They ranged from a little old gentleman, who looked like a gnome pretending to be an Italian Senator, to various lemon-coloured chits in their early teens. They were all talking at once and they were all enjoying themselves. The Latin races must be curiously insensitive to atmosphere, though possibly three generations and fifteen of you are able to create an atmosphere of your own.

Perhaps if there were fifteen of us, we could do something; but there are not, and we are ghosts. I have heard myself referred to, by members of the staff here, as "Number Twenty-Three," and it never occurred to me to resent it. I feel like Number Twenty-Three. I have no possessions beyond a suitcase of clothes and a little shelf of brushes, razors, and the like. I have no place of my own, for you cannot call a bedroom such a place. I am surrounded by people whose names and histories I do not know, just as if I were at the theatre or sitting in a bus. The waitress who brings me my food is pleasant and attentive, but if I were to drop dead in the street tomorrow she would not care a rap and within a day or so would be putting a slice of turbot or a cutlet in front of another Twenty-Three. The chambermaid only knows me as so much luggage and litter, a little different from the luggage and litter of the last Twenty-Three. The porter sees me as a possible five bob. The manageress hardly sees me at all, for what am I, with my mere fortnight or so, but a midge compared with the giant creatures who have booked Right Through The Winter? And how many of these creatures are there in all the residential hotels of London?

I think about them and am lost in a sad wonder. What epics of personal history have dwindled into breakfast, lunch, tea, dinner, bed, a south room, a corner table, in these places! You make your little pile or come into your own or win through, do something final and heroic, and then you find yourself a perpetual guest, honoured no doubt in the office, respected by the servants, but leading a spectral life. Nobody wants to hear what a trial Aunt Hilda was before she finally died and left you all her money. Nobody wants to hear your stories of India or Burma or China. How easy it must be to die in these places! — just a matter of not getting up one morning, of slipping away and booking right through a million winters.

ON VIEW

It is not true to say — as critics frequently do say — that flamboyant
romantic literature is not like life. Where that literature departs from life is
in being exciting, highly coloured, fantastic, all the time, in having no large
blank spaces. But there are times when life can only be expressed in a
flamboyant romantic fashion, for the fantastic stuff is there, under your
nose. We may spend months in a world as quiet and prosaic as Jane
Austen's and then suddenly we turn a corner — to find we have walked
into the Dickens world. It happened to me only yesterday.

We are staying in a little town on the Kentish coast, an old-fashioned
place but not Dickensy, far more reminiscent of *Black-Eyed Susan* and *All
in the Downs* and songs by Dibdin. Yesterday morning we noticed an
auctioneer's bill saying that the antique furniture and household effects of
Lilac Cottage, all to be sold by auction, were on view that morning. We
thought there would be no harm in looking over Lilac Cottage, which
might have a wonderful little walnut bureau or something of that sort
tucked away in a corner — you never know, do you? Nothing, you will
agree, could be more prosaic. We inquired our way to Lilac Cottage, at the
back of So-and-So Avenue. It took a great deal of finding. We were passed
from one helpful but puzzled townsman to another; we tried third turnings
to the right and fourth turnings to the left for at least half an hour. Finally,
we came near, but even then spent another ten minutes circling round the
house. Our last direction seemed to bring us to the railway lines, but we
discovered a very narrow little lane running by the side of the railway, and
at the end of this lane a small gateway leading to a garden that was a jungle
of weeds. We crept through gigantic briars and finally came to a little old
house. This was Lilac Cottage.

The threshold was simply so much rotten wood; you could have crumbled it in your hand. The interior was astonishing. I have never seen so
much dirt in all my life. Dust lay thick everywhere; huge cobwebs hung
from the walls; and every article of furniture was grimy beyond belief. The
atmosphere was choking. Long before you dared to touch anything, your
hand felt filthy. All the women were stepping delicately from room to

room, holding their skirts. All the men smoked furiously. You did not feel that the house had just been opened but that it had just been exhumed. The two rooms on the ground floor and the other two on the first floor were bad, but the other little places, where nothing was being sold, were horrors. I peeped into a kitchen in the basement, and then fled. The very rats must have left it years ago. And above there was a tiny bedroom — it had a bed in it and a straw mattress completely covered with thick black dust — that was a nightmare. In another little room I found a man with a long moustache kneeling on the floor and looking through an ancient box stuffed with letters. "I don't know how you can do it," I told him shudderingly. "I'm looking for stamps," he replied. "There's some been pinched already, stamps worth at least a fiver, stamps before the Penny Post came in. All pinched!" I had a picture of somebody creeping into that awful little house, groping through that box, looking for old stamps. Nearly all the things in the house were good. On the ground floor were dusty shapes that were discovered on examination to be charming old chairs, a spinet, bow-fronted chests of drawers, inlaid card tables, and the like. But it was the chief bedroom, where the women were so busy turning things over, that was most fascinating. On a fine four-poster bed were laid out exquisite old dresses and shawls and bundles of unused linen sheets. It was like finding fresh flowers in a dustbin. I heard some talk of wedding dresses. One was spread out, lighting up the room, a lovely shimmer of fabric. This, I was told, was a gem: a crinoline of silver and lilac brocade. There were other crinolines too, nearly as beautiful: green striped taffeta with black lace appliqué — so ran the expert description. The women there, forgetting the dust and their skirts and the spiders, turned over these and other garments and gave little cries of astonishment and delight. I had a sudden vision of a girl in the fifties, a very happy girl, pirouetting in these things before the mirror, trying this and trying that, wondering whether he would like her best in lilac and silver. There were some leather cases on top of a chest of drawers, and when I opened them they seemed at first to be nothing but slightly discoloured pieces of glass. But when I looked again, faces from a past age, girls with side-curls, whiskered young gentlemen with immense cravats, smiling or puzzled children, looked out at me. Probably among these faded daguerreotypes were several portraits of *him,* who would come down, like a whiskered and cravated god, to choose between the silver and lilac brocade and the green striped taffeta.

Yes, she had been a happy girl. Those vague faces of the daguerreotypes were once a host of approving relatives, smiling friends. And nobody had more luxuriant whiskers or cravats than he, who had said, again and again, that he loved her. And where could you find prettier dresses and shawls? Were not the very sheets the finest linen? There had been moments, probably when she was turning over these things just as the women were turning them over yesterday morning, when she had seen life stretching before her like a high road through one great golden valley. She had only to live on, just to breathe, to be happier and happier. And then, and then — dust, and more dust, first a grey film of it, and at last inches of black grime.

Do I imagine all this to be very romantic? I do. Do I know that I am being very sentimental? I do. Does it occur to me that I am merely a sentimental literary man who is not only embroidering but probably grossly distorting the facts? No, it doesn't, by Jingo! As I went through that little horror of a house yesterday, I learned some of the facts, and here they are and you can make of them what you will.

This house had been shut up for years. Its owner had lived there alone for a long period, and by the time she was middle-aged she was probably known to be cranky, eccentric, perhaps a little mad. I heard one woman, herself middle-aged, say yesterday: "She chased me many a time"; and I had a vision of this solitary woman, with the queer and even sinister reputation, running out of her remote little house to chase away the children who came to explore the fringes of the garden, climb the walls, and make faces at her. When she was past eighty she began to fail and at last had to be removed, filthy, horribly neglected, to the local workhouse infirmary, where finally she died, in her nineties. It was then discovered that she had been by no means penniless, as everybody imagined, but possessed a little fortune, something in the neighbourhood of ten thousand pounds. It is clear that she was a miser. But that is not why she kept all the crinolines, the lilac and silver brocade, the green striped taffeta, in which she would have peacocked through her honeymoon. Apparently the wedding was all arranged and then she was jilted. In fact, we have here another Miss Havisham. And those who like irony will enjoy the sequel to this old-fashioned story. There were the ten thousand pounds and this house and its furniture, and an heir had to be found. At last he was found, and he proved to be a rich American, who has recently been cruising the Mediterranean in his own yacht. When he was told about the furniture he is reported to have said: "Sell the lot. I don't care what it fetches."

So, yesterday morning, the antique furniture and household effects of Lilac Cottage were — like life — on view.

VIII. From SELF-SELECTED ESSAYS 1932

THE PROPHETS

There were four of them, three men and one woman, and I saw them in the public forum in Hyde Park. In the Nineties, which were crowded with professional Cockney humorists who gave us "glimpses of life" and jested desperately in and out of season, it was, I fancy, the fashion to regard these public meetings in Hyde Park as a magnificent free banquet of absurdity; the whole staff of *Punch* might have been seen any fine Sunday afternoon, pulling out their notebooks in the shadow of the Marble Arch; and women would titter and grow moist-eyed and men would roll about in their chairs and almost suffocate with laughter at the very mention of Hyde Park. In these days, now that we have exploded nearly everything, our gun-cotton, our ideals, and even our standard jokes, it is probably a sign of extreme youth or sentimental old age to think of these public meetings in the park as a glorious feast of fun. For my part, I have little interest in them, for they are usually conducted now by experienced tub-thumpers, old hands, and there is nobody more tedious after a first acquaintance than your old hand with his bag of cheap oratorical tricks, his face and voice of brass, his patched sordid dialectic. On the occasion when I saw this little group of four that I shall call the prophets, I walked round the assembled crowds without stopping to listen to any of the speakers. There seemed to be the usual meetings in progress: some orators roaring out their approval of God, others noisily assigning limits to His prestige and power, and others again loudly denying His existence; the philosophers, the saints and the angels were all being butchered by someone to make an artisan's holiday; and any idler present had the choice of some five or six entirely different universes. I was just turning away when I caught sight of the three men and the woman, the prophets, standing in a little empty space between two great knots of people. One was speaking and the other three were supporting him, and apparently they had no audience at all. Something about them, perhaps their pathetic isolation, rather attracted me, and I moved forward; but as I knew that if I planted myself boldly in front of them, all their eloquence would be directly addressed to me, I merely walked forward to the outskirts of the adjoining crowd and drew as near to my four as I could without appearing to listen to them.

This was sheer cowardice on my part and I suffered for it (as one always does), for I could not hear a word they said. On one side there was a noisy political meeting and a great deal of heckling and shouting and booing, and on the other, where I was standing, everybody was singing a very objectionable hymn under the leadership of a perspiring Salvation Army official. I had to content myself with watching my little group, apparently ignored by everybody else and at once absurd and pathetic in its isolation. All three men had beards. This was no mere coincidence, for there was something about these beards that suggested they were there on principle; they were all long beards that had obviously been allowed to go their own way, beards that had demanded and obtained self-determination. Two of the men were elderly and their beards were fairly full and satisfying, but the other, an under-nourished fellow with bulging eyes, was much younger, and his beard, though longish, was thin, patchy and straggling — a horrid sight. No doubt it was a rule in the tiny sect to which they obviously belonged that all male members should grow their beards. Many tiny religious sects have, I fancy, some such rule. There is nothing odd in this, because if a sect is only small enough all its members become prophets, and prophecy demands that the chins in its service should not wag uncovered. Indeed, there is a type of beard, long and full, that belongs to the prophet alone. This old and honourable connection between prophecy and beards is easily explained. Growing a long beard is the simplest way of going into the wilderness. The man who shaves is the man who has come to terms with this world. He who has foreseen the impending Doomsday cannot be expected to lather his face briskly every morning or come out of his apocalyptic vision in order to strop a razor; nor can a prophet, no matter how minor, consort with barbers, who care only for sport and sixpences and not at all for the wrath to come. Thus, the tiny sects, made up almost entirely of prophets, are right to insist upon beards, and these three men, in letting themselves be overrun by their strange growths, were only doing their duty.

When I first drew near, one of the two elderly men was taking a turn on the little wooden soap-box and addressing a heedless world, but after some time he was relieved by the others. They were all much less vehement (so far as my eyes could judge of the matter) and more restrained in manner than the general run of park orators; they gave me the impression of men who knew that it was their duty not to denounce, not to argue furiously, not to challenge and criticise, but to testify, without unnecessary violence, to the truth that was within them, a truth, I imagine, of which they had almost a monopoly. Every now and again, the little chorus of three, supporting the speaker, would nod their heads and make some exclamation to show their approval. The younger man, he of the vile beard and the under-nourished look, was the most interesting. When he mounted the soap-box, there happened to be a moment's quietness on either side, where the hymn-singing and heckling were still in progress, and I did actually catch the first two words of his discourse. In a thin reedy voice, the very tones of one who is nourished chiefly on starry and insubstantial fare, who feeds on tea and bread-and-butter and visions, he cried, "We believe . . ." And then the noise began again, and I did not catch another word, nor do I know to this day what they do believe. In all probability the doctrines of their micro-scopic sect are based on some strange little heresy that has persisted in odd corners, among bakers and saddlers in obscure towns, for centuries; and it is more than likely that there is much talk of the end of the world and the coming reign of the saints in the meetings of the sect. For all their quietness and mild glances, however, there was an apocalyptic gleam in their eyes, particularly in those of the younger man, and their beards had not sprouted on behalf of any shallow, time-serving sort of creed. Perhaps they knew the very date when the world was to be withered away and the stars were to drop from the sky like rotten fruit, and had travelled many a league with their soap-box to give us warning; perhaps they were there ready to barter an eternity of bliss for half an hour of our attention, and, because we did not choose to listen, already saw the angel of death making ready his sword above our heads. But no, if they believed that things were at such a desperate pass, surely they would not have been so calm, surely they would have raised their voices and not allowed every roaring fool in the park to catch the attention of the doomed city.

The woman did not speak, though, like the rest, she occasionally nodded her head in approbation. She was a sturdy middle-aged woman, who looked better fed and more sensible than her men-folk. Undoubtedly she had come with one of the men, and was probably his mother, wife or sister; she had accepted the creed when she accepted the personal relation, and being a motherly sort, she probably not only mothered the man, but mothered his poor little creed too. Against the background of these bearded fantastic, with all their starry folly, she looked robust and earthy, as solid as a hill. If her man had taken to drink instead of prophecy, she would have seen him through with that too, and would have gone with him into the public-houses to see that he did not take too much and get himself into trouble. As it was, she had come to Hyde Park to stand by the soap-box and nod her head with the rest, but doubtless all in a dream, her mind being busy with hurrying little images, with shifting faces, vague cries from the past, and the remembered grasp of little children; while outside the sun went down the sky, the crowds sang or cheered or heckled or drifted away, the voice just above her head droned on in the old way she knew so well, and she stood there ("like a fool," perhaps she thought) with aching feet, still nodding her head though no one listened or stopped to look.

As I watched this ineffectual quartet, in their motives like gods and in their wit like sheep, I pestered myself with vain questions. Where had they come from and where would they go to? To what strange place would they carry themselves, their beards and their soap-box? What did they do for a living? Did they go to workshops and factories and quietly endure the rough chaff of the others, comforted by the knowledge that they were men set apart, men guided miraculously by an inner light to the truth? Were they the only members of their set or were they merely the few who had volunteered for this particular duty? Where did they meet and what did they do? Of what would they talk when they were on the way home from the park? Were they always conscious of their mission, their great destiny, or did they relapse, on ordinary days, into commonplace artisans or shop-keepers, strangely bearded? Were they moved to come to this place by an ecstasy of conviction that left them no choice but to express themselves in public, whether they made converts or not? And supposing, I said to myself, that these people, whom you think absurd, whose beliefs you actually know nothing about, are in the right after all, that by some miracle they have stumbled upon the key to the universe and were busy on the soap-box tearing the problem of good and evil to shreds, that the date when these three men first met will be celebrated down the ages, that the younger one with the bulging eyes will ultimately turn human history in a new direction . . . what then? And I went on "supposing" and "what then"-ing to myself for some time, but nevertheless while I was doing this I was hurrying away from the three prophets and the woman, for I knew that time was getting on, and I was anxious not to be late for tea.

DISSOLUTION IN HAYMARKET

Surely there is hardly a street in London less morbid, more determined in its own sedate fashion to make something out of life, than Haymarket. Indeed, now I come to think of it, Haymarket is one of my favourite thoroughfares. It has a pleasant gentlemanly air, with just a suggestion of the eighteenth century, and has, too, all manner of interesting things in it. To begin with, there are its two large theatres, one of which is associated in my mind with a number of charming plays, and the other — I regret to say — only with camels. There are the Stores and a fine old tobacco shop, and, best of all, the shipping agents with their model steamers and little panoramas. Those steamers alone — and there are quite a number of them — lift the whole street high above the common level. The sight of them prevents London from closing in on you, for it suddenly opens some little windows in what seems the grey wall of the street, and through these windows come flashing the bright dunes and red roofs of Denmark or the shining peaks of the Sierra Nevada. If this is not enough, flanking them you have the actual windows of the little panoramas, which artfully combine in themselves the lure of travel and the excitement of a toy theatre. No, it would be hard to find a London street less morbid, less gloomy, more likely to augment rather than diminish one's zest for life.

Yet as I was journeying on a bus down Haymarket the other day, about the lunch hour, there suddenly came crashing down upon me a mood such as I have never known before. It was as if a huge black stone had been flung into the pool of my consciousness. It all happened (as we were told it would) in the twinkling of an eye. Everything was changed. The whole cheerful pageant of the street immediately crumpled and collapsed, with all its wavering pattern of light and shade, its heartening sights and sounds, its warm humanity, its suggestion of permanence, and I was left shivering in the middle of a tragedy. Not something magnificent, you understand, with funereal guns roaring out over the battlements of Elsinore or queens with bright hair dying for love, nothing after the high Roman fashion; but a dreary tragedy of cheated fools and illusions blown to the winds, of withering and decay, dust and worms. I saw this world for a moment or so through the hollow eyes of the prophets and the great pessimists, and what I saw left me shivering with cold and sick at heart. Nor did there remain with me that cosy painted chamber of the mind into which I might retire, there to forget in comfort, for it, too, was desolated, heaped about with cold ashes and with its tattered curtains flapping in the wind. All the stir and noise and glitter seemed nothing but fast shredding pigment on a dead face.

I might have been old Donne himself, brooding over corruption and putrefaction and the gnawing worm; and it was his words that returned to me: ". . . all our life is but a going out to the place of execution, to death." What was the bus I was in but a greasy tumbril, and what were all of us, jogging there empty-eyed, littered with our foolish paraphernalia of newspapers, umbrellas, parcels, but a company of the doomed? There we were, so many grinning skeletons masquerading in this brief and bitter carnival as fat citizens, charwomen, bus conductors, chorus girls; idly juggling with thoughts of our destinations, the offices, restaurants, clubs, theatres that claimed us; when, in truth, we had all but one sure destination — perhaps round the next corner — the narrow grave. "The sun is setting to thee, and that for ever." And on the face of everyone there, hurrying with me to the place of execution, I read the marks of weakness and decay, and seemed to see that untiring hand at work furrowing the brow and dimming the eyes. Everywhere was dissolution. The whole street was mouldering and rotting, hastening with all that was in it to its inevitable end. The crowds I saw through the windows seemed made up of creatures that were either gross or wasted, shuffling, bent, twisted in limb, already bleached and mangled by disease; and here and there among the crowd, in bright contrast and yet infinitely more pitiful, were the few who had youth and strength and beauty, who moved as if they thought they could live for ever — who had not yet heard, from afar, the hammering, the slow tread, the pattering of earth upon the coffin.

There was something more than the old thought, death is certain, festering in the heart of that mood. That, indeed, is a thought we are always quite willing to salute, with a mere wave of the hand, but are really very unready to entertain, except when we make its first acquaintance in childhood, when it has a trick of bringing a whole host of grimacing shadows about our bedsides. But there was something more behind that sudden tragic vision I had. There was a sense of universal dissolution, of this life as a pitiful piece of cheating, of bright promise all ruthlessly scattered. Nothing remained but the certainty of decay and death. The more you loved life, delighting in whatever it had of beauty and goodness to offer you, the more openly you bared your breast for the stroke of its dagger. I saw all of us there — my fellow-passengers in the bus, the driver and the conductor, the policeman and the hawkers, the playgoers waiting at the pit door, the crowds shopping or loafing — as the victims of this great treachery, lured into worshipping a loveliness that must fade and pass, trapped into setting our hearts upon things we can never keep with us, upon beings who smile for an hour and then miserably perish. It is well, I thought, for the grandest of our old preachers to say: "We long for perishing meat, and fill our stomachs with corruption; we look after white and red, and the weaker beauties of the night; we are passionate after rings and seals, and enraged at the breaking of a crystal," and then to make it plain that these things will not avail us. But other and nobler things, it seemed to me, would avail us even less, for the more we opened our hearts, making ourselves eager and loving, the more certain amid this universal dissolution was our ultimate misery. We are the poor playthings of Time, dandled for an hour and then flung to rot in a corner; and yet we are all born, as was said of Coleridge, hungering for Eternity.

So brimmed with such thoughts, feelings, old quotations, strange images, clustering together like the pieces in a kaleidoscope to form one tragic vision of things, I was carried down the desolated length of Haymarket, where man spendeth his vain life as a shadow. As those last words will suggest, my mood had by that time crystallised into the utter hopelessness of that other and greater Preacher. Vanity of vanities! Had I been a natural man instead of the smooth mountebank demanded by decency and encouraged by my natural timidity, I should have descended from the bus, put ashes on my head, and cried "Woe!" to the assembled hawkers and playgoers and policemen, stunning them with gigantic metaphors. That is what, in my heart, I wanted to do, so surely was I possessed by this sudden hopeless vision and by a mixed feeling of contempt and pity for my fellow mortals. Yet I sat there, quietly enough, and still well aware of the fact that I was on my way to lunch with two friends at a club not very far away. I was, as it were, purely automatically aware of this fact, for in those last moments, so rapt had I been in my vision, I had no sense even of personal identity. But I moved forward, as a man might over a darkening field of battle, towards the club and my friends, and arrived there and greeted them in a kind of dream; and then, suddenly, out of my dream, I looked at them sharply and curiously, these friends of mine, whose grim sentence and that of all they held dear still seemed to be ringing in my ears. How strangely childish, touchingly naïve, their smiling confidence, their little preoccupations, their chatter. I saw them seating themselves opposite me at the lunch table, and it was as if they were people acting on a distant stage; yet I did not feel completely detached from them, but, on the contrary, felt a kind of tenderness for them and all their little toys and antics. Then I heard one of these doomed creatures propose that we should drink Burgundy. I stood out for something lighter, for though I like a glass of Burgundy as well as the next man, I maintain it is far too heavy for lunch.

ON THE MOORS

If you go from Bradford to Bingley, from Bingley to Eldwick, then up the hill from Eldwick, you arrive at Dick Hudson's. Mr. Hudson will not be there to greet you, because he has been dead this long time. But the old grey inn that stands on the edge of the moors is called by his name and by no other. Even the little bus that runs up there now has "Dick Hudson's" boldly painted on its signboard. And there's a pleasant little immortality for you. "We'll go," they say to one another in Bradford, and have said as long as I can remember — "we'll go as far as Dick Hudson's." If you start from the other end, climbing the moorland track from Ilkley, you will inevitably come to Dick Hudson's when you finally drop down from the high moor, and if the hour is right, you will inevitably have a pint of bitter at Dick's. That is what I did, the other day. I returned, after years of southern exile, to the moors, and began by having two pints at Dick's. And I was mightily relieved to find it still there, the same old grey building, the same cool interior, still smelling of good beer and fried ham; for at any moment now, they may begin monkeying with the old place, turning it into an ice-cream parlour or some such horror.

If you live in Bradford, Shipley, Keighley, you kindle at the sound of Dick Hudson's. That is not merely because you have been so often refreshed there, but chiefly because you know it is the most familiar gateway to the moors. The moors to the West Riding folk are something more than a picnic place, a pretty bit of local country-side. They are the grand escape. In the West Riding towns you have something to escape from; for industrial mankind has done its worst there. But the moors are always waiting for you, and you have only to leave the towns for an hour or two, climbing the hills, to see them dwindle into a vague smoulder and a sheen of glass roofs in the valleys, then vanish, and perhaps be forgotten. The moors are there, miles and miles of country-side that has not changed for centuries, and you have only to squeeze through the little hole in the wall, just beyond Dick Hudson's, to take your fill of them. It does not matter who you are, for they are yours while you are there, and the richest wool man in the town can claim no more right in them than you can. Once through that hole in the wall, you have escaped miraculously; and if you were a favoured lad in a fairy tale you could have no better luck, no more elaborate transformation worked for you, for one afternoon. So if you are a stranger to those parts and should visit them, do not let the black streets, the monotonous rows of little houses almost set on end, the trams that drone away between factories, the whole grim paraphernalia of old-fashioned industrialism, depress you too much, but please remember that the winds that suddenly swoop down on the sooty slates have come over leagues of moorland and still have the queer salty tang in them.

Well, I had my pints at Dick Hudson's, went through the little hole in the wall, and climbed onto the moor, as I had so many times before and yet had not done for many a year. It was a weekday and very quiet. The sun was hot and seemed to smite these uplands, bruising every blade and blossom so that they sent out sharp odours. Once more I seemed to be walking on the roof of England. The singing larks only rose a little way from the ground, as if they were high enough now. The winds came sliding or shooting over the top, at no more than shoulder height, and there was in them the old magical scent, earthy enough and yet with always something of the sea in it, that strange saltiness. Against the brown hillsides I saw the tender green of the young bracken. There, once more, were the tumbled rocks, floating in and out of the great cloud shadows; the ruined byres and the mysterious stone walls; the granite dust of the moorland path glittering in the sunlight. I heard again the baa-ing of the moorland sheep, like complaining voices coming from great hollows. Everything there was as it had always been.

Down in the valleys, among the streets I once knew so well, they were putting up new buildings and tearing down old ones, they were going into bankruptcy or starting afresh, old men were dying and young men were marrying, and nothing was standing still. The life of the town was hurrying away from the life that I once knew, and down there, among the stalwarts that had so suddenly and strangely grown bent, grey and old, and the babies that had so suddenly and strangely shot up into young men and women, I was rapidly becoming a man from another place, a stranger. But up there, on the moors, there were no changes at all. I saw what I had always seen, and there was no sense that did not receive the same old benediction.

Yet it was not the same. I sat down on the smooth springy grass, with my back against a rock, and as I smoked my pipe in that high lonely place, I tried to disentangle it all. I was happy to be there again, and not a sight, a sound, an odour, that returned to me failed to give me pleasure, and yet in this happiness there was the strangest melancholy. It was as if there was between me and these dear and familiar sights and sounds a sheet of glass. I felt as if I had only to pluck the ling and heather at my side for it to wither and crumble in my hand. I might have been a man on parole for one golden afternoon from some distant internment camp. There were no tears in my eyes but I will swear my mind knew the salt glitter of them. If I had spoken to a fellow-traveller then, he would have concluded that I was a man who had once known great happiness in these parts and had then gone into some sad exile. And he would have been wrong. I am happier now than ever I was when I used to come to these moors week in and week out, when I was on the easiest and friendliest terms with them, and every rock and clump of heather spoke to me in my own language. When I walked these moors then, or stretched myself on the grassy carpet in the sun, hour after hour, I spent my time dreaming of the happiness that would be mine when I should be as I actually am now. I do not say that I was really unhappy in those days, for I was a healthy youngster with plenty of things to do and with many good friends, but I was certainly restless and dissatisfied and apt to be sulkily despondent in a world that did not appear to appreciate my unique merit. I thought I was a fine fellow then, but nevertheless I had not acquired that armour of conceit which begins to protect our self-esteem later in life, that armour which compels some elderly members of my profession to move so ponderously. I could be snubbed then, could retire in haste, all hot and pricking, from many a company. There is no doubt whatever that I am happier now.

What hocus-pocus, what sentimental attitudinising, was it then that made me feel so melancholy, the other afternoon on the moors? I was not an exile at all. If I want to live near the moors and visit them every day, there is nothing to prevent me. I could go there, and stay there, tomorrow, if I really wanted to. I know very well that I don't want to, that I would much rather live where I do live. I am well aware of the fact that the moors would bore me very soon and that I get more out of them by visiting them now and again than I ever would by living near them. Like most people, I have lost several persons very dear to me, but, there again, to be honest, I must confess that there is nobody who is associated with the moors in my mind who is now lost to me. The only possible person is that other, younger self, who had trod these very paths so often; but then, I do not mourn him. Let the young cub perish. First youth has gone, it is true, but I do not see that there is anything specially admirable in early youth. I have strength and vigour, a sense of fun and a sense of wonder, still with me, and I have not the slightest desire to be nineteen again. All this I pointed out to myself, as I sat against that rock and watched the great purple cloud shadows drift across the moorland, but that feeling of melancholy remained and would not budge. It was like one horn, amid the happy tumult of a full orchestra, ceaselessly sounding a little theme of despair. If the moors were real, then I was a ghost. If I was real, then all this sober richness of bracken and heather and tumbled rock and blue sky was a mirage, a bubble landscape that one determined forefinger could prick so that it gave a wink and then vanished for ever. I returned, a man in a puzzling dream, but also a hot and thirsty man, to Dick Hudson's.

THESE OUR ACTORS

I crossed Piccadilly Circus and then walked into another world. I did this by meeting a man I know, a man whose brother helps to run an agency for film actors. We began by threading our way through that little tangle of streets behind Regent Street and climbing some narrow stairs. At the top of those stairs was a small, noisy, smoky, and friendly club, used by people connected with the film industry, especially actors. These were not the people who go on with the crowd at a guinea a day, nor were they, for the most part, the stars. They were mostly character actors. We ate our cold silverside of beef and salad, surrounded by characters, who all ate, drank, smoked, talked, and gesticulated with such gusto that you would have sworn the whole scene was being taken down on celluloid. In the other room — the bar, lounge, or smoking-room — roistering companionship was being registered magnificently. Tall heavies, with colossal eyebrows and chins, roared "Hello, ol' man!" to family solicitors, doctors, and mild father parts, and slapped them on the back. Heroic young men with waved hair shook hands as if they had just encountered one another in the Brazilian jungle. Whiskies and beers were tossed down as if it was the young squire's twenty-first birthday and the Old Hall was ringing with the cheers of the assembled tenants. "How's it going, ol' man?" they asked one another, and to see them looking so intently at one another, eyebrows raised, hand outstretched, you would have sworn that the plot was thickening every second.

From this club we went to the office of the film agency. This office was mostly waiting-room. It was obviously a place where you waited and waited and waited. Photographs of that waiting-room ought to be supplied to anxious parents whose daughters have announced their intention of becoming film actresses. "You imagine," those parents ought to say to their daughters, "that in a very short time you will be at Elstree, on the 'lot,' playing the part of the beautiful Lady Helen, possibly extending your be-diamonded arms towards the handsome Jameson Thomas. You are wrong. You will be spending nearly all your waking hours in that waiting-room, hoping against hope that there is 'something for you,' that something being the chance of falling into a duckpond or jumping out of a car, at one guinea per day." We marched into the private office, which was full of photographs of noble profiles, signed by their delighted owners. A call came through the telephone, demanding the crew of a destroyer. Word was sent out at once that imitation sailors were in demand, and after a little interval, batch after batch of men were admitted, all neat and smiling, though it must have been weeks since some of them had earned even a guinea.

The two agents looked at them, very quickly. "Sorry, you're not tall enough," they would say to one man. "Sorry, too old," would dismiss another. And the men who were thus dismissed still smiled, and I think Drake or Nelson, seeing those smiles, would have signed them on, for their courage. This film agency business is no job for me; I should be too soft for the work, never finding it possible to turn one of these smiling waiting men away. They all deserve medals — to say nothing of guineas — for the way in which they keep themselves so trim, turning out every day with clean collars, creased trousers, and carefully brushed coats. I should like to have heard all their stories, and if I were a powerful producer, I should scrap the silly story on which I was engaged, and demand to make a film out of the lives of these hangers-on, beginning with a "shot" of one of them creasing his trousers in some distant and dingy little lodging before he set out to smile and wait, wait and smile.

A lady sailed in, very large, very dignified, the image of a duchess if duchesses really contrived to look the part. She leaned over the office table, superbly confidential. "Anything else for me, my dear?" she began. I gathered she was not too well pleased with the crowd work on which she was engaged. After a few sentences that I could not catch, she continued: "Mind you, my dear, I don't mind fighting with the Lascars at all. It's fun, so long as they're sober. But when they get filled with black beer, it's too much, really it is, too much. I'm black and blue," she concluded, smiling graciously. You would have thought she was opening a charity bazaar. "You do understand, don't you, my dear? That's right. If there is anything you know, just — er —" and, dropping the most condescending smiles all round, she departed.

She was followed by a confident young man with side whiskers. Was there anything for him? "Can you drop the side-boards?" he was asked. He shook his head. "Sorry, I can't," he said. "I'm on continuity with 'em." And so they left us, all three of them, the two whiskers and the young man they supported. There is in this queer film world a sort of hirsute gardening. An important producer can set beards and whiskers in motion for miles around. Apparently, the more fastidious producers will not tolerate false beards and whiskers: they must have the real thing. One of these gentlemen undertook to do a mid-Victorian film, a short time ago, and could not get a proper cast together at first, among so many shaven cheeks and chins. Within a month, however, those little streets running behind Regent Street or off Shaftesbury Avenue were bristling with full beards and Dundreary whiskers. The word had gone forth that hairy faces were wanted, and immediately all razors were put away. They have just been brought out again for the destroyer crew.

I was then taken round to the place where the humbler sort of film actors and actresses amuse themselves. I think it was once a night club, and its walls still bear traces of that determined jollity which is so depressing in night clubs. There is a good long room, with a dancing floor, little tables scattered about, and a refreshment bar. There are hardly any real people in that place; they are all types. Monocled dude drinks beer there with picturesque old artist type. Detective partners humorous landlady at bridge against middle-aged aristocrat and refined girl. Vamps and innocent girls fresh from Peroxideshire share a pot of tea and a great deal of chat. Rustics borrow matches and tobacco from East Enders (male). The Dear Little Mother explains to Sinister Hag just what she really did say to the assistant producer. In fact, there can be seen in that room all the faces you notice in any crowd scene on the films. Several of them deliberately registered things at me, being under the impression that I was a new producer, for they had never seen me before and I was there in the company of well-known agents.

I believe that all manner of film folk occasionally use this Guild club room, but obviously most of the people there were simply supers, on the guinea-a-day basis. Some of them, it was clear, were both young and ambitious, and hoped to rise in their strange shadowy profession. Others were not strictly actors at all, but men and women who had discovered that there was a market, some occasional demand, for their squint or broken noses or goatee beards or dignified appearance. Others again were old hands, who had once been on the Halls or the "Legit.," and were now taking an occasional toll of twenty-one shillings from the new thing that had closed so many theatres over their heads. I caught sight of one broken old man who had once topped the bill on the Halls, but now was lucky to get an odd day's work as a tramp or outcast of the slums in a crowd scene. I was told that between jobs he slept on the Embankment. You may see his ruined face, for five seconds, the next time you visit a picture theatre.

STRANGE ENCOUNTER

Yesterday, the people in the bungalow below took us to Hartland in their car. We went through Stratton, whose oldest inn has a notice that reminds you that the battle of Stamford Hill was fought just round the corner. And there are such perils, such hairbreadth escapes, in Stratton's narrow and twisting street, where gigantic buses miss you by an inch, that all the battles of that Civil War seem part of an idyll, old and happy, far-off things. We went, through Kilkhampton, where I saw nothing of interest except one of those queer families, those monstrous collections of odd humans, that you never see except when you are travelling. It is impossible to imagine them at home. We climbed to the top of a rustling moor, and then crossed it in happy solitude. We ran down steep and narrow lanes, and at last came to the headland where there is a crazy hotel and the ruins of Hartland Quay. A green sea shook itself now and again and then went creaming over the rocks. It was far below the shattered brickwork of the old quay, but you felt it was giving a glance in that direction every now and then, and muttering, "Just try building another breakwater, that's all! Just try it!" Lundy, that familiar speck, was now a big fat rock of an island, almost absurdly melodramatic. I spent a dreamy half-hour — and every scribbler will know how pleasant it was — vaguely planning a thriller that would have a Lundy chapter or two in it. The others, I believe, were trying to decide whether the blackbird fluttering about the face of the cliff really was a raven. Perhaps it was, as we shall see, and was trying to cry "Nevermore."

We walked to the top of the cliff, and watched some great buzzard hawks go wheeling up into the blue. There were sweet smells, an old intoxication, in the air. To have the heather about your feet and to look out to sea is to be happy, so happy that you feel it is incredible that you will not live for ever. But the shadow of mortality soon fell upon us. We arrived at Stoke Church. This church is miles from anywhere, except from the rocks and foam and the ruined quay, the gulls and ravens and hawks, yet it lifts a great tower to the sky, just as if the bustling plains of Flanders were beneath it. There are a few white-washed cottages, a few gnarled trees, and this church with its enormous tower. We wandered about the churchyard, in which a whole host has been buried, so that mounds and stones almost jostle one another. There you may meet generations of Chopes and Prusts and Okes, whole centuries of them. Their stones show a grim appreciation of the fact of death. Our ancestors may have had their weaknesses, but sentimentality about death was not one of them. They lived round the churchyard. Not a single passing coffin escaped their eyes. When they died themselves, they pointed out, in clear inch lettering in granite, that you would soon be dead too. The Shropshire Lad himself had not a better eye for all the signs of mortality, but they did not make the same fuss about it. Here was the older Western Front and all was quiet upon it, but decency and reticence had been given a turn too. In the lovely old interior of the church was a tablet to a local gentleman, and he was described, simply and superbly, as "a plain good man." I do not think that I am a plain good man, but I felt that here was a community in which I could have lived without frequently suspecting that we were all mad together.

And it was here, in this remote western corner, this place of foam and heather and great wild birds, among the unknown Chopes and Okes and Prusts, that I discovered my old publisher — John Lane. He lies in this very churchyard, and in the church itself there is a memorial tablet to him. It was the queerest, the most startling encounter. I knew that he came from some little place in Devonshire, but I had forgotten — if I ever knew — that it was Hartland, and that he was buried in Stoke Church. I stared and stared at his name. The memory of the man himself returned to me, very vividly. I only knew him during his last years. He was my first London publisher, and for several years I was his "reader." He used to give me lunch at his clubs, the Reform and the Cocoa Tree, and dinner down at Lancaster Gate. I saw again his short figure, his bearded face, his peering vague eyes. I heard again his curiously characteristic tones, at once a little hoarse and squeaky. It seemed only a month or two ago since we were sitting in some corner, heavy with cigar smoke, and I was listening to his rambling good talk about some portrait he had picked up or the idiosyncracies of one of his older poets. He was one of those men — and I mean only the men with whom one has business relations — of whom it might be said that they cannot be approved of or recommended and yet cannot be disliked. He was one of the old school of publishers, a sort of genial literary brigand, who believed quite sincerely that authors should not have any money, and so whittled down your terms to nearly nothing, but at the same time poured champagne and liqueur brandy down your throat and pressed upon you the largest cigars. He would give you anything so long as it was not a matter of percentages. The idea of an author who had an agent and a decent bank account and artful notions about dramatic rights shocked him. Authors to him were either people in society with incomes or wild geniuses who simply needed a good lunch or dinner now and again to keep them going. He always seemed to know about books, though I can never believe he ever read any. He was a character, and I liked him enormously.

Devon boys have roaméd about these heathery Hartland cliffs, gone out into the world and, after many Odysseys, have returned to this remote place to die. But few of them, for all the epics of Moorish galleys, sacked towns, and sunken gold, can have had a queerer history than this of John Lane. Only the day before I had been reading an advance copy of Miss Viola Meynell's delightful life of her mother, Alice Meynell, and John Lane had popped up there. He pops up everywhere in the Nineties. He was himself an intensely respectable man, a solid bourgeois, but as a publisher he had a flair and knew when the moment had arrived for naughtiness and fine writing and devil take the suburbs. As I strolled away from that church-yard, where cavalier's man, eighteenth-century farmhand, and Victorian coastguard all lie so peacefully together, and their times seem all one under that wide gull-haunted sky, I thought about the queer adventures of this wandering Devonian. How far away, how odd, seemed all the old activities of that Bodley Head! The "nest of singing birds." The "decadents." Beardsley and Harland and the Yellow Book. "I have been true to thee, Cynara, in my fashion." John Davidson, with his ballads and eclogues. Max Beerbohm's *Works*. Le Gallienne's *Quest of the Golden Girl*. The *Keynotes* Series. And the little man with the peaked beard and the near-sighted eyes threaded his way through these things, smoked his cigar at the Reform and the Cocoa Tree, surveyed his first editions and portraits at Lancaster Gate, conjured Anatole France into yellow-coloured English volumes, and then left what was mortal of him under the shadow of these Hartland Cliffs.

DIFFERENT INSIDE

I have been misunderstood and wrongly accused so many times that I ought to be able now to shrug my shoulders, not merely suffering in silence (for I know that protest is useless) but being indifferent, not suffering at all. Yet every other day or so something happens and I see once more what an ill-fated fellow I am. Only last night, for example, when we were playing bridge at my cousin's, she accused me of being far too pleased with myself when I contrived (not unskilfully, let me admit) to be four up in spades. The fact is, of course, that she was still rather annoyed because she had for once been overcalled, she who calls so wildly and unscrupulously and always forgets to pay, or at least forgets to pay me, when she loses. That is not the point, however, and I have no intention of discussing my cousin's fantastic ethics. The trouble is that I know very well she had evidence enough on which to base her accusation. No doubt my face was one vast ill-mannered grin of triumph, a revolting sight, and yet I was not feeling jubilant, ready to crow at my victory, but only mildly pleased with myself. I did not even know I was looking pleased, having forgotten for the moment the tricks my face plays on me. I can well believe, however, that I presented to the company a front that irritated everybody. Are other people, I wonder, as plagued by their faces as I am by mine, which thus monstrously exaggerates and distorts every feeling it is called upon to express; or do I suffer alone — a man with a calm philosophic mind but with a face that long ago decided to go on the stage, and the melodramatic stage at that, a man with his heart in the right place but with his features in Hollywood?

When I first entered adult life I imagined, like the young idiot I then was, that I had complete control of my face. I was convinced that I could permit myself to feel anything behind that bland disguise. When I went out for the evening and found myself becoming more and more bored by the company, I was sure that nobody but myself was aware of the fact. I set my face, as best I could from behind, to register a polite or even eager interest; I put on a smile and kept it there, left my eyes to sparkle away, and so forth; and then felt, even though the smile seemed rather stiff towards the end of the evening, that I could relapse with safety into comfortable boredom. As I never saw myself, it was some time before I was disillusioned. We never lose any of our illusions about ourselves in the company of strangers. But I made friends, and in this, as in other matters, they very quickly disillusioned me as they strolled, in the usual friendly fashion, through the house of my mind and casually opened a few windows here and there to let in the east wind. One would say: "Dullish at the So-and-so's the other night, I thought. You looked dreadfully bored." A succession of such remarks soon revealed to me the true state of things, and I realised that I had been deceiving myself. It was not for me to try to look one thing when I was thinking and feeling another. The idea of myself as one of your smooth fellows, made for diplomacy and the best society, for ever charming yet secretly tired of it all, would no longer hold, and, bearing in mind my newer and truer relations with my face, I was compelled to revise my estimate of myself.

There was, however, nothing alarming or even really disappointing in the situation. I was not sorry to be free from the strain of a diplomatic bearing, and congratulated myself on the fact that the higher types of human beings do not wear a smooth and impassive front. There is nothing better than an open, honest countenance, frankly expressing to the world its owner's feelings. I thought so then and I think so still, though now my opinion is worth more if only because it is more disinterested. I imagined then that mine was one of those open, honest faces, and was happy in this belief until the cumulative effect of a series of misunderstandings, of which that one last night is a good example, compelled me to take stock of myself once more, with the result that I was disillusioned once and for all. I found that people were always telling me not to be so angry when, in actual fact, I was only slightly annoyed, were for ever asking me why I was so jubilant when in truth I was only mildly pleased, were constantly suggesting that I should not glare furiously at strangers when I was only conscious of feeling a little curious. At last I realised the truth. My face did not even honestly reflect my mind but grossly caricatured it. I was carrying into all companies a monstrous libel of myself. It was as if I were compelled to wear a set of features that did not belong to me at all but to some other and very different kind of man. Small wonder, then, that I should be so frequently misjudged, for it is not unnatural that people should imagine that these facial antics, for which I am held responsible though they seem to be entirely beyond my control, are an indication of my state of mind. How are they to know that my face has apparently an independent existence, setting to work merely on a hint from my mind and then going on in a fashion of which I strongly disapprove.

That is the irony of the situation. My face would seem to belong to a type of man I dislike. It is a theatrical, temperamental affair, for ever rushing out to extremes, whereas I am all for moderation. I do not pretend to absolute philosophic calm and detachment, but — whatever my acquaintances, the deluded audience of this face, may say to the contrary — I am certainly not a man of strong feelings, one of those people who must be excited about something, who are not happy unless they are in the depths of misery or find all existence wretched because they do not feel ecstatic, who must be always yearning and burning, loving and hating, laughing and crying. Not only have I a contempt for such persons, but I could not imitate them if I would. Such emotions as I have are small and safe and never likely to get out of hand. Ecstasy and despair do not come my way and are never likely to be encountered in the easy rambles that my mind takes every day. My attitude towards my fellow-creatures is one of timid goodwill, tempered here by tranquil affection and there by a faint hostility. Even the kind of man who ought, at this moment, to be wearing my face only arouses a dislike that stops very far short of definite hatred. When, let us say (for last night still rankles), I win a game, I am only conscious of feeling a slight pleasure, spiced by just the slightest sense of triumph; and when I lose, as I do very frequently, I am certain that I am visited by nothing stronger than a tiny feeling of disappointment, a mere mental sigh. I have been guilty, in my time, of some meannesses and may have contrived, here and there, to do a kindness, but never yet have I played either the villain or the hero. If life is a melodrama — and sometimes it has every appearance of being one — then I am certainly a very minor character. In short, I am a well fed, comfortable, calm and not entirely unphilosophical adult male, with no desire for raging emotions and with precious few to rage.

That is what I am really like inside. Outside, apparently, everything is different, thanks to a set of features that totally misrepresent me. So far as I can gather, my face pounces on the least whisper in my mind, as it were, and transforms it into a shout. It grins insolently and sickeningly with triumph over a mere hand at cards. It scowls ferociously at inoffensive strangers, screams "You're a bore!" at prattling callers, and twists and writhes, lights up or fades out, falls into a sodden mass of depression, glitters with mischief, gapes or grins or glares, at every fresh turn the conversation takes. It transforms every hour into a benefit performance by a bad actor of the old school, strutting and mouthing insanely in the limelight. A talking ape with a megaphone could not produce a worse caricature of its master. While the company I am in is staring at this monstrous show, I sit there innocently behind it all, an unassuming fellow with nothing but a pleasant little rise and fall of emotion, entirely forgetting that this awful travesty of my mind is taking place until some strange misunderstanding bids me remember how grotesquely and unhappily I am situated. Am I alone in my trouble or has there been a general misdeal of faces? Perhaps there are other unfortunates for whom the situation has been reversed, who find themselves possessed of the most towering emotions, yet cannot make their passion felt because their faces refuse to express anything beyond a slight feeling of annoyance or a tranquil pleasure. If there are any such persons, I should like to meet one of them for the purpose of comparing our baffled sensations and of finally forming and consolidating a friendship. We could at least enjoy one another's faces.

IX. From DELIGHT 1949

PREFACE, OR THE GRUMBLER'S APOLOGY

I have always been a grumbler. All the records, going back to earliest childhood, establish this fact. Probably I arrived here a malcontent, convinced that I had been sent to the wrong planet. (And I feel even now there is something in this.) I was designed for the part, for I have a sagging face, a weighty underlip, what I am told is "a saurian eye," and a rumbling but resonant voice from which it is difficult to escape. Money could not buy a better grumbling outfit.

In the West Riding of Yorkshire, where I spent my first nineteen years, all local customs and prejudices favour the grumbler. To a good West Riding type there is something shameful about praise, that soft Southern trick. But fault-finding and blame are constant and hearty. The edge of criticism up there is sharpened every morning. So the twilight of Victoria and the brief but golden afternoon of Edward the Seventh discovered Jackie Priestley grumbling away, a novice of course but learning fast. A short spell of the Wool Trade — and in no trade do you hear more complaints and bitter murmurs — developed my technique. Then came the First World War, in which I served with some of the dourest unwearying grumblers that even the British Army has ever known, and was considered to hold my own with the best of them. After that, a rapidly ripening specimen, I grumbled my way through Cambridge, Fleet Street, and various fields of literary and dramatic enterprise. I have grumbled all over the world, across seas, on mountains, in deserts. I have grumbled as much at home as abroad, and so I have been the despair of my womenfolk.

Not that they ever understood what I was up to. We have always been at cross-purposes here. The feminine view appears to be that grumbling only makes thing worse, whereas I have always held that a fine grumble makes things better. If, for example, an hotel gives me a bad breakfast, I have only to grumble away for a few minutes to feel that some reasonable balance has been restored: the grumble has been subtracted from the badness of the breakfast. So it is no use crying to me "Oh — do be quiet! It's bad enough without your grumbling." My mind does not move along these lines. If I have not had a good breakfast, I argue, at least I have had a good grumble. Thus I have always been innocent of the major charge — that of trying deliberately to make things worse.

Another point for the defence is that I have always looked and sounded much worse than I felt. When I am displeased — but not when I am pleased, I gather — for some reason, still hidden from me, I tend to overact my part. Often when I am feeling merely annoyed, a little put out, I appear to be blazingly angry or lost in the deepest sulks. The appearance is larger than the reality. And I have suffered much from this suggestion of the theatre or the public platform in my private behaviour. Time and again my real feelings have been misinterpreted. I may not have been enjoying myself, but at least I have not been suffering as intensely as the rest of the company imagined. (When rehearsals are going badly, I am often rushed out of the theatre, given drinks, flattered, cajoled, simply to keep me out of sight of the players, those pampered creatures.) Once, years ago, at a large party, when I was grumbling as usual, a young woman who was a stranger to me turned on me fiercely and told me I had better go home instead of trying to spoil other people's pleasure. I was taken aback, and may be said to have stayed aback ever since. But though I would gladly send that woman an inscribed copy of this book — and regret I do not know her name, and hope all is well with her — the fact remains that she was misjudging me. The growling she overheard — for, dash it, I wasn't talking to her — was a kind of small talk, almost a social gesture. My discontent was not meant to be taken seriously. It was that old unconscious exaggeration again. And although perhaps I always ought to have been more careful, for this I am more to be pitied than to be blamed.

A final point for the defence. Much of my writing, I have no doubt, consists of adverse criticism of this life, and so is a sort of grumbling at large. There is some self-indulgence here, I will grant you, but there is also a speck or two of something better. For I have always felt that a writer, if only to justify some of his privileges, should speak for those who cannot easily speak for themselves. He may run into trouble — and I have gone headlong into whole cliffsides of it — but at least nobody is going to give him the sack, leave him with a mortgage and four children who need shoes, if he comes out and tells the truth. I have therefore often grumbled in print more on other people's behalf than on my own. Again, I am always led instinctively into opposition to the party in power and to all persons dressed in authority. I am a toady in reverse. I would not describe myself as a born rebel, for I have no fanaticism, but there is in me a streak of the jeering anarchist, who parts company even with his friends when they have succeeded to power. Moreover, having been fortunate in many respects, I have felt a dislike of appearing too conscious of good fortune, and some of my fault-finding and complaining has been a determined avoidance of *hubris,* like so much "touching wood." And of course this has meant more grumbling.

So many a decent fellow, showing a better face to his bad luck than ever

I appear to have shown to my good luck, must have cried in his exaspera-
tion: "Does this chap never enjoy anything?" And my reply, long overdue,
is this book. And nobody can complain that I have waited until everything
in the garden was lovely. The present state of the world — but no, we
know about that. We can also bolt the door of the madhouse of our
economic life, public and private, ignoring for once the mopping and
mowing throng of bank managers, accountants, tax collectors. But during
the period when I was trying to sort out, capture, record, these memories
and impressions of delight, I have had the nastiest flop I have ever had in
the Theatre, we have coped with two weddings, sundry illnesses, and the
longest and noisiest moving-house I ever remember, and I have had most
of my remaining teeth pulled out, two at a time at intervals nicely calculated to keep every nerve in my head jangling, together with a minor
sentence of forced fasting and reluctant self-mortification. In fact, most of
the anxieties and miseries of an author, a parent, a householder, and an
ageing sedentary male have been thrust upon me; and the life of Reilly,
which some people imagine me to lead, has been further away than a
fading dream. Nevertheless, through the prevailing thick and the occasional
thin, I have kept close to this little book on *Delight,* so that it could be my
apology, my bit of penitence, for having grumbled so much, for having
darkened the breakfast table, almost ruined the lunch, nearly silenced the
dinner party, for all the fretting and chafing, grousing and croaking, for the
old glum look and the thrust-out lower lip. So, my long-suffering kinsfolk,
my patient friends, may a glimmer of that delight which has so often
possessed me, but perhaps too frequently in secret, now reach you from
these pages.

ONE

Fountains. I doubt if I ever saw one, even the smallest, without some
tingling of delight. They enchant me in the daytime, when the sunlight
ennobles their jets and sprays and turns their scattered drops into diamonds. They enchant me after dark when coloured lights are played on
them, and the night rains emeralds, rubies, sapphires. And, best of all,
when the last colour is whisked away, and there they are in a dazzling

white glory! The richest memory I have of the Bradford Exhibition of my boyhood, better than even the waterchute or the Somali Village or the fireworks, is of the Fairy Fountain, which changed colour to the waltzes of the Blue Hungarian Band, and was straight out of the Arabian Nights. And I believe my delight in these magical jets of water, the invention of which does credit to our whole species, is shared by ninety-nine persons out of every hundred. But where are they, these fountains we love? We hunger for them and are not fed. A definite issue could be made out of this, beginning with letters to the *Times,* continuing with meetings and unanimous resolutions and deputations to Downing Street, and ending if necessary with processions and mass demonstrations and some rather ugly scenes. What is the use of our being told that we live in a democracy if we want fountains and have no fountains? Expensive? Their cost is trifling compared to that of so many idiotic things we are given and do not want. Our towns are crammed with all manner of rubbish that no people in their senses ever asked for, yet where are the fountains? By all means let us have a policy of full employment, increased production, no gap between exports and imports, social security, a balanced This and a planned That, but let us also have fountains — more and more fountains — higher and higher fountains — fountains like wine, like blue and green fire, fountains like diamonds — and rainbows in every square. Crazy? Probably. But with hot wars and cold wars we have already tried going drearily mad. Why not try going delightfully mad? Why not stop spouting ourselves and let it be done for us by graceful fountains, exquisite fountains, beautiful fountains?

SEVEN

On a dazzling morning in the early summer of 1919 I left the bus at Buckden, in Upper Wharfedale, to carry my rucksack over the pass into Wensleydale. I was beginning a walking tour. But no ordinary one. It was my first since I had left the army, from which I had recently been demobilised, after enduring four and a half years of what seemed to me its idiotic routine. I was out of uniform, a sensible civilian again, careless once and for all as to what purple-faced grunting military men might think of me. I

had an idle summer before me, after which I would go to Cambridge. But
that was not all. I took with me into the dales, like an enchanted passport,
a commission from the editor of the *Yorkshire Observer* to write several
articles on my walking tour, to be paid for at the rate of one guinea per
article. It was my first commission of the kind — though I had done some
journalism before the war, as far back as my middle teens — and I have
never had one since that meant half as much. To write what I pleased
about my walking tour — and to be paid for it — this was tremendous;
here was a literary career. Now add up all these items of felicity — the
bright morning, Upper Wharfedale, recent demobilisation, the editor's
commission — imagine what you would have felt yourself, *then double it.*
The track to Aysgarth — for it was still a track then, no motor road —
wound up toward the blue; larks sang above the moorland grass; the little
streams glittered and gurgled among the rocks; the sun was high, and a
wind blew from Paradise. I walked in delight, and now after thirty years I
have only to be quiet and to remember, to feel that spring in my heels and
my head towering in the golden air. Youth is perhaps an overpraised
season, but when all things conspire for it, as they did for me then, it lives
fabulously for an hour or two, rocketing into regions afterwards closed to
us for ever this side of Heaven. But the articles I wrote were not up to
much.

THIRTEEN

Cosy Planning. This can be delightful, and nobody I know has celebrated
it. There should be two of you — or at most, three. Committees are out. So
are strangers or acquaintances or even friends except the oldest and
dearest. You need wives or husbands, parents or children. Late evening is
the best time, and your own fireside the best place. What has to be planned
can be a move, an elaborate holiday, some new enterprise. (If both plan-
ners are female, then weddings will do.) You draw close to the fire; one of
you has paper and pencil, but there should not be much actual writing; the
cold chaos of the world has retreated; you are both alert, businesslike,
know all manner of sensible tricks and dodges, are intent upon getting

things done; but through all the pipes and channels of the plan there flows
the warm current of your feeling for each other, and the whole business is
securely and nourishingly rooted in a deep personal relationship. People
who believe they are going there often wonder what they will do with
themselves in Heaven. They make the mistake of assuming that the place
will be all complete, finished to the last bit of gilding, before they arrive.
But of course it won't be, and there will have to be lots of Cosy Planning.

SIXTEEN

Many playwrights enjoy attending performances of their own plays. Night
after night will find them lurking at the back of the dress circle, and if they
are discovered and challenged there they will pretend to be keeping an eye
on old Brown, who plays the doctor, or deciding whether there could be a
cut toward the end of Act Two. But — bless their hea.ts — they are really
there to enjoy themselves. Now I am not one of these playwrights. Once a
play is running smoothly I try to stay away from it. One reason is that I
have given the production so much close study during the rehearsal period
and have watched so carefully the first performances that I am weary of the
piece and want to think about something else. If it is a serious play, I am
more likely to be irritated than moved by it. If it is a comedy, then the sight
and sound of the audience laughing do not make me think what a fine
funny fellow I am, but arouse in me feelings of disgust. So there is no
delight here for me. That comes much earlier, at some point during rehearsal. After the preliminary readings, which are interesting rather than
delightful, you struggle along with moves and "business," and the actors
put aside their scripts and try to remember their words; and all this for the
author is rather like conducting a party of tourists across fields of glue. But
then, if you are lucky, there comes a moment when — suddenly, miraculously — the play is alive. There is no set, no lights, no costumes and makeup, no effects, no audience, yet perhaps the play is more alive than it ever
will be again for you. You forget that you are still messing about with
chairs and orange-boxes and chalklines on an empty stage lit with one
glaring bulb. You forget the cleaners still chattering and banging in the

upper circle, and the empties that are being noisily taken out of the stalls bar. You forget the traffic roaring outside. You forget that this theatre has merely been lent to you until five o'clock, and that as yet you have no theatre of your own. You forget all these things because now a miracle happens. The stage manager and his assistant, seated at their familiar table, marking the prompt script, fade from your consciousness. The horrible "working light" is no longer there; strange dawns or exquisite sunsets appear. The chalklines and orange-boxes turn into walls and tables and sofas, all perfect. Miss Thing, wearing her oldest clothes, her hair anyhow, with pinched features and a yellow complexion, suddenly transforms herself into the beautiful creature of your imagination. Young So-and-so — up to now a lout and a bad bit of casting — flashingly emerges as a gay and handsome breaker of hearts. Old Whose-it, who seemed to be a mistake, if only because he drinks too much and cannot remember a line, is now your lovable Old Smith to the last wrinkle and chuckle. And what pathos — what comedy — what suspense — what truth to life — what profound symbolism! Yes, it is here — as you first imagined it — no, better — much better — oh glory! Only for a few minutes at best; but while it lasts, this transfiguration, what delight!

NINETEEN

A photograph can do it, even a photograph without any personal associations. I cannot remember when and where I first saw Mrs. Cameron's photograph of the young Ellen Terry, but I know that then and there, ever since and everywhere, it has never failed to bring me delight. The girl herself, as she leans there with closed eyes, her right hand clutching at her necklace, her nose perfect in its tilted witty imperfection, is of course very beautiful, a lass unparalleled. But that is only the beginning. No doubt the long curve of neck and shoulder, catching the light, is exquisite. But though the aesthetic values are there, it is not they that do the trick. There is the fact that here, so suddenly confronting us, is the youth of somebody whom men of my generation think of in her old age; for here she is, that lioness, as she was nearly thirty years before I was born. And she is not only young

Ellen Terry or madcap little Mrs. Watts, she is Woman herself, her soul withdrawn behind those heavy eyelids, the mystery, the challenge, the torment, the solace. Yet it would not be all the same if this were not a photograph but a painting or drawing, some other man's vision. That would be art, but this, however artfully the sitter has been posed and the camera handled, is an objective record. This is how she was, on such a day, and not how she sang in some man's brain. But though a photograph indeed, this is an old old photograph, taken a long lifetime ago, with everybody who first admired it dead and gone. It is a legacy too from some tiny golden age of photography, some pure and massive Old Kingdom of lens and plate, of autumnal sunlight and sepia shadows. And all these facts and fancies, unrecognised at the time and only to be discovered and disengaged by analysis, come furiously crowding into the mind as our eyes meet this photograph; and because there is such a stir of them, then delight follows at once. Yes, even a photograph can do it.

TWENTY-TWO

Chamber music at home is delightful. Not for everybody of course; mere listeners, passive guest types, may have a hell of a time with it. (Let them go somewhere else and switch on their Third Programme.) No, this kind of music is delightful for actual performers, and for those who are loitering round the edge of performance, waiting to be asked to join in, and for those women — and a few wise men — who enjoy seeing the persons dear to them happy; let the notes fall where they may. There has always been to me a sort of cosy magic about it. (In *Bright Day* I made a musical family a symbol of magical attraction.) You are at home, all safe and snug, and yet are also wandering in spirit, through lost kingdoms, with the music. Even the best string quartets and trios will not always survive the atmosphere, chilly with determined culture, of those horrible little concert halls given up to chamber music. There is too a concert solemnity, as German as liver sausage, that blights many of the sauciest trifles. (We forget that a lot of music has been written *for fun*.) What a difference when you bring in firelight, armchairs, tobacco, and a tray of drinks! The execution — as it often is with us — may be sketchy and even downright murderous, but you can catch the mood of the masters, whether they are looking for the Holy Grail or a pint of wine and a helping of roast goose. (I fancy, though, that the late Beethoven quartets ought to be left out of the home programme.) You wish you could do it better, but you are delighted to be doing it at all. When, for example, Mary (violin) and her friend Joan (cello) and I (piano more or less) gave up most of a recent week-end to our struggle with the Smetana trio, I doubt if in any but the slowest passages I was hitting more than half the proper notes in the treble or a third of those in the bass; but the girls, aloft on their professional standard, enjoyed it, and as for me, floundering and grunting and sweating, I would not have missed a minute of it for a hundred pounds. Bestriding the hacked corpse of poor Smetana, I drank the milk of Paradise. We had no audience, and needed none, but went off, morning and night, into the Bohemian blue together. But I need not perform myself, nor be in my own home, to know this delight. As I write this, many rooms come flickering back, in Bradford and Cambridge, a Lakeland cottage, a studio in Chelsea, half-forgotten mysterious apartments abroad; and firelight and candlelight play tenderly among the instruments; and Mozart and Haydn, Brahms and Debussy, move among us again; and within the ring of friendly faces, ghosts these many years, the little worlds of sound shine and revolve like enchanted moons. Why — bless our bewildered souls! — every time a violin is taken up to the lumber room, a piano is carted away, and in their place is a gadget that turns music on and off like tap water, we move another step away from sanity and take to snarling harder than ever.

TWENTY-FOUR

When I was sixteen I was already writing articles and offering them to any kind of editor whose address I could discover. These articles were of two kinds. The first, which I signed portentously "J. Boynton Priestley," were serious, very serious indeed, and were full of words like "renaissance" and "significance" and "aftermath," and suggested that their author was about a hundred and fifty years old. And nobody wanted them. They could not be given away. No editor had a body of readers old enough for such articles. The other kind were skits and burlesques and general funny work, written from the grimly determined humorous standpoint of the school magazine. One of these was accepted, printed and paid for by a London humorous weekly. I had arrived. (And my father, not to be found wanting on such an occasion, presented me with one of his fourpenny cigars, with which, as I fancy he guessed, I had been secretly experimenting for some months.) The issue of the weekly containing my article burst upon the world. Riding inside a tram from Duckworth Lane to Godwin Street, Bradford, I saw a middle-aged woman opening this very copy of the weekly, little knowing, as I made haste to tell myself, that one of its group of brilliant contributors was not two yards away. I watched her turn the pages. She came to *the* page; she hesitated; she stopped, she began to read my article. Ah — what delight! But mine, of course, not hers. And not mine for long, not more than a second, for then there settled on her face an expression I have noticed ten thousand times since, and have for years now tried not to notice — the typical expression of the reader, the audience, the customer, the patron. How shall I describe this curious look? There is in it a kind of innocence — and otherwise I think I would have stopped writing years ago — but mixed a trifle sourly with this admirable innocence is a flavouring of wariness, perhaps a touch of suspicion itself. "Well, what have we here?" it enquires dubiously. And then the proud and smirking Poet and Maker falls ten thousand feet into dubiety. So ever since that tram-ride I have never caught a glimpse of the reader, the audience, the customer, the patron, without instantly trying to wedge myself into the rocks above the black tarn of doubt. As I do this, there is the flash of a blue wing — and the bird of delight has flown.

TWENTY-EIGHT

If I were kidnapped, taken to the Oxford or Cambridge Union, and told I must either debate a motion or be thrown into the river, I would propose: *That Shakespeare is the curse — and may prove the ruin — of the English Theatre*. For the Bard keeps popping up everywhere, and does no good to anybody in the professional Theatre. Managers do not mind him, because he asks for no royalties (if they had to pay him ten per cent of the gross, they would begin to wonder about him); he is Culture and a possible grant from the Arts Council; and you can always run extra matinées for the schoolchildren. Actors like him because they can gum on a lot of crêpe hair, bellow almost anything that comes into their heads, and then have their *King Lear* taken seriously by the critics. Actors have only to persist in playing the chief Shakespearean roles, and, although they may be so bad that I would not allow them to bring on a telegram in a play of mine, very soon they are regarded as ornaments of Our Stage and are given a civic lunch in Coketown. Leading actresses love Shakespeare because they started off with him at school and the Royal Academy of Dramatic Art, and adore wearing fancy costumes and using that smudgy breathy technique. And from neither sex is required any sharp outlining of character, any close observation of real life. If you offer the people in front a performance as a bank manager or a charwoman, those people have some notion of when you are hitting or missing the mark; but give them dim remote queens or armoured barons in blank verse and you are safe from genuine criticism. Whether most producers like doing Shakespeare, I have never been able to decide; but they set to work on him as if they hated the ubiquitous old William, as if the only thing to do with the Swan of Avon was to wring its neck. The result is nearly always the Theatre at its silliest. All that ranting and cooing, that guffawing and back-slapping, that comic business which would be thrown out of a third-rate touring pantomime! Oh — those anemic sighing maidens and roaring gallants, all wondering what they are saying; those neighing, chin-stroking clowns; those idiotic messengers from the battlefields! Oh — dear, dear, dear!

And yet once we are no longer clamped on to a heavy-handed production by the pros, when we come unexpectedly upon the smiling poet himself, what delight he gives us! One night we switch on the wireless and instead of a portentous talk, a half-wit's joke, or erotic laments from the swamp, we hear with up-rising hair —

> *O, wither'd is the garland of the war,*
> *The soldiers' pole is fall'n: young boys and girls*
> *Are level now with men; the odds is gone,*
> *And there is nothing left remarkable*
> *Beneath the visiting moon. . . .*

Or we visit a school at half-term and in the packed oven of the gymnasium, where the play is being performed, we recognise in the four-foot-nine figure of *Charles the Wrestler* one of the scarlet-faced boys whose giant tea we paid for at the "White Horse"; and then hear him pipe up, as unconcerned as a lark:

H

. . . They say he is already in the forest of Arden, and a many merry men with him; and there they live like the old Robin Hood of England; they say many young gentlemen flock to him every day, and fleet the time carelessly, as they did in the golden world. . . .

And — crikey! — call him Shakespeare, Bacon, Essex, Southampton or Uncle Tom Cobbley — what a chap!

THIRTY-NINE

Family silliness, domestic clowning. This cannot be described in any detail, and it would be disastrous to quote even the best of the jokes. A fairly large family is necessary, but nobody concerned need have any great sense of humour. You start with any bit of nonsense, usually at the dining table, and then everybody adds shaggy pieces of their own, until the whole table is roaring and screaming and the scarlet cheeks of the younger children are wet with tears of laughter. To a sensitive outsider the scene would bring no delight at all, and indeed would probably seem repulsive. But then it is not meant for outsiders, sensitive or otherwise. You have to be thoroughly in it and *of it* to appreciate its quality. Somewhere below this rowdy monkey business are deep hidden roots, and somewhere above it are invisible blossoms. A collective personality springs into being some time during this slapstick. Without a happy togetherness, the little farce would never begin. And it is scenes like these, without dignity, real wit or beauty, made up of screeching and bellowing and fourth-rate jokes about treacle puddings or castor oil, that a man who feels his life ebbing out may recall with an anguish of regret and tenderness, remembering as if it were a lost bright kingdom the family all at home and being silly.

FORTY-SEVEN

There was a time when merely wearing long trousers brought me delight. In those days, when I must have been about fifteen, I had only one suit — my best — with long trousers. My other suits had knee-breeches, buttoning tightly just below the knee and worn with thick long stockings, turned down at the top. There was really nothing wrong with my appearance when I wore these knee-breeches and long stockings, for after years of football I had muscular well-shaped legs; but whenever I wore them I felt I was still imprisoned, a shame-faced giant, in the stale miniature world of childhood. Condemned — and I use this term because there were strict rules at home about which suits could be worn — to wear these knee-breeches, I felt that no glimpse of my real self could catch the town's eye: I might almost have been sent to school in a pram. Conversely I felt that as soon as I put on the long trousers then appearance and reality were gloriously one; I joined the world of men; and even without doing anything more than wear these trousers — and leaving the other wretched things at home — I could feel my whole nature expanding magnificently. On the occasional days when I was allowed to wear the adult trousers to go to school, I almost floated there. Never did eighteen inches of cloth do more for the human spirit. On those mornings now when I seem to stare sullenly at the wreck of a shining world, why do I not remind myself that although I grow old and fat and peevish *at least I am wearing my long trousers?*

FIFTY

I can remember, as if it happened last week, more than half a century ago, when I must have been about four and, on fine summer mornings, would sit in a field adjoining the house. What gave me delight then was a mysterious notion, for which I could certainly not have found words, of a Treasure. It was waiting for me either in the earth, just below the buttercups and daisies, or in the golden air. I had formed no idea of what this Treasure would consist of, and nobody had ever talked to me about it. But morning after morning would be radiant with its promise. Somewhere, not far out of reach, it was waiting for me, and at any moment I might roll over and put a hand on it. I suspect now that the Treasure was Earth itself and the light and warmth of the sunbeams; yet sometimes I fancy that I have been searching for it ever since.

SIXTY-SIX

In our younger days we writers — or composers or painters — like to talk a lot about work and what we are going to do, but we do not like actually working, which usually means removing ourselves from the company of other great souls and toiling away in solitude. This becomes easier as we get older, and once we are well into our professional middle-age, instead of being reluctant we are often eager to disappear into our work and are angry when we are prevented from toiling in solitude. Indeed, I often feel delight now in merely surveying my desk and the rather pitiful implements of my craft (and here the painter has the advantage) laid out on that desk, all waiting for me. Typewriter, paper, pencils and erasers, notebooks, works of reference — they are all ready for me, these sensible old colleagues. Here is my own tiny world that I understand. The other world, so vast, so idiotic, is now shut out and can be forgotten for a few hours. And this gives me now as much delight as I used to feel, as a young man, when I was on my way to some party and imagined how I would astonish everybody. But although this change of outlook makes it easier to fulfil all contracts and earn a living, it has its dangers, as we can see from the dim and complacent work of so many elderly artists. It is possible to be too cosy on the job, to shut out the huge daft world too completely. This is in fact a dangerous delight, and has probably ruined more good men than booze and low company ever did.

SEVENTY-ONE

Dreams. Now and again I have had horrible dreams, but not enough of them to make me lose my delight in dreams. To begin with, I like the idea of dreaming, of going to bed and lying still and then, by some queer magic, wandering into another kind of existence. As a child I could never understand why grownups took dreaming so calmly when they could make such a fuss about any holiday. This still puzzles me. I am mystified by people who say they never dream and appear to have no interest in the subject. It is much more astonishing than if they said they never went out for a walk. Most people — or at least most Western Europeans — do not seem to accept dreaming as part of their lives. They appear to see it as an irritating little habit, like sneezing or yawning. I have never understood this. My dream life does not seem as important as my waking life, if only because there is far less of it, but to me it *is* important. As if there were at least two extra continents added to the world, and lightning excursions running to them at any moment between midnight and breakfast. Then again, the dream life, though queer and bewildering and unsatisfactory in many respects, has its own advantages. The dead are there, smiling and talking. The past is there, sometimes all broken and confused but occasionally as fresh as a daisy. And perhaps, as Mr. Dunne tells us, the future is there too, winking at us. This dream life is often overshadowed by huge mys-

terious anxieties, with luggage that cannot be packed and trains that refuse
to be caught; and both persons and scenes there are not as dependable and
solid as they are in waking life, so that Brown and Smith merge into one
person while Robinson splits into two, and there are thick woods outside
the bathroom door and the dining-room is somehow part of a theatre
balcony; and there are moments of desolation or terror in the dream world
that are worse than anything we have known under the sun. Yet this other
life has its interests, its gaieties, its satisfactions, and, at certain rare intervals, a serene glow or a sudden ecstasy, like glimpses of another form of
existence altogether, that we cannot match with open eyes. Daft or wise,
terrible or exquisite, it is a further helping of experience, a bonus after
dark, another slice of life cut differently for which, it seems to me, we are
never sufficiently grateful. Only a dream! Why *only?* It was there, and you
had it. "If there were dreams to sell," Beddoes enquires, "what would you
buy?" I cannot say offhand, but certainly rather more than I could afford.

NINETY

Not long ago we had to entertain a party of a dozen young people, and at
their request we took them to a smallish fashionable restaurant where they
could dance. I was commanded to stay for an hour or so, after which I
could leave the youngsters to enjoy themselves. And grumbling, I obeyed.
But after a few dances, first undertaken as a duty, it would have needed a
couple of policemen to drag me away from that crowded little floor. Sweating and grunting, a mad Old Man of the Tribe, I swept girls of all sizes
through all manner of dances, some of which were quite new to me. I was
still hard at it when the lads of the party, children of a decadent age, were
missing every other dance and cooling themselves with lager. I had never
been to the place before, and I have never returned to it since; but while I
was there and the alternating bands kept up their rhythm, I danced my
head off. And delighted in it. I cannot understand why I have not done
more dancing. Except for a short period in the late Twenties, when we
often used a large drawing-room for improvised dances with a group of
neighbours, I have never done any regular dancing. Nine times out of ten,
when I have danced, it is because I have found it difficult to refuse. (I am

not including here the fancy stuff in far-away places, where I will try anything from a Highland reel to a Georgian *pas seul*.) I do not know why I should be reluctant to dance. It is not because I consider myself a bad dancer. As middle-aged writers go, I am a good dancer. My sense of rhythm is excellent, and I am one of those heavy chaps who are yet light on their feet — an admirable type. But although I never want to go to any place where there is dancing, and even when bullied and hustled into such a place, I hesitate to begin, once I am launched on the dance floor I go on and on, and, if the music pleases me, am lost in delight. And as long as my partner moves easily, I do not care who she is. My close relationship is really with the music and not with my partner. In most novels, I have observed, dancing is regarded as an activity charged with sex, almost a form of making love; so that the characters of fiction have only to take a turn or two round the floor to be shaking with passion. And clearly this is how many of our moralists, too indignant to be perspicacious, regard the dancing that they denounce. But although this pastime has its roots in our erotic earth, it has never seemed to me a narrowly sexual activity at all. Dancing, I feel, restores us to the unlocalised sex of our early youth. We are moving in a faintly erotic atmosphere but seem quite free of passion ourselves. We may be dancing to the moans of the lovelorn but we are not lovelorn. It is to the rhythm that we delightedly bind our bodies. We achieve a symbiosis with a drum. And the sharp edge of consciousness is blurred, a backdoor is opened into the old forest, and we are no longer painfully ourselves, fixed in our time, but part of a long receding line of leaping and whirling folk, who enable us to blunt the sting of thought, to forget the ticking of the clock. Dancing, we are all Cinderellas at the Ball.

NINETY-THREE

Blossom — apple, pear, cherry, plum, almond blossom — in the sun. Up in the Dales when I was a child. In Picardy among the ruin of war. Afterwards at Cambridge and among the Chilterns, where I would read my publishers' manuscripts and review copies in their delicate shade. At the bottom of the canyons, at Bright Angel and Oak Creek, in Arizona. Here in our garden in the Isle of Wight. So many places, so much time; and yet after fifty years this delight in the foaming branches is unchanged. I believe that if I lived to be a thousand and were left with some glimmer of eyesight, this delight would remain. If only we could clean off the world from this Earth. But at least once every spring on a fine morning that is what we seem to do, as we stare again at the blossom and are back in Eden. We complain and complain, but we have lived and have seen the blossom — apple, pear, cherry, plum, almond blossom — in the sun; and the best among us cannot pretend they deserve — or could contrive — anything better.

NINETY-FIVE

Making stew. It is not often I am allowed to do this; and indeed my great stew-making time was during the darker hours of the war, when anything was about to happen. But I am always delighted to make stew. And it is unusually good stew. You might travel from Truro to Inverness, even today, and be offered nothing better than or as good as my stew. One of my children, without any prompting from me, once ate four large helpings of it. My stew is thick, nourishing and wonderfully tasty. It has meat in it, but almost any kind of meat will do. I add all vegetables that are in season and in the house. And when I am in the mood I toss in exquisite little dumplings. After hours of simmering and thickening and thinning, for I never rush the business and keep peering into the pan, tasting, muttering a spell or two, I add any red wine that I can lay my hands on, and then, at the last moment, drop in a spoonful of honey. The stew is then ready. The very smell is princely. All men and all children gobble my stew gratefully. The women, who hate us to master their little arts, pretend to taste dubiously, arch their brows, wrinkle their noses, ask what is in it, complain about the mess in the kitchen; but nevertheless they contrive in a rather absent-minded manner to eat their share of the noble dish. How can they help it? Here is a stew that has been seasoned with many onions, red wine and honey — and my delight.

NINETY-EIGHT

After a good concert. First, no matter how good it has been, I am glad it is over and that I need no longer keep still and quiet but can move about, talk, laugh, smoke, and perhaps eat and drink. But the music has done something to me. I feel refreshed inside, loosened up and easy, no longer an angry dwarf but a careless smiling giant. The night looks better than it did when I hurried into the concert hall. It too is larger and looser, and holds more promise in its glitter and distances. I like the look of people, perhaps for the first time that day. Strangers seem pleasant acquaintances; acquaintances turn into friends; and friends now seem well tried, old and dear. This is the hour, I feel, to give and receive confidences, confessions of the soul. Somehow the world outside the hall seems to reflect the noble patterns of sound. Still held aloft on the shoulders of Bach and Mozart, Beethoven and Brahms, I can take a longer view, a broader outlook, and can believe that the good life is not yet a lost dream. Ten minutes wait for a taxi — and the mood will be gone; but while it lasted and the green sap seemed to be rising in the Tree of Life — what delight!

ONE HUNDRED AND THIRTEEN

The secret dream: the hunger that can never be fed. All my adult life I have been more or less a Socialist Intellectual. I have tried to make myself — and other people — aware of the harsh economic and industrial realities of our time. Again and again I have taken my notebooks and typewriter to the factories, the mines, the steel mills. I denounced or jeered at those colleagues who would not look. I wrote some of the first detailed accounts of the depressed areas. Having been brought up on the edge of it, I knew what life was like "back o' the mill." I did not discover the proletariat at Oxford or Cambridge, for the West Riding working-class was in my blood and bones. I grew up among Socialists. I watched the smoke thicken and the millionaires who made it ride away. I saw broken old women creep back to the mills, and young men wither because there was no work for them to do and nobody wanted them. I knew the saddest waste of all, the waste of human beings. If Socialism was the way out, then Socialism we must have. If it meant more and bigger factories, then we must have more and bigger factories. If it meant larger and larger cities, more and more bungalows, cinemas, football grounds, greyhound tracks, motor roads, personal appearances of film stars, boards and committees, hostels, organisations for the right use of leisure, clinics, identity cards, radio night and day in every home, press officers and propaganda, party bosses arranging all our lives — very well, we had to have them. At the worst they were still better than the grey misery I had seen, the deep cancer of injustice. But there was never anything here for my own secret delight. Nothing for the hunger of the heart. Perhaps, for all my pretence of being up to the minute, I was not even living in the right age; and when I looked for my own enduring delight, I became an anachronism. When I caught myself off guard, last thing at night after too long a day, huddled in a train and too tired to read, coming out of a dress rehearsal into a wet Sunday midnight in Manchester or Sheffield, I would remember what I wanted, and it was always something quite different from what we were all demanding. Sometimes it seemed as if the capital of a tiny German dukedom, round about 1830, were nearer to my desire than anything my friends were planning or that I could help to bring into this world. I wanted a place with the dignity and style of a city, but reasonably small and clean, with genuine country only half an hour's walk from its centre, its single but superb theatre, its opera house, its symphony orchestra, its good restaurant always filled with friends. One little civilised place full of persons, with no name-less mob, no huge machinery of publicity, no glaring metropolis. To be myself in this one dear place, with a position as comfortable as an old slipper in a tiny sensible society; and not a caricature of myself in several continents. To come out of a late rehearsal and smell the lilac. To have a play done as well as it could be done, by tried colleagues, by friends, in the one familiar theatre; and not indifferently produced in a hundred different theatres, for large sums of money hastily removed from me by accountants and tax collectors. Not to be caught up and lost in the machinery of existence — as most of us are now — but to live simply and directly, like an artist, a philosopher, and in such a way that feeling, thought, action, were always closely allied, and last year's inspiration would be this year's achievement. No rushing about, no long-distance telephone calls, no expensive mountebanking, no losing touch with friends and admired colleagues, no running a career as if it were a damned great factory. Everything small but of fine quality, cosily within reach, and means and ends in sight of each other. Poky and provincial? Why, almost all the world's best work has been done in these conditions. Think of Athens, Florence, Elizabethan London, Weimar. And what has come out of Megapolis but rubbish and hysteria? But if I should be told — and my candid friends will be on to it before you can say *knife* — that now there never can be such a place outside a daydream left over from adolescence, then I can only nod and look away. But perhaps something like it, at least more like it than what we — no, no, I see. Fall in, comrades! Quick! But one of us, as we go, still hugs the notion of something quite different, the delight that never was, on sea or land.

X. From THOUGHTS IN THE WILDERNESS 1957

BLOCK THINKING

My children being too old for such things, my grandchildren still too young, I do not know if they still exist; but there used to be offered in the toyshops sheets of cardboard to which were fixed the miniature outfits of bus conductors, soldiers, cowboys, and so forth. A small boy presented with one of these outfits could at once transform himself, to his own deep satisfaction, into the fascinating figure of his daydreams. All you had to do was put on the hat, take the gun, the whistle, the badge: there you were, completely outfitted.

Now it seems to me that during the last twenty years there has been a great deal of this Complete Outfitting far away from toyshops, in the world of our beliefs and opinions. It might also be called Block Thinking. Neat sets of beliefs and opinions are fastened together; and you are expected to take the lot. Either live in one Block or go and find a room in the next Block. Stay in the street outside, and you will be sniped at from all the windows. A Completely Outfitted man, a good Block Thinker, would rather have a fellow from the other Block, properly Outfitted, than tolerate a ditherer without a Block and Outfit. Let him shuffle off to the wilderness where he belongs!

I remember the hours I spent in the Thirties arguing with people who thought they were much cleverer than I was. (I am not very clever, but a bit cleverer than I look, like many seemingly gormless West Riding men.) They would try to prove to me that I had no choice except between Fascism and Communism. Your money or your life? Black or Red? So they were joining the C.P.; and most of them since have written long articles and books — and not done badly out of them — explaining that when they were Communists they were not really Communists. It all seems sadly out of date now, of course, but the attitude of mind is still with us, the Blocks and Outfits still in fashion. Probably the same people, grown no wiser, have the same contempt for my lack of insight and decision now that they had then. What Block are you in? Where is your Outfit? Bah!

Let us say, for example, that you believe that when the men responsible for atom bombs and other horrors solemnly warn their audiences, composed of people who never asked for any of this, that they live in a perilous age, those audiences should throw their chairs at the platform, to show what they think of such impudence. Write something to this effect, perhaps omitting the chair-throwing but making your protest, and immediately messages arrive from the Pacifist Block, telling you that you only need more courage and consistency to be entitled to wear the Outfit. Yet you may be anything but a turner of cheeks. You may believe in the most murderous direct defence of your own homes and persons, with pistols and lead pipes for men, sharp knives for the girls, holding that if the other fellows do not want to be killed, they should not obey orders to leave their own homes and ruin other people's. You may believe, as I do, that if the citizens of Great Powers were more sharply militant, less like sheep, then States would soon be less like wolves.

Again, your attitude towards Science may be ambivalent, as mine is. You may be profoundly sceptical about scientific humanism and its air-conditioned cybernetics utopia round the corner. You may feel that pseudo-scientific thought about man and the universe, sinking into the popular mind, has done much to create a mood of despair, making men feel home-less exiles, caught in a blind machine. You may take a sour view of recent contributions of nuclear physics to human progress, and discover in its professors a certain irresponsibility. But if you say these things in print, there arrives a triumphant messenger from the Catholic Block, crying: "What did we tell you? Now admit, you are one of us." Whereas you may be not one of them at all, may feel entitled to be as sceptical about the Pope and the priests as you are about the British Association. A man may think that scientists should make narrower claims and take longer-term views and yet not want to climb on to the Angst-wagon of Original Sin and Guilt and Sex-lit-with-Hellfire.

This brings a loud cheer from the Rationalist Block. But it does not follow that you can join it. The accommodation it offers may seem much too small. For though you may not believe, with the Black gang, that man reached his noblest height in the thirteenth century and that the Renais-sance was a blot on our history, you may yet hold that men need some form of religion,·and that it is our misfortune if we find ourselves without one, among a litter of symbols that have lost their magic. You may know, as I do, men and women who never enter a church to worship there, yet seem more deeply possessed by genuine religious feeling than most of the ecclesiastical propagandists, hell-fire novelists, cold and cautious advocates of a Christian Society without faith, hope, or charity.

It is true that if a writer does not belong to a Block, goes about without a Complete Outfit, he suffers from many disadvantages. He has to think for himself, and thus may appear slow-witted as well as vague and "woolly."

(You are always "woolly" if you have no Outfit.) He has no access to a Block list of witty retorts and crushing counter-arguments. He may still be groping and fumbling about while his Outfitted opponent has whipped out the cowboy gun, the bus-conductor's bell, the policeman's whistle. A sound Block man has more respect for a fellow from the opposite Block than he has for woolly ditherers, and nine times out of ten would rather leave one Block for another than stay outside in the rain. Once they have worn a Complete Outfit, most men feel naked without one.

What is most important, however, is that a writer solidly established in a Block can count on its support. At a time when critical standards are uncertain, when independent judgment is fast disappearing, when the prizes are few and so increasingly valuable, this Block support is almost worth a gold mine. Thus, there are some aesthetic enterprises that are hardly likely to succeed without some assistance from the Inverts' Block — called by a sardonic friend of mine "the Girls' Friendly Society" — which enthusiastically gives its praise and patronage to whatever is decorative, "amusing," "good theatre," witty in the right way, and likely to make heterosexual relationships look ridiculous: all of which is probably the stiff price we are paying in London for our stupid laws against inversion.

Clearly nothing can be achieved in politics without a Block. Even those of us who mistrust Block thinking, Complete Outfits on cards, would have to form some sort of Block to assert our essential liberalism. (Though guerrillas have been known to succeed against regular armies.) Where I disagree with many of my correspondents is in believing that a man is not necessarily useless just because he remains outside the Blocks. Many of us feel that this is a time when it is better to be "woolly" than Completely Outfitted. For men are in despair. Most people who join the Blocks, accepting with relief some ready-made system, do it out of despair. That is why they are so often angry and intolerant, having arrived at their decision not by way of hope and love but through despair and terror. You can smell all this in the very air of our time: we seem to live among savage rats and screaming mice. We are in despair because we begin to feel that our problems are beyond our solution, our dilemmas intolerable. But the worst way out of this situation may be to hurry to the nearest Block and to man the guns there. This will settle nothing except perhaps the hash of Western Man.

We must think, and think in a fresh, creative fashion. One glimmering of a new idea, in our situation, is worth all the blaze and fury of the Block systems, with their propaganda and anathemas. For, as possible solutions, not as power systems, they are all out of date. The Outfit is Complete just because it is done with. Every Block known to me is old-fashioned, like all fortresses. Every man who joins one, proudly accepting its logic and consistency, has really stopped trying to shape the future. It is he, and not the vague woollies outside, who has given it up as a hopeless job. For example, what is the world's Number One Problem? Not one Block will give the right answer. Yet there it is glaring at us: "What can we do now that will prevent our great-grandchildren from eating one another?" But perhaps here I do some of the Block systems an injustice; for at least they are working hard to prevent our having any great-grandchildren.

Our remote ancestors, we are told, were not impressive creatures, they cut a poor figure among the great beasts of the forest; they had no huge claws and teeth, no scaly armour, no wings, no great turn of speed, not even the power of rapid reproduction: all the odds seemed heavily against them. But they had one miraculous trick — they could adapt themselves to make the best of changing conditions; they were flexible and experimental. And now that we have conquered — and nearly ruined — the earth, now when we ourselves change our conditions often at appalling speed and almost blindly, we are in sore need of all the adaptability our species can still discover in itself. We must think freshly, think fast, improvise, experiment, and be tolerant of one another's mistakes. Despair and hate are not going to help us. And neither, I fancy, is Block thinking.

THE HESPERIDES CONFERENCE

The Hesperides Conference was on the highest level and of exceptional size. Not only were all the leaders of the Great Powers there but also all their Foreign Ministers, Chiefs of Staffs, and top busybodies. Experts on foreign affairs and leading political commentators from America, Russia, Britain, and France descended upon the island, to grumble about the small back bedrooms that had been allotted to them. Articles discussing the possible results of the Conference appeared in the world's Press. They were as usual quite futile but at least provided their writers with a fair living. Highly paid reporters, flown to the island at enormous expense, told their readers, at an overall cost of about ten pounds a word, that the cigars smoked by the British Prime Minister seemed half an inch longer than usual, that the President of the United States was already playing golf, that the members of the Soviet Delegation had been seen eating caviare and drinking vodka. Newsreel men took the usual shots of bigwigs meeting and greeting other bigwigs at the airport. The FBI investigated the salad chef of the Hotel Bristol. The Russians installed two microphones (which did not work) into the smoke-room of the Savoy-Plaza Hotel. A member of the French Delegation plunged into a rapturous affair with a honey-coloured American secretary. An oldish member of the British Delegation began taking a strong interest in the piano-accordion player at the Beach Café-Bar. Two American correspondents, after four hours of bourbon-on-the-rocks, swung punches at each other and broke twelve glasses. The weather was beautiful. The Conference began.

It was during the third morning, when the head of the Russian Delegation was making a speech about everything, that several high-level personages first lost consciousness. As usual there had been plenty of yawns and several men had dropped off, but that was only to be expected. When, however, the session was adjourned for lunch, and the French Foreign Minister, among others, refused to wake up, it was realised that this was no ordinary bout of somnolence. By nightfall, after the British Delegation's cocktail party had been abandoned, all the leaders and Foreign Ministers had succumbed to this mysterious malady and had lost consciousness. Most of the Chiefs of Staffs and junior Ministers and expert advisers crawled to their beds during the following twenty-four hours. On the fifth day, the Hesperides Conference was in a coma.

Lord Ward and Sir Thomas Tittlemouse arrived by special plane from London. Doctors Elmer K. Jefferson and Herman Funf were rushed from Johns Hopkins to the American Delegation. Professor Oskarvitz, from Moscow, and Professor Nicolia, of Erivan, came to look after the Soviet representatives. Paris, Lyons, and Marseilles sent their finest specialists to examine the unconscious French politicians, soldiers, and officials. The games room of the Savoy-Plaza was turned over to the medical men, who began to hold a sort of conference themselves, and once they felt certain that their distinguished patients were in no immediate danger, began to enjoy themselves. The best resources of these hotels were now at their disposal. They were able to compare notes on this and other medical problems. The weather was still beautiful. The young Frenchman and the honey-coloured American secretary were still highly conscious, at least of each other, and had a glorious time.

Most of the foreign affairs experts, who had already begun sketching out articles called *After Hesperides — What?,* were victims of the strange sleeping sickness, remaining motionless in their little back bedrooms, now as good as any other. But the reporters in general had escaped the malady, and now they despatched hundreds of thousands of words to the astonished world, giving the verdicts of the assembled medical men and describing the amazing scene with all the wealth of adjectives at their command. The newsreel men were not allowed to film the unconscious great, but some excellent shots were made of less important victims and it was clearly indicated that if you had seen one you had seen, in effect, the lot. With the result that newsreel theatres in every capital city did wonderful business.

Bulletins were broadcast and published in the Press every few hours during the first days, and then daily after a week or two. There were as many theories as there were doctors on the spot. What was certain, after a week or so, was that nobody was in immediate danger, all pulses and respiration being excellent, that all the victims were in something more than a sound long sleep but in nothing more than a very light coma, and that there seemed no reason why they should not wake up as suddenly as they fell asleep. It was generally agreed too that the older delegates, who had existed under a severe strain for years and had made far too many journeys by plane, would probably benefit from this enforced immobility and lack of consciousness. One theory, indeed, took as its basis the idea that the root cause was mental rather than physical, taking the form of a group regression of libido.

Meanwhile, in all the countries concerned, no new appointments were made to places of power. The highest Offices of State remained vacant. Foreign Ministries, robbed of their most influential and forceful personalities and much of their authority, limited themselves to modest routine work. The various Governments, not feeling themselves competent to deal on a high level with foreign relations, concentrated upon home affairs, and even here tended to act with caution and restraint. The international situation remained as it was when the Hesperides Conference first assembled. And as most of the experts and leading commentators were themselves still unconscious on the island, and editors shrank from asking other writers to occupy their space, the more serious newspapers and periodicals in the chief capitals of the world devoted more and more of their columns to the discussion of non-political subjects, such as the arts, sciences, philosophy, travel, and the relations between men and women. And the discovery of two new fascinating games to be played on TV at once captured the more popular papers of the U.S., Britain, and France. In Russia, the Press, uncertain what line to take on any subject, dwindled until it almost disappeared.

As weeks passed into months, however, and the Hesperides Conference still remained unconscious, it was only in theory that the international situation stayed the same. As the Conference was officially still in progress, and had not yet announced its decisions, no action, no bold pronouncement in foreign affairs, was considered possible. This state of things soon brought about its own changes. For the first time for many years no important speeches were made, denouncing the West from the East, the East from the West. No new crusade against Communism was mentioned. World revolution was placed in cold storage. Neither God nor the historic destiny of mankind was loudly proclaimed an ally. No threats, no jeers, were exchanged. Even Anglo-American and Franco-British relations, being no longer examined and commented on at a high level, now failed to reach any crises. The Press no longer warned its readers that the hour was at hand. No radio talks asked listeners to stand firm.

Millions of people who had been weighed down with feelings of fear, hate, horror, and guilt now found themselves living in a different world. At last they could breathe freely. They began to make sensible long-term plans for the future. Many groups of scientists, freed temporarily from their researches into the possibilities of atomic and biological warfare, ventured, timidly at first but then with growing confidence, to divert their research into harmless and possibly useful channels. Having a chance at last to mind their own business, the countries represented at the Conference began making some effort to improve the conditions of life, to lighten the burdens of their citizens. Diplomats and minor officials, able for the time being to ignore time-old foreign policies that had never brought anything but disaster, often converted the very scenes of recurring crises into friendly meeting-places. As the chief representatives of the power motive were still unconscious, the power motive itself rapidly lost force and momentum. All the machinery of ideological and national propaganda, lacking the guiding hand, fell into disuse, and plans were eagerly made to spend the vast sums of money now saved, chiefly on various amenities that the overtaxed citizens had hitherto been unable to afford. Without Presidents, Prime Ministers, Foreign Secretaries, the Americans, British, and French did not know what was happening to Anglo-American and Franco-British relations; and for the first time for years began to get along quite nicely. There was even talk of temporarily suspending the rules and regulations about visas and passports. The easy freedom of the pre-1914 world was almost in sight.

It was then that a brilliant young pathologist from Barcelona arrived at the Hesperides. He had a theory, which he explained to the assembled doctors. He also had a small supply of a new and very powerful antibiotic, which he begged to be allowed to inject into three or four of the unconscious men. He was certain it would bring them out of their coma. Finally, he was given permission to treat one Chief of Staff, one Under-Secretary for Foreign Affairs, and one economic adviser. Within an hour, all three were not only awake but beginning to make angry speeches or to demand secretaries to attend them so that they could dictate aggressive memos. It

208   THOUGHTS IN THE WILDERNESS

was a triumph for the young man from Barcelona, who declared that if he
were given the necessary facilities, he could return within two or three
weeks with a sufficient supply of his remedy to revivify the whole Conference. As he announced this, through the long corridors where peace and
quiet had reigned for many months, loud angry voices were heard. The
medical men exchanged long inquiring glances. They were well aware of
what had been happening in the world during the time the Conference had
slept.

They escorted the young man back to their headquarters, the former
games room of the hotel, securely barred from the Press. They looked
thoughtfully at him. They exchanged more dubious glances. *What was their
decision?* No prizes are offered for the best replies.

EROS AND LOGOS

There are some people who become impatient and angry if they are con-
fronted by large, loose, wild generalisations. (They can usually tolerate a
few of their own: it is yours they object to.) Such people should not read
what follows. It is not for them. I must point out, however, that the object
of these pieces of mine is to provoke thought and discussion, chiefly by
their refusal to treat routine topics in a routine fashion. They do not
pretend to be the Word of the Lord, tablets of stone hauled down from the
sacred mountain. I am merely trying to arouse the interest of the English-
speaking middle class, overworked, worried, and on the edge of the last
ditch. So I am capable of using anthropological and other terms that will
set me at cross-purposes with some readers. For example: *matriarchy*.
What do I mean when I suggest (partly out of devilment) that a matriarchy might save us?

Certainly I do not mean that Cabinet offices, the Judiciary, the Higher
Command, the FBI, and the TUC should be taken over as soon as possible
by bustling, ambitious women. Nor that the images of fat fertility goddesses should be erected jointly by the Ministries of Works and Agricul-
ture. What I am suggesting is that we should begin substituting, in our
scheme of life, the values of the feminine principle, Eros, Yin, for those of

the masculine principle, Logos, Yang. These are not identical with male and female. I am myself a fairly robust male but I am devoted to Eros rather than to Logos. Much modern literature, as widely different as the novels of Mr. E. M. Forster and D. H. Lawrence, is a defence of Eros against Logos. On the other hand, many women, including the most aggressive feminists, are devotees of Logos, Yang girls. Not long ago I received a report of a women's conference in which the conclusions, which gave the impression that a woman was simply a neater, kinder sort of man, had clearly been arrived at under the spell of Logos. Those good ladies had not invited Yin to their conference: they probably knew she would not have behaved herself.

Risking the largest and wildest generalisations, let us consider the four Great Powers, America, Russia, Britain, and France, in terms of Eros and Logos, Yin and Yang. It is among the ironies of our time that the two main contestants, America and Russia, both represent societies that have too much Logos and not enough Eros. The rest of us have to choose not between Yin and Yang but between two Yangs. Which is yet another reason why we feel so uneasy, war or no war. We suspect that, whatever happens, Eros is out, not Yang.

Thus I cannot agree with my correspondent who declared that America is a matriarchy. Appearances there are deceptive. Girls may be made much of, there may be much sentiment about Mother, woman (being widowed early) may own much of the wealth of the country, yet American society does not show us Eros triumphant. Its chief values are masculine values. The restlessness, ruthless ambition, emphasis on change, inventions, gadgets, mechanical progress, rather pedantic idealism, the idolatry of business, are all masculine, Yang stuff. That famous phrase "The business of America is *business*" would seem to Eros the manifesto of a lunatic. Even the jazzing up of sex — the girl as "quite a dish" — is Yang at work. (In the world of Eros it is the mature woman and not the young girl who is important.) Fifth Avenue shows us Logos bribing Eros with silks and gems. Woman in urban America has everything except the deep and lasting rewards of Eros. I once saw a party of middle-aged American women, lined, nervous, haunted, being shown a group of Indian squaws, smiling, fat, sleek as seals. The white women, encouraged by the woman guide, were pitying the red women, who had to do so much of the hard work. But the red women were not pitying themselves: they lived under Eros, and kept on smiling, with just a hint of feminine insolence. Of course, they would have liked to have had washing machines and four sets of nylon underclothes. But not at the Logos price, thank you. Hard work or no hard work, they were living in the right world.

Eros has to come in somewhere, of course, but if the masculine principle is supremely triumphant, not properly balanced, then Eros arrives in an inferior form. The result is a taste for crude sex and hard liquor, sex without personal relationship, drink as a short cut to unconsciousness. Naturally there are a great many Americans who dislike this style of life, but nobody who knows urban America and the literature (often very powerful) that represents it could deny that it is a style of life much in favour there. Eros throws the party when the serious work of the day has been done. When the Yang is tired, he 'phones for the Yin. But the masculine values are the real values, shaping and colouring society.

The essential Russian character, as displayed by its great literature and even by Party members after ten glasses of vodka in a room without microphones, belongs more to Eros than to Logos, though it has always been haunted by a kind of wild Logos spectre. (Those country houses in Turgenev show us both the Eros values and the Logos speculation.) But Russian Communism is Logos gone mad. Revolutions nearly always start in an Eros atmosphere, with much talk of private happiness, much love-making and the swearing of eternal friendships, and then soon swing over to Logos, with more laws, more police, more demands for instant obedience. A State that ignores the claims, which ought to be primary, of lovers, husbands and wives, parents and children, represents the Logos at work without any check from Eros. It destroys private happiness, all those relationships and styles of life that are at the heart of Eros, for the sake of a theory, or mere power, or some vague dream of happiness that has never been realised yet. To Eros this is the substance being destroyed for the shadow, and therefore sheer lunacy. If Russia is not a complete hell on earth, that is because Eros, the Yin values, still keep breaking through, though their activities are never on the agenda.

Here, to keep the balance, I must add my belief that a society entirely dominated by Eros would sink into stagnation and sloth, and oddly enough, I suspect, would begin to develop its own cruelties, Yin being as cruel in her way as Yang can be in his. But we need not worry about this state of things. Our immediate dangers are far on the other side. The Yang has his foot pressed down on the accelerator.

We are between two vast and powerful societies that are governed, each in its own way, by the masculine principle not reasonably balanced by the feminine. That such societies should be piling up atom bombs should surprise nobody. This is Logos on the spree. And it is significant that in both these societies the emphasis is on quantities of things rather than on the quality of personal experience. Soviet propaganda and American advertisements often seem to speak with almost the same voice: the management is different but the enterprise is broadly the same. If I must choose, I would prefer an American victory to a Russian one, just as I would prefer writing

TV advertisements for Cornflakes to lumbering on thin cabbage soup in Siberia. But I do not want either of these Yang-heavy societies, which are less harmonious, less civilised, less capable of providing the deeper satisfactions, than the smaller and older communities they are dominating and then swallowing. We should have formed a neutral block, wearing the colours of the Yin, under the banner of Eros, who has not yet been completely banished from Western Europe.

Some people see in the Welfare State the handiwork of Eros. I wish I could agree with them. But though Welfare may belong to Eros, the State does not; and it seems to me that in the Welfare State the emphasis is on the State, with Logos firmly in command. (And I cannot help wondering if some of the results of the Welfare State do not show the re-entry of Eros in an inferior form, creating a dim passivity.) There is, however, in British life still a suggestion that Yin is with us. We find traces of her in the flexibility of our official machinery, in our lingering respect for private life, in a traditional piety towards earth, in the wealth of our odd hobbies and pastimes, in the wide network (to which we should cling) of our voluntary associations. Eros still broods over much of our country life.

If we want to see more of Eros, we should look across the Channel. Much of the condemnation of the French comes from the irritation felt by Logos for Eros. Try as they might to meet the Yang commitments, the French cannot help being guided by Yin values. That is why even the people who are most irritated by France, when they are discussing politics, want to spend their holidays there. They need the refreshment, the healing touch, of Eros. They want at least a little time away from the arid lunacies of Logos. And if I were a Frenchman, instead of being apologetic I would rise up in wrathful defence of my country's failure to turn itself into an efficient machine. I would declare that in our apparent Yin chaos, our wild Eros individualism, we were cherishing values that the other Great Powers were beginning to forget; that we were trying to preserve the sensible human scale; that we refused to sacrifice private happiness, discovered in the family, among lovers and friends, in the arts and genuine craftsmanship, for public bosh, power, and statistics; that we still knew, if other people had forgotten, what deep satisfaction came from the service of Eros and the Yin. There are of course many things wrong with France, just as there are with the other three countries, but you can still find there a zest and a sparkle hard to discover in New York, Moscow, or London. It is the twinkle in the eyes of Eros.

ON EDUCATION

When I was sixteen I left school and found myself a job in a wool office. I had no intention of settling down in the wool business; I had already made up my mind to be a writer, and indeed was already writing hard; but clearly there was no living to be made out of writing for some years to come, so into the office I went. That I was allowed to remain there until I joined the army in 1914 is a tribute to my personality, which then, if not now, was a peculiar mixture of the insufferable and the enchanting; for there cannot have been many young clerks worse than I was in the long history of the wool trade. After about four and a half years in the army I received an ex-officer's grant that took me to Cambridge but by no means kept me there, even on a diet of bread and cheese and boiled eggs, so that I had to eke out with journalism, coaching, odd lectures, anything to earn a guinea or two. Finally, I left Cambridge for London, with some vague introductions and capital of about forty-seven pounds.

Looking back, I can see quite clearly now that the great formative period for me was neither school nor the Cambridge years. It was 1911–1914, when nobody was trying to educate me nor paying for me to be instructed, when, in fact, I was working (though as little as possible) in the wool office. Our hours then were longer than most office hours are now: we had to be there at nine, took an hour for lunch, and usually finished sometime between six and seven. (If we worked after seven we received sixpence for tea money. No refreshment was provided before then.) We still sat on high stools like Dickens characters, and I was adroit at looking as if I were entering up the bag book, on my high desk, when in fact I was reading the poems of Yeats or Chesterton's last essays, lying inside my open drawer, which could be closed in a flash. I could also make a slower journey to and from the Bradford Conditioning House, losing myself in daydreams, than anybody else in the trade. Nevertheless, in spite of all these dodges, the office claimed me all the week and never let me go on Saturday until about half-past one. Nor did I live just round the corner from it, for our house, on the edge of the town, was at least two miles away. The fact remains, however, that this was the time when I learnt most and came along fastest. The State was not investing a penny in me.

(And here, for the benefit of those readers who believe in the State but not much in me, let me strike a rough balance. What have I had from the State? A very modest contribution towards my childhood and early youth, a grant that barely kept me alive at Cambridge, and a few fees for jobs undertaken from a sense of duty. What has it had from me? Fortunes in direct and indirect taxation, in Entertainment Tax on my plays and films, in foreign currency it badly needed, to say nothing about my services as a fighting soldier [no great shakes] in one war and as a day-and-night propagandist in another war. And if I should now go broke and dotty, I might receive with luck a Civil List pension of about two hundred a year. That is, if the country can afford it after meeting so many claims upon its generosity. I would have been ten times better off under George the Fourth.)

The truth is, I was fortunate during those years in my environment. My native city of Bradford is frequently mentioned, mostly by people who know nothing about it, as a kind of symbol of "muck and brass," a stronghold of North-country narrow provincialism. But when I lived there, as a youth, it was considered the most progressive city in the Kingdom. It was a Labour outpost. The first elementary school in the country where meals were provided was the one of which my father was headmaster. We had a Labour weekly to which, during this period, I contributed a regular page. Moreover, a number of Liberal German-Jewish families had settled there, as in Manchester, to give our West Riding dough a leaven of culture. Our Subscription Concerts followed the same plan as those at Leipzig. We also had our Permanent Orchestra and two great Choral Societies. We had three local daily papers as well as several weeklies. We had two theatres and two music-halls. We had a flourishing Arts Club and a Playgoers' Society. Our Central Lending and Reference Libraries were excellent. Bradford men were making their names in the arts and sciences. And though the town was ugly enough, the inviolable moors, where we walked and talked most week-ends, began only a tuppenny tram-ride away. For a few pence more, taking a train, you reached the Dales, the most beautiful country-side in England.

So there we were, walking towards our vast sevenpenny teas, arguing over our pipes of fourpenny Navy Cut, listening to Nikisch and Busoni, Casals and Kreisler, for ninepence, seeing Little Tich and Grock for fourpence, reading H. M. Tomlinson in the local paper and Chesterton's Saturday essay in the *Daily News,* buying our shilling classics or Nelson's old sevenpenny series. I am not growling and grumbling again. For all I know to the contrary, lots of youngsters in their late teens are having as good a life now. Here I am not contrasting two periods. I am explaining why, in my considered judgement, these years, when I was neither in school nor college, turned out the most rewarding years I ever knew. It was, I repeat, because I was fortunate in my environment. It was not that I went to the right sort of school, but that I was living in the right sort of town. (Of course it might not have been right for you, but it was right for me.) In theory no doubt it was all wrong that a "gifted youth" should spend his best years working long hours in a wool office. In practice it worked well. But it worked well, not because I happened to have massive determination and an iron will (I have never had either at any time), but because there was something in the atmosphere of that place at that period which encouraged me to develop and to grow. I do not think any school or college, by itself, could have done it. I would always have been wondering what was happening outside the walls. I would have been telling myself that this scholastic seclusion was not real life. I would not have taken anybody's word about what was going on in the outer world. But living as I did, I knew I was experiencing real life, exploring the outer world, taking what I wanted from my own town. Thus I was educating myself.

Let us take a look at what seem at first sight to be more formal processes of education. For example, at Oxford and Cambridge. In what lies their unique value? I would reply without hesitation that it lies in their successful creation (not quite what it used to be, perhaps) of an atmosphere of disinterested scholarship, an environment in which thought itself is triumphant. A young man can live for at least nine terms in a place that does not care a damn about the price of cotton and tin and the export trade. He can sit up all night arguing about God and Art. He can lock himself in, as I did once, with a tin of tobacco, a case of beer, and the whole of the Elizabethan Drama. In such places knowledge is in the very air. Not the formal courses of instruction but the atmosphere and the surroundings enrich the student. I have long thought it a shame that our students of music and acting have to live in London, lost among millions who care little or nothing for these arts. They would do much better if, as sometimes happens abroad, they received instruction in some place where the very landladies and bus drivers had a passion for music or the theatre, where the street outside was the ally of the school.

Now we have to spend so much on the school that we cannot afford to civilise the street. We are hoping that sooner or later the school will be strong enough to overcome the street, that a generation of teenagers will finally leave school to tear down the street and rebuild the town. If you argue with enthusiastic educationalists, they will admit under pressure that so far the street seems to have won, but they will declare their faith in the imminent victory of the school. I wish I could share this faith. But the odds seem to me too heavily in favour of the street, the town, the local environment. If their influence is not good, then the good influence of the school will not last long. To nine youngsters out of ten, the values of their home, their street, their town, seem far more important than anything learnt at school. There, outside, is real life, the world of the adults, towards which they are headed, away from the kid stuff of the classrooms. So it is largely a waste of time and money trying to persuade children that Shakespeare is our pride and joy if the town they live in cannot even boast one theatre, and prefers the films of Abbott and Costello to all that Shakespeare ever wrote. And if more and more youngsters leaving school want to read the *Daily Scream,* which steadily gets worse and worse, then what return is our national investment in education bringing? No doubt we need more teachers and should offer them better prospects. But what guarantee have we that they can successfully challenge the proprietors of the *Daily Scream,* the TV, radio and film experts, the advertising gang, the haters of the arts, the slow murderers of eager, hopeful living? Who, so far, is winning all along the line?

But no, I must not growl and grumble. I will simply state the case, as I see it. I owe most to a time when I was not being formally educated but when I enjoyed an environment favourable to a youth of my sort. I realise that youth still has its opportunities, perhaps more of them in some directions than I had, but it does seem to me that by and large the environment is far less favourable than it was, chiefly owing to the recent development of mass communications and of what might be called a mass pseudo-culture. (Where comparison can be made, for example, with the popular Press, the decline is obvious.) Meanwhile, we spend more and more and more on Education, hoping rather desperately that somehow and sometime the values of the school will triumph over those of the streets outside the school. And this costs us so much that we cannot afford to change and improve the towns that receive our boys and girls after they have left school. The environment they know in their later teens, probably their most formative years, is a dreary mess of cheap commercial values, in which any fire kindled in the classroom is likely to be soon damped down and smothered. Perhaps the educationalists are right, and we have only to turn a corner. Perhaps I am an odd fish and cannot argue from my own experience. But I cannot help feeling thankful that I grew up before we had achieved such progress.

ANOTHER REVOLUTION

The other day, reading the Prologue to Collingwood's *Speculum Mentis,* I came to the following passage: "The actual output of pictures and statues, poems and string quartets does not fail of its market because of its own low quality; for the purchasers do not buy the best, because they have not the skill to distinguish it; and anyone who doubts this can prove it to himself by merely walking round an exhibition of pictures and observing which of them are marked with red seals. . . ." This was written just over thirty years ago. Now I have walked round a good many exhibitions of pictures during the last ten years, often prepared to buy something I particularly liked, and it has been my experience that after the first few days, in an exhibition that is selling at all, it is undoubtedly the best pictures that bear the red seals and have already been bought. The purchasers have changed since Collingwood's time. They have probably less money but they have better taste and judgement. There has in fact been a revolution that, so far as I know, no social philosopher anticipated, and that even now deserves more attention than it has received. And it might save some of us a good deal of time and temper if we understood what has happened and is still happening.

I do not know what is happening to other nations, but I am certain that among us English the visual appreciation of things has increased while the literary sense is decaying. Years ago I noticed that my own children lived more through the eye than I had done at their age, and that at the same time they did not lose themselves in books as I had done. It did not occur to me then that perhaps a general shift of attention was taking place. Now I am sure that what had happened in my family had also happened in thousands of others. These post-war years have shown us the results of this change. Whatever appeals first to the eye attracts immediate attention. The important art exhibitions, as we have seen, draw big crowds at once. Even the more modest shows, if they are fairly representative, are always well filled. More and more art books are published and sold, in spite of their high cost. There are more and more books in which the text is a mere excuse for the photographs. It is the popular illustrated periodicals that survive. People must have something to stare at, as the advertisers know. It is the demands of the eye that must be satisfied first. What was once chiefly the method of the kindergarten, to catch the attention of very young children, is now imitated far and wide, for every possible purpose.

Post-war entertainment proves the point over and over again. Ballet uses music, but its chief appeal is to the eye, and the popularity of ballet shows no sign of waning. (Even here in the Isle of Wight, where we do not even pretend to be in the movement, the only Arts Council import that paid for itself, I understand, was rather sketchy ballet.) The ice shows, which play to fantastic business, pipe out some indifferent words and music, but they are of course designed for the eye. In order to survive at all, the Theatre, especially in its larger productions, has had to seduce the visual sense, whatever might happen to the mind behind it. The most successful directors are visual directors, often working as if they were producing ballet and not drama. It is this fashion that is working havoc with some Shakespeare productions, which will omit some of his most exquisite poetry so that there is more time for pageantry and eye-filling antics. The Bard has almost been turned into a clothes-line. His newest directors, who seem to have no feeling for words, are ready to cut any other line.

The Film may have lost some ground as all-round entertainment during these last few years, but as a modest art form, as a visual creation of director and cameraman, it attracts more and more of the young. This is proved by the success of the British Film Institute and the hundred-and-one local societies it encourages. From the ballet the young London highbrows go swarming to any West End cinema showing a film that has been praised by the more austere critics, those concerned with visual values. Very few of these youngsters are to be found at any unspectacular play, no matter how original and powerful it might be. They no longer want words and ideas, not even those of Messrs. Eliot and Fry. The visual sense must be fed and satisfied: they must have objective images, beautiful and significant if possible, but at a pinch almost any will do.

Finally — as the film boys say, the Big Pay-off — Television. Notice that it exists continually in a champagne atmosphere of ballyhoo and excitement that sound radio, even in its greatest days, never knew. Make two successful appearances in *Who's Your Father?* and the red carpets are rolled out from Lime Grove to the Caprice Restaurant. Here is the Giant Eye in fine frenzy rolling. One turn of a switch, and the images pour in. True, there may be words and music — and I will delightedly grant you that now this is anything but a "land without music" — but ask any television producer what his first concern is. It is the visual sense that must be tickled and flattered first. And with this medium, delivered on any hearth-rug, we are as yet only making a rough-and-ready start: a choice of programmes, larger screens, colour and closer definition, all are yet to come and all have been promised. And because its own chief appeal is to the eye, then its programmes will tend to emphasise more and more what appeals to the eye in the world outside. The children are its slaves. So a huge generation not of readers or listeners but of viewers is now moving towards what we hope can be called maturity. Unless there should be a sharp reaction — always a possibility among us pendulum creatures — the final triumph of the visual sense is assured. In the end will be The Eye.

If you are looking at pictures, photographs, ballet, ice shows and other spectacles, films and television programmes, you cannot be curled up in a chair with a book. Moreover, the mind finds it hard to use its interior eye with a lot of noise about, and quiet corners are harder to find than they used to be. (Sooner or later, some of us will have to buy an instrument that can switch on silence instead of sound.) Indeed, many youngsters are now so accustomed to noise that a quiet room seems sinister and they have to bring a radio set or a gramophone into it, for sheer security's sake. In this atmosphere it is impossible for the art of literature to flourish. All the conditions and habits of mind are against it. The inner eye cannot be exercised. A feeling for words, a sense of their magical potency, can no longer be acquired. Some interest in ideas, on which the appreciation of literature also depends, is hardly felt at all. (It has been noted by educators, particularly in America, that too much visual instruction can make a youngster's mind unfit to grapple with abstract ideas.) So the necessary equipment of a genuine reader has not been assembled. The password that opens the old treasure cave has been forgotten.

Here some critics, in my view, do more harm than good. These are the critics who take a lofty and somewhat arrogant stand, and seem to regard themselves as the ferocious theologians and grand inquisitors of the art. They announce, with that air of cold finality which impresses undergraduates and repels their fathers and mothers, that only a few books by a few carefully chosen authors can be regarded as Literature, and that all else is rubbish on which no time should be wasted. (The critic's own works, presumably, are an exception.) Thus, Stendhal is Literature, Dumas is not; Henry James is Literature, W. W. Jacobs is not. And nothing is gained, but much lost, by this hoity-toity treatment. It is better to assume that all writing not merely informative, all poems, novels, essays, even criticism, are *literature of a sort,* ranging from the shockingly bad to the good and glorious. A lad who has enjoyed Dumas may come to enjoy Stendhal. Jacobs, a genuine artist in his own kind, may lead to James. Because, in my youth, a lot of girls received at Christmas and birthdays their limp-leather editions of FitzGerald's *Omar,* many of them went on to buy and read newer poets, with the result that poetry found its way into the lists of all good publishers. So long as there are readers, trying this and that, there is hope for literature. It has been our misfortune that just when reading itself, as a pleasurable activity, was challenged, when the easier visual sense began to be immensely catered for, we should have developed a school of critics who spent more time warning people away from literature than encouraging them to enjoy it. They were the allies of the outer, not the inner, eye. If they are now appalled by the success of these visual things, partly at the expense of literature, it serves them right: they helped to steer people away from the bookshops.

Books come out, of course, and by the thousand, and publishers strangely multiply, to swell the chorus of *Ruin!* But it cannot be denied that we no longer behave as if we were primarily a literary nation. The space given to books and authors has dwindled. The mere attention, let alone the old excitement, is not what it was. (Dylan Thomas's tragic early death, more than his life and works, gave him sudden prominence.) To a writer the atmosphere of Paris seems quite strange now, because Paris is still a literary capital and London is not. Sartre, no towering genius, is capable of generating more excitement on both banks of the Seine than all of us could raise here, even if the whole Council of the Society of Authors marched along the Embankment in our underpants, making a last desperate appeal to the visual if not to the literary sense. The grim harrying of the educated middle class, which has long been both the chief producer and consumer of literature, has done something for this revolution too. If our rulers were to be photographed holding a book instead of patting a racehorse, both the important political sections of our people, the magnates and the trade unionists, would feel that some contact with the great heart of the nation had been lost. But even what is left of that middle class, which has given us most of these bearded young men and untidy girls with horse-tail hair, has been seduced by the visual appeal, is growing up to expect its images to be created for it, is forgetting the ancient magic of words and any passion for ideas. Sometimes I think they are being encouraged to go this way — for it is not our old art that receives the subsidies — because they will be all the easier to handle. The busy eye is less rebellious than the lively mind. No barricades will be manned by *montage* enthusiasts, balletomanes, and the patrons of *Desert Song on Ice*. (And if publishers think they can still discover a few lively minds, what about putting a few of them in the dock, to be bullied by lawyers, then fined or imprisoned? That ought to rattle these fellows.) Meanwhile, we writers must accept the fact of this revolution. Soon we may have to take in one another's washing. It will be a change from trying to cut one another's throats.

I

WHO IS ANTI-AMERICAN?

Most of the reviews of *Journey Down a Rainbow* have been friendly —
though there was the usual anonymous assassin in *The Times* — but too
many of the reviewers have assumed that our book is yet another attack
upon America. It is nothing of the kind, as we began the book by announcing. What I describe and denounce in my chapters is an economic-social-
cultural system I call *Admass*. But *Admass* and the *Admassians* are not
synonymous with America and the Americans, not even with Texas and
the Texans, as again I was careful to point out. The sharpest and most
urgent critics of *Admass* are themselves American. A large proportion of
American writing is now devoted to questioning, challenging, satirising,
and condemning the standards and values of *Admass*. This I know because
I read a great deal of contemporary American writing: unlike many reviewers, who do not seem to be reading even the specimens of contemporary English writing sent to them by editors.

On the other hand, as I have indicated in our book and have suggested
more than once in these columns, there is plenty of *Admass* now outside
America. No doubt one finds the biggest, richest, gaudiest samples of the
system across the Atlantic, but the rest of the world is hurrying to catch up.
Post-war Britain is one of the most progressive *Admass* colonies. That
banquet the other week at the Guildhall, to mark the inauguration of
commercial television, was pure *Admass* from soup to nuts. One reason
why we are having such argument and fuss about Royalty is that it is
caught between traditional Britain and the new *Admass* Britain, between
the yearly portrait and the *Daily Sketch*. As I have said before, we English
are more dangerously situated than the Americans because most of us, and
reviewers to a man, do not realise we are in any danger. We think that if
we can still toddle along to the Athenaeum, the Beefsteak, and Garrick
Clubs, the London Library, have our shirts made to measure, and hope to
be made a Knight Commander of the Grand Order of Gentlemen of the
Bedchamber, the *Admassian* jungle darkening the air all round us is no
nearer than New York.

These reviews will add to my reputation, built up over a quarter of a century, as an anti-American. For one of the public roles thrust upon me is that of *The Man Who Does Not Like America*. Except in private among a large circle of American friends, I have never been allowed to step out of this role. For twenty years, American reporters, after not being able to induce me to say anything rude about their country, have invented offensive remarks, all with a strong American accent, and have conjured them in and out of my mouth. I am the Gilbert Harding of Anglo-American relations. Dinner parties from Long Island to Santa Monica have been astonished when I have failed to insult everybody within hearing. Ordinary cheerful compliments have been probed for depths of savage irony. In descriptive essays of mine, filled with nothing but humorous exaggeration, there have been heard screams of anger, thunders of rage. And nobody has ever bothered to inquire — and this is where real irony begins — why this hater and denouncer of America should be always going to the trouble and expense of finding his way back there.

At this point, the cynical know-all jumps in, to tell me that I am a shrewd fellow (which I am not) who knows how to collect dollars. And he is quite wrong, years out of date, for it is some time since the Americans paid handsomely to be insulted by visitors. An anti-American reputation is now a poor dollar-earner. The frequent visits only just pay for themselves. The truth is astonishingly simple: I go to America not only because I have professional business to attend to there but also because I like going to America. I criticise and grumble, of course, but that is largely because I have now an affection for the place and the people and am beginning to feel almost at home there. After all, I do still more criticising and grumbling here, where I am completely at home, in a country and among a people I love. You don't catch me grousing about Afghanistan and Patagonia, the Bolivians and Albanians: I don't know about them and don't care. But about America I do know and care.

To begin with, I have seen more of the country than most Americans have. I have a ripening acquaintance with its history and literature. I count myself as a friend of this nation, and so take with me the curiosity, the affectionate concern, and if necessary the frank criticism, of a friend. But I refer now not to America as it figures in cartoons, in articles by economic and foreign-affairs experts, in statistics or statements by mysterious official spokesmen, in any abstract account of human affairs. I know and have a growing affection for the real America, the place itself where the real people live: for Central Park on a Sunday morning, the magical towers of New York at dusk; for those white villages among the flaring woods of New England in the fall; for the majestic rivers I have crossed so many times, the trains hooting so mournfully as night descends on the immense sad plains; for the sparkle and sharp fragrance, the blue air and distant violet ranges of the desert; for the Pacific dimpling beyond the solemn groves of giant trees; and for all the people, or most of them, I have talked to, eaten and drunk with, cursed or kissed, across those three thousand miles. I can write and talk American. I could pass for one, at a pinch, if the cops were after me.

There is a further irony. There are people here who are never accused of being anti-American, who are praised over there for their friendship. And many of these are the very people who secretly loathe the place and detest its people, who would not care a rap if tomorrow the Atlantic and Pacific oceans met above Kansas City. They merely go whoring after American wealth and power. So long as they can use the Americans, they will contrive to put up with them. What they say in public, when they are wanting something America can give them, is very different from what they say in private, as these battered ears can testify. If wealth, power, influence, passed from the northern to the southern half of that continent, these fellows would be making the same smiling after-dinner speeches about the Argentine and Brazil — and the United States would be out. The test of friendship does not lie in id e compliments and lip-service but in a close continuing interest and an affectionate concern, which may at times necessitate plain speaking. The weakness of America's present position, which is roughly that of a newly arrived rich man at a decaying fashionable resort, is that this test cannot be easily applied, the whole scene being too strange and bewildering, with the result that Americans too often do not realise where their true friends are.

There is another difficulty. We all tend now — and Americans more than most — to imagine that the world of political intrigue, newspaper and radio comment, public relations and propaganda, cartoon adventures, is the real world. Given this false assumption, then if we do not like the State Department's handling of the German problem, we do not like America, would never want to see again those crimson maples, huge rivers, plains, deserts, seacoasts both Atlantic and Pacific, would have done with all the hundred and fifty million persons who inhabit those regions. If we do not agree with Richard Nixon, any assorted Republican senators, the *Reader's Digest, Time,* the *Saturday Evening Post,* the Hearst Press, and Westbrook Pegler, then we cannot possibly want to enjoy another martini at the Coffee House Club, the Boston Symphony Orchestra, or the first sight of the desert from the Santa Fe *Chief.* It is as if when friends from New York arrived outside our door in the Albany, I did not invite them in until I had made sure they were in full agreement with our policy in Cyprus and were enthusiastic admirers of Eden, Butler, and Macmillan. Put like this, it seems altogether too idiotic, yet many "anti-American" reputations, referred to over and over again in the Press, are based on no better foundation.

Take this journal itself. It has a notorious anti-American reputation; I must have seen a hundred references to it in the American Press. And what does this mean? No more than what I have already suggested, namely, that it has a reasoned dislike of certain American political attitudes and policies, themselves equally severely criticised by a host of Americans. What it does *not* mean — and what it would mean if it were properly used — is that this journal is written by men and women who detest the country, the people, the whole American idea, who wish the War of Independence had been lost or that Lee had finally defeated Grant, who sneer at American customs, habits, manners, accents, who go out of their way to avoid meeting Americans, who find nothing to admire in anything that comes from such a people, who in their heart of hearts regard America and the Americans as the enemy. This is to be genuinely anti-American. And in London, Paris, Rome and elsewhere I have met these haters of America (and some distinguished members of my profession were among them); but they were not on the staff of this journal; and I never remember seeing one of them described in the American Press as being anti-American. The bricks are always thrown in the wrong direction.

When Mrs. Smith tells Mr. Smith that his trousers are baggy and he needs a haircut, nobody accuses her of being anti-Smith. Now I have actually spent more time in America than I have in any country except England; more than I have in Scotland, Wales, Ireland. I have more friends in America than I have in any country except England. If I were to be kicked out of this country, I should probably go to America, if it would have me. I have now an affection for it, and that is why I do not hesitate to criticise it. When I meet a friend I assume he would prefer my honest opinion to a vote of thanks. There is much in American life I do not like, just as there is much in English life that I do not like. But if I denounce *Admass* in *Journey Down a Rainbow,* that is not because it is largely American in origin and I long to have another crack at the Yanks. I do it because I believe the *Admass* system to be unworthy of the place, the people, and the astonishing revolutionary idea, unique in history, they represent. This is a nation that came out of a noble dream. If it is anti-American to remember that dream, which so many pro-Americans seem to forget, then I am indeed anti-American.

THE UNICORN

We are losing because we are backing the wrong beast. Our money should be on the Unicorn, not the Lion. We forget that a Lion, a creature of this world, is subject to time, that his claws are worn, his teeth mere stumps, his eyes cloudy with age, that he has lost his speed and his spring, that he has begun to shrink and is now dwarfed by eagles that darken the sky and bears that come rearing out of their winter caves as tall as fir trees. We have kept this Lion in captivity too long. He has yawned and dozed behind bars through too many years. When he roars now it is only because his dinner is late, and no longer because he wishes to challenge and terrify his enemies and ours. All sorts of shabby beasts come trotting up, give his tail a nip, screech in derision, and romp and prance within sight of his sad yellow eyes. Now that he is so old, Lion-taming is a corny act, well down on the bill. We know all this, but habit persists: we still put our money on him, and so lose it steadily.

Even now we are not risking the Unicorn, that odd creature which found its way onto our coat of arms one morning when all the sound types at the College of Heralds were busy elsewhere. Some unsound fellow, afterwards dismissed without a pension, opened a gate not marked on any plan of the establishment, to admit this fabulous monster. We tolerate him — after all, he looks pretty on summer afternoons, and the ladies, bless them, have always had a fancy for him — but, of course, no solid money, direct from the City, backs his chance, even at a sporting long odds. These are difficult times, when a fellow has to be careful, so all the important money must still go on poor old Lion. The careful, sound chaps couldn't agree with one another more: it's Lion or nothing, let's face it. And so that same nothing, a darkness in which now and again there glimmer phosphorescently some nightmare faces, creeps nearer and nearer.

We prefer not to remember that the Unicorn, just because he is not a creature of this world, escapes the withering process of time. Unlike the Lion, he is as young as ever he was, as swift and strong; his eyes are undimmed; his single horn as tense and unyielding as it was many centuries ago. He was magical then, he is magical now. The enchanted kingdom he represents may be largely forgotten, but it is still there, awaiting our discovery. But, of course, if we lose faith in the Unicorn, if we are secretly afraid of him, if we deliberately pretend he is not with us now, then he cannot help us, for he is fixed, motionless and powerless, until we speak the word that releases him. Perhaps we leave that word unspoken, even declare we no longer know what it is, because we think that any such happy magic won't work. Too many of us islanders now believe only in the other kind, a dark sorcery far removed from the Unicorn and all he represents, and because we believe in it we fasten its hold upon our minds.

Under the spell of this dark sorcery, probably designed to make us follow the social insects, we prostrate ourselves before the vast cement altar of the unimaginative, the uncreative, the unenterprising, the uninventive. It is the cult of a dreary conformity. Only the dullest is good enough for us. No man is fit to be trusted unless he is a bore. Anybody with an idea must be ignored, and soon may have to choose between exile and prison. Originality and insight and enthusiasm are a bar to advancement. A sound man — and we want no other kind — does not interrupt the march of the zombies. No risks must be taken; no crackpots encouraged; but under the guidance of thoughtful, responsible men, following a well-tried plan, we must move with care from one disaster to another. All gleams of hope may be extinguished, but in a decent, sensible manner. And mesmerised in the deepening gloom we hear the voices of authority in town halls, banqueting rooms, TV and radio, crying: "Mr. Chairman, friends, fellow somnambulists — tonight I hope to be as repetitious, uninspiring, and as utterly devoid of creative ideas as I was when I last had the honour of addressing you . . ." And amid this mournful sorcery we forget that we still have the Unicorn.

Here we come to the grand ironic illusion. We islanders wish to impress the world. We might have decided to spend our time, trouble, money, putting ourselves into such a position that it did not matter whether the world was impressed by us or not (in which case it would have been vastly and astonishingly impressed by us); but the decision went the other way, so that we are committed to the task of impressing the world. *Hurray for the islanders!* the world must cry. But we do not hear these cries. Their absence is mentioned in the House, deplored in leading articles. The world now refuses to be impressed; it shrugs, jeers, sniggers, roars with laughter. Sounder and sounder men, absolutely dependable types, present at great expense our famous old Lion act, but everywhere it is a flop. "But look, please," they implore the audiences, "this is our Lion. *The* Lion. The one you read about at school — the identical Lion. Give him a little pat if you like, only, of course, be careful. Stop throwing orange peel, please. No, don't go away. See — he's opening his mouth. He may roar in a moment. Yawning? Never mind — hang on, chaps. In just a minute the Member for Podbury West, already making his mark in the House, will place his head in the Lion's mouth. Or — say the word, and the chairman of the Cosy Tin Motor Company — he'll be along in a jiffy — will ride on the Lion's back. No? I must say, you people are a bit much." It is all no use: the act is a flop.

But does nobody care about us islanders any more? Is there not even a murmur of admiration, a glance of respect? This is where the irony begins. Now I have done some travelling during the past eleven years, and all the way from Copenhagen to Cuernavaca, Tiflis to Tokyo, the same thing happens almost everywhere. Fairly late in the evening, after a few rounds of bourbon-on-the-rocks, vodka, schnapps, saki, tequila, or whatever they are serving in those parts, the foreigners tell me that I am fortunate to be living in a country with such a noble creature, for which they have the deepest respect, the highest admiration. "Our Lion?" I exclaim, gratified but astonished. At once a barrage of emphatic negatives descends upon me. Who cares about that Lion? Please, is finish, that Lion. No, no, no, what is so wonderful about my island is its beautiful Unicorn. Boy, that's some beast! Comrade, we salute the British Unicorn! Honoured colleague, you must have for it much pride! And after another two rounds of whatever we are drinking too much of, they confess, most of them, that no such creature, so old and yet so young, so timeless, so potent in its magic, can be discovered now in their countries. And do we islanders realise how fortunate we are?

Unless the night is far gone, as a good Briton I pretend that always we are joyously aware of our good fortune. I suggest that the Prime Minister, the Chancellor of the Exchequer and all his senior officials, the Lord Privy Seal, the Leader of the Opposition, the Archbishops, assorted chairmen of federated industries, TUC, banks, coal and other boards, and anybody else of importance I can think of, are Unicorn attendants to a man. I describe how we cherish the lovely creature, taxing ourselves almost to bankruptcy to keep him glossy and proud. How can I reveal, at that time and place, the melancholy and ironic truth — that we are all so busy feeding and grooming and petting the mangy old Lion that we hardly notice the Unicorn? How can I confess my suspicion that some of my fellow islanders in authority, just intelligent enough to be aware of the Unicorn, only fear and hate him, and secretly hope that soon he will gallop away for ever? How can I explain that these men feel it would be safer to live where that fabulous single horn has reflected the moonlight for the last time? So although I may hear in my head these complacent or fearful voices, I say nothing about them to the foreigners, admiring me now as a visitor from the enchanted land of the Unicorn.

It is my belief — and nearly every bulletin I read or hear adds confirmation to it — that the Lion can do no more for us, that only the Unicorn can save us now. We have reached again, as we must do at irregular intervals, the hour of the Unicorn. I am seeing it, of course, as the heraldic sign and the symbol of the imaginative, creative, boldly inventive, original, and individual side of the national character. It is such qualities and what they have contributed to our national life and culture that are so genuinely and warmly admired by the rest of the world. It is the Britain of the poets and artists and scientific discoverers and passionate reformers and bold inventors and visionaries and madmen that still dazzles the world. If we want to impress it, this is what impresses it — the Britain of the Unicorn. If, as I believe, this country is in danger of decline, only the Unicorn qualities can rescue it. If we continue to suppress this side of ourselves, refusing to be imaginative, creative, inventive, experimental, we are lost. But now there is hardly an unsound Unicorn man to be discovered in our public affairs, hardly a single gleam of that legendary horn. Yet what else have we to offer the world that it wants from us? The Lion leaves it hostile or derisive. The old roar is wheezy, only displaying the worn teeth. Nothing there to awe distant peoples into submission, nor even to earn their respect. Commerce, then? Not without the Unicorn touch; not simply routine sound trading. Are we more industrious and painstaking than our competitors? (Don't make me laugh, chum.) What advantages now have our factories? Have we even many skills not easily acquired by disgruntled customers? Do British salesmen outwit all others? What, in short, have we still got that our rivals haven't got?

To that final and terrible question I can only reply — *the Unicorn and all it represents.* Tricky, of course, risky, of course; mistakes will be made; all manner of rules and regulations may have to be broken; but a better prospect than that of millions on meagre rations, standing about again in hopeless streets, the victims of routine policies, timid conformity, minds without insight, courage and gaiety. So — up with the Unicorn! Make way for the unsound types, all those who made such a bad impression on the committee! Forward the imaginative men, the creators and originators, even the rebels and cranks and eccentrics, all those with corners not rubbed off, bees in their bonnets, fire in their bellies, poetry in their souls! It's nearly now or never. For if we don't back the Unicorn against the Lion, if we are not a boldly imaginative, creative, inventive people, a world that expected more of us will soon not even let us keep what we have now. The only future we can have worth living in is the one we greet, bravely and triumphantly, riding on a Unicorn.

SHAW

Nearly forty-five years ago, when I began writing a weekly page for the *Bradford Pioneer,* I became acquainted with a group of enthusiastic Shavians, who lived for the Master's next work or pronouncement. When they attended one of his plays, everything in it — costumes, wigs, and all — brought screams of laughter from them. They seemed to me then rather silly people, and I doubt if I would change my mind now. They also gave me a prejudice against their wonderful, inimitable G.B.S. and it took me years to get it out of my system, if ever I completely did. I met him on a good many occasions, not only on committees and at parties but also under his own roof and mine; but though we had the theatre as common ground, I never felt at ease with him: he was too much my senior, nearly forty years; he might be considerate both as host and guest, as indeed he was, but it was clear that I was heavily addicted to all the smaller vices from which he was free; on the other hand, he seemed to me the victim of two vices from which I felt myself to be reasonably free, namely, talking too much and showing off. But of course by this time he was fixed in his rôle of The Ancient of Days; I never even caught a glimpse of him — though I might easily have done, for he often visited Bradford — in his earlier and greater rôle as a red-bearded, Jaeger-type Mephistopheles.

It was the greater rôle because, to my mind, that was when his best work was done. Although he became almost a symbolic figure of old age, it was G.B.S. in early middle-age who wrote the plays that will last longest. I am not even excepting *Saint Joan* and *Heartbreak House.* For a time I thought the latter his supreme masterpiece, but on the last occasion when I took in that third act, when we were all sitting under a giant bomb, its emotional impact seemed inadequate. This inadequacy has to be faced in Shaw. When I was a boy, ordinary stupid people thought him a self-advertising intellectual clown, who would say anything to attract attention. This view of him was dismissed with contempt even by those, like Chesterton, who sharply disagreed with him. And, of course, it was nonsense. Yet there was in it, as there often is in the judgements of ordinary stupid people, a valuable grain

SHAW   229

of truth. He held many beliefs but he did not hold them as most of us do.
He never appeared to be emotionally committed to them. He could advance or defend them without anger. His warmest admirers tell us that this
was because he was almost a saint. The opposite party say it was because
he had a great deal of the charlatan in him. What is certain is that his
peculiar relation to his beliefs gave him both the strength and the weakness
characteristic of him.

He and Wells, whom I knew better than I did Shaw, offered some
valuable contrasts. Wells always behaved far worse than Shaw; he was too
impatient; he made mischief; he lost his temper and screamed insults and
slander (Belloc once said that Wells was a cad who didn't pretend to be
anything but a cad; that Bennett was a cad pretending to be a gentleman;
that Shaw was a gentleman pretending to be a cad.) These tantrums threw
into relief Shaw's patience and good humour and courtesy; and in any
debate between these two, G.B.S. would win easily on points. Yet for my
part I was always admiringly and affectionately aware of H.G.'s honesty of
mind, his frankness, his raging desire to discover and to announce the
truth. To those redeeming qualities it seemed to me that Shaw opposed
something personally attractive and polemically formidable, but disingenuous and dubious.

Thus, Shaw might win the argument about Stalin and the Soviet Union,
but it was Wells who was nearer the truth, and was not playing any
monkey tricks with his own values. Sometimes, both when I read him or
heard him in private, I felt that Shaw deliberately switched off his imagination when dealing with certain topics. It is not that he was downright
dishonest, but that he refused to follow his debating points into the world
of flesh and blood. So he could defend or even admire dictators when he
must have known that he could never have endured their authority. He
could cheerfully advocate the "liquidation" of anti-social types, as if they
were merely being barred from a summer school. He did not see them as
real people, shrieking and bleeding, but as creatures of paper and ink,
characters with no entrances in the third act.

I never felt he came through into the world that followed 1914. Often he
seemed to have persuaded himself that we were all still in the Edwardian
world of debate, where the man who disagreed with you so violently on the
public platform would be found, smiling a welcome, at the next week-end
house-party. During that long fine afternoon it was fun to listen to a witty
Irish Socialist, even if you did not believe a word he said. Later, especially
after 1917, it was different. There had arrived the world of passports and
visas, secret police and strange disappearances, labour camps and gas
chambers. Even in England there were changes. The Socialist was no
longer a crank but a menace; it was fortunate for G.B.S. that he now

became a grand old man, and escaped most of the new hard abuse and the elaborate smearing.

Again, there is to my mind something dubious, disingenuous, too, reminiscent of those rather fatuous Shavian groups, in much of his handling of our non-intellectual, emotional life. He would pretend to be through with sex, as if it were fretwork or stamp-collecting, when really he had hurriedly by-passed it. This pretence almost ruins some of his plays. Those maternal managing heroines of his ought to have had fourth acts composed for them by Strindberg. As for his assorted kittens, from Cleopatra to Orinthia, they are hygienic toys with never a gland in working order between them. No wonder that his greatest part for an actress is Joan of Arc.

All this seems very damaging, and so it would be if it were not for the fact that most of his plays rest on his strength as well as on his weakness. Because he could hold his beliefs in his own peculiar fashion, keeping them free of negative emotions, he was able to create his own kind of comedy, good enough to put him among the world's great dramatists. This comedy of his has light without heat. The superbly theatrical wit crackles and dazzles and strikes without wounding. Behind the cut-and-thrust of the talk, like some smiling landscape behind a battle scene, is a vast golden good humour. The master quite early of a magnificent debating style, he heightened it and orchestrated it to provide us with this comedy of argument, the Mozartian opera of witty debate. And this is not far-fetched, for it was opera and not other men's plays, the stuff he had denounced as a critic, that offered him models. He told me himself how he nearly always began without any ground-plan of action, hearing and not seeing his characters, trying a duet, then a trio, then perhaps a full ensemble. It is this method, together with an absence of fine shades and atmosphere, that explains why repertory companies in a hurry so often choose a Shaw play. You have only to learn the lines, slam them across, and the piece comes to life.

Treat Chekhov in this hell-for-leather style and you have nothing that the Russian master had in mind. For these two, the best who have written in this century, are complete opposites. And here is an odd thing. It is the dramatically simple, forthright Shaw and not the delicate, evasive Chekhov who is the dangerous influence. No playwright was ever the worse for being influenced by Chekhov. But Shaw's direct influence has been the kiss of death: no survivor is in sight. This is not hard to explain. Chekhov opened out a new dramatic method, whereas the Shaw play is a highly personal *tour de force,* demanding his unique style and temperament. I never felt myself that G.B.S. was really interested in dramatic method, though, of course, he may have tired of the theatre by the time I knew him. He despised the content of the plays he criticised in the *Saturday Review,* but he was not above using some of their oldest tricks. When an act was getting a bit dull he would bring on a gorgeous uniform or some fancy dress; and some of his deliberate clowning, as distinct from the expression of his wit, is just embarrassing.

Saint or charlatan, he was Irish, not English. What would have been fighting words in a Cockney or Lancashire accent seemed delicious banter in that rich, soft brogue. His debating tricks, which were often outrageous, were in the Dublin tradition, and so, of course, was his assumption of a public character part, starring in a cast that had Wilde, George Moore, Yeats, "A.E.," James Stephens, all playing character parts. Like Chekhov's Gaev, he was "a man of the Eighties" — with some Edwardian ripening. After that, he was with us but not of us. Like a man in a cautionary fairy tale, he had his wish granted — to live a long time — and it was all different and wrong. He became — and who can blame him? — a very vain old super-V.I.P. I remember once coming across him at the Grand Canyon, and found him peevish, refusing to admire it, or even look at it properly. He was jealous of it. Later still, the crisply assertive style, which he kept almost to the very end, deceived people into imagining that he was still thinking hard when he was often being rather foolish. His wife was no intellectual giant, but it seemed to me that her mind was still open long after his had finally closed.

You might say that he made up his mind too early, which gave him an immense advantage in debate, arming him at all points, but cost him something in wisdom. Bertrand Russell, who had known him a long time, said that G.B.S. was an immensely clever man but not a wise man. He seemed to me to have a sort of natural wisdom in his ordinary dealings with life (he must have given people in private more really good advice than any other man of his time), but to be perverse, obstinate, cranky, wrongheaded, in his positive philosophy. He was, in fact — and came at just the right moment — a great destroyer, head of the Victorian rubbish disposal squad. He hid any doubts he might have about his positive wisdom in quick mocking laughter, just as he hid so much of his face behind a beard, red and white at the proper seasons. But because he was an iconoclast, this does not mean, as many people imagine, that all his work will "date" itself into obscurity. I suspect that all the "dating" that can happen has already happened. His best pieces, those comedies unique in style and spirit, have the vitality that defies time and all social changes. Their character, their appeal, may be different — for notice how early plays like *Arms and the Man* and *You Never Can Tell,* once thought to be grimly shocking, now seem to bubble and sparkle with wit and delicious nonsense — but they will be alive. And existing still behind the work will be the memory and the legend of the man, half saint and half clown, preposterous in his Jaeger outfit and assorted fads, glorious in his long stride towards some kingdom worthy of the spirit — the wittiest of all pilgrims, humming an air by Mozart.

TELEVIEWING

Down here on the island, where I have rented a fine large set and where we have a powerful transmitting mast not far away, I am a Viewer. We keep the set in a room originally intended for music, and I can sit in the dark there, viewing and viewing, without disturbing the rest of the household. I lie back in an armchair, put my feet up on a stool, and smoke and view away. Except when there are Test Matches, I do all my viewing after dinner. Wheezing a bit, heavy with food and drink, I waddle along the hall, switch on the set, drop into my chair and put my feet up, then peer into my magic mirror like a fourteen-stone cigar-smoking Lady of Shalott. At first I told myself that I watched the set and its antics for strictly professional and technical reasons, but lately I have not had even a shadow of that excuse. I am simply one of the Viewers. I have already passed uncounted hours half-hypnotised by the jiggling and noisy images. Sometimes I wonder if I am going out of my mind. We have been told that the worst is over after about four years, but long before that my outlook will have been so completely changed that I shall be a different person. I shall probably be removed to an old man's home. Let us hope these places are equipped with good TV sets.

In my capacity as a Viewer, I have no intention of criticising adversely and in detail the way things are done. Given this strange medium and their own particular responsibilities, the people directing and handling the medium do almost all that can be reasonably expected of them. Most of them, I know, are enthusiasts; if removed from TV they would feel they were in exile. I don't imagine I could do it better myself. I think I would be far worse than they are. Most of the familiar jeers and sneers at their efforts seem to me quite unfair. The difficulties they have to face are too lightly disregarded. The critics who attack them make little or no allowance for the black magic of the medium itself, always discussing the entertainment provided as if they had not been staring at a set but sitting in a theatre, a cinema, a concert hall, a cabaret. So not a word that follows must be taken as unfriendly criticism of TV personnel. Good luck to you, boys and girls! Thanks a lot, Mary, Peter, Sylvia, Derek! But I am a Viewer too, one of the regular customers, even though I never ring up to complain that one of my precious prejudices has been ignored, and now I feel I must explain, as honestly as I know how, what the thing is doing to me.

The general line about TV — I took it myself before I became a Viewer — is that it is terrifically exciting, immensely powerful, potentially very dangerous. Here is this miraculous medium that pours into the home, hour after hour, night after night, images so dazzling and enticing that it immediately outbids all other media for its tenancy of the mind and imagination. It can transform any licence-holder into a well-informed and thoughtful student of all public affairs. It can turn children into future scholars of Trinity and Girton or into gunmen and molls. So we are playing with fire and dynamite — but what fire, what dynamite! This is the kind of stuff I wrote and talked myself before I became a real Viewer. Now that I know what happens, I can no longer write and talk in this strain. Certainly the medium produces its own particular effects, undoubtedly has an influence all its own; but these effects and this influence are very different from what they are generally imagined to be. Unless I am a very peculiar Viewer, the alarmists have all been looking in the wrong direction. They are like a man who expects a wolf at the door when he ought to be attending to the death watch beetle in the woodwork.

Instal a set, turn a switch — and hey presto! — here in a corner of the living-room is an ever-changing image of the whole wide, glittering, roaring world. Or so they say. But that is not quite how my viewing works. To begin with, it does not seem to bring the outside world closer to me but pushes it further away. There are times, after I have played the Lady of Shalott longer than usual, when this world is not here at all; I feel I am taking a series of peeps, perhaps from the darkened smoke-room of a giant spaceship, at another planet, with whose noisy affairs I am not involved at all. Let me stare and idly listen long enough and I seem to have arrived at some theosophical astral-body-life-after-death. I am as little involved in or perturbed by all these conferences, departures and arrivals of shadowy Ministers, crashes and floods, strikes and lockouts, aircraft and racing cars, atomic plants or fishing villages, scientists and film stars, as some Great White Master, a thousand years old, gazing into a crystal ball in Tibet. At most, these are — as one of Yeats's characters observed in another connection — the dreams the drowsy gods breathe on the burnished mirror of the world. I remember an old retired nannie, rather weak in the head, who when she visited the silent films thought everything she saw was part of one vast confused programme, an astonishing but acceptable mixture of the Prince of Wales and cowboys and Indians and Stanley Baldwin and sinking ships and *It*-girls and the Lord Mayor of London. She was an early Viewer. I know now exactly what she felt. Perhaps I am rather weak in the head too.

No sooner is any subject under review and discussion on the screen than it is drained of all reality. The instrument itself, probably guided by some satanic intelligence hostile to our species, adds a fatal dream effect. Even what I thought were urgent burning problems stop being problems at all. They are not settled, but their hash is. Somehow I no longer care what happens about Oil or Married Women At Work or Youth And The Churches Today or What We Do With The Old People or Whither Britain. I just view them. They might be bits from untidy and badly acted plays. Sometimes I don't know — and don't care — if the gesticulating image of a Foreign Minister belongs to a real Foreign Minister or to an actor in one of those political plays we are always having. Here on the screen the difference between Yugoslavia and Ruritania is hardly worth bothering about. After half an hour of The Future Of Our Fisheries or Africa At The Crossroads, the programme personalities, bursting with fisheries or Africa, stare accusingly at me and ask me what I propose to do about it. They might as well know now that, as a Viewer, I don't propose to do anything about it. After they have given me a final earnest look and asked their last question, I stare at the credit titles, listen dreamily to the end music, wonder idly why Malcolm Muggeridge looks handsomer on the screen than off, where Woodrow Wyatt has acquired his new haughty accent, light another pipe, and float into the next programme.

Perhaps it is *Picture Parade* or something of the sort, in which all the imbecilities of the film studio hand-outs and the fan magazines are given a kind of idiot dream life, especially — ah what golden moments! — in the foyer at a gala première where celebrities of screen and stage consent to smile at us and tell us how exciting it all is, as if we didn't know, and are wished lots of luck. As a Viewer I try not to miss one of these occasions. To view one, smoking in the darkened room with your feet up, is much better than actually being there, what with all the dressing up, the heat and fuss, the pushing and shoving to get nearer the mike or the Press photographers. It is a dream glimpse, carefully focused and timed, of a dream world. But it is all so *exciting,* as everybody keeps telling us Viewers. Perhaps that is why I so often find myself laughing — all alone, there in the dark — probably only a nervous excitement.

Some nights there seem to be dozens and dozens and dozens of people being interviewed, not just about films but about everything. We go all over the place — inside and outside Ministries, home and abroad, to airports and railway stations, to sports grounds and factories. The organisation of it all, the sheer technical achievements, are a credit to our civilisation. The courtesy and friendliness are admirable: all the persons interviewed are for ever being thanked and wished good luck. People under Cabinet rank and sixty years of age are on Christian name terms at once. It is a wonderful and happy world, this of TV interviews. And perhaps that is why it is not a world in which anybody ever says anything. That might spoil it. Between the cordial *Hellos* and the charming *Good-byes* nothing much seems to happen. We are either going to the interview or coming away from it. "Let us," they say proudly, "go to Coketown and talk to the Mayor himself — so now *It's Over To Coketown* — This is Coketown and here in the studio is the Mayor of Coketown, who has kindly consented to talk to us — Very good of you, Mr. Mayor — er what about this er campaign of yours, Mr. Mayor? — Well, Reg, I think er I can say er we here in Coketown er hope to get it started fairly soon — Thank you, Mr. Mayor, and the best of luck — Thank you, Reg — And now we return you to London — This is London and that was the Mayor of Coketown being interviewed by our representative, Reg Rowbottom — and *now* —"

At first, when I was a new Viewer, a stranger in this magic world, I wanted the Mayor to say something, if only to justify all the trouble that had been taken to flash his image across the country. Now I know that this does not matter at all, that what is important is that we should keep jumping around, stare at a fresh face for a moment or two, then be off again. The instrument likes to do this, and it is the instrument that has us in its power. In this world of the magic tube, all the values are different. Here we are more interested in what the interviewer sounds and looks like than we are in what the interviewed person says. Viewing, I accept these topsy-turvy values. It is only afterwards, coming to my senses and thinking things over, I begin to question them. Staring at the set, my mind almost a blank, I am quite ready to believe in TV personalities, the elite and aristocracy of this dream world. I do not ask what they have done, what massive talents they possess. They still have personalities where I, as a Viewer, a captive of the screen, have little or none. Not this Christmas but possibly the next, when I may have said good-bye to reality, I shall have no party of my own, perhaps will no longer understand what arrangements could be made for one; I will attend, as a Viewer, a party of TV personalities, to enjoy the sparkle of the wine in their glasses, to listen with joy to the crunching of their mince pies; and one or two of them may look straight in my direction, to wish me a Merry Christmas Programme, a Happy New Year's Viewing.

Meanwhile, sitting in the dark with my feet up, I feel I have *had* Fisheries or Africa or Youth And The Churches Today. I couldn't agree more about Married Women At Work or What We Do With The Old People or Whither Britain, and could hardly care less. We Viewers know now that we are such stuff as dreams are made on, that all is Maya, that *For in and out, above, below, 'Tis nothing but a magic shadow-show.* So it is easy to imagine oneself viewing the next war, dreamily watching whole cities crumble to radioactive dust, catching a last glimpse of Manchester or Leeds in between a thirty-minute detective play and some light music and a gipsy dancer. Never did a medium of information and entertainment arrive more opportunely, to soothe the tormented mind, to ease the bewilderment of the soul. We may emerge from our four or five years' bondage to it, having at last achieved detachment, for ever untroubled and smiling, finally victorious over the technique and the instrument. Already we Viewers, when not viewing, have begun to whisper to one another that the more we elaborate our means of communication, the less we communicate. Some words on a page can be unforgettable. The memory of an actor, moving and speaking on a platform, may haunt us all our lives. Then the inventors and technicians arrive, the costs rise prodigiously, the complication sets in, and we get film and radio, far less potent and memorable. The inventors and technicians, in a frenzy, with millions of money behind them, invade the home with TV, adding more and more images to sound, performing miracles with time and space, bringing in colour, stereoscopic sight, everything. And out of this mountain of invention and technique, finance and organisation, comes a little dream mouse. "Not bad," we Viewers cry. "What next?"

XI. From the SATURDAY EVENING POST December 12, 1964

WOMEN DON'T RUN THE COUNTRY

A thousand times I must have read or heard that American society is now a matriarchy. I disagree. Here I may be told I am not an American, don't live here and only pay occasional visits. My personal opinions may not be important, but if I can persuade a few hundred thousand readers that this matriarchy idea is all wrong, I shall be doing this country a great service. The saving in analysts' fees might soon amount to several million dollars a year.

Nobody believes, of course, that America is a matriarchy in the anthropologists' sense of this term: "A state or stage of social evolution in which descent is reckoned only in the female line, all children belonging to the mother's clan." In such a society the chief deities would be Mother Goddesses, magically potent symbols of fertility. (In many places they began to be ousted by several law-making male deities about three thousand years ago.) What a large number of men do believe, however, is that America is well on its way to becoming a new kind of matriarchy, increasingly ruled by mothers and dominated by Woman. In a superficial sense, American women do seem to have the upper hand. They appear to call the tune while their men pay the piper. They sweep in triumph along Fifth Avenue. This is their place, their hour. But it is all mere surface fuss, a little almond icing on the cake. In its fundamental values, tone, organization, American society is moving *away* from rule by Woman. American women make a fuss because they find themselves in a *man-made* society. The men who denounce this fuss should criticize the society they have created, and stop talking nonsense about women.

In a matriarchy it is feminine and not masculine values that are dominant. In such a society women feel completely at home. It provides the kind of life they want. It is shaped and colored by Woman's deepest feelings. It satisfies not her superficial wants — a washing machine, a new TV set — but her profoundest needs. What are these needs? They are not concerned with things at all; they are concerned with personal relationships. Woman enjoys things — furs, gowns — simply as toys of love, which to her is *the* gigantic blazing reality, compared with which defence, invention, politics, legal and financial systems are simply so much masculine hocus-pocus. In a true matriarchy, love, personal relationships, home-making, family-creating and taking root in a settled society are at the top of all lists of priorities. They come first, and all the things that men are always arguing about come a very bad second.

A matriarchy is always a small society, deeply rooted in the earth and in tradition and custom. It would never attempt large-scale industry because one of the first things that such an industry does is to break up families. Then it keeps people moving about and prevents them from sinking any roots. All this, from the matriarchal point of view, is not progress but a barbarous invasion of the kingdom of love. It puts things before people, and in the feminine scale of values, this is a terrible crime, the ultimate treason.

I suspect that in most matriarchies the women work hard and the men take it easy. This should not surprise anyone who remembers that in these societies sexual love is much more important than business. A wife who sees her husband primarily as a lover, not as a provider, does not want him to work until he is ready to drop. A tired man makes a poor lover. And a man forever worried will not make the best husband and father.

In a matriarchal system a woman might toil for the comfort and well-being of her family, but she would see no sense in drudging away to add to the profits of some vast corporation. And we can bet our boots that in such a system nobody would be encouraged to travel at supersonic speeds, to land on the moon, to invent devices for destruction on the largest possible scale. These elaborate imbecilities are the products of the masculine mind, and they would not be tolerated in a society run by women. Men who even dreamed up such ideas, much less demanded that everybody make sacrifices on their behalf, would be given a very rough time by the females in charge.

Whatever else may be said about the character of contemporary American society, it certainly represents the triumph of the masculine principle. Nor is it hard to see why this should be so. American traditions, from Puritanism to pioneering, are severely masculine. The immense development of industry upholds the masculine principle. The emphasis upon invention and machinery and the prominence given to finance and commerce, characteristic of America, are essentially male. And up to now American society has been steadily offering Woman not more and more but less and less of what she really wants. Never were her superficial needs more elaborately attended to. Never were her deepest needs so often ignored. Remember, what she really wants is not a lot of "things," but love, a secure family life, taking root in a stable community. And nine times out of ten she has a longing to be close to living, growing things, and does not want to find herself on some vast plain of cement.

Why do American men imagine that their society is turning into a matriarchy? It is because their women demand so much attention, spend so much on themselves, invade one masculine region after another, and now exercise tremendous economic power. (This last point is often because husbands overwork and worry themselves into early graves. In a matriarchy, these men would have been encouraged to take it easy, for most women prefer live husbands to blocks of shares and seats on the board.)

It is precisely because they find themselves in an alien society that so many American women demand so much attention. If this society represented their own deepest values, they would feel at home in it and therefore they would not be crying, "Look at me. Attend to me." They feel that unless they make a fuss, they will be in danger of disappearing from sight, like wives who have gone with their husbands to inspect some vast new machine which is entrancing to the male.

It is true that far more is spent on feminine adornment in America than anywhere else on earth. There are two reasons for this, and neither of them even suggests that women rule America. The first is that this immense trade in feminine frippery is good for business, oiling innumerable wheels of production and consumption. But this idea of an ever-increasing turnover, together with the colossal amount of sheer waste, is itself essentially masculine and, I suspect, repugnant to Woman on her deeper levels, where she is a frugal creature. In societies that approach the matriarchal, the women are not forever buying new clothes but tend to be conservative about their dress, preserving through generations the same native costumes. Behind the whirl of fashion in America are men who are keeping an eye on their balance sheets.

The second reason for all this feminine adornment is that women are indulged just because they are in an alien society. They are like girls in a mining camp being rewarded with gold nuggets. Because they are out of place, they must be given a treat. Moreover, the woman elaborately adorned is a kind of tribute to the male, who can show her off. The natural woman enjoys dressing up occasionally, but she does not see herself as a kind of model. What she wants is an erotic relationship, offering her emotional security, a relationship in which she is clearly seen, appreciated, loved, *as a person*. And if she is accepted and loved as a person, she does not want to be expensively dressed up all the time — this is the illusion of men who do not see women as real people — and can be quite happy messing about in an old housecoat and wearing no makeup.

If American women often do make excessive demands — and here I am only repeating what I have heard many American men say— this may be a kind of revenge. They marry men who wear themselves out, make themselves unfit for conjugal companionship — but not for something noble and glorious, to which a woman can also dedicate herself, but for something

242 THE SATURDAY EVENING POSTTHE SATURDAY EVENING POST

that by the feminine principle seems contemptible and ridiculous — like selling 100,000 more boojums this year than last. It is worth pointing out here that nearly all courageous and truly dedicated men, not engaged in merely increasing profits, arouse intense feminine loyalty. It is the men who grind themselves away on ignoble and idiotic work who largely have to meet women's excessive demands. If Man has turned himself into a provider, then let him do more and more providing. If he believes cars and fur coats are more important than kisses and companionship, then she will demand bigger cars and richer fur coats. *But this is not what she really wants.*

It has been said — and here again I am only repeating what I have heard many times — that too many American women are sharply aggressive in an unfeminine way. And this aggressiveness has been put forward as proof of the growth of a matriarchy here. And again, this is completely wrong. It is precisely because American society reflects masculine and not feminine values that so many women become aggressive. They are putting on aggression as they would put on fur coats and boots in an arctic climate. If their world seems to them so determinedly masculine, then they feel they must adopt male characteristics. It is no use speaking in soft, gentle tones if everybody else is shouting. To make themselves heard at all, then they must shout too. Deep down they do not want to be aggressive but the manner is forced on them. And this makes for further dissatisfaction, and this in turn may mean that the aggressive manner is now heightened. It is our old enemy — the vicious circle.

During the last fifty years American women, chiefly through inheritance, have come to possess a formidable amount of economic power. This is a country of rich widows. The extent of their influence has helped to create this legend that women are in charge. But this does not go down to the roots of American society, does not change its fundamental character: It is still dominated by the masculine and not the feminine principle. How do I know? Well, here is a quite simple test. At the present time America possesses sufficient instruments of destruction to kill every man, woman and child on earth. This macabre achievement, which has demanded an astonishing amount of technical skill and superb organization and the expenditure of billions and billions of dollars, not only represents the masculine principle triumphantly asserting itself but also suggests the male mind coming to the end of its tether. Where is the feminine principle, where is Woman, in this madness? Where is the feminine emphasis here upon love, on the happiness of persons? Is this how women want their money spent? We have only to ask the question to know the answer. Here is a society shaped and colored by male values. It is about as much like a matriarchy as the Marine Corps.

Now here I must make an important point. If I say, as I do, that a swing over from the masculine to the feminine principle is now urgently necessary, I do not mean that women must leave the professions and the businesses and return to the kitchen and the nursery. (After all, I am married, and most happily married, too, to a brilliant archaeologist and writer, who has her own career.) What I do mean is that society itself must be as thoroughly permeated by womanliness as it is by masculinity, that *as a community*, not simply as separate persons, we must accept feminine values with their emphasis upon love, people, relatedness, synthesis as opposed to analysis, intuitiveness as distinct from purely intellectual discourse.

We live in a sick world. It is sick because it is now hopelessly unbalanced. It is unbalanced because the masculine principle has been given too much freedom and the feminine principle has been fettered and stifled. This means that women feel frustrated and unhappy. And women who feel frustrated and unhappy find it hard to bring to men that idea of relatedness, that sense of wholeness, which most men ask from Woman. For the *psychological need* of each sex for the other (which women understand better than men) is unfathomably deep, going down to the very roots of our being. America is not a matriarchy, and I do not think it ever will be. But it will be a good day for both men and women when America begins to behave as if it *wanted to be a matriarchy,* turning from the bleak insanity of the unchecked masculine principle to the glow and warmth of the feminine principle, from the icy glare of Logos to smiling Eros.

XII. From THE MOMENTS AND OTHER PIECES 1966

THE MOMENTS

All my life, I now realise, I have been nourished and secretly sustained by certain moments that have always seemed to me to be magical. If I have completed the tasks and shouldered the burdens all the way, finishing the marches without handing over my rifle and pack or dropping out, it is neither conscience nor energy that has kept me going but the memory and the hope of this magic. It has visited me before; it will come again. Sooner or later I would taste the honey-dew once more. And if this is to have a romantic temperament, then I have a romantic temperament. If there is immaturity here, then I am still immature in my seventy-first year.

But here I shall fire a few rounds in the direction of the enemy camp. People who in their confident maturity reject this magic, who have instant "nothing-but" explanations of everything, are either kept going by their vanity — and the vanity of severely rational persons is astounding — or not sustained at all, existing hungrily in despair, seeking power at all costs, trying various brutal excesses, or stiffening into automata. I can imagine an age, in which this magic has been explained away, that would cover the world with zombies all manipulated and directed by power-maniacs. In such an age, power and organisation and machinery would be everything, poetry would be nothing. How far off is it?

Sometimes I have wondered if the seemingly inexplicable *rages* of the young, violently destructive now in so many different countries, might not be explained by the nonarrival of these magical moments. Something expected, promised at birth, is missing. Where among all these prompt deliveries of Grade-A pasteurised is the milk of Paradise? However, it is true that for one lad who is breaking windows there are a hundred, not mentioned in the papers, who never pick up a brick. And it is not for me to say that our Pop culture never brings its magical moments. But what is certain is that it does not attempt the grand and sublime, which is what we cry out for in our youth. On the other hand, it is equally certain that whenever the Eroica or the Choral Symphony is being performed, the cousins of the brick-throwing lads will be there, if necessary standing for hours. The contemporary scene is now so wide and complicated that anything can be proved from it. I must return to myself.

Describing an innings by Jessup, Neville Cardus wrote: "He at once took the game out of the prison of cause and effect." That is what these moments have always done for me. That is why they are magic. Two and two suddenly make twenty-five. In a flash they add another dimension to existence. They award us, for as long as they last, a bonus, huge, irrational, glorious. We win a prize from God knows where. It isn't earned and deserved; that would be justice or fair dealing, a decent cause producing a satisfactory effect; whereas this is magic. It belongs to the fairy-tale world, in which the idlest of the three lads in the forest meets the princess, and hardly anything that happens could be explained by experts writing in the weekly journals. Indeed, the moments are entirely beyond the reach of experts, who, I am convinced, never experience them. They favour the woolly minded, of whom, I am proud to declare, I am one. Brush away all wool, give yourself a first-rate razor-sharp intellect, and you will go far, and probably a hell of a long way from this magic. This is one reason why men who have arrived where they have always wanted to be are impressive but not much fun to be with, so that their women so often look depressed. Whatever they may say, women believe in a magical world. They are seen in the prison of cause and effect only on visiting days.

It is my experience that these moments arrive as and when they choose. They cannot be summoned, nor even induced, beckoned. But of course some circumstances are more favourable than others. It is just possible I might be visited by one of these moments while reading a report on the tin-plate industry or a list of arthritic patients in Bedfordshire, but all odds are heavily against it. On the other hand, I have found the arts most generous with these magical moments, and this is one good reason — there are several others, mark you — for hanging around with them. If this last phrase suggests an absence of painstaking study, anxious application, then it is doing what I intended it to do. I suspect — though of course I am writing within the limits of my own temperament — that you have to hold yourself a bit loosely, not bothering about cultural improvement, for the magic to work.

In the long run, which is where I am now, music has worked best for me, though when I was younger I think literature and drama were neck-and-neck with it. The visual arts have given me enormous enjoyment — and indeed I am a bit of a holiday painter myself — but for some reason obscure to me they have rarely brought me these magical moments. Perhaps my ear provides a shorter cut to enchantment than my eye. Certainly music may do the trick when it is far below its highest level. Let nobody imagine I have to wait for Bach's B minor Mass or Beethoven's late quartets. To give the first example that occurs to me — and I could offer dozens — in the opening movements of his Cello Concerto and his D minor Symphony, Dvorak makes his woodwind trail after his main themes

— they are like sunlit wisps of dissolving cloud — and to this day the magic has not utterly faded from them. Again, listening recently to a new recording of Elgar's First Symphony (which I had long thought I didn't care for), I found that with the muted trombones at the end of the third movement, the Adagio, the sudden magic seemed almost numinous, as if the gods walked the earth again. Enough, enough!

How far and with what complexity and depth the arts interact with life, we do not know, though some brave writers — Proust, for instance — have refused to avoid the subject. It may be that people who know and care nothing about the arts have known as many magical moments as the rest of us have — perhaps even more if they happen to be introverts living in lonely places. (But probably far fewer if they happen to be ambitious politicians, editors of sensational newspapers, brisk salesmen, New York taxi drivers.) There seems to me no difference in quality between the moments coming by way of the arts and those that arrive, quite unexpectedly, in our ordinary daily life. These are more remarkable than the immensely heightened moments of travel, of which most of us could furnish examples — and perhaps too often do. In my life I have suddenly known the greatest happiness always when *there was no apparent reason for it* — when out of nowhere there came floating up the great blue bubble. I shall never forget walking once, some years ago, along Piccadilly and across Leicester Square in a blinding snowstorm, which made walking difficult and did not seem to me at all picturesque and romantic, and yet I walked the whole way in a kind of ecstasy, as if in another world, magical and immortal. And there was no reason for it at all, not the tiniest scrap of any possible cause.

It is the same, at least in my experience, with personal relationships. I have never needed any help from manuals on how to get rich in the private commerce between the sexes; but even so, I think we are now inclined to make too much out of the bedroom scenes in our love stories. It is my experience that even in love the magical moments come when they please, often when we are wearing all our clothes and are far from the bedroom. I can remember a moment of complete insight and perfect understanding, as if one had been given the freedom of a strange continent, that arrived in a dreary little teashop near the ministry from which I had extracted the lady of my choice. There were not even any words, just a meeting of eyes above the teacups, but a magical meeting, in which there was the promise of many happy years, an unearned bonus if there ever was one.

So long as we experience these moments, we live in a magical world. (And don't let anybody talk you out of it, boy.) I was arguing the other day with a clever young man who said that we are machines — extraordinarily elaborate, intricate, delicate, subtle — but machines. I said that we weren't so long as we remained open-ended, with one end open to the

250   THE MOMENTS AND OTHER PIECES

collective unconscious, the whole heritage of earth life, and the other open
to influences beyond our understanding. And perhaps it is when we are
suddenly opened a little more at either end that two and two seem to make
twenty-five, another dimension is added, we taste the honey-dew, and all is
magical. Of course the moments do not arrive as often as they did, but I
soldier on in the belief that I have not yet used up my ration, that there are
still a few more to come.

TOBACCO

I have just realised that I have been smoking a pipe for half a century. I
grew up among pipe smokers; my father was one and so were most of his
friends. Fifty years ago in the north there were still some real tobacconists,
who knew how much Latakia and Perique to add to Virginia, who did not
earn a living by hiring girls to push packets of cigarettes across the counter.
In those days men offered their tobacco pouches to one another. Some of
them in the north may still do it, but not for years and years have I given or
received a fill. Perhaps I don't live right.

To this day you will find pipe tobacco improves as you move up the
map. It is better in the north of England than it is in the south. In Scotland
it is better still. The Scots like to boast, but it is strange they never mention
the debt owed to them by the world's pipe smokers. There is some good
tobacco in Ireland too. On the Continent, especially in the northern half,
there has been some improvement since the war; but most of it, now got up
to look British, is still very poor stuff. Most American pipe tobacco is too
sweet, as if meant for eating not smoking. I remember that George Doran,
the publisher, used to smoke a Los Angeles mixture that had a chocolate
flavour. If any pipe-smoking reader is planning to stay in America, he
should make a note of a mixture, medium and broad-cut, that comes from
St. Louis and is called Hayward Mixture. I have carried yellow pound tins
of it into almost every state of the Union. Sometimes when I wondered if I
was going out of my mind, a few pipes of it have restored my sanity.

When I started smoking a pipe, fifty years ago, I bought Cut Cavendish
from Salmon and Gluckstein at 3½d. an ounce. It was very strong, and
there were times when, after puffing furiously as youngsters nearly always

do, I felt queasy and my surroundings began to shift about and dissolve. Since that hard beginning, I have been able to smoke anything, though not of course always with enjoyment. But I would rather have bad tobacco than no tobacco. In Egypt, earlier this year, I was compelled to smoke some of their local muck, wondering as I coughed and cursed why the United Arab Republic, which you are never allowed to forget for a moment, did not make sure that Syrian tobacco reached Egypt. Probably President Nasser does not smoke a pipe.

Those people now ready to write and tell me I am a slave to a dirty habit need not waste time, paper and stamps. I admit I have been long enslaved by tobacco. But all men are enslaved by something, and there are worse masters than the weed. By encouraging me to reflect, at the same time freeing me from spiritual pride, it has kept me from more dangerous forms of slavery. Nor have I ever been able to see that smoking is a particularly dirty habit. It is absurd of course, this continuous puffing out of smoke, but no dirtier than most of our habits. You have only to be sufficiently fastidious, and life itself is one huge dirty habit. Purity is reached only in the crematorium.

We are told, usually by people who dislike tobacco, that smoking injures the health. That may be so, though it is worth pointing out that the contributions to a world civilisation of men careless of their health far exceed those of the health-seekers. (*Fit for what?* still seems to me the best joke *Punch* ever achieved.) There may be something in this lung cancer idea. Yet when I was young, and good tobacco was far less than a tenth of the price it is now, I was surrounded by heavy smokers, but nobody seemed to be suffering from lung cancer.

I suspect a good deal of disguised puritanism among medical men, especially in America. They denounce various forms of enjoyment but never suggest that the whole modern way of life is idiotic. A man who sits with ten telephones in Wall Street, desperately trying to outwit his competitors, might be healthier if he did not smoke, did not drink, ate no fats. He would be healthier still if he got to hell out of Wall Street and forgot the rat race.

But look at the money we waste on tobacco. No, madam, in Britain we are not spending all that money on tobacco, but on taxes. If we all stopped smoking tomorrow, several hundred million would have to be found elsewhere, for rockets that must never be fired and other imbecilities. The ever-increasing duties on tobacco, making its price about twelve times what it was when I started smoking, show our Establishment at its worst — uncreative, lacking all ingenuity, lazy-minded, mean and callous. I am not thinking of myself now, when I call this completely inequitable taxation mean and callous. I am thinking of men of my generation trying to keep going among the never-had-it-so-goods on wretched tiny pensions.

K

You are seventy and have always enjoyed a smoke. Now, no longer active and with a lot of time on your hands, you enjoy a smoke more than ever. To ponder and remember over a pipe is probably now your greatest pleasure. So what do they do to you, these smirking Chancellors of the Exchequer, with their annual Budget performance, these first-class minds of the Treasury, the pick of Oxford and Cambridge? Every time they need more money, they empty your tobacco pouch, robbing you of the last enjoyment life offers you. There is no fire in the grate, the cupboard is nearly bare; the road at the end of the street is noisy and dangerous with cars; your friends are dead or dying; so they screw another sixpence out of you, before you are carted away to rot in an overcrowded understaffed hospital; and if you haven't the sixpence then you suck an empty pipe while you read, in the paper you borrowed, all about the tax-free millions that have been made out of property deals.

In restaurants all pipe smoking is sharply discouraged, not because of the food, cigar smoke being even stronger, but probably because there is no profit to be made out of it. (The profit on cigars is fierce.) It is the banning of the pipe from aeroplanes — and I bet the British started that — which has brought me hours of misery. Only on the old Stratocruisers could one go below to the little bar and light a pipe, and more than once I have bumped across the Atlantic, reading and smoking the night away while all the other passengers were asleep. On one flight, without the little bar below, I was able to smoke my pipe all the way to Montreal, but that was because I had deliberately chosen a Friday the thirteenth and had the plane almost to myself. This does not mean I am not superstitious. I was born on a thirteenth and so feel free of its sinister influences.

Pipes of course can smell foully, though the worst of them are probably more easily endured than the reek of the last inch or so of soggy cigars. To my mind the gravest offender is that favourite of all authorities — the cigarette. It is not the tobacco but the paper that is so offensive. A room crowded with cigarette smokers is like a papermill on fire. Again, it is not the cigarette that is being smoked that afflicts eyes, nose and throat, but the cigarette smouldering in the hand or on the ash tray, the Virginian joss stick. The behavior of cigarette smokers has always puzzled me. Why, for example, do they want to light up ten seconds before a meal, then puff again between meat and pudding? Many of them, I feel, do not consciously enjoy smoking, as I most genuinely do, but wish to avoid the pain of not smoking. I do not include them among the friends of tobacco.

Cigars can be things of beauty, works of art, but on this level they are harder and harder to find, evil entropy being at work here as elsewhere. (This is called by my friends Iris and John Bayley "Jack's Law.") On a much lower level I would now just as soon smoke a Jamaican cigar as a

Havana; and I have spent many a pleasant hour abroad — never finding
them in London — with those large black Brazilian cigars, banded a
threatening scarlet and emerald green, that are so surprisingly mild and
friendly, as if some flashing-eyed Carmen in a gipsy cave came across, took
your hand, and talked quietly and sensibly.

A cigar rounds off a substantial meal, but when, being short of pipe
tobacco in distant places, I have found myself compelled to smoke them all
day, I have soon got tired of them. Perhaps if Sir Winston, round about
1944, had taken to a pipe, we might have all been living today in a happier
world. But the pipe smoker's appearance of solidity and wisdom is of
course illusory. Some of the biggest chumps I have ever known have had
pipes stuck in their faces. Even so, I fancy they were great relighters and
puffers and knockers-out of dottle, and perhaps never filled a pipe when
they were by themselves. There is a kind of pipe smoking that belongs to
actors on the stage and clergymen having a jolly good yarn with the chaps.

It is just possible that a few readers may decide either to try smoking a
pipe for the first time or, what is more likely, to have yet one more shot at
it. To them, after this half century, I venture to offer some advice. Many
men have defeated themselves as pipe smokers. They start the wrong way.
They buy a small light pipe and probably fill it with some rubbed-out
yellow flake, at which they puff away. In a few minutes they have a furnace
in their hands and too much saliva in their mouths; there is no fragrance,
no flavour; the pipe, almost too hot to hold, begins to gurgle disgustingly;
so they decide pipe smoking is not for them — "Tried but can't manage it,
old boy — wet smoker." I would be one as well with that equipment.

To begin with, do not buy one pipe but at least three. If you cannot
afford pipes by well-known makers, do not buy cheap imitations but search
the tobacconists' for throwouts. Some of the best pipes I have ever had I
have picked out of the baskets of throwouts. Here I must add, after my
fifty years, that just as you choose a pipe, so a pipe chooses you. I have had
as presents magnificent pipes, cut from the finest straight-grain brier, that
never gave me ten minutes satisfactory smoking. Either they were not right
for me or I was not right for them. There is something like a personal
relation here. And until you are used to smoking a pipe, avoid small thin
light pipes: they get hot too quickly. You will be happier at first with fairly
large pipes, even if they seem too heavy. And do not scrape out all the
carbon, for it keeps the pipe cool.

But why three pipes? Because you must never refill a warm pipe: it is
precisely this that has left us pipe smokers in bad odour. I have watched
with horror men smoking the same pipe hour after hour, smelling like
gardeners' bonfires. Always I carry three pipes in my pocket. On my desk
there may be a dozen or more. I buy and use a great many pipe cleaners.

On the other hand, I remove from all pipes any aluminium tubes or similar devices. I have been sent pipes that had most ingenious arrangements for collecting nicotine, but they always seemed to me to taste nasty. The pipe, I suspect, is an enemy of gadgetry.

Now for the tobacco. Do not make a start with light Virginia leaf or mild mixtures. They can easily be hot and tongue-burning. Try a darker flake or a mixture with a fair amount of Latakia and Perique in it. Out of the strong comes forth sweetness. Fill your pipes carefully, using the third finger not the first to complete the filling. The trick then is to keep the tobacco smouldering, smoking as slowly as possible, for the hotter it is the worse it tastes and smells.

A cool clean well-packed pipe that is just being kept alight pleases the smoker and anybody who comes near him. All over the world people have said to me, "What wonderful tobacco you must be smoking!" I have even gone through Customs (but not in England) on fragrance alone — when in fact there was nothing remarkable about the tobacco itself: it was being treated properly.

If I were a youth today perhaps I would never start smoking, if only to thumb my nose at these appalling prices. But after fifty years of it, I regret nothing. Man, the creature who knows he must die, who has dreams larger than his destiny, who is for ever working a confidence trick on himself, needs an ally. (Woman I include here in Man.) Mine has been tobacco. Even with it I have too often been impatient and intolerant. Without it I should have been insufferable. You may retort that I am insufferable anyhow, but with a pipe nicely going, I do not believe you.

WRONG ISM

There are three isms that we ought to consider very carefully — regionalism, nationalism, internationalism. Of these three the one there is most fuss about, the one that starts men shouting and marching and shooting, the one that seems to have all the depth and thrust and fire, is of course nationalism. Nine people out of ten, I fancy, would say that of this trio it is the one that really counts, the big boss. Regionalism and internationalism, they would add, are comparatively small, shadowy, rather cranky. And I believe all this to be quite wrong. Like many another big boss, nationalism is largely bogus. It is like a bunch of flowers made of plastics.

The real flowers belong to regionalism. The mass of people everywhere may never have used the term. They are probably regionalists without knowing it. Because they have been brought up in a certain part of the world, they have formed perhaps quite unconsciously a deep attachment to its landscape and speech, its traditional customs, its food and drink, its songs and jokes. (There are of course always the rebels, often intellectuals and writers, but they are not the mass of people.) They are rooted in their region. Indeed, without this attachment a man can have no roots.

So much of people's lives, from earliest childhood onwards, is deeply intertwined with the common life of the region, they cannot help feeling strongly about it. A threat to it is a knife pointing at the heart. How can life ever be the same if bullying strangers come to change everything? The form and colour, the very taste and smell of dear familiar things will be different, alien, life-destroying. It would be better to die fighting. And it is precisely this, the nourishing life of the region, for which common men have so often fought and died.

This attachment to the region exists on a level far deeper than that of any political hocus-pocus. When a man says "my country" with real feeling, he is thinking about his region, all that has made up his life, and not about that political entity, the nation. There can be some confusion here simply because some countries are so small — and ours is one of them — and so old, again like ours, that much of what is national is also regional. Down the centuries, the nation, itself so comparatively small, has been able to attach to itself the feeling really created by the region. (Even so there is something left over, as most people in Yorkshire or Devon, for example, would tell you.) This probably explains the fervent patriotism developed early in small countries. The English were announcing that they were English in the Middle Ages, before nationalism had arrived elsewhere.

If we deduct from nationalism all that it has borrowed or stolen from regionalism, what remains is mostly rubbish. The nation, as distinct from the region, is largely the creation of power-men and political manipulators. Almost all nationalist movements are led by ambitious frustrated men determined to hold office. I am not blaming them. I would do the same if I were in their place and wanted power so badly. But nearly always they make use of the rich warm regional feeling, the emotional dynamo of the movement, while being almost untouched by it themselves. This is because they are not as a rule deeply loyal to any region themselves. Ambition and a love of power can eat like acid into the tissues of regional loyalty. It is hard, if not impossible, to retain a natural piety and yet be for ever playing both ends against the middle.

Being itself a power structure, devised by men of power, the nation tends to think and act in terms of power. What would benefit the real life of the region, where men, women and children actually live, is soon sacrificed for the power and prestige of the nation. (And the personal vanity of presidents and ministers themselves, which historians too often disregard.) Among the new nations of our time innumerable peasants and labourers must have found themselves being cut down from five square meals a week to three in order to provide unnecessary airlines, military forces that can only be used against them and nobody else, great conference halls and official yachts and the rest. The last traces of imperialism and colonialism may have to be removed from Asia and Africa, where men can no longer endure being condemned to a permanent inferiority by the colour of their skins; but even so, the modern world, the real world of our time, does not want and would be far better without more and more nations, busy creating for themselves the very paraphernalia that western Europe is now trying to abolish. You are compelled to answer more questions when trying to spend half a day in Cambodia than you are now travelling from the Hook of Holland to Syracuse.

This brings me to internationalism. I dislike this term, which I used only to complete the isms. It suggests financiers and dubious promoters living nowhere but in luxury hotels; a shallow world of entrepreneurs and impresarios. (Was it Sacha Guitry who said that impresarios were men who spoke many languages but all with a foreign accent?) The internationalism I have in mind here is best described as world civilisation. It is life considered on a global scale. Most of our communications and transport already exist on this high wide level. So do many other things from medicine to meteorology. Our astronomers and physicists (except where they have allowed themselves to be hush-hushed) work here. The UN special agencies, about which we hear far too little, have contributed more and more to this world civilisation. All the arts, when they are arts and not chunks of nationalist propaganda, naturally take their place in it. And it grows, widens, deepens, in spite of the fact that for every dollar, ruble, pound or franc spent in explaining and praising it, a thousand are spent by the nations explaining and praising themselves.

This world civilisation and regionalism can get along together, especially if we keep ourselves sharply aware of their quite different but equally important values and rewards. A man can make his contribution to world civilisation and yet remain strongly regional in feeling: I know several men of this sort. There is of course the danger — it is with us now — of the global style flattening out the regional, taking local form, colour, flavour, away for ever, disinheriting future generations, threatening them with sensuous poverty and a huge boredom. But to understand and appreciate regionalism is to be on guard against this danger. And we must therefore make a clear distinction between regionalism and nationalism.

It is nationalism that tries to check the growth of world civilisation. And nationalism, when taken on a global scale, is more aggressive and demanding now than it has ever been before. This in the giant powers is largely disguised by the endless fuss in public about rival ideologies, now a largely unreal quarrel. What is intensely real is the glaring nationalism. Even the desire to police the world is nationalistic in origin. (Only the world can police the world.) Moreover, the nation-states of today are for the most part far narrower in their outlook, far more inclined to allow prejudice against the foreigner to impoverish their own style of living, than the old imperial states were. It should be part of world civilisation that men with particular skills, perhaps the product of the very regionalism they are rebelling against, should be able to move easily from country to country, to exercise those skills, in anything from teaching the violin to running a new type of factory to managing an old hotel. But nationalism, especially of the newer sort, would rather see everything done badly than allow a few non-nationals to get to work. And people face a barrage of passports, visas, immigration controls, labour permits; and in this respect are worse off than they were in 1900. But even so, in spite of all that nationalism can do — so long as it keeps its nuclear bombs to itself — the internationalism I have in mind, slowly creating a world civilisation, cannot be checked.

Nevertheless, we are still backing the wrong ism. Almost all our money goes on the middle one, nationalism, the rotten meat between the two healthy slices of bread. We need regionalism to give us roots and that very depth of feeling which nationalism unjustly and greedily claims for itself. We need internationalism to save the world and to broaden and heighten our civilisation. While regional man enriches the lives that international man is already working to keep secure and healthy, national man, drunk with power, demands our loyalty, money and applause, and poisons the very air with his dangerous nonsense.

THE MAD SAD WORLD

Our more sensible and sensitive film critics have already told us that *It's A Mad, Mad, Mad, Mad World* is not really funny at all, but violent and cruel. I believed them but I felt I had to see it for myself. Having seen it, I have now reached the conclusion that it must be the oddest example of film making there can ever have been. I never remember before sitting in a place of entertainment and feeling at such complete cross-purposes with the providers of the entertainment. It is as if we belonged to different planets.

The programme, which cost a steep five bob at the Coliseum, is full of information about how the film was made. From its conception to its release, we are told, it took three and a half years, 166 shooting days, 636,000 feet (approximately 125 miles) of exposed film, finally reduced to 21,939 feet — a "running time of 210 minutes, including intermission." Some 1,700 drawings, blueprints and models of the exterior and interior settings were needed. There were 217 items of special effects — "a conglomeration of unworldly devices such as pemberthy siphons, gunpowders, squibs and squib hooks, dynamite caps, pulleys, cranes, compressors, popping matches, air rams, hydraulic rams, smoke pots, smoke blowers, cables and wires and opaque paint." For one effect alone, a car going off a cliff in the opening sequence, they had to have "a radio-controlled pilot put together with bits and pieces of electronic equipment they acquired from the laboratories of the California Institute of Technology and nearby aerospace plants." Here, we may say, was our new technological age, nowhere better represented than in southern California, happily at play. The backroom boys were having fun. And the result is murderous.

Stanley Kramer, the producer-director, is an experienced and courageous film man. He is quoted as saying: "Bill Rose's script was the funniest ever written. If the motion picture isn't the funniest ever made, the fault will lie with the man I see in the mirror." (An odd but perhaps significant way of putting it, for in the mirror we see our outward selves, embodying *our conscious intention.*) We read that:

He sought to brew an unheard-of mix of onscreen chicanery, calamity, disaster and suspense, requiring more performing talent and behind-the-camera artistry and cunning than any entertainment recipe ever before devised, and to come up with an explosive celluloid of belly laughs. He aimed to fashion a giant blend of slapstick and whimsy to the end that audiences of all ages, lands and mores would find delirious divertissement.

Even the writer of the programme, we feel, is straining so hard that he may rupture himself.

William Rose, responsible both for the original idea and the final script, is a writer of very considerable talent, an American who spent some years over here and gave us *Genevieve,* surely one of the best comedy films made in this country. Moreover, the cast reads like a convention of film and TV comedians. Never since Hollywood began have so many funny men been assembled by a film producer. And never have funny men been less funny. They all work like whipped blacks at it, and hardly raise a smile. There are some laughs of course, but they are mostly of the shocked nervous sort, in response to yet another realistic catastrophe on the huge screen and a new barrage of amplified sound. We never find ourselves chuckling. Strictly speaking, there is no humour.

Now what can have happened? Where did these experienced film makers, with so much talent and time and money at their command, go wrong? How could they set out to achieve the funniest film ever made and end with something that leaves us stunned, repelled, saddened? What became of all the fun that they and we were going to enjoy? To what desert did the river of laughter find its way, thinning out and drying up and vanishing in the hot dust? Why is it that the slapstick films of thirty-five to fifty years ago are still a joy — often making us laugh more now than they did when we first saw them — when this immensely ambitious new attempt at a comic masterpiece fails so dismally?

Before trying to answer these questions, I will make a point in passing. A few years after the war, a company that not only produced films but that could also distribute them, offered me the chance of writing and co-producing a feature-length slapstick film. Delighted, I said I would do it, and then I retired to the country to consider what I would do. Some days later, I found myself declining the offer. I realized that such a film, to succeed, would have to create for itself an artificial world in which everybody and everything would be ridiculous, as they were in the genuine old slapsticks, in which the very roads and trees, automobiles and trains, were comic characters. I was neither clever enough nor, what was even more important, sufficiently strong-willed and ruthless to create, simply for one film, such a world, so different from ours. Many thanks but nothing doing!

Now this is the trap into which Messrs Kramer and Rose and their colleagues have rushed headlong. Not only have they not attempted to re-create the old artificial world, the dream empire of slapstick, populated entirely by clowns, but they have been at the greatest possible pains and expense, calling on our new technology for all its formidable resources, to show us — in panoramic breadth and full colour — our actual world as it exists today in southern California. It is there to the smallest puff of dust and can of orange juice. I know that region fairly well, and as soon as the film began, with wide shots of the twisting desert roads, like tape tossed on a moulting hearth rug, I was back there. And I knew that the MAD-4 boys were stuck with it; they could never come out laughing.

Then — at least this is my guess — something else happened. I think they worked so hard and so long at this Super-Jumbo-Comedy that, without being aware of what was happening, they began dredging up out of the dark of their minds more and more disgust and contempt and hatred. A sardonic lama and a communist intellectual, collaborating to attack contemporary American life, could not have done a more ruthless job. It is southern California on the rack and having its bones broken. It is the American Way drenched in wormwood solution and sulphuric acid. There is in it not a glimmer of affection for anybody or anything. All its huge explosions and bashings are not so much overdone attempts at slapstick as they are the outward and exaggerated expression of an unconscious violence, of disgust and contempt and hatred, once concealed, now boiling over. What it offers us is no "giant blend of slapstick and whimsy," but a savage rejection of contemporary American society and its values and status symbols.

All the people, condemned from first to last to a frenzied chase, are moved by nothing but greed, the hope of getting money without working for it, the fear of missing a soft buck. If all these comedians are never funny (and they aren't) it is because they are not allowed time and space in which to deploy themselves; they are tied to a story line that is really a fizzing string of firecrackers. The characters are all contemptible people, inevitably doomed to disaster. They are all screaming their heads off for something they will never be allowed to have and that would do them no good even if they had it. They are loveless, without dignity and self-respect, suspicious and treacherous and stupid; and any society breeding more and more of such creatures is moving away from any true civilisation.

Machinery and property are held in high respect in the American way of life, seen near its peak in southern California. So in this savagely violent film, more machinery and property are wrecked than ever before. Automobiles, no longer sacred objects, clash against one another, lose wheels and other essential parts, run off the roads, tumble down gorges, fall off cliffs. Aeroplanes are bashed about as if they were cheap toys. A whole filling station is reduced to a heap of boards. Neat rows of canned merchandise, fit for any supermarket, are hurled from their shelves, split open, ruined. The mere existence of a wall, any wall, is a signal for somebody or something to come crashing through it. Nothing is safe from this appalling violence and explosiveness. Even the things that normally try to save life are here a menace to it, so that in the last sequence a gigantic firemen's ladder is transformed by some evil magic into a monstrous catapult, hurling one character after another through doorways and windows far below. And everything that had a kind of dreamlike comic innocence in the old slapstick films now seems menacing, relentless, cruel. This is the world of the nuclear deterrent trying to have fun. It is the high jinks of a ruthless technology. Behind my shrinking gaze and battered hearing, my blood ran cold.

I cannot help suspecting that many of the episodes were chosen not for their comic possibilities but as symbolic presentations of our various predicaments. (In this department it is far superior to the film made out of Kafka's *The Trial*.) As disgust and contempt, hatred and despair, came boiling up from the unconscious, such symbolism was inevitable. It explains the long and wearing adventures of the pair who found themselves locked in the basement of the ironmonger's, together with enormous stocks of explosives, fireworks, fuses and blowlamps. It explains the episode of the two idiotic youths in the fine private aeroplane, whose owner, a drunk, was unconscious; they did not know how to fly it; while the men in the control tower of the airport were themselves no longer in control. It explains why the good old honest cop (Spencer Tracy, no less) was the craftiest crook of them all. I could go on and on; but why should I? Either you have seen the film or you haven't.

As an attempt not merely to revive but to enlarge, magnify, lengthen and strengthen and bring bang-up-to-date the old slapstick film, demanding a maximum of "belly-laughs," *It's A Mad, Mad, Mad, Mad World* seems to me a huge and appallingly expensive flop, wasting more comic talent than any film has ever done before. But as a savage satire of the kind of society, really a sort of Hell, we are striving so hard to maintain, prepared if necessary for its protection to turn the world into a radioactive cinder, it is in an eye-straining, ear-battering, nerve-shattering class of its own. It makes the blackest of the avant-garde Theatre-of-the-Absurd playwrights seem like tepid protesters playing at charades. And what I wonder now is whether Stanley Kramer and William Rose and their colleagues can go on making motion pictures in southern California. Purged, purified, free to meditate in peace, they ought to be making arrangements to enter Tibetan monasteries or caves in the Indian forest.

GIVING UP CONFERENCES

For all I know other people may turn down more invitations to conferences than I do. However, their percentage of refusals cannot be higher during these past few years because mine is one hundred per cent. Down they are turned, these invitations, one after another, *flat*.

Not that I am rude about them. I always offer an excuse. I am not very well, I have other long-standing engagements, I am wrestling with some great opus. I bring in a lot of reluctance, am filled with regret. But I make it quite plain that I am not going. And here I behave better than some of my distinguished colleagues, who accept such invitations, allow their names to go into print, and then never turn up. This is bad. I am ashamed of such distinguished colleagues and sometimes doubt (*a*) if they are all that distinguished and (*b*) if they really are colleagues.

But before I explain why I do not attend them, let us be clear about conferences. They are apparently on a high, wide and handsome level. I am not concerned here with a week-end in Wolverhampton in August or three nights at Worthing in February, with delegates arriving by bus and being sent to a Youth Hostel or the Gladstone Temperance Hotel. Any man over thirty and in his right mind will refuse that sort of invitation.

Most of these conferences I turn down are international, and fares will be paid to Switzerland, Italy, the Island of Rhodes. Rooms have been booked at the Bristol or the Grand. There may be sight-seeing tours laid on, to say nothing of official luncheons and cocktail parties and seats at the opera. They look like Continental holidays for nothing. Why should a man boast (it is a weakness of mine) of turning them down? Is he trying to suggest that he is *so grand* that he can afford to refuse — and even sneer — at such magnificent invitations?

No, madam. (For it is about thirty to one that the last query was feminine.) It is the old hand in me that writes the refusals. I have had my share of these doings. And now I know — and it is high time I did — the limitations of my own temperament and tolerance. Lady, I know what it will be like, and probably you don't. Just listen now.

In the ten years following the War, when public spirit still moved in me, I attended a number of international conferences. On several occasions I was actually the Chairman. This is, I must admit, not as bad as it sounds. In fact I would rather "chair" a conference than simply attend one as a delegate. My method as a chairman was to make a speech, brief but rousing, at the opening session, make another, just as brief, at the closing session, and during the three days in between do nothing official and boring at all, having divided the work among all the other people, who would be toiling over resolutions and amendments and final reports while I was sitting at ease in the nearest bar. But with whom, you may ask. The answer is — with a few rebellious and choice souls who had marched out of their subcommittees or working parties. And sometimes that is how the real work of the conference was done, well away from the conscientious gasbags.

My first complaint against international conferences is that there are so many foreigners attending them. I have a great store of international goodwill except when I am surrounded by foreign delegates, who suddenly seem altogether *too foreign*, as if they were playing irritating character parts. Some I don't mind — usually, the Scandinavian, the Dutch, the Swiss, the Austrian. The worst of the Europeans — and I say this with regret, being a greedy man and fond of France — are the French. M. Toulemonde and his delegation from Paris are conference-wreckers to a man. (They never used to send any women in my time.)

To begin with, they always pretended not to understand a word of English, fighting a rear-guard action for their own language. On being introduced to them, you would mutter a few words of your own miserable French, and then later they would corner you and pour out floods of rapid and idiomatic French, which you nodded and muttered at, hoping they were complaining about the Grand or Bristol Hotel food. Afterwards, to your horror, you would discover, at some plenary session, that you had apparently already given your support to some monstrous proposal of theirs. Their other trick was to arrive late, in a body, at some meeting, insist upon discussing something not on the agenda, and then depart furiously in a body if they were called to order. No wonder they have to have a de Gaulle.

Delegates from much further afield usually belonged to one of two groups. Either they spoke little but when they did speak could not be understood at all, or they were orators and went on and on and on. Many South Americans, in my conference time, were capable of wasting hours and hours, chiefly for the benefit of the reporter from the *Uruguay Gazette* they had persuaded to attend the session. In Paris once, as chairman, I was challenged to a duel by one such orator, whom I had accused of wasting our time. And if this seems a bit much, I must add that once as chairman

THE MOMENTS AND OTHER PIECES

in the Central Hall, Westminster, I had fireworks thrown at me, even though I was not rebuking anybody.

Even apart from the boredom of most of the procedure, I have never been able to escape feeling a fool at most of these conferences. There is, I think, something silly about us, the way in which we all arrive together, hand in our names (though I have never yet worn one of those badges they give out) and queue up for programmes, tickets, labels, time-tables, city plans and guides, like sheep who have suddenly developed a taste for print. I may have been too self-conscious and oversensitive, but I always felt that the other people in the hotels and the local citizenry regarded us as so many self-important asses. Moreover, I always had a suspicion that the hotels and restaurants, the ones in which we dined en masse, had earlier been beaten down to their lowest possible prices, so that we figured in their eyes as a miserable lot of cut-rate guests who did not deserve much attention.

And the receptions by the Minister, the Burgomaster, and the rest, did nothing to restore my self-esteem. I felt that in their eyes we were just part of yet another official chore. "What have I to do tonight?" they probably asked. "Oh — those fellows. No way of getting out of it, I suppose?" If they hadn't said anything like that, they always seemed to me to look as if they had. After all, who in his senses wants to Welcome a Conference? What is there to say that would not be better left unsaid? What sane man (I am not sure about women) enjoys routine official hospitality?

Not I, for one. Coming close to my idea of Hell is the official diplomatic life, with its endless luncheons, cocktail parties, dinners, receptions, suppers, all packed with the same people saying nothing in particular. It is boring to receive such hospitality, and it must be still more boring to give it. You cannot even drink yourself out of tedium, because either the booze is not strong enough (that thin white wine that does not seem to come from anywhere) or, if potent, then there is not enough of it. And when there are a hundred or so of you — and there can easily be far more at a big conference — all wearing badges and fixed grins, then everything is much worse. The tipple may easily be one part of cheap Barsac and one part of Riesling to four parts water. The only conference guest who has a chance is the chairman, who, if he knows what's what, may escape to a back room and whisky.

Then there is that *Morning* or *Afternoon Sight-seeing,* with which the trap is so often baited. Anything is probably better than listening to men droning on and on in a stuffy room, until you have covered your agenda with doodles, but I am not one who enjoys an official tour of the city and its environs accompanied by special guides who let you off nothing. "This book," said the little girl when returning it to her teacher, "tells me more about penguins than I want to know." And guides are like that. I took to painting partly in order to avoid sight-seeing when on holiday. And this was private and conjugal sight-seeing, whereas on conferences there may be three or four coach loads of you, yawning and yawning or wondering what could have been wrong with the *fruits-de-mer* served at the cut-rate lunch.

As for those free seats at the opera, it depends where you are. In Vienna — fine! But in Boojum or Snarksy, you may be in for a terrible evening — and five hours of it too. And if the alternative is the Municipal Theatre, it is ten to one they will be doing, specially for you, a very long and quite incomprehensible historical play ending about quarter to twelve, by which time you would be ready to rat on the conference's chief resolution if anybody offered you cold beer and hot sausages.

Finally, there is too often about the conference's whole proceedings an air of futility. Gasbags, who love these affairs, will have nearly asphyxiated you. Point-of-order sticklers will have infuriated you. Chairmen (not me) will have said nothing in longer and more pompous terms than you have ever known before. Final resolutions, adopted in despair after the last oxygen has left the room, will seem quite meaningless. And — but here I exclude scientific and technological conferences — instead of feeling more optimistic about international cooperation, you may now have lost all belief in it.

Certainly, madam, I am exaggerating and I am being unfair and it can't be as bad as I say it is. The fact remains though, I turn the invitations down *flat,* even though they come from Venice, Ascona, Dubrovnik, Stockholm. I'm not going. I've given it up.

THE HAPPY INTROVERT

Our civilisation is monstrously lopsided, so overextroverted and so ignorant or contemptuous of man's inner world that it is now in danger of destroying itself. Across the road we have been travelling for the last hundred years or so, turning it into a dead end, is the H-bomb. This progress towards a time of terror was foreseen by Dostoievsky and Nietzsche. The age being so onesided, it is not surprising then that the arts, attempting to restore a balance, are more deeply introverted than they were

in earlier ages. What is regarded as "serious modern literature" — not
unreasonably, even though many leaders of literary opinion have been
themselves not well balanced — has been the creation of introverted writers, often almost lost in their inner worlds. Nor is it surprising that so many
of these writers should have been hysterically defiant, despairing, wretch-
edly unhappy. Artists want to go their own way but they also want to be
widely understood and appreciated, not misunderstood and rejected by
their own age. The unhappy introvert in modern literature, his work often
darkened and distorted by his feeling of frustration and his bitterness, is to
be expected. What is unexpected and so really surprising is a writer of
power, as deeply introverted as the others, who seems as happy as the rest
seem unhappy. John Cowper Powys is an original, perhaps in this sense a
unique figure in modern writing, because he can be fairly described as a
happy introvert.

The best evidence leading to this judgement — and he would agree at
once with this himself — is to be found in his fiction. But here I am not
concerned with his novels, and so would point to various minor works,
such as *A Philosophy of Solitude* and *In Spite Of,* and above all to what is
a major work, his astonishing *Autobiography.* The story it tells, ending in
the early 1930's (it was published in 1934, probably a year or so after it
was finished) and bringing him into his sixties, is no record of fortune's
smiles and gifts. He was for ever suffering from stomach ulcers, which
landed him in hospital on many occasions. Both in England and America,
too often he went from one lecture engagement to the next wrestling with
pain, nausea, vomiting, sustained somehow by mournful diets of bread-and-
milk and the like. For thirty years he lectured for a living, chiefly in
America, spending days and nights in trains, sometimes on his way to
familiar audiences that knew and loved him, at other times arriving in
women's clubs, packed with ladies searching for "the finer things" who
probably regarded him with bewildered suspicion and hostility. Manfully
he paid his way, facing squarely his family responsibilities, but it must have
been almost always a near thing. And what was worse was that time was
running out; he was the eldest and the genius of the gifted Powys family;
both Theodore and Llewelyn were enjoying literary reputations when he
was still unknown, except to some scattered and dazed lecture audiences;
and he was well into his fifties before he could begin writing in earnest.
Moreover, from first to last he was carrying a load of neurotic obsessions
that would have sent most men tottering towards a psychoanalyst's couch.
And he was a sensualist — it is his own term — debarred in one way or
another from almost everything the average sensual man enjoys most. Yet
we can call him the happiest of the deeply introverted moderns.

It is true that in the end everything came right. The books were written, then read, enjoyed, admired, at least by those, not necessarily critics, capable of appreciating originality, genius as distinct from talent. The life-long semi-invalid entered a vigorous and productive old age. The neurotic load was lightened by will, imagination, humour: no analysts were needed; Powys was his own — and far superior — medicine man and magician. But when he wrote the *Autobiography* — or, for that matter, the earlier and longer novels — this serene and almost cosy ending was not in sight. Then, the way was still hard, the weather dubious, the goal hidden. But we have only to read the *Autobiography* to discover him as the strangely happy introvert. And if I seem to be labouring this point, I would say to the objectors — name me another modern of anything like this size, deeply introverted, taking his stand in his own inner world, who is so free from bitterness and despair, who has such breadth and buoyancy, such ease and prodigality. It is as if from the mouth of some familiar black pit we saw Pegasus come winging out, white and dazzling.

Round about page 500 in the original English edition of Jung's *Psychological Types,* we can find some account of John Cowper Powys, not of course the man himself, the complex personality of the writer, but as a basic type. He is — with some differences of his own — among the Introverted Sensation Types. These bring sensations of the outer world into the magical depths of their inner world, where all is mythology and — to quote Jung — "men, animals, railways, houses, rivers, and mountains appear partly as benevolent deities and partly as malevolent demons." Such a one might stare at a flower, a patch of moss, the corner of an old wall, or what might seem to another a commonplace stretch of road, and know strange forebodings and fear or an uprush of ecstasy. What would seem dull to most of us would seem alive and magical to him. But to enjoy his peculiar temperament he would have to demand what so many people now dread — solitude, loneliness. This is not, I suspect, a rare type, though not to be found at most cocktail parties or indeed at meetings of authors. It could easily be discovered among men who despise gregariousness and cheery good citizenship, who often break away to lead what seem to us to be hard and monotonous lives, like some of the leathery oldish men I met years ago in the Arizona desert, where they were "dry-washing" for gold, earning just enough to keep them in bacon, canned beans and tobacco. The type seems uncommon because such men do odd unsocial jobs, live in out-of-the-way places, and when encountered, though not unfriendly, are tongue-tied or close-mouthed after much solitude. But it really is uncommon, a rare odd fish indeed, when it has at its command a wide culture and astonishing gifts of expression. And now we arrive at John Cowper Powys.

Let us dip into the *Autobiography,* quoting one out of scores of similar passages:

How can I find the right expression for the feelings that came to me in those days when the wind blew in a certain way as I followed some muddy grass-track along the edge of the Ely Road or the London Road? How can I describe the feeling I got, as if all the scarce-noticed sensations that had come lightly and incidentally to long generations of my ancestors, when they met the rain, or felt the sun, or heard the calling of rooks or the twittering of sparrows, or saw the smoke rising from human hearths, were rushing over me, in a hardly bearable flood of ecstatic happiness, simply because, on that undistinguished road to the railway station, I heard some patient shop assistant mowing his scrap of grass behind a privet-hedge?

I know perfectly well that everybody born into the world has the feelings I am describing, is visited by these indescribable and apparently causeless transports. I am not in the least suggesting that I am peculiar in this. But why, in the Devil's name, then, do we go on making a cult of everything else except these? Why must politics, religion, philosophy, ambition, revolution, reaction, business, pleasure — all be considered intensely important, and these rare magical feelings not be considered at all?

And then we can add to this passage another, again one of many that might be quoted, from *A Philosophy of Solitude:*

The hour is at hand when an immense number of men and women in all countries of the world will revolt — secretly, passionately, obstinately — against the crowd-opinions that have turned man's heart away from its rightful world and made it a slave of the unessential. The hour is at hand when thousands and thousands of men and women will recognise that the utmost all the Governments, all the Revolutions and Reactions, all the economic upheavals and improvements can do, is to supply them with a minimum of livelihood, a minimum of security and peace, a minimum of labour and its reward.

Let the revolutionaries and reactionaries, let science and machinery give us our bare living, and bare security against famine, our bare peace of mind, and they have done enough. Their States and their State-Upheavals, their Politics and Economics, their Inventions and Industries, are but means whereby men and women can enjoy the few years of harmless happiness that intervene between the two great Silences, between the eternal Un-born and the eternal Dead.

It is a strange madness to lay the life-stress upon anything less significant, less mysterious than life itself. By all means let the whole world be organised into one great Productive Machine, into one great Productive Economic State. By all means let us each labour, like obedient slaves, for this World-Organisation, for four or five hours every day, and receive, as our return, food, shelter and freedom from panic. But for the rest, the important thing is not external at all, not social or gregarious at all, not necessarily human even. The impor-

tant thing is how, as individual solitary spirits, who might have been
born on Uranus or Saturn rather than upon the earth, we are going
to strengthen, deepen, intensify our ecstatic happiness in life and our
philosophic acceptance of death. . . .

Now to innumerable introverted sensation types, indeed to all deeply introverted types, people who may have never read a word of his and feel
baffled and frustrated and in despair as the man-made world closes in on
them, Powys offers a way out, a new and more satisfying kind of life. And
they should certainly read *In Spite Of*, which Powys, writing in his eightieth
year, boldly described in its subtitle *A Philosophy For Everyman*. But
Everyman may well be a gregarious extrovert. There is a certain innocence
in Powys's assumption that behind all our various disguises and antics we
are really at heart so many introverts of his own sort, to be saved by long
solitary walks. And he had not looked hard at the political scene, even in
the earlier 1930's when he wrote the passage I quoted above, if he could
imagine that modern men can be safely indifferent to "all the Governments,
all the Revolutions and Reactions, all the economic upheavals and improvements." The Nazis would not have left him in peace among the Welsh
hills. Communists might not allow him to publish anything at all. A World
Organisation, regarding cheerful anarchy as treason, demanding absolute
loyalty to itself, might order him to be brain-washed. And a nuclear war
might leave nothing to enjoy and nobody to enjoy it. We can no longer
afford to ignore the politicians; they are not simply arguing a long way off;
they are busy trying to mould, shape and colour our lives; therefore we had
better discover which of them would do us the least harm.

    Objections of this kind, however, are really out of place. It is as if we
interrupted an orator to ask him to define a term or to point out that he is
not being entirely consistent. Readers of the *Autobiography* will remember
that not long after he had left Cambridge, when he was earning a very
modest living as a weekly lecturer at various girls' schools along the South
Coast, Powys decided, as he told his brother Littleton, that he had invented
a new art, the art of *Dithyrambic Analysis*. This is the sort of thing high-
and-mighty young men tell one another, and Powys, in the middle of
describing his youthful fears, follies and obsessions, is humorous about it.
But in fact he must have come near the truth. He brought out of those
years of lecturing in America, where he was immensely impressive on the
platform, a famous "spellbinder," something that might fairly be described
as being dithyrambic and analytical. It is writing that is oratorical; not
words arranged to catch the eye but an eager voice in print; yet a voice that
while it seems to be eloquently improvising — and we are told he could do
this for a couple of hours on the platform — serves a mind that can be
most delicately perceptive and aware of the finest shades. He might be said
to address us from two very different levels. On one, where he is a figure

larger than life in a rather theatrical fashion, a Henry Irving of prose, he performs gigantically, in modes tragical, comical, philosophical, grotesque and fantastic. On the other level, far from the limelight, on the dusky edge of the unconscious, where he is a poet not a performer, he can catch and illuminate a look, a tone, a mood, a memory, that would escape most writers of our time. Readers who have dipped into Powys and do not like him have usually not given themselves the chance of enjoying him on this second level, having been antagonised by the antics and dithyrambs, the drums and trumpets, on the stage above. Such readers should try again. For my part, though at times feeling exasperated (and it is major writers in their large and loose fashion, without the tact of little masters, who *do* exasperate us), I can enjoy almost everything on both levels.

Llewelyn Powys, who came close to worshipping his eldest brother, thought the major part of the *Autobiography,* describing John's first forty years, a marvel of truthful narration and self-analysis; but he disliked the final chapters, covering their author's next twenty years, because in them narrative and analysis give way to dazzling performances in an intellectual three-ring circus. This is severe family criticism, and there is no reason why we readers should echo it. Indeed, there are as many good things in these final chapters as there are earlier in the book. One of them is my favourite quotation from Powys, who, after describing an old friend, goes on to say: "He combined scepticism of everything with credulity about everything; and I am convinced this is the true Shakespearean way wherewith to take life." (People who do not understand this observation at once should forget about it; it is not for them.) There are too passages here about America that seem to me beyond the range of any other English visitor there. We have all been compelled to read and to listen to an immense amount of claptrap about Anglo-American understanding; here in the *Autobiography* we can discover a real understanding being created out of experience and perception, poetry and philosophy. He admires and lovingly describes much that the visitor in a hurry, trapped in the cities, never discovers in America; yet he is equally eloquent, in a manner not without grotesque humour, about what he calls the "phantasmagoric horror" of America:

> The horror can be very big. But it can also be very small. Most things of this sort can be detected by their smell; and I think this particular horror is usually found — like the inside of an American coffin after the embalming process has run its course — to smell of a desolate varnish and unspeakable decomposition. The curious thing about it is that it is a horror that can only be felt by imaginative people. It is more than a mere negation of all that is mellow, lovely, harmonious, peaceful, organic, satisfying. It is not a negation at all. It is a terrifying positive. I think at its heart lies a sort of lemur-like violence of grue-

some vulgarity. It certainly loves to dance a sort of "danse macabre" of frantic self-assertion. It has something that is antagonistic to the very essence of what the old cultures have been training us to for ten thousand years.

In the *Autobiography* as a whole, as he remembers himself in this place or at that time, recapturing the finest shades of feeling and yet, so to speak, creating out of himself a huge half-comic character, he is a better advocate of his basic type and the life of introverted sensation than he is in the books devoted to this subject. We are shown directly how obvious disadvantages — ill-health, lack of money and position, neurotic obsessions — were more than cancelled out by advantages belonging entirely to temperament and outlook. Always, except of course when deliberately remembering, he lived in the present, making the most of whatever it offered him. He lived without ambition, that great destroyer of sensuous satisfaction and easy contemplation, forbidding that inheritance of the earth which rightly belongs to the meek. In this sense, though obstinately, toweringly, his own man, Powys here is one of the meek. And his astonishing frankness, which to my mind never becomes embarrassing as some other men's confessions do, has behind it this genuine humility, not towards other people but towards life itself, together with what I have already suggested as a humorous enlarging, heightening, caricaturing of himself. So we have here the life-story of a Comic Character in a book that is deeply serious, often profound, at times entrancing in its beauty. It is magical because it is the work of a man who believes, as he has told us more than once, that by living intensely between our outer and inner worlds, bringing sensation to our depths, we can indeed work magic. It is a masterpiece revealing the happiest of our modern introverts.

WHAT HAPPENED TO FALSTAFF

No Shakespearean character has received more enthusiastic praise than Falstaff. More ink and print may have been devoted to the enigmatic figure of Hamlet, but it is Falstaff who has turned critics into a rapturous chorus. Among the loudest applauders of the fat knight may be found professors of Eng. Lit. who, after their glass of barley water, have never stayed up later than eleven, and careful men of letters who would no more think of roistering in a tavern than of breaking into a bank. Falstaff is not only wonderfully written in himself but the cause that good writing has come out of other men. But is there anything new to be said about him? I think there is, but only after we have stopped chuckling and clapping, have begun to explore the mind of Falstaff's creator, and have seen both the character and the poet who made him against the widest possible background of English literature and life.

In order to understand what happened to Falstaff, how he was built up and then knocked down, how in this instance the dramatist in Shakespeare conquered the poet, we must first return to some familiar ground. Here we shall keep company not with Shakespeare the poet but with Shakespeare the astute man of the Theatre, anxious to provide his company with plays and to please his large audiences. *Richard II* and *Henry VI* had already been written, and, if there were to be more historical plays, based like the others on Holinshed's *Chronicles,* clearly they ought to fill this gap between Richard II and Henry VI. Moreover, within this gap, waiting for Shakespeare to bring him to life on the stage, was the one triumphant popular figure among all these monarchs — King Henry V. Audiences loved him, for even bad plays about him had proved successful. As a hero-king of drama he seemed to promise everything: first, the madcap youth, the despair of his father; then the gallant prince who helped his father to put down rebellion; and finally the king, now free of all folly, who proved to be a greater man than his father. Such a figure was worth more than one play; there could be matter for two dramas in his wild youth and subsequent gallantry on the battlefield, and for yet another in his reign as king. So Shakespeare devised *Henry IV, Parts One* and *Two,* and *Henry V.*

The legends of Prince Hal's youthful follies could not be ignored. Indeed, without them there could hardly be a play worth seeing. The serious matter, what could be made out of the rebellions against Bolingbroke, was inferior to that in *Richard II* and *Henry VI.* The scenes containing Prince Hal and his boon companions would be a welcome change from those showing the harsh dry king and his court or the stiff anger of the barons in rebellion. A drama on two different levels was possible here, as Shakespeare saw from the first. (Here I must add, to be rid of the subject, that he accepted the theatrical tradition that Prince Hal's chief boon companion was Sir John Oldcastle. It is generally supposed that the character was renamed Falstaff because Oldcastle, executed as a Lollard, was regarded as an early Protestant martyr. But it is also likely that Shakespeare was glad to give this giant creation a name of his own. And to us he is Falstaff, so that we can forget Oldcastle.) It was a brilliant idea to present the drama of Henry IV and his son on two different levels, dividing it between the court and the tavern, the top people and the riffraff, and giving the historical play a new breadth and depth. But technically it was tricky. If the comic scenes of low life were not good entertainment, all was lost. But if they were too good, the balance of the drama would be destroyed. Again, if Prince Hal were shown rollicking with tedious buffoons, as the heroic central character he would suffer just as the play itself would. The future hero-king must at least frolic in amusing company. There must be somebody in the tavern, leading him on, more or less his own size and weight. And while this character must be good enough to sustain all the comic scenes, he must not divert any sympathy from Henry when, as king, Henry has to reject him. For unless we are ready, at the end of the second part of *Henry IV*, to join in the cheering for the new young king, soon to be the all-conquering hero of the play of *Henry V*, something will have gone badly wrong. And, as we know, it did go wrong. After Falstaff has been rebuked and rejected, then carried off to the Fleet prison, we stare after him in dismay and cannot do any cheering for King Henry. *Hurray for what?*

It went wrong not because the technical job was altogether too tricky. When his mind was considering every aspect of his work, Shakespeare was equal to any technical problem, no matter how tricky, but often his stage-craft slipped because he was not attending to it properly, not bothering, not caring, just pasting the thing together ready for next Tuesday. What happened in *Henry IV*, however, was not the result of indifference. Here Shakespeare the successful man of the Theatre, the planner of a series of plays about English kings, was defeated by Shakespeare the poet, the creator working out of his unconscious depths. It is the dramatist's experience, craft, talent, that present us with Henry, both as prince and as king; but the character of Falstaff comes out of the poet's genius. This was felt by audiences from the very first, for there are contemporary references to the two parts of *Henry IV* as the Falstaff plays. The fat knight, originally intended as a foil to the prince and so much comic relief, steals both the *Henry IV* plays, and he would have walked away with *Henry V* too if Shakespeare, breaking the promise of the *Henry IV* epilogue, had not killed him offstage. So that the hero-king could live in all glory, Falstaff had to die. In the two earlier plays, Shakespeare does his best for Henry — we can see him working at it trying to keep to his conscious plan — but Henry is overshadowed, almost extinguished, by that huge, triumphant, *effortless* creation — Falstaff.

I repeat — effortless. A character of such size, scope and vitality, a character who seems himself a genius, cannot be sustained by conscious effort. He arrives, pulsing and glowing with life, from the unconscious depths. No writer, not the cleverest who ever lived, could coldly contrive, put together, consciously set in motion, a Falstaff. If such characters seem magical, as indeed they do, that is because they come, like figures in some marvellous enduring dream, from the magical part of man, the innermost recesses and unfathomable depths of his being, the region far within where "he on honey-dew hath fed, And drunk the milk of Paradise." These giant characters come unbidden, and when they arrive, they do as they please. Shakespeare, consciously planning his historical series, with one eye on his more important patrons, wanted a useful comic foil to Prince Hal, some fat old fool who would amuse him and us for a time and could then be shrugged away; but what he got, rising magnificently out of his creative depths, was Falstaff, who not only does not fit into the drama's planned structure but finally succeeds, at least for many of us, in wrecking it. At the end of *Henry IV, Part Two,* we are not ready for a play about *Henry V* — let the treacherous prig stew in his oil of anointment! — but are eager to follow Falstaff to the Fleet prison or wherever he chooses to go, and would echo the cry of Bardolph when he hears that Falstaff is dead: "Would I were with him, wheresome'er he is, either in Heaven or in Hell!" It is not fanciful to suggest then, as I do again now, that here Shakespeare the poet, the creative man, by conceiving a character so out of scale, so much in excess of what the drama needed, rose up and rebelled against Shakespeare the careful and practical man of the Theatre. It is not unreasonable to regard Falstaff as the retort, the huge protest, of one side of Shakespeare, the inner and hidden side, to the other, the outward, belonging to the smiling and prosperous playwright, already with an eye on some sound property and a possible coat-of-arms.

If Falstaff is much bigger and richer than he was originally designed to be, this is because the life in him was created by an explosion of rebellious energy. Out of this same eruption, which was to be followed soon by the explosions and earthquakes and shuddering darkness of the tragedies, came much else, not offered for our enjoyment now: scorn and disgust and the beginning of horror, all the imagery of disease that increasingly finds its way into this two-part drama of Henry IV and his son. The wretched king, dying by inches, who has sacrificed so much for power and enjoyed it so little; his friends and enemies alike, clanking metallic figures that seem to talk in clanking metallic verse; the brassy pride, the anger that can be released at a word, a touch; the cold treacheries, the meaningless battle-fields still smoking while the next set of pompous lies are being composed and uttered — we are made more and more aware of all these, together with sores, poxes and plagues, as the drama of *Henry IV* moves to its close. The common folk make no better show than the baronial ironclads; they are senile and doting, like Shallow and Silence, or bleating caricatures of common men like those pressed into military service by Falstaff. The bright shield of chivalry is reversed and seems to be crawling with maggots. None of this is realism, simple and direct as it would have been in Chaucer, for example; there are too many diseases, too much scorn and disgust; it is a voice from a man's inner world condemning the outer world of power and glory, to which one side of the man himself may have been too much committed. He is protesting and rebelling against himself. Yeats said that we make poetry out of the quarrel with ourselves; and until his last years, Shakespeare, with his rich but deeply divided nature, was always ready for this quarrel. One half of him, the more outward and conscious half, admired order and detested all forms of disorder; we could fairly describe it as conservative, respectable, conformist. The other half of him, which seized the pen whenever he was being fully creative, was in hot rebellion against the ordered world, and it was the fiery energy of this hidden self that went into his greatest characters, all of them rebels of one sort and another, like Hamlet, Cleopatra and Falstaff.

The secret of Falstaff is that he is masterfulness, quickness, energy, genius, everything that makes a great commander of men, all in the service not of power and glory but of delight. When we see him on the stage we miss these essential qualities because the overpadded actor is so busy being a fat old man, puffing and wheezing and grunting. But Falstaff wears his years and fat as if they were a comic uniform, using them as matter for more humour, so that all the best jokes about his age and size are his own. We must not be deceived by his sprawling bulk; his eye misses nothing; his mind is wonderfully clear, quick and commanding, working like lightning — but summer lightning, hurting nobody. He is a great man, far greater than Bolingbroke or any of his brawling nobles, but he is a very unusual great man because instead of giving himself to ambition and power, he chooses ease, pleasure, good fellowship, his and our delight. He is the Alexander, Caesar or Napoleon, not of battlefields, victory marches and ruined kingdoms, but of rollicking evenings and circles of happy faces. If wit, humour and enjoyment should have an emperor, then this is he. And why should not the qualities of a master of men, everything that makes for greatness, serve for once far removed from the standards of ambition, cruelty, death? The triumph of Falstaff down the centuries is not explained by the fact that his scenes offer comic relief from the grim chronicle of Bolingbroke and his adversaries. To go as we do from Bolingbroke's kingdom to Falstaff's is to experience a glorious expansion of the spirit; the glitter of steel is transformed into firelight, candlelight, and the gleams of gold in the sherris-sack; the men of power and war, rigid in iron, all vanish, and we are among boon companions, the enchanted air is filled with "nimble, fiery and delectable shapes." Where the two kingdoms come together and clash, as in the battle scenes, Falstaff still commands our allegiance and sympathy. He knows he is ridiculous, therefore there is in him a detached intelligence that demands our respect; the others, for all their pride and high places only like so many brutal boys, are ridiculous without knowing it. In a third kingdom, the invisible but enduring realm of intelligence and spirit, Falstaff is not their butt, he is their master.

His raffishness, his lying and cheating, his astounding impudence, must be accepted, but we are mistaken if we imagine that we have only to add wit and humour to them to complete the character. He is something more than just another lovable rogue. Odd elements, usually opposed and excluding one another, are mixed in him, fused together in his personality. His judgements are absolutely realistic; he is easily the most clear-sighted person in the play; he is entirely free from the common English vice of self-deception; the world in which he moves, so superbly sure of himself, is the real world, where wounds are wounds, corpses are corpses, and cant and nonsense are cant and nonsense. And yet, though he talks prose, Falstaff is undoubtedly one of Shakespeare's great poetical creations; he exists in an atmosphere in which there is an element of poetical idealism; he is almost an archetype, a symbol of the self raised to its highest power of wit and humour, ease and enjoyment; he belongs to some haunting dream, perhaps as old as drink and firelight, of a gigantic wonderful night out, a hell of a party. When we are no longer haunted by this dream, we have finished with our youth for ever. So when Falstaff tells the travellers he is robbing that "young men must live," or, with sublime impudence, says to the Chief Justice, "You that are old consider not the capacities of us that are young," he is not merely making a joke out of his white hairs, for we cannot help feeling he speaks out of a spirit enduringly youthful. When, after seeing through Shallow and Silence at a glance, he says to us, "Lord, Lord, how subject we old men are to this vice of lying!" we still feel this spirit, dead in them, is alive in him, that his eye is still clear and bright while theirs are misty with age, self-deception and foolishness. That fine critic, Walter Raleigh, in his life of Shakespeare, brings the poet and his creation together here: "With the passing of Falstaff," he tells us, "Shakespeare's youth was ended. All that wonderful experience of London life, all those days and nights of freedom and adventure and the wooing of new pleasures, seem to be embodied in this great figure, the friend and companion of the young." This could hardly be said better, but we must examine this relation between the poet and the character he created far more closely than Raleigh did.

We have already seen that Shakespeare the popular dramatist, the careful successful man of the Theatre, wanted to write three plays about Henry, first as Prince Hal and then as the triumphant hero-king, Henry V; but he had received from Shakespeare, the poet, the creative and rebellious man, far more than was necessary to keep the story going. Falstaff, a tremendous character, threatened the whole structure of the drama, diverting sympathy from where it was needed, just because he took up so much room and attracted so much attention. And if we follow Falstaff through the two parts of *Henry IV*, we can catch more than a glimpse of the conflict between the Shakespeare who merely wanted to use him as a comic foil and the other Shakespeare who could not help enlarging, deepening, illuminating the character, this figure symbolic of and sustained by his own rebellious energy, his love of a life not found in courts and on battlefields. In the first scene, set in the prince's apartment, Falstaff says some good things but has not arrived at his full stature. Indeed, here he plays the part originally assigned to him, simply as the leading figure among the prince's idle companions. It is of course at the end of this scene, after what we may call the Gadshill plot has been worked out between the prince and Pointz, that the prince, left alone, begins:

> *I know you all, and will awhile uphold*
> *The unyoked humour of your idleness*

and tells us that he will imitate the sun, sooner or later emerging from the clouds and then admired all the more. It is a detestable speech, going much further in cold calculation and self-approval than the situation demands. Quiller-Couch, while accepting it, rightly, as Shakespeare's, suggests that it was added to the scene, after the play was written, because the leading actor, playing Henry, insisted upon some speech of this kind, detaching the prince from his low companions. This is possible, but my own view is that the speech is overdone, clumsily losing sympathy, because Shakespeare, already fascinated by the possibilities of Falstaff, is forcing himself to keep the story as he originally planned it. He gives Prince Henry what is at best a tactless speech because he is already beginning to feel divided about him.

Taste in humour is personal. I can only speak for myself when I say that the Gadshill scenes and the long tavern scene that follows them do not show us the great Falstaff, except in a few flashes. My guess is that they were originally planned to keep the prince dominant, with Falstaff his butt, but as the scene in the tavern developed, after the robbery, Falstaff began taking charge of the proceedings. Even so, he is still not quite his richest and ripest self. He reaches this towards the end of Act III, perhaps in that opening speech to Bardolph which concludes with "Company, villainous company, hath been the spoil of me." When we find him at the war he is fully ripe: notably, in his account of how he first recruited well-to-do timid fellows, who immediately bought out their services, leaving him to fill his ranks with riffraff:

. . . you would think that I had a hundred and fifty tattered prodigals lately come from swine-keeping, from eating draff and husks. A mad fellow met me on the way, and told me I had unloaded all the gibbets, and press'd the dead bodies. No eye hath seen such scarecrows. I'll not march through Coventry with them, that's flat: nay, and the villains march wide betwixt the legs, as if they had gyves on; for, indeed, I had the most of them out of prison. There's but a shirt and a half in all my company . . .

Equally rich are his exchanges with Prince Henry and Westmoreland on the subject of these men — "food for powder, food for powder; they'll fill a pit as well as better"; the famous soliloquy on Honour; and then of course our various glimpses of him during the battle of Shrewsbury. Here, among the *alarums* and *excursions,* he is allowed to make some characteristic observations, as for example: "I like not such grinning honour as Sir Walter hath: give me life, which if I can save, so; if not honour comes unlook'd for, and there's an end." But the dramatist, now in charge of these final scenes of *Part One,* takes the opportunity here to raise the prince high above Falstaff. Notice the prince's speech when he thinks that Falstaff is dead:

> . . . *Poor Jack, farewell!*
> *I could have better spared a better man:*
> *O, I should have a heavy miss of thee,*
> *If I were much in love with vanity!*

Falstaff, shamming death, overhears the whole of this speech and he should have taken better note of the last two lines I have quoted. The business that follows — his taking the body of Hotspur on his back and then pretending to have killed him — is not very happily contrived, at least to our taste, even though Falstaff's account of the matter contains one of those exact details that always suggest a master of lying: "I grant you I was down and out of breath; and so was he: but we rose both at an instant, and fought a long hour by Shrewsbury clock. . . ." And if, as I feel strongly, there is something unsatisfactory about these scenes that conclude *Part One,* something hurried, forced, overcontrived, I believe it is because the dramatist, as distinct from the poet, has to take charge almost brutally, has to make his points, round off his action, get the thing done. This is a contracting process; Falstaff, like humour itself, is essentially expansive, so he has to suffer some loss.

We do not know exactly when and how these two plays of *Henry IV* were written. Dr. Johnson, and most critics since his time, have not unreasonably regarded them as being what they are described to be, two parts of one drama, divided simply for the convenience of production. It is

possible that Shakespeare went straight on from *Part One* to *Part Two,* as
if he were writing one long play. But this seems to me unlikely. I think
there was a considerable interval between the writing of these two pieces,
and that this interval accounts for the fact, as I see it, that *Part Two* is not
a mere continuation of *Part One,* even though it shows us most of the same
people during the same king's reign: it is a different play. It moves, as all
Shakespeare's plays do, in its own atmosphere. Its highlights are brighter
than those of *Part One,* its shadows darker; it is both a more comic and a
more tragic play. It is divided more equally between public life and private
life, between the two realms, the kingdom of Bolingbroke and Prince
Henry and the kingdom now triumphantly Falstaff's; and the gap between
them is wider until the end, when of course it is brutally closed. It is as
if the opposites in Shakespeare's mind and spirit were each given more
freedom to do their best or their worst: at one extreme, the politic dramatist bent on celebrating the arrival at last of public order and national
unity, represented by Henry V, and at the other extreme, the poet and
humorous anarchist who could create Falstaff. These opposites are stronger
than they were in *Part One;* but also, here in *Part Two,* we are aware
of a third Shakespeare, beyond these opposites: it is the spirit of the man
himself, never directly revealed, only to be guessed at, but seeming to
many of us to be moving, now at this time, through a darkening world from
bewilderment to a loss of hope. There are no droller scenes in all Shakespeare than these in *Henry IV, Part Two;* we must not be surprised if they
were born of a growing despair. Tragedy, black and raging, will soon arrive; but here, in the dusk, there is still time to enjoy the fireworks of wit,
the bonfire of humour, and Falstaff before he is carted away like a felled ox.

Notice Falstaff's first appearance in this *Part Two.* There is now no
pretence that he is merely the oldest, fattest, wittiest of the prince's companions. Not only does he exist in his own right; not only is he enormously
and victoriously himself; he might even be said to be now more than
himself, as if aware of his archetypal nature. For what does he say, a minute
after he has arrived on the stage?

> Men of all sorts take a pride to gird at me; the brain of this foolish-
> compounded clay, man, is not able to invent anything that tends to
> laughter, more than I invent or is invented on me: I am not only witty
> in myself, but the cause that wit is in other men . . .

Here, in *Part Two,* he exists independently of Prince Henry; in his own
kingdom he is now absolute monarch. In all his best scenes — with the
Chief Justice and then with Hostess Quickly, with Doll Tearsheet and
Pistol in the tavern, with Justice Shallow, the recruits and Master Silence — he is not seen here with Prince Henry. Again, tastes differ, but to

my mind the long tavern scene — with Doll Tearsheet's immortal "Come, I'll be friends with thee, Jack: thou art going to the wars; and whether I shall ever see thee again or no, there is nobody cares" — loses far more than it gains by the entrance of the prince and Pointz, in disguise and playing the last of their uninspired farce tricks. But there is one remark by Pointz that should be remembered: "My lord, he will drive you out of your revenge and turn all to a merriment, if you take not the heat." What a wonderful gift this is, to be able to drive any man, or any combination of men, out of any thought of revenge and turn all to a merriment! A Falstaff at the United Nations would be worth all the billions we spend on arms.

The scenes in and around Justice Shallow's house in Gloucestershire, on or off the stage, have perhaps never been equalled since in any English comic writing. Shallow and Silence and the rustic recruits may be broad caricatures, rapidly sketched by the hand of a master; but no man who has spent any time in the remoter parts of rural England, and has kept his eyes and ears open, would agree they are caricatures of types that have long ceased to exist: they are all with us still, down to this day, and only Falstaff — alas — has vanished from the scene. And even among these hearty drolleries there are flashes of truth and deep feeling: for example, the confusion of past and present in the old men's chatter of Shallow and Silence; or in Feeble's sudden manfulness: "By my troth, I care not; a man can die but once; we owe God a death: I'll ne'er bear a base mind." For my part I could sit for hours after dinner in Shallow's garden, over the wine and apples and caraway seeds, listening to Master Silence being so unexpectedly merry "in the sweet o' the night." Somehow we are made to feel that behind the hiccoughing and belching, the jokes and drunken snatches of song, there is the enduring poetry of the English rural scene. This poetry is exquisitely suggested in the pastoral interlude towards the end of Elgar's *Symphonic Study: Falstaff,* a work too little known, perhaps his masterpiece, certainly superior to his familiar *Enigma Variations.* Across the centuries a lantern lit by Shakespeare's mind illuminates and inspires the Edwardian composer's score.

We have been asked, fairly enough, to notice how Shakespeare, in these last scenes, compels Falstaff to put himself in the wrong with us. We know very well of course that Falstaff will get what he can out of this silly old Shallow — that is his way and we have come to expect it — but his winks and nudges, being forced, are too gross. In the same fashion his expectation of power and influence, now that Hal is king, is deliberately pitched too high and given an ugly sound: "Let us take any man's horses; the laws of England are at my commandment." There is *hubris* here, asking to be toppled down; but it is not quite Falstaff as we have come to know him; we feel he is being pushed and hurried by the dramatist, now busy preparing us for the rejection scene. But before these sinister preparations have reached their height, we have had the most elaborate of Falstaff's soliloquies, ostensibly celebrating the virtues of sherris-sack. It follows, we must remember, an encounter with the cold and correct Prince John of Lancaster, who has just put down the rebellion by an appalling act of treachery. As he goes, Lancaster says:

> Fare you well, Falstaff: I in my condition,'
> Shall better speak of you than you deserve.

To which Falstaff, alone now, retorts:

> I would you had but the wit: 'twere better than your dukedom. — Good faith, this same young sober-blooded boy doth not love me; nor a man cannot make him laugh: but that's no marvel; he drinks no wine . . .

We are then told by Falstaff how a good sherris-sack

> . . . ascends me into the brain; dries me there all the foolish and dull and crudy vapours which environ it; makes it apprehensive, quick, forgetive, full of nimble, fiery, and delectable shapes; which, deliver'd o'er to the voice, the tongue, which is the birth, becomes excellent wit . . .

This may be wine at work but it will do very well too for the imagination, which our Prince Johns, bent on power and a career, then and now, prefer to avoid: they find it no help in the rat race.

It is this same Prince John who has the last word, after the King has cried, "I know thee not, old man: fall to thy prayers" and all the rest of it, banishing Falstaff, on pain of death, "not to come near our person by ten mile." Prince John re-enters, with the Chief Justice and his officers, who carry Falstaff and his followers to the Fleet Prison; and it is he who cries, "I like this fair proceeding of the King's," and later adds, to round off the play:

> I will lay odds that, ere this year expire,
> We bear our civil swords and native fire
> As far as France . . .

To which we can add that this native fire, after consuming a hundred castles, villages, towns, crowded with folk who only asked to be left alone, put a torch to the faggots under Joan of Arc. So Henry, turned away from his former self, is now in the saddle, with brother John at his elbow; and Falstaff we never see again. The play of *Henry V* could not have contained him; so he has to die offstage. Shakespeare can no longer trust himself to do two contrary things at the same time, to give equal play to the divisions in his own nature; the furious creative energy that went into Falstaff — and is nowhere to be found in the drama of *Henry V* — must now wait for the great tragic figures, who arrive when the lid comes off and history and politics are forgotten. The poet gives a shrug, as the dramatist insists upon taking charge; and Falstaff has to die. A character having the same name and appearance and a trick of speech copied from the original Falstaff finds his way into *The Merry Wives of Windsor,* a farce so uninventive that it yawns in our faces, though I shall take care it never yawns in mine again; indeed, we do Shakespeare's memory a service if we refuse to produce this botched hack job. We see the last of the real Falstaff, being carted off to prison, at the end of *Henry IV, Part II*. Perhaps the offstage character who repents and dies in *Henry V* is no more our Falstaff than that fat buffoon at Windsor, for the one we treasure is both unrepentant and immortal.

The rebellious poet in Shakespeare created a better man than *Henry V,* but the other Shakespeare, the Globe Theatre playwright and "sharer," the careful man, felt compelled to sacrifice him to Henry. The patriot hero-king must have his play to himself. The English nation, so desperately warring against itself in so many of these historical plays, must now be seen united behind a strong popular king, almost as if the Tudors had arrived. But this unity of Crown and People, this appearance of the English nation, and this common understanding between Establishment and mob, all represented by Henry's change of heart and mind, his rehabilitation, his welcome into the ranks of sound decent people in authority, can only be achieved if Falstaff is denounced, banished, jailed. When, earlier, Falstaff and the Chief Justice met in the street and fought a duel of words, Falstaff won handsomely. He did it in his own harmless fashion, not having the Chief Justice carted off anywhere but simply making him forget his anger, luring him into wit and humour, turning "all to a merriment." But now King Henry, reassuring the Chief Justice, has said to him:

> *There is my hand.*
> *You shall be as a father to my youth:*
> *My voice shall sound as you do prompt mine ear;*
> *And I will stoop and humble my intents*
> *To your well-practised wise directions.*

And one of the first of these well-practised wise directions is to have Falstaff taken to the Fleet Prison. The Chief Justice, not as Falstaff left him at the end of their duel, tolerant, indulgent, humorous, but in all the intolerant bad temper of the law lord, can claim complete victory. Falstaff is out. The nation unites, Crown and People find themselves in harmony, the Establishment waves and smiles as the mob cheers; and Falstaff, together with all he stands for, is very firmly — we might say even ruthlessly — rejected. England goes her way without Falstaff.

Now of course there is a great deal in this disreputable character that will not do at all, and that we English, then and now, are better without. Idleness, gluttony, drunkenness, lechery, lying and cheating, cannot be approved. Shakespeare deals very honestly with us here. He never forgets that these historical dramas are taking place in a real and not an ideal world. Oberon and Puck have already had their turn; Prospero and Ariel have not yet arrived: here among these chronicles of kings, though dramatic liberties may be taken with men and events, our feet are kept to the ground, no magical tricks and transformations are allowed, causes inevitably bring effects. If Shakespeare shows us plainly what the desire for power can do to a Bolingbroke or an Earl of Northumberland, he also makes it clear that irresponsibility and the lusts of the flesh can turn Sir John Falstaff into a lying old toper, ready to swindle any senile acquaintance foolish enough to trust him. This is not a pleasing picture. As King Henry says in his notorious rejection speech:

> How ill white hairs become a fool and jester!
> I have long dream'd of such a kind of man,
> So surfeit-swell'd, so old, and so profane . . .

No doubt this is what is being banished. Both King Henry and his brother, John of Lancaster, tell us that Falstaff must reform himself before the Court will consent to set eyes on him again. "All are banished," says Lancaster, "till their conversations" — and by this he means not just talk but general manners and behaviour — "till their conversations appear more wise and modest to the world." But a Falstaff who appeared wise and modest to this cold-blooded young prince would not be recognisable as Falstaff; in fact, he would not be Falstaff at all. He could then no more "turn all to a merriment" than Lancaster himself could. We would not waste five minutes listening to such a character. On the other hand, the unreformed Falstaff, the one who has to be banished, has been applauded by three centuries of critics, many of them sterner moralists than I can even pretend to be. So if official England, represented here by Henry V, totally rejects Falstaff — for this is what is happening, because a reformed Falstaff, acceptable to Lancaster and the Chief Justice, would not be a Falstaff at all — then this England deprives itself of the whole Falstaffian quality. It may want to have its cake and eat it, but in fact it rejects what is good in Falstaff as well as what is bad. And as we have already seen, there is much in Falstaff that is wonderfully good. But let us take a closer look at what is being dumped overboard from the ship of state.

To begin with, though capable of uttering the most gigantic lies, most of

L

them never intended to be believed, Falstaff is remarkably free from the vice of lying to himself. He may deceive others, although he does that only rarely, but he never deceives himself. Instead of deliberately befogging his mind, as so many of the English do, especially when they are in authority, Falstaff keeps his mind clear, open, marvellously perceptive. His judgements, as I pointed out earlier, are absolutely realistic. When he talks nonsense, he knows he is talking nonsense, and is indeed turning "all to a merriment." What he does not do is precisely what the official English have been accused of doing for hundreds of years — that is, talk a lot of cant, solemn and dangerous nonsense, born of hypocrisy or elaborate self-deception. England has produced mountains of it, which Falstaff would have seen through at a glance. If an example is needed, there is one in the passage already quoted from King Henry's speech reassuring the Chief Justice. Here it is again:

> There is my hand.
> You shall be as a father to my youth:
> My voice shall sound as you do prompt mine ear;
> And I will stoop and humble my intents
> To your well-practised wise directions.

I think that is cant. To quote Shakespeare for once against himself, it represents "that glib and oily art/To speak and purpose not." When King Henry promises "to stoop and humble" his intents to the directions of the Chief Justice, then if he believes what he is saying he is deceiving himself, and if he knows he will never keep this promise, then he is being hypocritical. Either way he is talking cant. One glance from Falstaff would have shrivelled this solemn humbug to a wisp of smoke and a nasty smell. That is one good reason why King Henry had to banish Falstaff, and why Shakespeare, who may or may not have known that a lot more cant was on its way, had to kill him off.

Ever since then, we English have had no more Falstaff but an ever-increasing load of cant. Over a hundred years ago, Peacock's Mr. Crotchet grew warm on this subject: "Where the Greeks had modesty," he says, "we have cant; where they had poetry, we have cant; where they had patriotism, we have cant; where they had anything that exalts, delights, or adorns humanity, we have nothing but cant, cant, cant." If there has been much improvement since Mr. Crotchet's time, it has not been noticeable. We now have cant from the pulpit, blessing hydrogen bombs. The reputation of the English Establishment and its admirers for smug self-deception, hypocrisy and perfidy, has long had some notoriety in the outside world. We are famous for our pious treacheries. King Henry, John of Lancaster and the Chief Justice lead an immense procession of personages, heavily titled

and glittering with orders, all saviours of the nation, all masters of cant.
Now, after print has reeked of it for three centuries, the air is filled with it.
But it is only fair to add that the banished Falstaff has had his followers
too, keeping alive and bright the perceptive eye, the unfogged open mind,
the realistic judgement, the humorist's temperament. In their different
ways, Swift and Dr. Johnson, Fielding and Sterne, Hazlitt and Carlyle,
Dickens and Peacock and Meredith, Wilde and Shaw and Wells, to name
no more, all spoke out against cant, risking — and sometimes suffering —
banishment of one sort or another. After all, Falstaff and the poet who
created him were Englishmen too. The antidote grows in our island as well
as the poison. But now I hope it will not be thought utterly unreasonable to
discover something symbolic in that final scene of *Henry IV, Part II,* with
its rejection of Falstaff. It is as if there floated into Shakespeare's mind,
which must have broadened like some vast spreading flood when he was at
work, a vague precognition of what was to happen to England and the
English down the centuries. It is as if he were given access for a moment to
"the prophetic soul of the wide world dreaming on things to come."

If we turn now to the more positive side of Falstaff's personality, then
the symbolism of his rejection, in the light of what has happened since in
English social history, is still more striking. Here let me repeat what I said
earlier: the secret of Falstaff is that he is masterfulness, quickness, energy,
genius, everything that makes a great commander of men, all in the service
not of power and glory but of delight. He is a very unusual great man
because instead of ambition and power he chooses ease, pleasure, good-
fellowship. A large and influential section of English opinion, from Shakespeare's day to ours, has felt that this attitude of mind should be discouraged. No empires can be founded on it, no fortunes made out of it, no
power hunger satisfied by it. That a formidable character like Falstaff, with
a kind of genius, at once perceptive, commanding and ingratiating, should
leave the highroad for the byroads, the court and camp for the tavern,
profit and power for merriment, seems a shocking piece of treachery.
Banish the fellow, jail him, hurry him out of sight and hearing, so that the
solid business of the country can go on, Parliament be summoned, money
be raised, and France invaded again! Remember — *My lord, he will drive
you out of your revenge and turn all to a merriment, if you take not the
heat.* This corrupting spirit must be resisted: there are fortunes to be made,
great positions to be won, French villages to be burnt and peasants to be
hanged. Falstaff, who would keep us loitering and laughing in taverns,
must go.

Already, while Shakespeare was writing "I know thee not, old man: fall
to thy prayers," a dark suspicion of all enjoyment was common in England,
spreading and gathering force. Falstaff, we might say, was being rejected

and carted off to jail every day. For example, we like to think of this as the Glorious Age of Elizabethan Drama, and even our politicians, after an exceptionally good dinner, have mentioned it favourably. But already the suspicion of all enjoyment was at work on it. The City Fathers, the London Council, disliked actors and playgoing so much that the theatres were built just beyond the city bounds and their control. Attending the play was denounced as an "unthrifty waste" of money. When Shakespeare was a boy in Stratford-on-Avon it had been visited by various companies of actors; but about the time he was making his hero-king banish Falstaff, the Stratford Council was banishing the Drama itself. Here it was only following, as it said, "the examples of other well-governed cities and boroughs." Jumping forward to our own time, the years since the last war, I must add that during these years no fewer than 175 theatres have been closed in Britain, not through any fierce puritanical opposition but because of public indifference and neglect, people preferring now to sit at home with their television, staring at advertisements of detergents and toothpaste. Incidentally, which is worse — to condemn actors because you believed, as the old Puritans did, that they were "fiends sent from their great captain Satan," or to neglect them in the Theatre because you would rather see them in advertisements pretending to be ecstatic about lubricating oil and mouthwash? Give me the old Puritans, for something can come out of people who can talk about the "great captain Satan," and something did — Cromwell and Milton, for example; whereas out of the imbecilic prey of advertising agencies nothing can come but more advertising agencies and more imbecility.

We know that from the early years of the seventeenth century onwards England acquired a reputation, the reverse of her former character as Merrie England, for being peculiarly joyless, taking her pleasures sadly. Foreign visitors increasingly left our shores shrugging their expressive shoulders, delighted, in spite of the terrors of the Channel passage, to turn their backs on the dreary island. Now this is generally attributed to the influence of the Puritans. But puritanism is to blame only if we take it in its very broadest sense, in which it has little to do with what was thought and felt by the genuine old Puritans, with their vision of an angry God and an ever-busy and infinitely artful Satan. Here, with Falstaff still in mind, we must discriminate. After all, Henry V, John of Lancaster, the Chief Justice, were not Puritans. Shakespeare, who created Falstaff only in the end to humiliate him, was like all the dramatists and actors an enemy of the Puritans. Yet Falstaff has to be knocked down and carted off. Why? Because he represents something anarchic, ungovernable, outside the pattern of power, property-owning, social standing, mockingly critical of all solemn official cant, just as the playhouses themselves did to the mayor and aldermen of the City of London. What happened to him symbolises, almost as if Shakespeare had caught a glimpse of his country's future, a strange division in the English national character and life, in which Falstaffs are being for ever created only to be rejected. The negative side, the rejectors, the haters of ease and merriment, wit and humour, are not God-haunted salvation-seeking Puritans, comparatively only a few. They are all those, from the top men of the Establishment down to the crowds outside their gates, who want anything from supreme power to the greyest respectability that is darkly suspicious of candour, an open mind, and merriment. Falstaff must go. We cannot afford him. This spirit, suspicious and sullen, can be discovered at work among the merchants and empire-builders, behind the black horrors of the Industrial Revolution from which every foreign visitor shrank appalled, in the elaborate hypocrisies of the Victorian Age detested and denounced by every great Victorian writer. It is still with us, this Falstaff-rejecting spirit. For example, to this day, as all our friends from abroad realise with astonishment, at an hour when in other capital cities the glasses are being filled again, on behalf of merriment and goodfellow-ship, in London the glasses are removed and tavern lights begin to be extinguished. Our legislators, who have their own glasses filled at all hours, are afraid that Falstaff might walk in again and take command.

Given time and space I would undertake to show how this negative spirit, this suspicion of enjoyment, this fear of Falstaff, has come between England and her men of genius, often darkening their lives. It has happened time after time, one age after another. But there is a place here for only one example, that of Oscar Wilde. Now Wilde talked and wrote a lot of solemn and often tasteless nonsense about art, to which, in fact, he was too idle and self-indulgent to devote himself properly, as an artist should. What was real, what was good, about this overdressed, curled and scented giant was his genuine Falstaffian quality, the ease and merriment, wit and humour, that made him irresistible in all companies. All we know about him proves him to have been generous and compassionate; he cor-rupted nobody but was the easy prey of youths other men had corrupted; the pederasty, for which he was jailed and broken, was so common in London that he might as well have been arrested for using eau de cologne. The cold ferocity of the Law, the orgy of cant in the Press, the jeering and yelping of the crowd, revealed the English, high and low, at their worst. Wilde was really a victim of this negative drive, this suspicion or envious hatred of gaiety, colour, brilliance, whatever refused to serve the power motive or broke the drab pattern of respectability and conformity. Falstaff was rejected and banished again. The prophecy latent in that final scene of *Henry IV, Part II*, was being fulfilled, as it has been over and over again, in ways too numerous and various to be listed here. But in all this we are keeping to the shadow side of the national character and life; after all, Shakespeare is English and so is Falstaff too. All that immortal ease and merriment, the wit and humour, are as English as the apples in Shallow's orchard. The shadow in us, which I think was there in Shakespeare, may condemn and reject these qualities and gifts, but the sunlight in us, when it has not been kept out by power drives or a timid conformity, welcomes and cherishes them. So these days, more and more English people save their money, consult the innumerable travel agencies that have sprung up in all our towns, and then go abroad for a summer holiday, anywhere from Norway to southern Italy. Why do they do it? Partly, I think, because being English they secretly hope for a magic hour somewhere abroad to turn all to a merriment, so fine, so gay, so careless, that there will be in it a kind of poetry, all those nimble, fiery and delectable shapes. Perhaps some of these people, knowing him to be immortal, are looking for Falstaff.

XIII. From THE NEW STATESMAN 1966–1967

DANDY DAYS

A bit of me, the other morning, travelled some million times faster than the speed of light. I am assuming now that what some people tell us is true — that we may be moving along the fourth dimension (in what I like to call Time One) at the speed of light. And that morning I returned in a flash to 1910, covering fifty-six light-years in a second. How many miles I don't know and don't care. But the end of the journey found me not perhaps bronzed and really fit but no worse than usual — and smiling, ready if necessary to be interviewed and photographed greeting my wife.

What happened was this. I was sitting in a taxi and as it slowed up for a light I saw through the window of the taxi and the window of a haber-dasher's a pink shirt with a black tie draped over it. And as soon as I noticed them I was back in 1910, when I was sixteen and pink shirts worn with black knitted ties were the latest and most wonderful thing, and I felt that my life was a blank without them. I longed for them as I long for nothing now, not even the peace of the world, the prosperity of Britain.

It was a longing at once pure and passionate. The pink shirt (liberally displayed by the type of waistcoat then fashionable, at least among pro-vincial young bounders) and the knitted black tie represented not a means but an end. I would have been happy just wearing them. I wasn't thinking in terms of admiring glances, of envy, of social prestige — no damned *status* nonsense. Pink-shirted, black-tied, I felt I would have been com-pletely and gloriously myself, whereas without them I was nothing but a drab caricature of the real Jack Priestley. I may add here that I never did acquire one of these shirts; my father, who would have had to provide the money, was no admirer of them; and a year or two later, when I could afford to buy some clothes for myself, pink shirts and black ties were out.

They were, of course, summer wear. But I had a terrible winter longing too. It was for one of the huge overcoats that were fashionable at this time among dashing young men and the actors I used to see, as I queued for the gallery at the Theatre Royal, moving majestically towards the stage door. These overcoats had gigantic lapels and reached down to the ankles. They were altogether different from the decent, sensible overcoat I had to wear.

They belonged to another world, not decent, not sensible, a world not of high teas but of late suppers at the Midland Hotel, perhaps with entrancing beings like Phyllis Dare. But it was not of Miss Dare I was thinking when I longed and longed for one of those overcoats. All I wanted was simply to wear one, not to do anything special in it or with it, just to move around, rather slowly, with it on. I seem to remember that at times I walked with bent knees, trying to make my decent, sensible overcoat look longer and grander, but of course it was hopeless as well as tiring.

When, a little later, I was able to choose my own clothes — and not yet out of my dandy period, which ended just before the First War — I behaved with courage if not, as I realise now, with good taste. There were those powder-blue socks with a single — or was it a double? — gilt stripe. And I recollect very distinctly the sports coat I had made, of light green tweed, longish, rather waisted and then full below. With it I used to wear light-grey trousers that were definitely and defiantly peg-top, and I was not afraid to complete the outfit, really belonging to Murger's *Vie de Bohème,* with a floppy bow tie. It took guts to dress like that as a junior wool clerk in Bradford round about 1912.

I didn't do it for the girls, even though they were never long out of my thoughts. (I doubt if they were for the next forty-odd years, and if they are now, it isn't because I'm old but because so many of them look so scrawny and unappetising.) Of course if any of the girls thought I *looked interesting,* I was delighted, but I was not really putting out my bright plumage then to attract the other sex. My main motive, going beyond pure dandyism, belonged to self-assertion and defiance. I was already a writer of sorts, earning a guinea here, a guinea there, and though there was no sensible reason why I should look like somebody from the Rue Jacob in the 1840's, at least nobody could say I looked a typical young clerk in the wool trade. I was, in a muddled sort of way, trying to wear a uniform.

Well, it wasn't long after this that I found myself wearing uniforms of various kinds throughout four and a half years, and I never remember particularly enjoying it. But then khaki was never one of my favourite colours. If, however, I had returned home from the war to discover that writers were entitled to wear specially designed suits — velvet perhaps and of a deep plum shade or an unfathomable indigo — I think I might have happily saved up to buy one. I happen to have been given honorary doctorates in three different countries, which were all alike in insisting upon our dressing up, and this was always the chief fun of the thing — covering yourself with crimson and gilded robes and putting on, at a rakish angle, a huge velvet cap out of the sixteenth century. One of the many reasons why I like Arnold Wesker is that he always seems to be wearing a suit that he has just invented for himself.

The best I can do here is to appear at solemn, white-tie, decorations-will-be-worn functions attired, rather beautifully I like to think, in a maroon velvet jacket, which the ladies — bless them — at least pretend to admire, and the men — saying nothing — secretly envy, stung by its suggestion of Naboth's vineyard. Now we seem to live in a universe where all tracks are circular, and of course what is happening is that I am returning gradually and stealthily to something like myself of fifty-odd years ago. As I shall move backward in time I shall go through this semi-dandy phase of self-assertion and defiance to the purer dandyism of a year or two earlier, roughly you may say from 1912 to 1910, when my whole being cried out for the pink shirts and the gigantic overcoats. I don't know yet what I shall be crying out for in vain, but it is just possible, the way things are going, I may be found weeping silently in an old men's home over pictures of Carnaby Street and the livelier inspirations of Hardy Amies.

What you won't find me doing, I promise you, is getting red in the face and furious because some of the boys enjoy dressing up. Who are we, far more responsible than they are for the idiotic world they are living in, to sneer and jeer because they want to be dandies for a few years? A lad who lives in a dingy back street and does a boring stupid job all day is surely entitled to change into some colour and do a little swaggering. He is in a sense defiantly wearing his uniform, that of his individual male youth, turning himself from a work unit, herded to and from a factory, into a unique Jimmy Brown or Ted Smith.

It is the young men at the opposite extreme from these gaudy lads that I regard with some prejudice and suspicion. I am thinking now of those young men who don't work in factories but in superior offices. They wear tight-fitting suits, thin darkish ties, narrow-brimmed bowlers tilted forward, and always carry rolled umbrellas. I don't understand why, for I have no evidence of any sort, but I always feel there is something vaguely but disturbingly fascist about these young men as if they were already wearing the uniform of some mysterious half-crazy Right Wing, the equivalent here of the John Birch movement in America. And if this is reading too much into what is merely a genteel conformity, then I apologise. But even while apologising, I will admit I don't like the look of these chaps.

No doubt they don't like the look of me. Why a bright yellow or dusty-pink tie? Why that squashed-in broad-brimmed hat? Why that peculiar over-coat almost as loose as a cloak? And if such questions should be asked, I have my reply here. I am inevitably being carried back, if not on a circular then on a spiral track, towards my 1910 self, that yearning immature dandy. I feel as frustrated now as I did then, but for quite different reasons. Then I saw those dazzling things but couldn't afford to buy them. Now when I see them, I know I can't afford to wear them. I am, let's face it, the wrong shape. Let us by all means bring in a note of the carnival, a touch of the harlequinade — it is one of the weaknesses of Communism, though it has virtues we too often refuse to acknowledge, that it does seem to create a general scene that is altogether too damnably drab — but nobody wants a fat Harlequin. A man of my size can risk a tie like a daffodil or a rose, but a shirt with an 18½ collar bright yellow or pink would be overpowering, unendurable. A two-hundred-pound rainbow would not win friends.

As for the hats, they have to be broad-brimmed because the now customary narrow-brimmed hat makes me look like a Lancashire comedian, engaged for the season at the Central Pier, Blackpool. They always look like the same hat, worn for ever. But in fact they have to be constantly renewed by Scotts. I lost one in Australia a few years ago, and another, fairly recently, in Soviet Armenia. But as soon as I have a new hat — and there is genius here — I can make it look like an old one. This is where that lad of 1910, who longed in vain for a pink shirt, has arrived. He can at least wear a succession of new hats that everybody takes to be the same old one. It is hardly dandyism; it is not what he was aiming at; but — dash it all — it is *something*.

FACT OR FICTION?

Somebody must like the stuff that editors seem to buy more and more of for their magazines and supplements. I am thinking of those Now-We-Show-You-People features:

Mrs. Thing is 34, has been married ten years, and has three children. Her husband is a trombone-slide technician working in North-West London. The Things have been able to buy through a building society a six-room semidetached bungalow in a new housing estate, Betjeman Vistas. They own a car (a Mini-Mini), a 19-inch TV set, a washing machine, an electric mixer, and one of the new low trolleys for TV snacks. Mrs. Thing doesn't smoke but enjoys an occasional gin-and-orange. Mr. Thing smokes, preferring the odd cheroot now to cigarettes, but never drinks anything stronger than gingerale. On fine Saturday mornings they go out shopping, taking the children with them, for it is only half a mile to the nearest supermarket. If it is wet, then Mrs. Thing takes the car and their eldest child, a boy, leaving her husband to amuse the two younger children. They rarely go out in the evening . . .

And so on and so forth and so forth and so on. And usually of course with photographs. There are not many reasons now why our society should exist in its present form, but one of them seems to be that at least it keeps its photographers busy and — we hope — happy.

For my part — and according to some reviewers my part seems to be that of a decaying Edwardian gentleman, which is in fact about the last damned character I could play — I say, for my part, I find all this Mrs. Thing stuff, people-in-the-goldfish-bowl, increasingly boring or irritating — boring if I am feeling sleepy, irritating if I am feeling alert and wanting to know about people. I don't want persons — trimmed, flour-dusted, cooked in a moderately hot oven — served up to me in this fashion. I am no shy and oversensitive introvert myself, but I suspect and indeed dislike this super-extraverted approach to people. I am not in the Consumer Research business — thank God! I want to keep well out of the sociologists' status-symbol world. Neat and bright accounts of habits and possessions don't reveal actual persons, my brothers and sisters. Their real life, what happens in the mind, what warms or freezes the heart, is entirely left out. We may be shown two men who walk round to the pub every Saturday morning, but one may have just fallen in love and the other may be planning a murder.

It seems to me savagely ironical that at the very time when so many of our editors commission these factual features, our novels receive so little attention. Never in the last two hundred years has our fiction been so neglected as it is today. Certainly, novels and tales are published by the hundred. The free libraries, though not the bookshops, are crammed with them. But they are chiefly regarded as a kind of reading fodder. They have almost completely lost any importance they ever had in the public mind. Even literary editors rarely take them seriously, merely handing them over in batches to any reviewer willing to run through six of them in under a thousand words. Younger novelists will hardly believe this, but I can remember when early long novels of mine had full big pages devoted to them. And in those days the arrival of any new book by an established novelist was accepted by conscientious editors as an event. Moreover, educated people talked and talked — and indeed when I was a youngster we argued for hours, far into the night — about these new novels.

Their place has been taken in the literary pages (such as they are), in the bookshops, the library lists, the literate sector of the public mind, by ghost-written memoirs, biographies, tarted-up history and sodden slabs of sociology. These are supposed to represent serious reading. Fiction is for women of the more frivolous sort, idling away an afternoon with a novel and a box of chocolates. Listening to politicians and other public men being interviewed, over and over again we have heard something like this: "Reading? Well, yes, I try to read as much as I can — memoirs, biographies, history — that kind of thing. No novels — after all I *am* a busy man, y'know." He is also telling us that he is a *serious* man, one who wants to learn something from his reading and not waste his time among a lot of purely imaginary characters. None of this fancy light stuff for *him!* So he pays his money — and several guineas of it too — to read what Churchill said in 1903 and what Mr. Harold Macmillan thought in 1936. And I am not saying he shouldn't do this. Nevertheless, I am not impressed by his account of himself as a serious reader. And if he is a politician and boasts of never looking at a new novel — he is a solemn ass.

It is the very books he ignores, the despised novels, that can bring him closest to his fellow countrymen of these 1960's. It is the novelist who can make him live their lives, enter into their minds and hearts. Nobody else can do it half as well, not even — and I add this reluctantly — the dramatist. Films and TV and radio programmes can do something, but the novel has not to submit to many of their limitations. As for this documentary journalism (*Mrs. Thing is 34*), it is all on the outside, in the Consumer Research world, where there are no persons, no individual thinking and intimate feelings, not far from the idiot realm of the advertisers where whole families are in ecstasy over a breakfast food, a new toothpaste, a bar of chocolate. If I were an American editor — and there's a flight of fancy for you! — appointing a London correspondent, I would tell him not to bother about public opinion polls and all this documentary stuff but to read twenty or thirty recent novels, which would take him where the British really live.

I am making no attempt here at literary criticism. I am not thinking in terms of literature. It is no use the politician, let us say, retorting that, if we were producing great novelists, he would be reading them. (He might, and then again he might not.) Our time is not favourable to good novelists — though we have some — and, I suspect, simply could not begin to supply the nourishment a great novelist needs. Vast wars, revolutions, kaleidoscopic societies, are the enemies of fiction on its highest level. And an enemy of fiction on any reasonable level is the stealthy but persistent dehumanising process now at work in our society. It is significant that the most widely read recent tales have taken us into the world of espionage, where humanity is very thin indeed and gadgets seem more important than men.

If the churches could stop arguing about how far young Ted and little Kate should go, late on Saturday night, they might take a longer and sharper look at this dehumanising process, and then begin to defend the individuality and dignity of Man. (Watch the Post Office machine-men, who already want to abolish our addresses and may soon ask us to believe we would do better off without names. And the technological crackpots who think we could be happily mated through computers, which in fact know as much about the unique and enchanting relationships between men and women as sewing machines or vacuum cleaners.) And this dehumanising process, in a subtler form, can be discovered in this neglect of the novel, which brings us close to people and compels us to live with them, and in this too-objective documentary approach to people — *Mrs. Thing is 34,* and the rest.

Let me make this clear. I have no dislike of facts. I rather enjoy them, and have spent many a cheerful hour just pottering about among statistics laid out like new towns. Every conscientious writer, I feel, should occasionally explore the figures and facts. But no genuine creative writer will ever imagine that here will be found the truth about people. It is precisely what is left out of the account of Mr. and Mrs. Thing and their three children and their semi-detached bungalow that would tell us what these people are really like, would bring them to life as our brothers and sisters. It is this concentration on fact that is keeping them at a distance, which is where many influential contemporary types, short on empathy, want them to be, taking the essential humanity out of them and seeing them as consumers, voters, units of various kinds. I have suggested that all this is savagely ironical — and so it is. For the facts turn into fiction — and bad fiction at that. And it is good fiction, so largely ignored now, that brings us so much closer to the real facts. And the men who say they want to know, because they are in authority over us, refuse to listen to the very persons who do know. Finally, the fashion for describing and reporting on more and more people but all from the outside, giving us Mrs. Thing and her habits and possessions but not telling us *what it feels like to be Mrs. Thing,* is itself part of the dehumanising process of our dangerous time.

A last word, addressed more to my reviewers than to readers. If these, yet again, are merely the nostalgic ruminations of a decayed Edwardian, then I apologise for them. To my mind, perhaps already muddled and dim, this seems quite a topical subject.

DISTURBING?

What has been puzzling me for some time now is this. Why does everyone worth reading, hearing, looking at, have to be *disturbing*? That is, according to all *in* reviewers and critics. (We don't have to bother about elderly men in the provinces.) But among the men and women who count, the pacesetters in taste, the highest term of praise is *disturbing*. Not only is our neo-Elizabethan age, really a kind of Renaissance, astonishingly rich in genius, but all this genius is here to disturb us. Briggs, Higgs, Niggs, in their day — two years ago — could disturb, but the new man, Figgs, who'll be in the colour supplements any week now, can disturb until we're ready to scream. And if we want to know what we look like when we scream, there's always Francis Bacon, a disturber if there ever was.

It must be a moot point — though I can't be sure because I've not been invited to attend the moot — whether the newest novel is more disturbing than the newest play, the film from Prague more disturbing than the sculpture from Brooklyn, New York. But what is certain is that as they are all significant works of contemporary art, then give them a chance and they will disturb the hell out of us. That is what the critics say, and they ought to know, many of them having devoted themselves to criticisms since 1961.

The day may arrive soon when there is little or no difference between advanced art and a disturbance. Already we have avant-garde types who don't play pianos but hack and bash them to pieces in what they believe to be a meaningful fashion. Soon there may be plays in which stinkbombs are hurled into the audience at the end of the first act and nobody sees the final scene of the second act because of the tear gas. There may be novels that will explode as page 193 is turned. We want to be disturbed, do we? Well, the arts will be right in there with us.

But now I must ask a question that will show how far out of touch I am. Why do I have to be disturbed all the time? Why do the newer novelists and playwrights (sometimes on TV too) and their critics and admirers think it is necessary I should be disturbed? Why should *disturbing* be the term of highest praise now? Why am I supposed to regard this as the strongest recommendation? What do they think I ought to be disturbed *out of*? Where the devil do they imagine I've been all my life — lolling in a rose-garden? I could tell these boys a thing or two. However, let's forget me and consider the public in general. Why do *they* have to be disturbed all the time? For my part I can't believe it is necessary. All this disturbing business — and now comes the bitter stroke — seems to me old-fashioned. After all, we are living in 1967 not 1867.

There are of course a certain number of stupidly complacent people in this country who would be better after a jolt or two. They can be found in small residential hotels in or near watering places or in country houses full of cats and dogs. Some of them, no doubt, find their way from shops and offices on to town or county councils. They may be discovered presiding over stalls and tombolas at Conservative fêtes. They are usually well represented in local weekly papers and the like. Oh yes, such people exist and no doubt they ought to be disturbed.

They ought to be, but they won't be. Not for them the "disturbing" novels, plays, films, painting, sculpture, music. They keep well away from such things. They take care to guard their complacency. They go to some trouble to choose only nice novels and plays. And as they still have some money to spend on books and the theatre, this partly explains why the disturbing novels (unless they're obscene) don't sell and the disturbing plays have to be subsidised by the Arts Council.

When we move away from these people to the population at large, the very notion of a general complacency that needs a shock is laughable. Never have the English felt more disturbed. They wonder day and night where the money's to come from and where it goes to. Crime increases and the prisons are overcrowded. Mental homes are packed out and psychiatrists desperately overworked. People take barbiturates and pep pills as they took acid drops when I was young. They spend not hundreds but thousands of millions on gambling, amusements, cigarettes and booze, not out of confidence or any excess of joy but largely out of an attempt to cope with worry, anxiety, deep-seated feelings of unease.

What they don't spend their money on is all that work, so fashionable among the intelligentsia, which is praised because it's disturbing. No bloody fear, chum! They want, as they say, to be taken out of themselves, not further into themselves, where it's all churned up anyhow. They don't want to pass their evenings being told what life's like, they've had that all day, thank you. And yet, being the children of their ancestors, not some race newly created, when they watch their favourite television series or go to the pictures, they are really groping for what our age has deprived them of — mythology, the timeless world of gods and heroes, unchanging and shining immortals. Which is why a Perry Mason or a Dr. Kildare, going on year after year, never ages a day. There must be some beings, they feel, who are not being hurried by time into senseless oblivion.

Now we come to the inner circle of the educated, the sensitive, the cultured, the people to whom these reviews and notices of novels, plays, films, the visual arts, are being addressed. It is for their sake, to attract their attention, that *disturbing* is trotted out over and over again, with an occasional change to *deeply disquieting*. You might imagine that these critics have overheard their readers saying to one another: "We really must try to rid ourselves of this stupid complacency of ours, this easy acceptance of everything, this blank refusal to feel any anxiety. Darling, we've simply got to be *disturbed*."

The truth is of course that these are the very people who have been feeling disturbed for years. They have grown up under the Bomb. They have hope neither of heaven nor of earth. They are hagridden by anxieties that some of us, who are older, have never even dreamt of, such as loss of identity, alienation, the difficulty or impossibility of real communication. There is nothing to shout for, nobody to cheer. Just when the vodka martinis are taking hold, there falls the shadow of Vietnam, Africa and Oxfam's empire of hunger. Even falling in love means more worries about sex. And while the admen persuade you to spend more and more, the state tells you to spend less and less — except on itself.

Disturbing these people seems to me like watering the Thames. Just a little more, all deeply disquieting, and some of them will need a week's sedation. I shall be told of course that the really significant writers and artists of our time are *expressing* what such people feel. It is their duty to keep right on disturbing the disturbed, just as it is the duty of the intelligent and conscientious critic to single out and recommend whatever will best disturb the disturbed. And to show them what they may not have noticed, that what they thought was still dark grey is in fact now a deep black.

And, indeed, just as the detergent admen are trying to prove that white can be washed much whiter, the disturbers are now making black much blacker. There is among them and their admirers a kind of new snobbery of pessimism. Oh — you felt it was all rather hopeless, did you? Well, wait till you hear this new man! So we are told all over again, with perhaps a few original and more appalling examples, that man is an accident, that life is futile, that the universe is absurd. And if we have any sense, if we haven't been quite disturbed out of our wits, we'll refuse to swallow this miserable stuff, much of it egoism gone sour.

If the universe were absurd, we'd never realise it, having nothing to compare it with. Life can be grim and horrible but it cannot be entirely futile or we would never be able to recognise its futility. And while it may be fun — to annoy your uncle, the Dean — to declare that man is an accident, at least some part of you, standing aside to make the declaration, is far from being accidental. Life can be disturbing of course, but it can't be all disturbance, without any point of reference outside it; and I feel it's about time we kept this in mind — while we still have minds.

THE SKULL CINEMA

Unless it is raining hard I go for a walk every afternoon, usually round this village though sometimes into Stratford. The chief object is of course exercise, to keep my carcase briskly on the move for at least one bit of the day. Some people imagine — and I know because they have told me that on these walks I am thinking about the book I am writing or the one I hope to write next. I believed in this myself at one time, because it is easy to accept other people's more flattering fantasies, to wear an image — loose overcoat, broad-brimmed hat, pipe, stick — of the thoughtful elderly author. But I have known now for several years that during these walks my mind is compelled to visit a tenth-rate cinema.

I don't want to return to this appalling cinema every afternoon, and I would be much happier if my mind would do one of three things. The choice lies between real constructive thinking, staring ecstatically, or switching the mind off and going blank. I will settle happily for any of those three, but so far they are all beyond my reach.

It is rather odd that I can't manage any real thinking because up to now — and I realise that I may go off rapidly — I have been able to concentrate far better than most men can do. I have lectured many times without a single note. I have delivered public speeches with hardly any preparation. Interviews on television or radio don't worry me. And if I have written more than most authors, this is not because I have been exceptionally industrious — I am in fact rather lazy — but because I can concentrate quickly on my work. On the other hand, I have never thought constructively. My mind moves in a series of intuitive flashes. Whenever I have sat down to work out a complicated plot, let us say, nothing has happened and I have found myself wandering away from the notebook — I buy notebooks but never make proper use of them — to clean some pipes or search for a book. Then an idea jumps into my mind while I am shaving or in the bath.

So the first choice, some real constructive thinking while I walk, is out. I haven't a hope. However, I would gladly accept number two — staring ecstatically. This is the John Cowper Powys thing. You see a bit of old wall or a tangle of roots or even three broken bottles, and, without doping yourself to do it, you suddenly understand in a rush of happiness how beautiful, how deeply significant, they are. I don't say this has never happened to me but I certainly don't know how to lay it on for my walks. Perhaps Powys or a Zen Master could move from ecstatic trance to trance every afternoon, but the experience is so rare with me that it is no use my trudging round day after day, waiting for it. So I must do something else with my mind.

This brings us to the third choice — switching the mind off and going blank. If I could do this, I would have forty minutes of it every day and even walk further to enjoy more of it. How refreshed one would feel afterwards! What energy would be saved. Where then would be all those imbecilities and obscenities? Stride out, switch off! But I have tried and tried and I can't do it. (And none of the usual dodges for inducing sleep works for me, I may add.) I tell my mind to go blank, then I begin thinking about my mind going blank, and sentences form themselves, and then thoughts and images come streaming in — and I am back, a prisoner, in that tenth-rate cinema.

I remember an actual cinema of this sort in Tahiti, more than half a lifetime ago. There was a performance every ten days or so, and it was advertised by young men going round in a lorry, banging drums. The films — silent, of course — seemed to be made of bits of everything strung together. One minute you would be looking at an old newsreel, and the next minute at Pearl White or Francis X. Bushman, jerky but heroic in some perilous situation. Travel pictures of Ceylon or the Canadian Rockies would explode into glimpses of Fatty Arbuckle or the Keystone Cops. Custard pies would vanish to reveal one of the Gish sisters in rags, despair and tears.

When I am on my walks I seem to open and then lock myself into a cinema even worse than the one in the South Seas. The stream-of-consciousness programme, which I didn't devise, never asked for, is a dreadful muddle, not worth a moment's attention. I dislike it as much here as I do when I find it in fiction, where it is easy to write and damnably hard to read, being so tedious. Even when used by brilliant performers this stream-of-consciousness method soon becomes boring, and when lesser novelists attempt it they might as well offer us conversation pieces painted in tomato sauce, mutton broth and mud. Thank heaven it is now draining out of fiction!

I have realised for a good long time now that I need not accept any responsibility for this thought-stuff rattling through the old projector at the

back of my mind. This rotten cinema does not belong to me. I may have to
sit in it but I am not running it. In other words, I am not really thinking
these thoughts. They are, so to speak, thinking me, just because, as I
suggested earlier, I don't know how to stop them. And I don't want anybody to write and tell me how it is done in India, after much meditation in
the lotus position. I am too old, fat, determinedly occidental, for any
Indian remedies.

Even so, I do agree with the late Maurice Nicoll, who wrote much on
this subject, that these thoughts are not ours but are just visiting us, that we
must keep ourselves detached from them and not identify with them. For
as soon as we identify with them, they have nailed us.

It is a fact — and I wish I knew some way of establishing it — that
murderous thoughts don't visit me. Nothing suggesting them appears on the
screen when I am sitting helpless in that bad cinema. But, to take an
extreme and dreadful instance of identifying, I can imagine a murder-
thought that keeps returning until it has fixed its man and turned him into a
murderer. It is a pity we have abolished the Devil — this has probably
been his greatest triumph — otherwise we might have attributed to him
such terrible predatory thoughts.

It is possible, of course, for there to be flashed across this interior screen
not merely random thoughts and images but something like whole scenes.
In such scenes the sole patron of the Skull Cinema is himself or herself the
chief character. Because I have to create scenes for imaginary people in
order to earn a living, I rarely waste time and energy projecting incidents
from *J.B.P. Turns at Last* or *Priestley's Surprising Success*. But you have
only to watch people to discover that they are hard at it being producer,
director, leading actor or actress, distributor, exhibitor, audience, of *My
Wishing Self Films*.

Mrs. Fred Smith is at a bus stop. Her eyes are open but they are not
really looking at anything. Her lips are moving. She is waiting for a bus and
will not hang back when it arrives. Nevertheless, at the moment she is busy
with a scene from *Fred Smith Gets Told a Thing or Two*, which has been
running off and on for several years now in this particular little cinema.
Would Mrs. Smith be any better off if she stopped this form of entertainment, in spite of its cheapness and convenience? For my part I think she
would be much better off. She is probably preventing herself from coming
to a real understanding with her Fred. She is indulging her worst faults
instead of frankly acknowledging them. And this triumphant imaginary self
is inferior to her real self.

I suspect that the huge development of our urban industrial life has
favoured these self-indulgent sessions in the secret cinema. For example,
take a look at the people sitting at lunchtime in the windows of popular
restaurants or snack bars in London or New York. (Especially in the

business districts of New York.) If they are alone, and very many of them
are, then four out of five have a Mrs. Fred Smith look about them. Strictly
speaking they are not eating at all. They are not really attending to the food
they are consuming. It may be flavourless, but even if it had an exquisite
flavour, they wouldn't know. They are all in their own little cinemas,
concentrating on such programmes as *How a Clerk Corrected a Big Execu-
tive* or *A Middle-aged Married Man Can No Longer Resist a Young Secretary's Beauty and Charm*. This is one reason why cheap food in London
and New York can be so bad. Hardly anybody is tasting it.

You may have noticed what I have done in this piece. I have done what
we are always doing. Stealthily but surely, I have moved from an inferior
position — that of a man who doesn't know what to do with his mind when
out walking — to a superior position, that of a man contemptuous of the
idle and self-indulgent daydreaming of ordinary foolish people. And it isn't
good enough; honesty must come back. I am still the one who on his
afternoon walks cannot attempt any real constructive thinking, finds it
almost impossible to do any ecstatic staring, and has still not discovered
how to switch off his mind, to sit refreshingly in his Skull Cinema in front
of a dark and silent screen.

As it is, I am constantly reminded of a restaurant or night club to which
Raymond Chandler took me in La Jolla, where he lived. One wall of its
lower floor was an enormous illuminated window under the sea. My mind,
out walking, has something like that, but the images that float past, the
thoughts that flash and dart out there, are rarely beautiful, hardly ever
arrestingly strange — just, as people like to say now, a load of old rubbish.
And I don't even believe it's *my* old rubbish.

OFF-SHORE ISLAND MAN

Nobody has asked me yet if I want to go into the Common Market, just as
nobody asked me if I wanted to be defended by the Bomb. And I will
remark here in passing that there seem to me to be certain decisions so
important that they burst the seams of our parliamentary democratic
system. In these rare instances we ought to be asked. As it is, I may wake

up one morning to find I am already in the Market, and perhaps discover sooner or later that if arrested and charged I shall be presumed to be guilty unless I can prove my innocence — and God knows what else. Of course I can see the noble possibilities of a federated Europe, but creating this and bashing into the Market seem to me to be very different activities.

One reason why I feel dubious about the Market is that most of our practical, hardheaded, no-nonsense men are strongly in favour of it. For thirty-five years now I have been at odds with these men and have been called a literary sentimentalist or a crackpot, and it seems to me that I have always been right and they have always been wrong. (I could prove this, and may do so, one day.) The point about these men is that, while they are practical and hardheaded about bank loans, costs, profits, ledgers and petty cash, as soon as they consider very large questions and issues their minds go hazy and dreamy. But though ignorant and an innocent in many practical matters, I am in the dream business, know all about self-deception (our national vice), and in this region I am a realist.

So I feel that many of these no-nonsense Market enthusiasts write and talk about going into Europe quite unrealistically, out of a golden haze. They tell us in effect that once we are in then all will be different *but* — not to worry — somehow just the same. Or, if you like, what we want to be different *will* be different and what we want to remain unchanged will stay the same. But this is not coming to an agreement with tough types across the water, representatives of French peasants, German steel men, Belgian financiers — it is strolling through fairyland, picking unfading flowers. The practical men, the hardheaded fellows, are at it again.

Smacking their lips over the magic cake you can eat and still have, they tell us that once in the Market, up against some ruthless competition, management and labour here will rise "to face the challenge." Now I know that we can face challenges if necessary, as we did so magnificently in the war. But that was another sort of challenge, very different from business. The truth is — and we might as well face it — we English find it hard to develop an overwhelming passion for business. (We are a nation of hobby-horse riders, and out of our pursuits and pastimes, from birds and flowers to football and tennis, has come an astounding contribution to world civilisation.) I don't believe myself that any cutthroat competition in the Market will turn us into people who can hardly think about anything but production curves, sales graphs, rising profits, people who talk on and on and on about business. Certainly we have to earn a living. But not an existence — *a living*. Being *alive*.

Now, if we go into the Common Market and can't face this challenge, I feel we shall be worse off than we are at present. London, Birmingham, Manchester will be swarming with cleverer business men than we are. But what if we go in, boldly face the challenge and triumph? As I see it, we shall still be worse off than we are now. There may be more money about, but a lot of it will benefit the wrong people while many of the people I like will be staring in horror at the household bills. At the same time we shall be turning ourselves into a business-first community. Already too much Admass rubbish about Executives (business men seen through a haze) is creeping into our advertising, and we are being shown the planes, cars, trains, hotel suites fit for Executives.

All right then, we encourage Executives (with wives who have passed the necessary tests) to beat their brains out, risk ulcers and coronaries, and pile up the money, but under a Labour government we take most of the money away from them (we hope) and distribute it, with the help of 500,000 civil service clerks, among the needy. That might be worse — and it would be under the Tories — but to my mind it doesn't offer an attractive picture of a society. I see us all existing in the shadow of weary-Titan Executives, now our great men, and of public filing cabinets two hundred feet high and a quarter of a mile long. Will this release and ennoble the spirit of man? It will not.

But what — and you can hear the voices of the Marketeers rising higher and higher — is to happen to us if we don't go in? Do I want to find myself living merely on an offshore island? And the trouble is — I do. I am an offshore island man. If there were a great West European combine to secure better terms for writers (and we could do with some), I wouldn't join it. If I did I might soon find myself wearing a skullcap, reading my new works aloud and plotting day and night to obtain a prize for Jimmy Wood, Jean Dubois or Heinrich Wald. And this isn't my style, isn't our style, it is the Continental not the island style.

Am I being frivolous when I ought to be considering money and business, size of markets, imports and exports and tariffs? I don't think so. It is the enthusiastic Marketeers who are being unrealistic. For example, it is absurd to believe you can happily join the Common Market by turning it into something else. Some of these Marketeers are like a woman doctor trying to become a member of a club of male barristers. Either you want to go along with these Europeans, who understand one another much better than they do us, who are in closer touch, who share certain traditions strange to us — or you don't. If deep down you don't, then stop the fuss. If you do, if you realise that the Common Market isn't going to transform its character just to please us, that sooner or later the whole style of our national life will have to be changed, then be ready to face the consequences. I'm not.

Much of this desire to get into Europe seems to me to have its origin in a bad idea. A nation must have trade but it is not primarily a trading concern. Britain is not a super-ICI but the home of the British people. Because of the balance of payments, the trade gap, the tremendous influence of the economists, the effect on the people in general of Admass (how can you live without colour television?), we are beginning to believe that the gross national income is more important than anything else. But a country might have a gigantic and rapidly increasing gross national income and yet be crammed with dissatisfied and miserable people, hating the sour flavour of their lives. I believe Mr. Wilson and his colleagues would agree with this, but circumstances are compelling them either to rush us into the Market or to drag an enormous *son-et-lumière* herring across the trail. They have to do something in order to lighten the atmosphere.

A few years ago, in a piece here called "Ambience or Agenda," I argued that a change of atmosphere, a different climate of values, ideas, opinions, was even more important than the most elaborate party programme. The ambience would produce the agenda, not the agenda the ambience. But it seems to me that Labour, though meaning well, has so far been all agenda and no ambience. Instead of being made to feel we must make sacrifices out of love of our country, we have been encouraged to suspect that we are being punished for something. Again, while we can live more frugally, we would do it with a better heart under an obviously frugal government. Finally, we don't feel we are living in an audaciously creative country but in a rather stiff and disagreeable one.

And while all manner of outworn or bogus traditions are allowed to waste time, money and temper, real and valuable traditions — the cheap food policy, for example — may soon be in danger of being scrapped. We might find ourselves in a still more disagreeable country, irritated by all sorts of alien demands, perhaps tied to ruthless big-business types whose methods and values we despise, and forbidden to make any generous social experiments of our own. Somehow the Common Market doesn't smell like the possibility of any noble federation. And the Tory rush to get into the Community arouses my suspicion. These have never been the men I have wanted to follow.

But how can we go our own way, so many eccentric islanders, who don't want to work too hard or think and talk about business day and night? The answer is — and I write in all earnestness — not to have our corners rubbed off by chaps from Clermont-Ferrand, Essen or Liège but to turn ourselves into even more eccentric islanders. There are two sides to our national character: one represented, we might say, by Francis Chichester, the other by the town clerk of Bumbledom. The latter and his sort and their whole attitude of mind weigh us down like a lead poultice. The adventurous, the original, the inventive, the imaginative, can hardly breathe. We have a well-meaning, careful government that may take us cautiously into the Market, behind high tariff walls. But we might be happier out in the wind, risking the loss of colour television, holidays in Spain, more and more cars, prepared to make audacious experiments, so many odd but exciting islanders. We might then have youth on our side.

GROWING OLD

It is not life but essay competitions that have made me think about old age. I acted as judge for one such competition, and I have been running a miniature competition in this village, the subject being What Old People Need. Nearly all the little pieces have been written by women. All of them mentioned the usual things — a room of their own, warmth, an occasional visitor, some means of sending a distress signal — but several of them added that they needed to be needed. And surely it is too often forgotten that the old can give as well as take.

Many of our arrangements cut the ancient lifeline between the old and the very young. There can be a rewarding relationship between the sevens and the seventy-fives. They are both closer to the world of mythology and magic than all the busier people between those ages. When I was very young we had my grandmother living with us, and whenever my parents went out for the evening, my grandmother fed and entertained me. After we had eaten our rice pudding, she revealed to me the daily life, customs and folklore of the West Riding in the 1840's and 1850's. Ten university lecturers and twenty certificated teachers could not have given me as much as she did — in sheer quantity, yes, but not in quality. What was there, illuminating everything, was the magic that begins with personal experience and demands a certain detachment, close to wonder and far from worry, often common to childhood and old age. After seven we start disinheriting ourselves, and after seventy, with any luck, we begin to unload a lot of the damned rubbish that has been weighing us down for fifty-odd years.

It is chiefly the humbler old folk who are ready to write little pieces explaining what they need. It is this humility that prevents them from declaring outright what I think is implied in their pieces, and as they won't say it, then I, one of them, will say it for them. In spite of all this "problem of the aged" stuff, all the arrangements and possible arrangements, all the

national or regional councils and societies, this is a bad world, perhaps the
worst there ever was, in which to reach old age.

To begin with, ours is a world that changes too quickly. Even I, fortunate in my work and circumstances and tougher than most old people, have
now had about as much as I can take. I feel already that I am half in
science fiction. The sensible world I knew how to cope with is vanishing.
What a lad of twenty takes for granted, I regard with increasing horror.
Those monster blocks of flats that are going up everywhere, from here to
Hong Kong! (I saw an interrelated group of them in Singapore that could
house the whole population of Cambridge.) Or, where people won't live in
flats, those detached or semi-detached villas that go on for ever! Or those
bewildering networks of motor roads, as on Long Island or in southern
California, where the cars never stop, looking at a distance like an invasion
of beetles! All the more and more with less and less variety! As if sheer
numbers might turn us soon into something like insects, whose lives might
ultimately be controlled entirely by machines! I am willing to believe that
the young see it all quite differently; I have lived too long to interpret the
huge changing scene in ordinary human terms.

I cannot help remembering, though, that for thousands of generations
not only were the old able to cope with the world but it was agreed that it
was they who were better able to cope than anybody else. They were in fact
respectfully consulted as experienced copers. Grandfather was not a problem but a solver of problems. And clearly there is much to be said in
favour of societies that honoured old age and did not put all the emphasis
on youth. All the people in those societies had something to look forward
to. Everybody was moving towards the prizes and not away from them. To
flatter and pamper the young for ten years is to leave them increasingly
dissatisfied for the next fifty. If being young *isn't* wonderful, then why all
the fuss? If it *is* wonderful, then the young creatures who enjoy it can stand
being given a few orders and shouted at. Why put everybody on a conveyor
belt to disenchantment and despair?

There would be some excuse for me if I took to drugs "for kicks" or
went out at night to smash things, because after all, in what is now the
fashionable view, I am old and almost done for and might as well play
merry hell before I am bedridden. If I don't do these things, then it is
because I have more sense and know better. But the prevailing philosophy
of our society suggests I haven't more sense and don't know better, just
because I am no longer young. Meanwhile, the youngsters who get up to
these antics may be influenced by the idea that theirs is the only time of life
worth having, that they have nothing to look forward to, so in secret
despair they take something "for kicks," or satisfy their inward rage by
smashing things that don't belong to them.

Both in life and in the arts, no doubt, it is best if there is a certain give-

and-take between the generations. But if in the arts it is bad for the old to be in the saddle, it is even worse for the young to be there, galloping to nowhere. Fifty years ago, art students were taught to draw, often by severe and sarcastic professors. After that, if they had a genuinely original personal vision, they could rebel against accepted forms, each in his own way. But now we have art students who won't be taught anything, being young and therefore geniuses. This is not really a rebellion against the standards of the old but against art itself. In this growing chaos we are threatened with the disappearance of the artist himself, the man who really knows how to do something that most of us cannot do. There are signs that music, literature and the drama are going the same way.

When I was young we were just young, we weren't Youth. In those days, Youth hadn't arrived. Now, not only has it arrived but there seems no escaping from it. Illustrated periodicals, especially if they use colour, all appear to be passionately devoted to Youth. One of them ought to produce a special number, all deep purple and black, describing the tragedy of a thirtieth birthday. This new cult of Youth is largely an Admass device. What Admass (my term for a system, not for a number of people) wants to do — and nobody can say it isn't succeeding — is to persuade us that first and last we are consumers. We are here on earth to earn, spend, consume. (And this must be the lowest view humanity has ever taken of itself. The social and psychological consequences may be discovered all round us.) Youth is now the big spender. The young have more money to chuck about than anybody except the really rich. They snow pound notes on certain industries. So in those periodicals in which the advertisements and the editorial matter begin to seem all one, we have this cult of Youth. The young are switched on; the rest of us have long been switched off; and as any sign of maturity is a disaster that must be postponed, the young will soon be younger still, schoolchildren being given more and more attention.

Another reason why this is a bad world to grow old in is that it is a world increasingly devoted to technology. I am no enemy of technology and gladly accept whatever benefits come my way. But its enormous importance puts the elderly into the shade. Just as we imagine that we are superior to our ancestors because we have technology and they hadn't, so our young men feel they are better than their fathers and grandfathers because they are closer to technological expertise. Yet a man may have an impressive amount of mechanical ingenuity, sufficient to put other men into space, but behave like a spoilt child or a maniac in his personal life and be hypnotised by ideas that are wildly irrational. If this is the great technological age, it is also the age of collective psychoses in which money, time and effort have been wasted on fantastic illusions. I see no signs therefore that technology, for all its benefits, makes men wiser. It is true that age is no guarantee of wisdom — and God knows it is wisdom we need — but we might agree that an increasing knowledge of electronics is not an adequate substitute.

There is a final reason why we who are growing old must face a sharp challenge. In the later afternoon of life, going down the other side of the hill, we look towards Death. Just as youth must prepare itself to live, we must prepare ourselves to die. This doesn't mean we must mope and sicken; on the contrary, we must live fully but in a different way, broadening our base, losing much of our egoism to religion or culture, already reaching out, we might say, to immortality. Like Cleopatra, we should have immortal longings, though our immortality should belong to the spirit of man. (As this is one of Jung's favourite themes, I refer the reader to him. Try, as a generous tasting sample, his *Psychological Reflections,* edited by Jolande Jacobi.) Now we cannot pretend we live in a society that encourages this attitude of mind. Death it tries to ignore; the very word itself is avoided. Religion and culture are both shaky. There is a pretence that we are all on the morning side of the hill, and might soon, with the help of goats' blood or sheep's glands, stay there longer and longer. But if we who are growing old are wise, we shall reject this pretence, go unprotesting down the other side of the hill:

> Be absolute for death; either death or life shall thereby be the sweeter. . . .

We could do with a duke or two as wise as that one.